LEARNING TO SERVE
Promoting Civil Society Through Service Learning

OUTREACH SCHOLARSHIP

Editor:

Richard M. Lerner
Tufts University
Medford, Massachusetts, U.S.A.

SERVING CHILDREN AND FAMILIES THROUGH COMMUNITY-UNIVERSITY PARTNERSHIPS: Success Stories
Vol. 1   ISBN 0-7923-8540-3   T.R. Chibucos, R.M. Lerner

FAMILY DIVERSITY AND FAMILY POLICY: Strengthening Families for America's Children
Vol. 2   ISBN 0-7923-8612-4   R.M. Lerner, E.E. Sparks, L.D. McCubbin

SOCIAL CHANGE, PUBLIC POLICY AND COMMUNITY COLLABORATION:
Training Human Development Professionals for the 21st Century
Vol. 3   ISBN 0-7923-8659-0   P.A. Ralston, R.M. Lerner, A.K. Mullis,
                                    C.B. Simerly, J.P. Murray

TRANSFORMING SOCIAL INQUIRY, TRANSFORMING SOCIAL ACTION: New Paradigms for Crossing the Theory/Practice Divide in Universities and Communities
Vol. 4   ISBN 0-7923-7787-7   F.T. Sherman, W.R. Torbert

THE JUVENILE OFFENDER: Theory, Research and Applications
Vol. 5   ISBN 0-7923-7222-0   R.D. Hoge

TRENDS IN YOUTH DEVELOPMENT: Visions, Realities and Challenges
Vol. 6   ISBN 0-7923-7451-7   P. Benson, K.J. Pittman

LEARNING TO SERVE
Promoting Civil Society Through Service Learning

edited by

Maureen E. Kenny
Boston College

Lou Anna K. Simon
Michigan State University

Karen Kiley-Brabeck
Fordham University

Richard M. Lerner
Tufts University

KLUWER ACADEMIC PUBLISHERS
Boston / Dordrecht / London

Distributors for North, Central and South America:
Kluwer Academic Publishers
101 Philip Drive
Assinippi Park
Norwell, Massachusetts 02061 USA
Telephone (781) 871-6600
Fax (781) 681-9045
E-Mail < kluwer@wkap.com >

Distributors for all other countries:
Kluwer Academic Publishers Group
Distribution Centre
Post Office Box 322
3300 AH Dordrecht, THE NETHERLANDS
Telephone 31 78 6392 392
Fax 31 78 6546 474
E-Mail < services@wkap.nl >

 Electronic Services < http://www.wkap.nl >

Library of Congress Cataloging-in-Publication Data

Learning to serve: promoting civil society through service learning / edited by Maureen
E. Kenny ... [et al.].
    p. cm. – (Outreach scholarship ; 7)
  Includes bibliographical references and index.
  ISBN 0-7923-7577-7 (alk. paper)
  1. Service learning—United States—Case studies. I. Kenny, Maureen. II. Series.

  LC220.5 .L43 2001
  378.1'03—dc21

                                                    2001050310

TABLE OF CONTENTS

vi

FOREWORD

This book comprehensively covers the growing community service movement in higher education. Additionally, it focuses attention on the very encouraging transition from an emphasis on service learning, alone, to a new concentration on how such activities contribute to civic engagement and active citizenship.

While some forms of community service have been part of the higher education landscape for many years, particularly in the land-grant institutions, education for active citizenship, as we call it today, or civic education, as it was referred to in the past, tended to be treated as an isolated subject area, if at all. Previously, students may have encountered civic education in their high school government classes, or perhaps in undergraduate political science courses. Viewed retrospectively, that approach to civic education was terribly limited and, as a result, treatment of this important subject was often isolated and totally inadequate. Many felt it was irrelevant to a liberal arts education and very few attempted to connect civic education with engagement.

Realizing this deficiency, a small group of presidents founded Campus Compact in 1985, with the purpose of promoting and supporting community service and active citizenship at our nation's colleges and universities. Those founding presidents were deeply concerned about the attitudes of the then enrolled college students, whose focus on only their own personal needs and desires had led them to be dubbed the "me generation." That is not to suggest that many students were not then volunteering to serve their local communities in their free time, but they were doing so without the benefit of receiving institutional recognition or support. The presidents felt that they and their colleagues should take responsibility for fostering community service efforts and for the creation of educational institutions where the impulse to serve could flourish. The three institutions that originally comprised Campus Compact have now grown to over seven hundred, with more than 700,000 students contributing more than seventeen million hours of community service annually. In fact, national data indicate that more than one-third of all students at Campus Compact member institutions volunteer in the community at some point during each academic year.

All this is to merely point out that the higher education community service movement is now thriving and numerous outstanding programs are now being offered by individual institutions, as well as through institutional collaborations. People at all educational levels and in many roles at our colleges and universities – faculty, staff, students, department heads, and even presidents – are working hard to build, maintain, and strengthen community service initiatives.

Student volunteerism in the past decade has become more sophisticated, more extensive, and more integral to the student's overall educational experience and satisfaction. Furthermore, it has become abundantly clear that collegiate service experiences tend to be most effective, in terms of learning, when they are integrated into the academic curriculum and when they draw on and reinforce the institution's educational mission. This recognition has been the genesis of the powerful and popular national movement called service learning, based on the realization that when the academic experience and educational mission of an institution combine to support democratic purposes, education for active citizenship is an inevitable outcome.

While much has been achieved in this domain, many questions remain unanswered. For instance, what obligations do our institutions have to encourage the impulse to volunteer and to tie it to the values and skills that sustain our democracy? How do we support our students in their transformation from campus leaders to global citizens? How do we effectively cultivate in our community-minded students the passion, concern, and the entrepreneurship that will inspire them to go out into society and make a difference after graduation? These are just some of the challenging questions for which there are no easy answers, particularly for colleges and universities where change tends to be more evolutionary than revolutionary, where departmental structure typically funnels students toward greater specificity and a more narrow focus in their studies over time, and where the core value of education for active citizenship — which does not fall obviously into one particular department or discipline — can easily be overlooked or simply ignored.

The authors in this timely book have, in a thoughtful and insightful fashion, attempted to initiate a dialogue on these and many other related issues. Concurrently, they describe a number of innovative approaches being utilized to link community service and civic education. This is an important work that will be of interest to all who are dedicated to civic education and to the proposition that our colleges and universities are responsible for not only graduating students who can succeed in their chosen careers, but who also possess and practice the attributes of good citizenship.

John DiBiaggio
President
Tufts University
Medford, MA
July, 2001

PREFACE

Contemporary colleges and universities aspire to creating successful alumni, people who will contribute positively to their own lives and to the lives of their families and communities. In turn, today's higher education institutions seek to reach out to communities, and to use their research and educational programs to add value to civil society. Through providing opportunities for student civic engagement and through outreach activities, higher education institutions may integratively create a cadre of educated and engaged citizens graduating from community-collaborative, or engaged, universities. Accordingly, higher education institutions attempt to weave civic engagement into the core educational experiences of students. A dialectic is created wherein students not only learn to serve but, as well, serve to learn, for instance, through service learning programs.

This book presents a rich sample of the ways in which a range of higher education institutions — community colleges; liberal arts, undergraduate institutions; comprehensive state universities; land-grant universities; independent universities; and faith-based institutions — integrate through service learning programs undergraduate civic engagement and university outreach within their institutional missions. In addition, this book includes a range of local, state, and national community-based perspectives about the important contributions colleges and universities may make to civic life and civil society through programs such as service learning.

We believe that this book provides a unique discussion of how service learning functions as a critical cornerstone of outreach scholarship. Service learning contributes significantly to student development, to the vitality of higher education, to enhancing the quality of community life, and to the promotion of a more just and civil society. Such service learning provides, then, a value-added dimension to the undergraduate experience. It converges with the current call by undergraduates and young Americans more generally to participate in community service and to "give back" to their society.

This volume includes perspectives pertinent to university administrators and faculty members involved in promoting service learning as part of university engagement with communities. As such, the book will be of interest also to community leaders of those organizations and programs partnering with universities in the context of outreach scholarship and service learning.

We believe as well that this book gives unique voice to the ways in which the issues involved in fostering civil society through service learning enhance student, academic-institutional, and community outcomes.

As such, we believe the book will contribute to the knowledge base for establishing "engaged" universities that promote civil society and successfully integrate outreach scholarship and service learning with the traditional university missions of teaching, research and service.

We are grateful to several colleagues for their contributions to this book. We thank John DiBiaggio, President, Tufts University, and President, Campus Compact, for his generous foreword. We are deeply indebted as well to the contributors to this volume. Their vision and passion for enhancing the lives of students and communities are well represented in this volume. Their creativity, collegiality, and collaborative spirit made this book possible.

We are grateful as well to Lisa Marie DiFonzo and Karyn Lu for their dedicated and able editorial assistance, and to Holly Maynard whose administrative skills enabled our work to proceed more efficiently. We appreciate also the stewardship and support of our editor at Kluwer Academic Publishers, Michael Williams. His faith in and support of this project were invaluable sources of encouragement and motivation for us. We thank as well the numerous colleagues at our respective home institutions — Michigan State University, Boston College, Fordham University, and Tufts University — for their support and encouragement throughout the time we spend working on this project.

Finally, we are grateful to our respective families for their love and devotion through the process of developing and completing this book. Their contributions extend well beyond those we can list or acknowledge.

M.K.
L.A.K.S
K.K.B.
R.M.L.

CHAPTER 1

PROMOTING CIVIL SOCIETY THROUGH SERVICE LEARNING: A VIEW OF THE ISSUES

Maureen Kenny
Boston College
Lou Anna K. Simon
Michigan State University
Karen Kiley-Brabeck
Fordham University
Richard M. Lerner
Tufts University

INTRODUCTION

There is a lot more that can, and ideally will, be gained from a college education than the knowledge and skills inculcated through the various major, minor, or elective courses offered in the curricula of colleges or universities. Most higher education institutions hope that the opportunities that students are provided during their four undergraduate years will imbue them with more than an academic education. Most colleges and universities aspire to creating successful alumni, people who will contribute positively to their own lives and to the lives of their families and communities.

There is a lot more that college and universities can, and ideally will, contribute to the health and positive functioning of the communities within which they are embedded than only the education of students who will occupy jobs associated with the knowledge and skills inculcated through curricula offerings. Most higher education institutions aspire today to reach out to communities, and to use their research and educational programs to add value to civil society (Lerner & Simon, 1998a, 1998b).

Thus, through providing opportunities for student civic engagement and through outreach activities, higher education institutions may integratively create a cadre of educated and engaged citizens graduating from community-collaborative, or engaged, universities (Kellogg Commission, 1999; Spanier, 1999; Votruba, 1999a, 1999b). In fact, the increasing pressure placed by politicians, boards of trustees, alumni, community stakeholders, and civically engaged students for universities to use their educational and research resources to add value to the lives of the individuals and families of their proximal and distal communities (Lerner & Simon, 1998a) has created a historically unprecedented impetus for leaders of higher education to merge education and outreach in manners that serve communities.

Higher education institutions have responded by attempting to weave civic engagement into the core educational experiences of students. A dialectic is created wherein students not only learn to serve but, as well, serve to learn. For instance, service learning, experiential learning, participatory action research experiences, or practicuum placements are among the strategies that colleges and universities pursue to make student civic engagement and university outreach an integrated part of their educational curricula and a value-added feature of the outreach role of the college or university in the life of its community.

This book presents a rich sample of the ways in which a range of higher education institutions — community colleges; liberal arts, undergraduate institutions; comprehensive state universities; land-grant universities; independent universities; and faith-based institutions — integrate student civic engagement and outreach within their institutional missions. Service learning programs, as well as other community-collaborative strategies for such integration, are discussed as the chief means for such syntheses. In turn, this book samples a range of local, state, and national community-based perspectives about the important contributions colleges and universities may make to civic life and civil society through programs such as service learning.

Together, these higher education and community-based perspectives reflect both the reasons for and the approaches to community engagement by contemporary American higher education institutions. The chapters of this book represent the major reconceptualization that is emerging today about the nature of the undergraduate experience, of the importance of providing both high quality education and the inculcation of values and skills pertinent to civic engagement. Finally, this book offers some insight into the ways that community-based organizations are reacting to (e.g., welcoming, accepting, or finding the need to significantly supplement) the work of the engaged university and its cadres of civically interested and service-providing students.

THE CONTEMPORARY CHALLENGES FACING HIGHER EDUCATION

Across the chapters of this book we believe that one point is clear from the perspective of either higher educational institutions or community-based organizations. Arguably, the major challenge facing contemporary higher education is to enhance its relevance and connectedness to the issues and problems faced by the broader society — as these problems are defined by community members, and not by academics acting independently of the views of non-academic community members. Indeed, perhaps the most consistently identified "problem" in higher education, as reflected in the comments and behavior of taxpayers, legislators, governing boards, funders, parents, students, and businesses is that the academy is not playing a visible role in contributing to the improvement of the lives of people in the community — as their lives are lived on a day-to-day basis.

Traditionally, such contributions have not been regarded as a part of the mission of colleges and universities, as such missions were generally understood by academics (Bonnen, 1998; Boyer, 1990). However, both Peter Magrath (1993, 1998) and Ernest Boyer (1994), among others (e.g., Graham Spanier, 1997, 1999; and James Votruba, 1996, 1999a, b) remind us that in both public universities, especially land-grant ones, and several private institutions (for example, those, such as institutions in the Jesuit tradition, founded to have a direct role in the promotion of social justice in communities), there is a long and rich history of directing scholarship to address the "practical" problems of life — as those issues are defined by the communities within which universities are located. Simply, there has been a long tradition of "outreach scholarship" (Lerner and Simon, 1998a) in America — a tradition which, while perhaps dimly remembered in some quarters in modern academe (e.g., see Bonnen, 1998), is gaining renewed attention.

A key reason for attention to outreach scholarship — and to the collaborations between universities and communities that may foster it — is that contemporary pressures in and on higher education institutions foster such work. For example, federal policy makers (e.g., Kennedy, 1999) and national philanthropic organizations (Richardson, 1996; Sherrod, 1998, 1999a, b) are pressing universities and colleges to use their learning resources and to engage in scholarship that will add value to the lives of youth, families, and communities. Outreach scholarship integrates community based expertise relative to the needs, networks, and values of the community with the theoretical and scientific knowledge of university scholars in efforts to provide solutions to community problems, to develop and evaluate interventions, and to further social and scientific knowledge. It furthermore enhances student educational experiences through opportunities for applied scholarship.

Colleges and universities are also under pressure to develop tomorrow's leaders and to successfully prepare their undergraduates for entry into the most competitive graduate programs and employment positions. At the same time, education is at risk of becoming outmoded. As technology makes university learning resources more accessible (e.g., through distance learning programs), it is arguably the case that when members of the public think of the best source of knowledge available to them, the name of Bill Gates comes to mind more readily than their nearest institution of higher education. Through the synthesis of outreach scholarship and civic engagement experiences that may be provided by programs of service learning, which offer students the opportunity to participate in the community-based outreach scholarship of faculty and graduate students, colleges and universities may meet these challenges and realize their individually defined goals for promoting student development, citizenship education, participatory action, and generating knowledge and service that is of benefit to the community.

CIVIL SOCIETY AND SERVICE LEARNING

Examples currently exist of successful university-community outreach scholarship (Chibucos & Lerner, 1999; Lerner & Simon, 1998a), many of which have at their core a strong tradition of service learning. This book provides a discussion of how service learning functions as a key instance of outreach scholarship. As illustrated by the chapters from the administrative and faculty leaders of the colleges and universities represented in this book, service learning — and related programs promoting student civic engagement — may contribute significantly to student personal as well as academic development, to the vitality of higher education, to enhancing the quality of community life, and to the promotion of a more just and civil society — that is, a society wherein its institutions (including governmental and non-governmental organizations, public services, and the public problem solving roles of businesses) balance the rights "granted to individuals in free societies and the responsibilities required by citizens to maintain those rights" (O'Connell, 1999, pp. 10-11).

Stephen Bailey's (1977) appraisal of more than two decades ago remains relevant today: "This nation is in woefully short supply of people equipped to look at problems as a whole, at life as a whole, at the earth as a whole. Without a sense of the whole we have no way of evaluating the parts, no way of appraising the importance of the expert" (pp. 257-258). There exists today a clear call for people who have academic knowledge, who have achieved personal development, and who have problem-solving skills to work on solutions and programs promoting a just society.

Accordingly, across the sections and chapters of this book, evidence is marshaled in support of the idea that undergraduate service learning, infused throughout the curriculum and coupled with outreach scholarship, is an integral means through which higher education can be responsive to the people and institutions of the communities of this nation (Boyer, 1990, 1994; Kellogg Commission, 1999). We believe that the evidence provided indicates, furthermore, that such engagement perpetuates civil society (e.g., O'Connell, 1999). Predicated on the vision of enabling colleges and universities to become "engaged institutions" (Kellogg Commission, 1999), and contributing to the enhancement of civil society through university-community collaborations involving outreach scholarship, this book provides evidence of the special role that student civic engagement — for example, as exemplified through service learning experiences — can play in higher education institutions committed to linking their teaching, research, and service endeavors with the communities they serve.

ELUCIDATING THE ASSOCIATION BETWEEN CIVIC ENGAGEMENT AND SERVICE LEARNING

This book presents multiple models of student civic engagement, most notably involving service learning. In conjunction with outreach scholarship, such student activities enable community service and civic engagement to be more central to the scholarly life of the university, to address challenges regarding relevance that are confronting higher education, to make value-added contributions to communities, to foster civil society, and to contribute to the holistic education of the person. It is useful to specify in some more detail the vision on which this book rests and then to describe how the organization of the book pursues this vision.

SERVICE LEARNING: NEW WINE IN AN OLD BOTTLE

As discussed by Lerner and Simon (1998b), there are considerable pressures on higher education institutions to add value to the community. In order for universities to engage in outreach in a manner that is both valuable to and sustained in the community, the mission of outreach must be integrated throughout the university; it must become part of the intellectual life of faculty and a core component of university culture; it must be part of the research and teaching missions of the university and not a separate activity that can be (and historically has been) marginalized (Bonnen, 1998).

Student civic engagement, as represented by service learning programs, also shares a history of marginalization in many universities. For example, service learning curricula are sometimes viewed as promoting affective development, at the expense of more rigorous academic content (Howard, 1993). Courses that provide a service learning component are typically more common among courses in the social sciences, education and humanities, and less prevalent among the hard sciences. Faculty may spend substantive time developing service learning components for courses, but these efforts are often not linked to their scholarship and are thus not highly rewarded by university promotion and tenure committees.

The marginalization of service learning, and the alienation of students from engagements with the institutions of civil society that such marginalization produces, presents risks to the viability of programs of service learning (or of civic engagement more generally) at a time in history when the need for such engagement may be at its greatest. Given the growing importance of technology in our lives, young people may be becoming increasingly disconnected from the human values that can only be learned through direct interaction with others. The opportunity to develop compassion, empathy, moral reasoning, and multicultural understanding through activities such as service learning may be an important rationale for university investment in such programs at a time when accessing information can be accomplished through technology and distance learning (Boyte & Kerin, 2000). Service learning may thus be an educational mechanism for developing the fully educated person, a person who can apply the lessons of technology and the professions in ways that promotes a more civil society (Eckert & Henschel, 2000).

Because of the previously noted risks to contemporary higher education, such a contribution of service learning programs may be timely and possibly critical to the health and viability of American higher education. As we have emphasized, higher education is under external scrutiny to produce research that is relevant to problems of the real world and to add value to the community, while university faculty also experience internal pressures to produce high quality scholarship that contributes to the knowledge base of their field and is published in leading journals (Lerner & Simon, 1999b, c). Universities are also under pressure to successfully prepare their undergraduates for entry into the most competitive graduate programs and employment positions. At the same time, higher education must also find a means to pursue — and make visible — programs of outreach that, consistent with institutional missions, advance the university's teaching and research functions and educate the whole person in a way not possible through distance learning.

We believe that the cutting-edge of the successful synthesis of teaching, research, and service is outreach scholarship coupled with service learning that imbues undergraduates with the sense of the need, and provides them with the opportunity, to participate in the community-based outreach scholarship of faculty and graduate students (e.g., in regard to evaluation research, asset mapping, needs assessment, issues identification, demonstration research, or participatory action research) (e.g., see Chibucos & Lerner, 1999). Through such a linkage, the quality of undergraduate education is enhanced by providing students with the experience of adding value to communities; this integration helps students experience the value of combining knowledge and service (Ralston, et al., 1999).

The learning cycle is reciprocal, however. Just as undergraduates add knowledge and application to the communities in which they serve, the communities also teach undergraduates valuable lessons related to their fields of study. The community provides the ecological component of knowledge (Bronfenbrenner & Morris, 1998); it affords the student the ability to understand how knowledge-based actions are, may, or must be transformed when embedded in a given community, cultural, environmental, policy, or historical context (Bronfenbrenner & Morris, 1998; Lerner, Sparks, & McCubbin, 1999).

Service learning provides, then, a value-added dimension to the undergraduate experience. It converges with the current call by undergraduates and young Americans more generally to participate in community service and to "give back" to their society (Sax, 2000). Service learning may provide lessons in contextualizing action and in appreciating the sources of change within the social system of which students are a part (cf. Brandtstädter, 1998, 1999). Through such experiences undergraduates may be part of the knowledge generation and application process they are studying in their courses.

Through such a merger of civic engagement and scholarship, universities are able to better market the education they provide. A quality education is coupled with valuable contributions to society; students are imbued with the value of using knowledge to serve their community and acquire skills to do this. Moreover, this action orientation to knowledge and to student development reflects cutting-edge ideas about human development and motivation, ideas that focus on the dynamic relations between developing people and their changing social ecology (Brandtstädter & Lerner, 1999).

As such, service learning may be a means to promote positive outcomes of these person-context relations; it may be a vehicle for building civil society and for promoting social justice (Lerner, Fisher, & Weinberg, 2000). Students may come to see themselves as active agents of change in the settings in which they live and work; they may come to regard themselves as active contributors to the prosperity of their community.

The expected benefits for the student and university are numerous. Consistent with traditional models of service learning, students may be expected to make gains in moral development and values acquisition (Damon, 1997; Noddings, 1984). The connection of academic learning with applied experience in the community provides opportunities for the development of practical skills that enhance the relevance of classroom learning (Benson, 1997; Damon, 1997; Crews, 1997; Scales, et al., 2000). The volunteer activity provided by students should also benefit the community (AAHE, 1992), and the outreach scholarship of the faculty should contribute to the production of knowledge that provides solutions to real world problems (Harkavy & Puckett, 1994).

Of course, some of the above outcomes may be valued and emphasized more heavily than others by some institutions of higher learning or by different segments of the university community. Service learning is not a monolithic entity.

This vision requires, then, either a broader, more inclusive definition of the civic engagement or service learning concept or, in turn, a differentiation of the expectancies that are currently subsumed under the label of service learning. The integration of the university missions of research, teaching, and service through service learning and outreach scholarship may be nothing more than "new wine in an old bottle." Service learning that integrates all facets of the mission of higher education may enable institutions to return to fostering the traditional core vales of what it means to be an educated person (Bonnen, 1998; Boyer, 1990). Having an education may mean (again) being able to translate one's academic knowledge (including technological knowledge) into information of value to one's own life and to those of one's family, community, and society (Boyer, 1994).

As a consequence of this potential impact on students and their world, there has been a growing national interest in service learning among students, educators and administrators. The National Society for the Study of Education recognized the growing relevance of service learning as a mechanism for educational reform and devoted its 96th Yearbook to the topic, examining the theory and practice of service learning and its value in achieving a variety of educational and social outcomes in both higher education and K-to-12 schools (Schine, 1997).

Interest in service learning grew, in part, from dissatisfaction with current educational practices that do not prepare students for roles as active and concerned citizens, dissatisfaction with socially irrelevant university-generated research, and the desire to restore an emphasis on relevant instruction and student learning to the heart of the university. Consequently much of the writing in service learning has focused on pedagogical issues related to integration of service learning into the curriculum (Bringle & Duffy, in press; Jacoby, 1996; Rhoads & Howard, 1998) and to the use of service learning as a mechanism for preparing students for intercultural citizenship (Guarasci & Cornwell, 1997) and for promoting ethical development (Fried, 1997).

Existing literature, thus, has focused heavily on the identification of practices to enhance student learning and development, with less attention to practices of community collaboration, research concerning impact of service learning for all collaborators, or institutional factors that are critical to the support and sustenance of service learning programs.

Waterman (1997) addressed this gap, in part, by editing a volume that examines the role of research and evaluation in assessing and informing service learning. Zlotowski's edited volume (1998) contributed significantly by focusing on successful service learning programs and how they transformed the organizational culture of their university to gain acceptance and funding.

However, across the extant literature it is clear that what is needed is a consideration of the multiple models of service learning and of the potential for and/or proven ability of each to promote civil society by enhancing student learning and development, by collaborating with the community in producing outreach scholarship, and by developing an institutional structure to support this work. Accordingly, it is useful to discuss the organization of this book and how it provides this contribution.

THE PLAN OF THE BOOK

Service learning may be a central component in university-community partnerships that integrate the university missions of teaching, research, and service. Indeed, we believe that the impact and sustainability of service learning programs will depend upon the ability of colleges and universities to successfully integrate the university mission of teaching, research, and service by infusing service learning with faculty outreach scholarship.

To explore this integration, this chapter considers the nature of service learning, the individual (student development and academic achievement) and community (outreach scholarship) levels of impact such learning may have, and how service learning programs may enable colleges and universities to address the risks/challenges facing contemporary higher education. In addition to this introductory chapter, Chapter 2 considers the history of service learning and the development of different models through which universities seek to involve students in the life of the community. Across the first two chapters of this book, the importance of understanding the diversity of definitions of service learning are juxtaposed with a stress on the opportunity offered by service learning to return higher education to its historically core conception of the meaning of an educated person — and thus of linking the "products" of higher education (knowledge and students with knowledge) with service to society's institutions and thus with the advancement of civil society.

Chapter 3, which concludes the first section of this book, explores the opportunities to promote such a vision for service learning at America's universities and within its communities. This chapter, authored by leaders from Campus Compact, a national organization dedicated to promoting service learning and citizenship education, identifies critical "indicators" by which a university can evaluate its level of community and civic engagement.

Major examples of the range of exemplary service learning programs that exist are presented in the second section of the book, "University models of service learning." We expect that these examples of university practices will contribute to the knowledge base for establishing "engaged" universities that promote civil society. Here, chapters were written by the leaders of service learning programs associated with a range of two- and four-year colleges and universities across the nation. These institutions vary in regard to size, public versus independent status, and secular versus religious affiliation. They also vary in regard to the developmental status of their service learning and outreach scholarship programs. For example, Fordham University is at the "introductory" level where service learning is practiced and building toward formally institutionalizing its program. Other campuses are at the intermediate or "advanced" levels. Advanced service learning programs have many service learning course offerings and are engaged in many different types of community outreach activities. Service learning is active, valued and widespread across the campus (Campus Compact, 1999).

This range of institutions and developmental levels afford an examination of a broad range of treatments of the key issues involved in building and sustaining service learning programs and evaluating their impact on both (a) student development in regard to academic achievement, service commitments, community-relevant skills, and social responsibility; and (b) community enhancement and the promotion of civil society. The examples reflect the differentiated concepts/models of service learning. For example, Kansas State University emphasizes citizenship education and the values of diversity, justice, equality, tolerance and integrity. The University of Colorado at Denver strives to meet the civic responsibility of an urban university by providing practical and theoretical education that meets community needs and by supporting faculty work that contributes to the solution of social problems. Faculty members at Wheelock College, a private college dedicated to the improvement of the quality of life children and families, participate in community sites with students so that they learn "side by side." Students at Northern Kentucky University participate on boards that make decisions about granting university funds to community based organizations as part of the Mayerson Student Philanthropy Project. As a rurally located state land grant college, Penn State promotes public scholarship as a means of integrating student civic participation, faculty research and discovery-teaching methods, thereby enhancing the legitimacy of service learning and citizen participation as methods and goals for student learning. Alverno College, a private, faith-based, undergraduate liberal arts college, offers a comprehensive service-learning program infused throughout many aspects of the curriculum and college structure to a student body of traditional and non-traditional college students. Portland State has undertaken a process of comprehensive institutional transformation in efforts to build a sustainable institutional capacity for civic engagement.

Each college or university included in this section focuses, then, on the relationship of service learning to institutional mission, how the institution has sought to integrate teaching, research, and service through service learning, and the institutional factors that have served to facilitate and hinder that integration. Each example specifies the model (definition, conception) of service learning found at the institution, and thus the options for service learning experiences offered to students. Each example is coupled, furthermore, with a discussion of how the multiple dimensions of service learning (student learning, outreach scholarship, and community impact) have been and should be evaluated. That is, each example specifies the student, institutional, or community outcomes sought for the university's service learning program, as well as the challenges to the development, implementation and evaluation of such programs.

In the past, service learning programs have been scrutinized for their contributions to student academic gains and, at times, to citizenship education. Today, most evaluations concerning the effectiveness of service learning emphasize academic outcomes. However, given the range of definitions of service learning that exist, and thus the different models used and outcomes sought by institutions, college or university enhancement (e.g., greater numbers of students seeking enrollment in the university), moral development, citizenship education, social responsibility development, community and/or civil society enhancement are additional outcomes envisioned for service learning programs. If one goal of service learning is student affective and/or citizenship development, it will not be sufficient to evaluate the program based solely on student academic gains. If civic responsibility is a goal of service-learning, program evaluation must consider benefit to the community. Institutions must clearly define the outcomes sought and evaluate accordingly.

Of course, the value of any given outcome can only be determined by the college or university, as well as by the communities it serves. Accordingly, the third part of the book presents selected community and agency perspectives on the value and limitations of outreach scholarship and service learning and what is needed to enhance university-community partnerships. Contributions are provided by community-based organizations having local, state, or national programs. Across the sample organizations represented in this section we will see that there exist a range of ways in which community partners respond to and ally with varied models of university collaboration and the varied institutional cultures and missions represented by the universities. For example, Jump Start, an early literacy division of the national AmeriCorp program, and Tufts University have created a partnership that enrolls undergraduates as corps members. Students work with a child for a minimum of one year on literacy and school readiness skills. Participating children often are enrolled in Head Start and are socioeconomically disadvantaged. Jump Start members have the opportunity to apply their academic knowledge, reflect on their service experiences, and grapple with social justice issues. Also on a national level, 4-H has long recognized the potential of young persons to contribute meaningfully to their communities. Through the past century, 4-H provided national leadership in creating opportunities for youth to engage in service. With awareness that the involvement of young people in solving community problems is essential to preparation for citizenship, 4-H has established priorities that will prepare youth to contribute to the creation of a civil society in the 21st century.

FUTURE VISIONS

Across the chapters of this book both university and community contributors discuss their visions of how to build civil society through university-community partnerships. Among the core conceptual issues raised across the chapters of the book are ones that enable an action plan for program design, delivery, and evaluation. There are learnings about how to develop effective, appropriately scaled, and sustainable service learning programs that derive from across the discussions by the colleges, universities and community organizations represented in the book.

This volume presents a vision of the college/university with service learning as a central component and a focus on university-community partnership as a unique way of integrating the university missions of teaching, research, and service. The examples constituted by the university practices described in this book contribute to the knowledge base for establishing "engaged" universities that promote civil society and successfully integrate outreach scholarship into the core fabric of the institutional agenda.

We hope that the discussions in this book of diverse models of service learning and outreach scholarship — and of their challenges, successes, problems, and future plans — will contribute to the generation of new local and national efforts to prepare students for becoming fully engaged citizens contributing to civil society. To the extent that this book enhances knowledge about and is associated with more robust attempts to integrate civic engagement and outreach scholarship into the agendas of community-collaborative, engaged universities, it will have met the aspirations of its editors and contributors.

REFERENCES

American Association for Higher Education Assessment Forum. (1992). *Principles of good practice for assessing student learning.* Washington, DC: AAHE.

Bailey, S.K. (1977). Needed changes in liberal education. *Educational Record, 250-258.*

Benson, P. (1997). *All kids are our kids: What communities must do to raise caring and responsible children and adolescents.* San Francisco: Jossey-Bass.

Bonnen, J. T. (1998). The land-grant idea and the evolving outreach university. In R. M. Lerner & L. A. K. Simon (Eds.), *University-community collaborations for the twenty-first century: Outreach scholarship for youth and families* (pp. 25-71). New York: Garland.

Boyer, E. L. (1990). *Scholarship reconsidered: Priorities of the professoriate.* Princeton, NJ: The Carnegie Foundation for the Advancement of Teaching.

Boyer, E. L. (1994, March 9). Creating the new American college. *The Chronicle of Higher Education,* A48.

Boyte, H. C., & Keri, N. N. (2000). Renewing the Democratic Spirit in American Colleges and Universities: Higher Education as Public Work. In T. Ehrlich (Ed.), *Civic responsibility and higher education* (pp. 37-59). Phoenix, AZ: American Council on Education/ The Oryx Press.

Brandtstädter, J. (1998). Action perspectives on human development. In W. Damon (Series Ed.), & R. M. Lerner (Vol. Ed.), *Handbook of child psychology: Vol. 1 Theoretical models of human development* (5th ed., pp. 807-863). New York: Wiley.

Brandtstädter, J. (1999). The self in action and development: Cultural, biosocial, and onotgenetic bases of intentional self-development. In J. Brandtstädter & R.M. Lerner (Eds.), *Action and self-development: Theory and research through the life-span* (pp. 37-65). Thousand Oaks, CA: Sage.

Bringle, R. G., & Duffey, D. K. (Eds.) (in press). *Collaborating with the community: Psychology and service learning.* Washington, DC: American Association for Higher Education.

Bringle, R. G., & Duffy, D. K. (1998). *With service in mind: Concepts and models for service-learning in psychology.* Washington, D C.: American Association for Higher Education.

Bronfenbrenner, U., & Morris, P. A. (1998). The ecology of developmental process. In W. Damon (Series Ed.) & R. M. Lerner (Vol. Ed.), *Handbook of child psychology: Vol. 1 Theoretical models of human development* (5th ed., pp. 993-1028). New York: Wiley.

Chibucos, T., & Lerner, R. M. (Eds.) (1999). *Serving children and families through community-university partnerships: Success stories.* Norwell, MA: Kluwer Academic Publishers.

Crews, R. J. (1997*). The University of Colorado at Boulder service-learning faculty handbook, second virtual edition.* University of Colorado, Boulder: The Office of the Director of Service-Learning.

Damon, W. (1997). *The youth charter: How communities can work together to raise standards for all our children.* New York: The Free Press.

Eckert, P., & Henschel, P. (2000). Supporting community involvement in the digital age. In T. Ehrlich (Ed.), *Civic responsibility and higher education* (pp. 197-207). Phoenix, AZ: American Council on Education/ The Oryx Press.

Freid, J.(Ed) (1997). Ethics for today's campus: New perspectives on education, student development and institutional management. In M. J. Barr, & M. L. Upcraft (Sereis Editors), *New Directions for Student Services, Number 77.* San Francisco: Jossey Bass.

Guarasci, R., & Cornwell, G. H. (1997). *Democratic education in an age of difference: Redefining citizenship in higher education.* San Francisco: Jossey-Bass.

Harkavy, I., & Puckett, J. L. (1994). Lessons from the Hull House for the contemporary urban university. *Social Service Review, 68,* 299-321.

Howard , J. (Ed.) (1993). *Praxis I: A faculty casebook on community service learning .* Ann Arbor, MI: OCSL Press.

Jacoby (Ed.) (1996). *Service learning in higher education: Concepts and practices.* San Francisco, CA: Jossey-Bass.

Kellogg Commission on the Future of State and Land-Grant Colleges. (1999). *Returning to our roots: The engaged institution.* Washington, DC.: National Association of State Universities and Land-Grant Colleges.

Kennedy, E. M. (1999). University-community partnerships: A mutually beneficial effort to aid community development and improve academic learning opportunities. *Applied Developmental Science, 3*(4), 197-198.

Lerner, R. M., Fisher, C. B., & Weinberg, R. A. (2000a). Toward a science for and of the people: Promoting civil society through the application of developmental science. *Child Development, 71,* 11-20.

Lerner, R. M., & Simon, L. A. K. (Eds.) (1998). *University-community collaborations for the twenty-first century: Outreach scholarship for youth and families.* New York: Garland.

Lerner, R. M., Sparks, E., & McCubbin, L. (1999). *Family diversity and family policy: Strengthening families for America's children.* Norwell, MA: Kluwer.

Noddings, N. (1984). *Caring: A feminine approach to ethics and moral education.* Berkeley: University of California Press.

Magrath, C. P. (1993). Comments to the Board on Home Economics on November 12, 1993. Washington DC: National Association of State Universities and Land-Grant Colleges.

Magrath, C. P. (1998). Foreword: Creating a new outreach university. In R. M. Lerner & L. A. K. Simon (Eds.), *University-community collaborations for the twenty-first century: Outreach scholarship for youth and families* (pp. xiii-xx). New York: Garland.

O'Connell, B. (1999). *Civil society: The underpinnings of American democracy.* Hanover, NH: University Press of New England.

Ralston, P., Lerner, R. M., Mullis, A. K., Simerly, C., & Murray, J. (Eds.). (1999). *Social change, public policy, and community collaboration: Training human development professionals for the twenty-first century.* Norwell, MA: Kluwer.

Richardson, W. C. (1996). A new calling for higher education. Paper presented at the John W. Oswald Lecture, The Pennsylvania State University, University Park.

Rhoads, R. A., & Howard, J. (1998). Academic service learning: A pedagogy of action and reflection. *New Directions for Teaching and Learning,* No. 73, Jossey-Bass.

Sax, L. J. (2000). Citizenship development and the American college student. In T. Ehrlich (Ed.), *Civic responsibility and higher education* (pp. 3-18). Phoenix, AZ: American Council on Education/ The Oryx Press.

Scales, P., Benson, P., Leffert, N., & Blyth, D. A. (2000). The contribution of developmental assets to the prediction of thriving among adolescents. *Applied Developmental Science, 4,* 27-46.

Schine, J. (Ed.) (1997). *Service learning: Ninety-sixth yearbook of the National Society for the Study of Education* . Chicago: The University of Chicago Press.

Sherrod, L. (1998). The common pursuits of modern philanthropy and the proposed outreach university: Enhancing research and education. In R. M. Lerner & L. A. K. Simon (Eds.), *University-community collaborations for the twenty-first century: Outreach scholarship for youth and families* (pp. 397-418). New York: Garland.

Sherrod, L. (1999). "Giving child development knowledge away": Using university-community partnerships to disseminate research on children, youth, and families. *Applied Developmental Science, 3*(4), 228-234.

Spanier, G. B. (1997). Enhancing the capacity for outreach. *Journal of Public Service and Outreach,* 2(2), 7-11.

Spanier, G. B. (1999). Enhancing the quality of life: A model for the 21st century land-grant university. *Applied Developmental Science,* 3(4), 199-205.

Votruba, J. C. (1996). Strengthening the university's alignment with society: Challenges and strategies. *Journal of Public Service and Outreach, 1*(1), 29-36.

Votruba, J. C. (1999a). Implementing public policy education: The role of the university. In P. Ralston, R. M. Lerner, A. K. Mullis, C. Simerly, & J. Murray (Eds.), *Social change, public policy, and community collaboration: Training human development professionals for the twenty-first century* (pp. 117-120). Norwell, MA: Kluwer.

Votruba, J. C. (1999b). Afterword. In P. Ralston, R. M. Lerner, A. K. Mullis, C. Simerly, & J. Murray (Eds.), *Social change, public policy, and community collaboration: Training human development professionals for the twenty-first century* (pp. 141-145). Norwell, MA: Kluwer.

Waterman, A.(Ed.) (1997). *Service-learning: Applications from the research.* Mahwah, NJ: Lawrence Erlbaum Associates.

Zlotowski, E. (Ed.) (1998*). Successful service learning programs: New models of excellence in higher education.* Bolton, MA: Anker Publishing.

CHAPTER 2

SERVICE-LEARNING: A HISTORY OF SYSTEMS

Maureen E. Kenny
Laura A. Gallagher
Boston College

INTRODUCTION

From an historical perspective, service-learning is a relatively new phenomenon in American higher education. The term was first coined in 1967, in reference to an internship program that was sponsored by the Southern Regional Education Board and through which college students gained academic credit and/or federally funded financial remuneration for work on community projects (Sigmon, 1979). As a pedagogical practice in higher education, service-learning was limited to a small group of participants until the mid 1980s. By the late 1980s, service-learning was gaining in prominence and was clearly distinguished from community service by its attention to the integration of service with academic study (Hollander, Saltmarsh, & Zlotowski, 2001). The 1990s have witnessed tremendous growth in service-learning, such that it is now regarded as a "vital force in educational change" (Liu, 1999, p. xi). Colleges and universities have espoused a renewed commitment to civic responsibility, with service-learning as a central vehicle for fulfilling this commitment (Ehrlich, 2000).

Despite its short history, the conceptual antecedents of service-learning can be found in the historical commitment of American higher education to public purpose, in the political and educational philosophies of John Dewey, and in American traditions of volunteerism and social activism (Jacoby, 1996; Morton & Saltmarsh, 1997). Goodwin Liu (1999), for example, described the current movement as a "phase in the evolution of a more general aspiration to bring theory and practice, schools and communities, and thought and action closer together" (p. xii). Examination of the roots of service-learning is helpful in understanding its current manifestations and the ways in which service is linked to the missions of a variety of diverse educational institutions. The specific goals of university-based service-learning programs vary depending upon the heritage of the institution and the ways in which service-learning addresses the mission of the college or university. As is evident by the chapters comprising this volume, service-learning program goals include a focus on the development of citizenship and preparation of students for participation in an active civic life, the moral and religious development of students, the preparation of students for careers through engagement in real-world activity, and the partnering of the university and the community in ways that enhance both the learning of university students and the intellectual, economic, and social resources of the community. The historical roots of service-learning provide a framework for understanding the variety of existing programs, help to clarify what is similar and what is different across varied service-learning initiatives, and prompt us to ponder the trajectory of service-learning as it evolves in a period of rapid growth. This chapter identifies the varied systems that have contributed to the current burgeoning of service-learning in American higher education and examines contemporary challenges that service-learning faces as it seeks to promote civil society in the 21st century.

COMMITMENT OF AMERICAN HIGHER EDUCATION TO PUBLIC PURPOSE

The history of higher education in America includes a clear, if not sustained, commitment to public purpose. Colleges in colonial America focused on preparing students for leadership of the new nation (Altman, 1996). Among the first U.S. colleges, education of character was of equal importance to intellectual development (Colby, Ehrlich, Beaumont, Rosner, & Stevens, 2000). Harvard College, for example, was founded in 1636 to prepare citizens for active involvement in community life. In the late 1800s, university commitment to the solution of social problems of the surrounding community was exemplified at the University of Chicago through the establishment of Hull House, a social settlement founded by Jane Addams and Ellen Starr (Harkavy, 1996). The philosophy and practice of the land grant universities and extension education programs exemplify another longstanding commitment by higher education to practical education and community outreach. The land grant system was created through the Morrill Act of 1862, with a focus on excellence in scholarship and the application of scholarship to the practical needs of the community (Bonnen, 1998; Lerner et al., 1996). The second Morrill Act of 1890 founded the historically Black land-grant colleges with a directive towards combining work, service, and learning. The Hatch Act of 1887 created agricultural experiment stations and the Smith-Lever Act of 1914 provided for extension services beyond the boundaries of the college campus. This series of legislative acts affirmed the central importance of service and community outreach, along with teaching and research, to the mission of American higher education. Commitment to service has also been present historically among the large number of religious and church-related institutions that have formed an important part of the higher education landscape in the United States. Jesuit higher education, for example, has been committed to educating students to participate in a just society, to reflect on experience, and to become empowered through knowledge acquisition (Fleming, 1999). Founded with a commitment to meet community needs and to link education with preparation for practical work in community settings (Barnett, 1996), community colleges represent the newest and largest segment of American higher education dedicated to public purpose.

Despite the historical commitment of higher education to public service, several trends detracted from this focus. In the early 1950s, for example, Cold War fears fueled competition with the Soviets, directing national attention and federal funding to the advancement of scientific knowledge, with less focus on domestic issues. The university responded to this societal need by elevating the status of basic scientific research above teaching, service and applied community-based research (McCall, 1996), thereby reducing the connection of higher education to real world problems (Gamson, 2000). The status and prestige of the American university grew because of the importance of university-based research for the development of defense-related technology and for the education of a growing middle-class workforce to meet labor market needs (Bok, 1992). Social critics, such as Bellah et al. (1985), maintained, however, that the specialization of the research university led to the "impoverishment of the public sphere" (p. 299). Additionally, according to some observers (Altman, 1996), the aftermath of the Cold War led not to a renewed concern for social responsibility, but rather to an attitude of increased individualism and entrepreneurial spirit across our country and university campuses.

Recent interest in service-learning is, in part, a response to the view that higher education abandoned its historical commitment to the community and should now reestablish its responsiveness to society and its relevance to public life (Boyer, 1990, 1994). The supposedly objective knowledge promoted by the research university has been criticized as inadequate in meeting the civic and social crises that confront our nation (Battistoni, 1985; Gamson, 2000). In recognition of this gap, Boyer (1994) called for a "New American College" that would successfully connect thought to action and theory to practice and "give new dignity and status to the scholarship of service" (p. A48). More recently, the Kellogg Commission on the Future of State and Land Grant Universities (1999) called for the state and land-grant colleges to return to their roots as "engaged" institutions, serving "local and national needs in a more coherent and effective way" (p. i). Colleges and universities are thus experiencing external pressures, as discussed in Chapter 1 of this volume, to become more active in solving problems of the local, regional, and national communities of which they are a part. Evidence of increased university civic engagement is accruing. For example, the American Council on Education developed a forum on the Civic Responsibility of Higher Education in 1997. During the following year, a Wingspread Conference on the Civic Responsibility of Research Universities was attended by scholars, university administrators, foundation personnel, and members of higher education organizations. The concept of university-community collaborations that utilize outreach scholarship of faculty to enhance the well-being of communities is emerging as a viable concept and strategy for integrating university research and civic responsibility (Lerner & Simon, 1998).

INTELLECTUAL AND PHILOSOPHICAL ROOTS

The intellectual and philosophical roots of service-learning have been attributed to the conceptualizations of democratic society put forth by Alexis de Tocqueville in the 1830s and John Dewey in the early twentieth century. De Tocqueville (1835/1969) noted that social commitment is critical to the functioning of democracy in a competitive and individualistic society like the United States. De Tocqueville maintained that individual strivings for advancement in the United States must be countered by a social commitment to civic, religious, and moral freedom. In his writings on democracy, Dewey (1916) similarly emphasized the need for democratic citizens to understand and consider the welfare of the society as a whole. In order to balance their personal needs with the needs of others, citizens must gain an understanding of the lives and experiences of other citizens. The philosophies of de Tocqueville and Dewey resonated with social critics of the 1980s and 1990s who noted increased individualism and a distancing and disillusionment of Americans from civic participation. Bellah et al. (1985) suggested that many Americans had withdrawn from social and political involvement because they felt isolated and powerless to deal with the complex problems of contemporary society. Political theorists, like Barber (1992) and Battistoni (1985), turned to the writings of de Tocqueville and Dewey for guidance on enhancing social and political understanding and embraced service-learning as a means to promote experiential understanding and motivate civic participation. In a similar vein, Robert Coles (1993) advocated for student involvement in community service as a means for building moral character and social action.

As an instructional pedagogy, service-learning is indebted to the ideas of Dewey and other proponents of experiential education, from Jean Piaget to David Kolb and Donald Schön (Jacoby, 1996). For Dewey, a commitment to the collective goal, in conjunction with academic growth, could best be attained through project-based and experiential learning (Dewey, 1938/1963). Dewey (1938) maintained that students would not be prepared for life in a changing society by memorizing static facts and information passed along by society's elders. Instead, genuine education would be derived from life experience that was accompanied by opportunities for discussion and reflection. In the absence of reflection, experience by itself has the potential for "mis-education," or a faulty interpretation of experience. Contemporary educators maintain that experiential learning, coupled with reflection, offers a pedagogy well-suited to educating students to understand and offer creative solutions to societal problems. Donald Schön (1995), for example, suggested that an epistemology of "knowing-in-action" is useful for identifying solutions to practical, applied problems that occur in the real world and are not fully comprehended by the objective decontextualized methods associated with pure science. The instructional pedagogy of service-learning has thus been advanced as a method that is better-suited than traditional professor-dominated instruction for preparing students for involvement in civil society.

TRADITIONS OF VOLUNTEERISM AND SOCIAL ACTIVISM

Service-learning also clearly builds on traditions of volunteerism, service, and social activism in American culture. A communal ethic of service and activism has accompanied and countered the American focus on individualism (Bellah et al., 1985). A commitment to helping one's neighbors was important, for example, to the survival and advancement of the individualistic American pioneers. Voluntary associations with a focus on community service, such as 4-H, YMCA/YWCA, and scouting have introduced many youth to the concepts of service and community involvement. Grassroots movements such as the abolition of slavery, women's suffrage, and civil rights reflect traditions of social action for the purposes of community betterment (Stanton, Giles, & Cruz, 1999).

As early as 1910, William James proposed the notion of nonmilitary national service in his essay on "The Moral Equivalent of War." Numerous national service programs have developed since that time. The Civilian Conservation Corps (1933), which served as a forerunner for future youth service programs, was designed to resolve depression-related unemployment by engaging youth in work/service projects. The Youth Conservation Corps of the 1970s involved 38,000 youth between the ages of 14 and 18 in summer conservation programs. The Vietnam protests and Civil Rights movement of the 1960s challenged students and colleges to be more socially responsive. The Peace Corps, VISTA, National Teacher Corps, Job Corps, and University Year for ACTION emerged during the social activist climate of the 1960s and early 1970s and engaged young people in addressing social and economic problems in the U.S. and abroad. The National Civilian Community Corps (NCCC), enacted as part of the 1993 Defense Authorization Act, was modeled after the depression-era Civilian Conservation Corps and U.S. military service. Economic and human resources made available as a result of the conclusion of the Cold War were devoted to the solution of domestic problems through the NCCC.

The popularity of social activism and experiential learning in the 1960s and early 1970s, in conjunction with student demands to increase the social relevance of university education, contributed to the birth of service-learning. The momentum of this movement was relatively short-lived, however, as a result of shifts in the political and social climate of the country and the shortcomings of early service-learning programs. Early service-learning programs were not integrated with the central mission and goals of schools and agencies, conveyed an attitude of paternalism and charity toward community partners, and assumed that service by itself would ensure student learning (Jacoby, 1996; Kendall, 1990). With awareness of these shortcomings, a number of community leaders and educators sustained a commitment to service throughout the "me-generation" of the late 1970s and 1980s and developed standards that would be critical for the successful implementation and continuation of service programs.

THE EVOLUTION OF SERVICE-LEARNING IN ITS CURRENT FORM

The mid 1980s and early 1990s witnessed major developments in service-learning. Astin and colleagues' 1989 survey of college students provided a reminder to educators and the public that materialism ranked high among student values, with 73% of students reporting that "being well off financially" was essential or very important them, whereas "participating in a community action program" was rated as very important to only 22% (Astin, Parrot, Korn, & Sax, 1997). Service-learning regained attention as one possible antidote to youth political withdrawal, materialism, and social alienation. Pioneers from the service-learning initiatives of the 1960s and 1970s had learned from early mistakes and responded to public concerns regarding youth civic disengagement by presenting a theoretically and pedagogically sound base of practice to inform service-learning initiatives (Kendall, 1990).

In 1984, the Campus Outreach Opportunity League (COOL) was formed by a group of recent college graduates to encourage college students to serve their communities. Campus Compact, the only national higher education organization whose primary purpose is to support campus-based public and community service, was established in 1985 by college and university presidents who expressed a commitment to helping students develop the values and skills of citizenship through participation in public and community service. These college presidents felt that students on their campuses had been misrepresented as the "me-generation," with many students holding a strong commitment to serve others (Ehrlich, 1996). Campus Compact focused attention on the integration of service into the academic curriculum of the university and thus sought to reduce the status of service learning as a marginal campus activity (Ehrlich, 1996). Concern for the establishment and dissemination of sound service-learning practice led to the Wingspread Conference of 1989, sponsored by the Johnson Foundation, a private operating foundation that co-sponsors conferences on issues of public interest. Principles of Good Practice for Combining Service and Learning were developed at the 1989 Wingspread Conference. In 1991, a second Wingspread Conference was co-sponsored by the National Society for Experiential Education, which resulted in the creation of a Research Agenda for Combining Service and Learning in the 1990s. In response to a call for published research, the first academic journal dedicated to service-learning, the Michigan Journal for Community Service, emerged in 1994.

Federal legislation of the late 1980s and early 1990s gave a tremendous impetus to voluntary service and service-learning on a national level. Campus Compact supported efforts for federal legislation that would promote public and community service and provide incentives for higher education to expand student volunteerism and create partnerships with community agencies. The National and Community Service Trust Act of 1990 represented the culmination of President Bush's campaign promise of a "thousand points of light," which had also inspired the creation of the White House Office of National Service in 1989. The National and Community Service Trust Act of 1990 created a new independent federal agency, the Commission on National and Community Service, and a non-partisan, non-profit organization, The Points of Light Foundation. The Points of Light Foundation was founded to expand service initiatives, following from an assumption that societal disconnection is a core element of current social ills. The Community Service Provisions of the 1992 Reauthorization of the Higher Education Act stipulated that 5% of work-study program funds allocated to institutions of higher education must be used to pay students engaged in community service. As part of his 1992 presidential campaign, Bill Clinton called for an expansion of national service. The National and Community Service Trust Act of 1993 drafted by the Clinton Administration and members of Congress established the Corporation for National Service to operate three initiatives, Learn and Serve America, AmeriCorps, and the National Senior Services Corp. Learn and Serve America supported service initiatives in K-12 schools and in higher education. Through the AmeriCorps national service program, volunteers receive post-service educational stipends that can be used either to pay off their educational loans or to finance further education or training (Corporation for National Service, 2000; Learn and Serve America, 2000). The Learn and Serve National Service Learning Clearinghouse was created in 1993 to promote the integration of service with the academic curricula of schools and universities. In 1994, President Clinton asked college presidents for help in fostering service among students, which led to the January 1995 Colloquium on National and Community Service organized by Campus Compact and the American Association of Higher Education, as well as a series of additional meetings, workshops, and materials.

In 1996, America Reads was launched by President Clinton as part of a comprehensive children's literacy program to insure that all children can read well and independently by the end of the third grade. Federal Work Study Funds have been a primary source of funding for America Reads' tutors, because the federal government waived the usual requirement that educational institutions match the funding provided by federal monies. Responsibility for administering and organizing the America Reads program is often housed in college community service offices and is one of the largest community needs filled by college community service programs (Campus Compact, 2000). As a result, many college students have become involved in community service by tutoring children in reading and have funded their college studies through this activity.

The Points of Light Foundation, along with the Corporation for National Service, co-sponsored the Presidents' Summit for America's future in April 1997 in Philadelphia. The purpose of the summit was to celebrate America's commitment to its youth and to create an interest in volunteerism and community service across the nation. Service was conceptualized as a civic responsibility and an opportunity for young people to give back to society. The summit was attended by more than 4,000 people, including Retired General Colin Powell, President Clinton, Vice President Al Gore, former First Lady Nancy Reagan and former presidents George Bush and Jimmy Carter. Volunteers joined with political leaders in a cleanup of Germantown Avenue in Philadelphia. At the end of the event, President Clinton signed a Summit Declaration, proclaiming that the duty of Americans to take responsibility for one another. Representatives from communities across the nation met in small groups to discuss ways to take the ideas and energy of the summit back to their home communities, schools, communities of faith, and workplaces.

Higher education organizations have dedicated events and resources to enhance service-learning, as well as civic responsibility, and community partnership, thereby helping to move service-learning from the margins to the mainstream of higher education. The American Association of Higher Education (AAHE) Conference in 1995 focused on ways to link service with learning. AAHE has also produced an 18 volume series on the integration of service-learning across a variety of academic disciplines. These discipline-based monographs provide a resource for faculty wishing to explore and initiate community-based learning in their courses and across their campuses. Consistent with their mission to meet community needs, the American Association of Community Colleges (AACC) has promoted the value of service-learning among the 1200 two-year institutions in the U.S. (Barnett, 1996). In 1994, the AAAC received a grant from the Corporation for National and Community Service, with additional support from the Kellogg Foundation, to train community college faculty to implement service-learning and to strengthen institutional support for service-learning within and across community colleges. National resources targeted towards community colleges include the Campus Compact Center for Community College and the AACC Service-Learning Clearinghouse. Since 1997, Campus Compact has broadened its vision to promote "engaged" campuses, with a focus on educating students and all members of the university as engaged community and national citizens (Hollander & Hartley, 2000). Nearly 400 college presidents signed a Declaration on the Civic Responsibility of Higher Education at the Presidents' Leadership Colloquium organized by Campus Compact and the American Council on Education on June 29-July 1, 1999 at the Aspen Institute (Ehrlich, Hollander, et al., 1999). The Council of Independent Colleges, in conjunction with the National Society for Experiential Education and Campus Compact, developed an informational network among colleges and universities that are involved in developing community partnerships (Hollander & Hartley, 2000).

Government enthusiasm for national service has been accompanied by the championing of service in the private sector. Voluntary service has been embraced as a solution to contemporary social ills and an alternative to expensive government assistance programs (Gerson, 1997). America's

Promise, a not-for-profit organization, was founded in April of 1997 under the leadership of Retired General Colin Powell, and has been dedicated to changing the lives of at-risk youth in the United States. America's Promise has solicited talent and resources from corporations, service providers, state and local governments, and not-for-profit organizations to form an alliance that would provide critical resources to children and youth in need. A number of private foundations and private corporations have lent important financial support to fund service initiatives.

CURRENT STATUS AND CHALLENGES

The popularity of community service and service-learning by a broad constituency across the public spectrum marks a high point in its history. The broad acceptance of service-learning in higher education is reflected by a large membership of Campus Compact, which in 1999 numbered 639 colleges. More than 13,000 faculty and 374,333 students across these campuses are involved in service learning (Campus Compact, 2000). The tremendous growth of service-learning and the expanding commitment to build civil society provide an occasion to reflect on the history, current status, and future directions of this movement. Although service is a popular educational activity, it is not free from controversy and challenge. The challenges that confront service-learning as it attempts to further civil society stem from its multiple and complex agendas to promote student citizenship, meet national and community needs, and transform university structures.

Although service-learning is wide-spread across university campuses, programs remain diverse, shaped by unique histories and missions. Some programs were inspired by a commitment to social action, community partnership, civic renewal, and the enhancement of economic, social, and intellectual resources available to the community. Other programs evolved through a belief in the pedagogy of experiential learning, and others developed primarily from a commitment to enhance the moral, religious, and/or civic development of the student body. The service mission of the university may be defined differently at community colleges, liberal arts colleges, research universities, and professional schools, and is often reinterpreted and renegotiated as the national climate of social, political, and cultural forces change (Pollack, 1999). How a college interprets its service mission and the relationship of service to research and teaching will inevitably impact its approach to service-learning and the location on the campus in which service activities are housed. The extent to which service-learning is part of the formal curriculum developed by the faculty, is a co-curricular activity sponsored by student affairs, or is a community outreach function implemented through a separate university structure remains a source of tension on many university campuses (Kezar & Rhoads, 2001).

The contributions of this volume reflect the varied service missions of contemporary universities, including citizenship and civic responsibility, academic development, professional preparation, the quest for social justice, and community partnership/public problem solving. We believe that diversity of missions is necessary because it reflects responsiveness to the varied contexts of the colleges/universities and their surrounding communities. This diversity also contributes to ongoing dialogue concerning the ways in which service-learning should educate its citizens. Given the variety of current models, Chapter 1 of this volume suggests that contemporary definitions of service-learning must be either more inclusive or more differentiated. Yet, if service-learning is to survive and flourish as part of the mainstream of academia, current models must also effectively integrate the missions of community outreach/service, research, and student development. Continued debate on definitions, purpose, and models of service-learning is recognized as a means for strengthening the field and connecting service-learning with on-going dialogues about educational reform (Stanton et al., 1999).

Despite their diverse origins, recent events related to the advancement of service-learning, including a proliferation of government and private programs and expansion of service-learning knowledge, have inevitably transformed colleges and universities, such that service-learning programs of the new millennium differ significantly from programs that first surfaced from varied missions. The chapters in this volume document many changes that have occurred in university service-learning in recent years as a result of these developments. The institutionalization of service-learning has created dilemmas for social change advocates, who worry about how service-learning has been transformed in the process of meeting mainstream agendas (Stanton et al., 1999). Liu (1999), for example, questioned whether service-learning programs can assimilate or transform the norms of the academy and whether the development of a national service-learning movement supports or undermines local autonomy and self-determination. National organizations, common standards, and federal funding have helped to move service-learning from the margins to the mainstream of higher education. The popularity and consensus that currently surround service-learning reflect a political, social, and economic alliance that could be difficult to sustain. Kahne and Westheimer (1996) suggested that efforts to find common ground between conservatives and liberals, business leaders and community activists, have contributed to a tendency to overlook controversial issues.

Proponents and critics of service-learning are also asking difficult questions concerning student preparation for civil society. Service programs in public education have been criticized by some for promoting and indoctrinating a liberal social and political agenda (Garber & Heet, 2000). Other critics have expressed concern that service-learning teaches students to fit into and reap the benefits of the existing social order, rather than to bring about a change in social institutions. Kahne and Westheimer (1996) lamented that much service activity involves a focus on charity rather than change. They claimed that students are not typically taught about social transformation, but rather perform a civic duty and service that makes them feel good, but does little to change society. Ward (1997) similarly maintained that service-learning can be a transforming experience when students are challenged to examine underlying beliefs, yet claimed that too few programs critically examine the structural issues that create the need for services in the first place. Boyte (1991) criticized service curriculum for insufficient examination of the complex dimensions of power, race, and class that are created when middle class youth go to serve in low-income areas. According to Kezar and Rhodes (2001), an essential philosophical issue, exemplified by current tensions around service-learning in higher education, is whether the learning goals of service-learning should focus predominantly on the development of citizenship and social responsibility, of multicultural understanding, or of critical thinking and writing.

Although many universities have integrated service-learning into their curricular or co-curricular activities, the success of the university in solving societal problems through outreach scholarship has not been widely documented. Maybach (1996), for example, criticized university programs for their emphasis on student development and relative inattention to community needs and benefits. Harkavy (1996) suggested that when service-learning fails to address itself to the solution of core community problems, it "is merely the pedagogical equivalent of exploitative community-based research" (p. 58). Gerson (1997) maintained, however, that volunteers cannot be counted on to solve critical social problems. Volunteers often respond to short-lived crises and seldom commit to the most difficult social problems that require large and sustained sacrifice and commitments of time and money. The political consensus that fueled the Philadelphia Summit may thus be fragile and short-lived as it was based in part from a flawed expectation that volunteerism can provide a sound replacement for social welfare.

Visions of civil society through service-learning might be threatened by uncertain financial support. Federal legislation is credited with an expansion of service-learning programs across the nation. The extent to which these programs are dependent upon federal funding or represent a broad and sustainable movement towards renewing community and reforming education is yet to be determined (Kraft, 1996). University and societal willingness to contribute time and money to resolving social ills flourished amidst the resounding economic boom of the 1990s. During times of economic down-turn, contributions of private donors to social causes usually drop, and government and university funding for programs beyond the essentials becomes tight. Students may return to a narrow focus on vocational preparation, with less investment in "giving back" to society. University commitments to community engagement and civil society will likely be tested during times of economic uncertainty.

Despite concerns that the goals of service-learning have been diffused and are supported by a fragile consensus, service-learning has also been heralded as offering a potential for coherence in the fragmented world of higher education. Some have claimed that the university missions of research, teaching, and service can be unified through the integration of service-learning and outreach scholarship (Lerner & Simon, 1998; Zlotowski, 1998). Excellence in research, teaching, and service can be combined without sacrificing one endeavor for the other. Kenny and Gallagher (2000) reviewed best practices in service-learning in higher education to identify models and methods that simultaneously advance the multiple agendas of service-learning. Continuity in service to communities that cannot be sustained by individual volunteers can be sustained by institutional commitments. The Combining Service and Learning in Higher Education: Summary Report (Gray, Ondaatje, & Zakaras, 1999), which evaluated programs funded by Learn and Serve America: Higher Education, indicated that programs are generally successful in simultaneously increasing student civic commitment and social responsibility, providing services that are valued by the communities, and building university structures that will help to sustain service-learning programs after federal funding has ended.

It is the premise of this volume that colleges and universities can respond to the identified challenges and commitments to merge student academic, moral, and civic development and outreach activities to serve communities by studying and building upon current efforts as presented in this book. Elsewhere, Zlotowski (1998) maintained that service-learning practitioners should not fear the movement of service-learning from the margins to the mainstream, as it is only through the wide-spread institutionalization of service-learning that resources have been garnered to overcome barriers to its implementation. Hollander and Hartley (2000) suggested that a social movement that transforms and reconnects higher education to its civic roots will best be accomplished through the expansion of national networks of organizations and resources linking information and expertise. The growing number of scholarly resources, outcome research, and refereed publications now devoted to service-leaning and outreach scholarship should contribute to increased recognition of the academic legitimacy of this work by university promotion and tenure committees. The obstacles to the development and sustenance of successful service-learning programs have not vanished as a result of its recent popularity. However, the varied models and programs that have emerged nationwide and are presented in this book provide a wealth of data for examining best-practices, for creating dialogue among scholars, practitioners and community partners, and for forging the future of service-learning in a reflective manner that is consistent with its intellectual, civic, and social action roots.

REFERENCES

Altman, I. (1996). Higher education and psychology in the millennium. *American Psychologist, 51*, 371-378.

Astin, A. W., Parrott, S. A., Korn, W. S., & Sax, L. J. (1997).*The American freshman: Thirty year trend*. Los Angeles: Higher Education Research Institute.

Barber, B. (1992). *An aristocracy of everyone: The politics of education and the future of America*. New York: Oxford University Press.

Barnett, L. (1996). Service learning: Why community colleges? In M. H. Parsons, & C. D. Lisman (Eds.), *Promoting community renewal through civic literacy and service learning. New Directions for Community Colleges*, (No. 93, pp. 7-15). San Francisco: Jossey-Bass.

Battistoni, R. (1985). *Public schooling and the education of democratic citizens.* Jackson, MS: The University of Mississippi Press.

Bellah, R. N., Madsen, R., Sullivan, W. M., Swidler, A., & Tipton, S. M. (Eds.). (1985). *Habits of the heart: Individualism and commitment in American life.* Berkeley, CA: University of California Press.

Bok, D. (1992, July/August). Reclaiming the public trust. *Change,* 18.

Bonnen, J. T. (1998). The land-grant idea and the evolving outreach university. In R. M. Lerner & L. A. K. Simon (Eds.), *University-community collaborations for the twenty-first century: Outreach scholarship for youth and families* (pp. 25-71). New York: Garland.

Boyer, E. L. (1990). *Scholarship reconsidered: Priorities of the professoriate.* Princeton, NJ: The Carnegie Foundation for the Advancement of Teaching.

Boyer, E. L. (1994, March 9). Creating the new American college. *The Chronicle of Higher Education,* A48.

Boyte, H. C. (1991). Community service and civic education. *Phi Delta Kappan, 72,* 765-67.

Campus Compact. (2000). 1999 Campus Compact member survey. Retrieved January 26, 2001 from the World Wide Web: http://www.compact.org/news/stats/2-student-service.html.

Colby, A., Ehrlich, T., with Beaumont, E., Rosner, J., & Stephens, J. (2000). Higher education and the development of civic responsibility. In T. Ehrlich (Ed.), *Civic responsibility and higher education* (pp. xxi-xliii) Phoenix, AZ: American Council on Education/The Oryx Press.

Coles, R. (1993). *The call of service.* Boston: Houghton Mifflin.

Corporation for National Service. (2000) About us: Legislative history. Retrieved November 10, 2000 from the World Wide Web: http://www.cns.gov/about/leg_history.html.

De Tocqueville, A. (1945). *Democracy in America.* New York: Vintage Press.

Dewey, J. (1916). *Democracy and education.* New York: MacMillan.

Dewey, J. (1963/1938). *Experience and education.* New York: Collier.

Ehrlich, T. (1996). Forward. In B. Jacoby (Ed.), *Service learning in higher education: Concepts and practices.* San Francisco: Jossey-Bass.

Ehrlich, T., Hollander, E., et al. (1999). Presidents' Fourth of July declaration on the civic responsibility of higher education. Providence, RI: Campus Compact. Retrieved March 16, 2001 from the World Wide Web: http://www.compact.org/resources/plc-declaration.html.

Fleming, J. (1999). The emerging role of service learning at Jesuit universities. *Explore, Spring,* 6-10.

Gamson, Z. F. (2000). In T. Ehrlich (Ed.), *Civic responsibility and higher education* (pp. 367-372). Phoenix, AZ: American Council on Education/The Oryx Press.

Garber, G. P., & Heet, J. A. (2000). Free to choose service-learning. *Phi Delta Kappan, 81,* 676-677.

Gerson, M. (1997, April 28). Do do-gooders do much good? *U.S. News & World Report, 122,* 26-30.

Gray, M. J., Ondaatje, E. H., & Zakaras, L. (1999). Combining service and learning in higher education: Summary report. Santa Monica, CA: RAND.

Harkavy, I. (1996). Back to the future: From service learning to strategic, academically-based community service. *Metropolitan Universities, 7,* 57-71.

Hollander, E., & Hartley, M. (2000). Civic renewal in higher education: The state of the movement and the need for a national network. In T. Ehrlich (Ed.), *Civic responsibility and higher education* (pp. 345-366). Phoenix, AZ: American Council on Education/The Oryx Press.

Hollander, E., Saltmarsh, J., & Zlotowski, E. (2001). Indicators of engagement. In L. A. K. Simon, M. Kenny, K. Brabeck, & R. M. Lerner (Eds.), *Learning to serve: Promoting civil society through service learning.* Kluwer.

Jacoby, B. (Ed.). (1996). *Service learning in higher education: Concepts and practices.* San Francisco, CA: Jossey-Bass.

Kahne, J., & Westmeier, J. (1996). In the service of what? The politics of service learning. *Phi Delta Kappan, 77,* 593-599.

Kendall, J. C. (1990). (Ed.), *Combining service and learning: A resource book for community and public service* (Vol. 1). Raleigh, NC: National Society for Experiential Education.

Kellogg Commission on the Future of State and Land Grant Universities. (1999). *Returning to our roots: The engaged institution.* Washington, DC: National Association of State Universities and Land Grant Colleges.

Kenny, M. E., & Gallagher, L. (2000). Service-learning as a vehicle in training psychologists for revised professional roles. In F. S. Sherman & W. R. Torbert (Eds.), *Transforming social inquiry, transforming social action: Creating communities of practice at the university and in the community* (pp. 189-205). Norwood, MA: Kluwer Academic Publishers.

Kezar, A., & Rhoads, R. A. (2001). The dynamic tensions of service learning in higher education. *The Journal of Higher Education, 72,* 148-171.

Kraft, R. J. (1996). Service learning: An introduction to its theory, practice, and effects. *Education and Urban Society, 28,* 131-159.

Learn and Serve America. (2000). About Learn & Serve: Service-learning. Retrieved January 15, 2001 from the World Wide Web: http://www.nationalservice.org/learn/about /service_learning.html.

Lerner, R. M., Ostrom, C. W., Miller, J. R., Votruba, J. C., von Eye, A., Hoopfer, L. C., Terry, P. A., Taylor, C. S., Villarruel, F. A., & McKinney, M. H. (1996). Training applied developmental scientists for community outreach: The Michigan State University model of integrating science and outreach for children, youth, and families. In C. B. Fisher, J. P. Murray, & I. E. Sigel (Eds.), *Applied developmental science: Graduate training for diverse disciplines and educational settings* (pp. 163-188). Norwood, NJ: Ablex Publishing Corporation.

Lerner, R. M., & Simon, L. A. K. (Eds.). (1998), *Creating the new outreach university for America's youth and families: Building university-community collaborations for the twenty-first century.* New York: Garland.

Liu, G. (1999). Foreword. In T. K. Stanton, D. E. Giles, & N. Cruz (Eds.), *Service-learning: A movement's pioneers reflect on its origins, practice, and future* (pp. xi-xiv). San Francisco: Jossey-Bass.

Maybach, C. W. (1996). Investigating urban community needs: Service-learning from a social justice perspective. *Education and Urban Society, 28,* 224-236.

McCall, R. B. (1996). The concept and practice of education, research, and public service in university psychology departments. *American Psychologist, 51,* 379-388.

Morton, K., & Saltmarsh, J. (1997). Addams, Day, and Dewey: The emergence of community service in American culture. *Michigan Journal of Community Service Learning, 4,* 137-149.

Pollack, S. (1999). Early connections between service and education. In T. K. Stanton, D. E. Giles, & N. Cruz (Eds.), *Service-learning: A movement's pioneers reflect on its origins, practice, and future* (pp. 12-32). San Francisco: Jossey-Bass

Schine, J. (Ed.). (1997). *Service learning: Ninety-sixth yearbook of the National Society for the Study of Education.* The University of Chicago Press.

Schön, D. A. (1995, November/December). Knowing in action: The new scholarship requires a new epistemology. *Change,* 27-34.

Sigmon, R. (1979). Service learning: Three principles. *Synergist, 8,* 9-11

Stanton, T. K., Giles, D. E., & Cruz, N. (Eds.). (1999). *Service-learning: A movement's pioneers reflect on its origins, practice, and future.* San Francisco: Jossey-Bass.

Ward, J. V. (1997). Encouraging cultural competence in service learning practice. In J. Schine (Ed.), *Service learning: Ninety-sixth yearbook of the National Society for the Study of Education* (pp. 136-148). The University of Chicago Press.

Waterman, A. (Ed.). (1997). *Service-learning: Applications from the research.* Mahwah, NJ: Lawrence Erlbaum Associates.

Zlotowski, E. (Ed.). (1998). *Successful service learning programs: New models of excellence in higher education.* Bolton, MA: Anker Publishing

CHAPTER 3

INDICATORS OF ENGAGEMENT

Elizabeth L. Hollander[1]
John Saltmarsh[2]
Edward Zlotkowski[3]
Campus Compact

INTRODUCTION

As institutions of higher education reshape their organizational and administrative structures and functions in alignment with community-based education and civic renewal, there has emerged a framework for the "engaged campus." This essay traces the emergence of the engaged campus in the late 20th century as the developments in service-learning converged with widespread recognition of a national crisis defined by civic disintegration. Working from the conceptual framework of an engaged campus, the authors identify and provide current examples of ten critical "indicators" of community and civic engagement that indicate that an institution is establishing the essential foundations for engagement.

---

[1]Elizabeth Hollander is the executive director of Campus Compact. Previously, Hollander served as executive director of the Monsignor John J. Egan Urban Center at DePaul University, which works with the University to address critical urban problems, alleviate poverty and promote social justice in the metropolitan community through teaching, service and scholarship. She also served as the president of the Government Assistance Program in Illinois and is the former director of planning for the city of Chicago under Mayor Harold Washington. Hollander is the author, most recently, of "Civic Renewal in Higher Education: The State of the Movement and the Need for a National Network," in Thomas Ehrlich, ed., *Civic Responsibility and Higher Education*, (Orynx, 2000).

[2] John Saltmarsh is the Project Director of Integrating Service with Academic Study at Campus Compact. He taught for over a decade at Northeastern University and as a Visiting Research Fellow at the Feinstein Institute for Public Service at Providence College. His essays on service-learning and experiential education have appeared in *the Michigan Journal for Community Service Learning*, the *Journal of Experiential Education*, the *National Society for Experiential Education Quarterly* and the *Journal of Cooperative Education*. He is also the author of "Emerson's Prophesy," in Ira Harkavy and William Donovan, eds., *Connecting Past and Present: Concepts and Models for Service-Learning in History*, Washington, DC: American Association for Higher Education (2000).

[3]Edward Zlotkowski is Senior Faculty Fellow at Campus Compact and directs the Compacts initiative on service-learning in the disciplines. He is a Professor of English at Bentley College, in Waltham, MA, where he founded the Bentley College Service-Learning Project in 1990. He has written extensively on service-learning and is the author *of Successful Service-Learning Programs: New Models of Excellence in Higher Education* (Anker, 1998) and is the series editor for the American Association for Higher Education 18 volume Series on *Service-Learning in the Disciplines*. He is also a Senior Associate at the American Association for Higher Education.

INDICATORS OF ENGAGEMENT

The Emergence of the Engaged Campus

Campus engagement with local communities can take many forms, emerge from a variety of motivations, and have vastly different roots depending upon institutional culture, history, and geography. A historically black college has a rationale for engagement that differs significantly from that of a land grant university, which differs again from that of a private university in an urban center. From decade to decade, to a greater or lesser degree, holding close to or wavering from their mission, each institution shapes its public purpose accordingly. Over time, experiments in engagement have produced highly successful examples of programs, policies, and organizational and administrative structures that in concrete and visible ways can be identified as "indicators" of engagement. These indicators have emerged from experience with a range of institutional engagement strategies over the past quarter-century.

From the perspective of Campus Compact, a national coalition of over 750 college and university presidents committed to the civic purposes of higher education, a portrait of an engaged campus has emerged from the experiences and examples of hundreds of institutions across the United States. At its beginning, Campus Compact's perspective on campus engagement was focused on community service, which was embraced by both students and campus administrators as a counterweight to the characterization of contemporary students as a self-centered "me generation." Students' creation of COOL (Campus Outreach Opportunity League) in 1984 and the Compact's founding by college and university presidents in 1985 implicitly affirmed that students were seeking and that campuses were willing to provide opportunities for altruistic, socially responsible activity through community service (Morton and Troppe, 1996; Stanton, et al, 1999).

By the late 1980s service-learning had risen to prominence, marking a distinct evolution from community service to service that was integrated with academic study. During the early 1990s, service-learning spread across college campuses as a pedagogy of action and reflection that connected student's academic study with public problem-solving experiences in local community settings. As increasing numbers of faculty became involved in redesigning their curricula to incorporate service-learning, new questions emerged regarding such larger institutional issues as the definition of faculty roles and rewards, the value of community-based teaching and research, definitions of faculty professional service, strategies for maintaining community partnerships, and the role of the university in assisting community renewal (Zlotkowski, 1998; Jacoby, 1996; Rhoads and Howard, 1998, Eyler and Giles, 1999).

By the mid 1990s, these service-learning developments had converged with a range of critical and often contested issue — pedagogical, epistemological, institutional, and political — in higher education. Campuses were widely viewed as disconnected from social concerns and unresponsive to public needs, indeed, as largely deficient in meeting their civic obligations. When the National Commission on Civic Renewal issued their 1998 report on civic disengagement, it offered no role for higher education in providing solutions aimed at rebuilding civic life. (National Commission on Civic Renewal, 1998; Damon, 1998). Instead, the report in many ways echoed what the community organizer Saul Alinsky had written in the late 1940s about higher education's relationship to community building; namely, that "the word 'academic' is often synonymous with irrelevant" (Alinsky, 1946). However, while a contemporary could have objected that Alinsky's critique failed to reflect the significant contribution higher education was making to meeting the country's international crisis during the 40s, no such mitigating consideration was available in the 90s.

Indeed, institutions of higher education were highly responsive in helping to meet the needs of the country as defined by the cold war, and allowed themselves to become in large part structured and organized around the demands of the military-industrial complex. This meant that their culture celebrated science and technology, their faculty emphasized objectivity and detachment, and their value system elevated the role of the scientifically educated expert over that of ordinary citizens in public affairs (Bender, 1993; Mathews, 1998).

Yet the crisis we now face at the beginning of a new century is a crisis in our civic life. Success in addressing the cold war meant that colleges and universities became shaped in ways that are not necessarily those needed to meet the challenge of transforming our civic life. The ethos of professionalism and expertise that defined higher education's response to the national crisis of the cold war now contributes to public disillusionment with institutions that represent and legitimize a system that no longer addresses our most pressing national needs (Boyte, 2000; Sullivan, 1995). For this reason, many higher education institutions, in their struggle to meet our need for civic renewal, have found themselves returning to their founding missions, which in some part express the aim of serving American democracy by educating students for productive citizenship. At the same time, they look to pedagogies of engagement such as service-learning to prepare students with the knowledge and skills needed for democratic citizenship. Service-learning not only transforms teaching and learning, but also has the potential to surface a broader vision of the engaged campus (Hollander and Saltmarsh, 2000; Campus Compact, 1999A). Such a campus, centrally engaged in the life of its local communities, reorients its core missions — teaching, scholarship, and service — around community building and neighborhood resource development.

- Pedagogy is centered on engaged teaching; that is, connecting structured student activities in community work with academic study, decentering the teacher as the singular authority of knowledge, incorporating a reflective teaching methodology, and shifting the model of education, to use Freire's distinctions, from "banking" to "dialogue" (Friere, 1970; Dewey, 1916; Saltmarsh, 1996).

- Scholarship of engagement is oriented toward community-based action research that addresses issues defined by community participants and that includes students in the process of inquiry (Boyer, 1990).
- Service is expanded beyond the confines of department committees, college committees and professional associations to the application of academic expertise to community-defined concerns (Lynton, 1995).

The vision of the engaged campus also suggests a wider democratic practice, one that goes beyond a reorientation of the institution's professional culture and a revisiting of its academic mission to include changes in institutional structure and organization. Reciprocal, long-term relationships in local communities imply institutional structures — what Mary Walshok calls "enabling mechanisms" (Walshok, 1995) — to connect the campus to the community. Faculty roles are reconsidered, as is the reward structure, to acknowledge, validate, and encourage a shift in teaching, scholarship, and service toward community engagement. Additionally, traditional campus divisions such as those between student affairs and academic affairs, and between disciplines and departments are suspended in the interest of a broader view of educating students as whole individuals whose experience of community engagement is not artificially confined by disciplinary distinctions. Further, the institution embraces a view of the campus as a part of, not as separate from, the local community. Such a view reconceptualizes the resources of the college or university as community-related resources, impacting issues like community economic development, hiring, purchasing and the investment of capital in community revitalization (Ehrlich, 2000). It is this larger sense of institutional alignment that Ernest Boyer had in mind when he employed the concept of "the scholarship of engagement," by which he meant "connecting the rich resources of the university to our most pressing social, civic, and ethical problems." Higher education, claimed Boyer, "must become a more vigorous partner in the search for answers to our most pressing social, civic, economic, and moral problems, and must reaffirm its historic commitment to what I call the scholarship of engagement" (Boyer, 1996).

Indicators of Engagement

When Campus Compact is called upon to assist a campus in moving toward deeper engagement in a local community, our response is shaped by the experience of our member campuses over years of experiments and challenges, and draws upon a wide range of experiences and examples. We look specifically for the existence of certain institutional activities, policies, and structures. These, as they stand individually, can be considered "indicators of engagement." Any number of these indicators occurring together on a campus suggests wider institutional engagement and the emergence of an "engaged campus." However, it is unlikely that all will be apparent on any one campus. These indicators should not be regarded as prescriptive; their value lies in the possibilities they suggest. They include:

1. *Pedagogy and epistemology*: Are there courses on campus that have a community-based component that enhances the acquisition and creation of disciplinary or interdisciplinary knowledge (service-learning courses)? Is gaining knowledge through experience accepted as an academically credible method of creating meaning and understanding?

2. *Faculty development*: Are there opportunities for faculty to retool their teaching methods to employ a reflective teaching methodology that maximizes the value of integrating community-based experiences with the academic aims of a course? Is there administrative support for faculty to redesign their curricula to incorporate community-based activities and reflection on those activities?

3. *Enabling mechanisms*: Are there visible and easily accessible structures on campus that function both to assist faculty with community-based teaching and learning and to broker the relationships between community-based organizations (community partners) and various curricular and co-curricular activities on campus?

4. *Internal resource allocation:* Is there adequate funding available for establishing, enhancing, and deepening community-based work on campus – for faculty, students, and programs that involve community partners?

5. *External resource allocation:* Is there funding available for community partners to create a richer learning environment for students working in the community and to assist those partners to access human and intellectual resources on campus? Are resources made available for community-building efforts in local neighborhoods?

6. *Faculty roles and rewards*: Do the tenure and promotion guidelines used at the institution reflect the kind of reconsideration of scholarly activity proposed by Ernest Boyer, whereby a scholarship of teaching and a scholarship of application are viewed on a par with the scholarship of discovery (Boyer, 1990)?

7. *Disciplines, departments, interdisciplinarity*: Is community-based education relegated to a small number of social science disciplines, or is it embedded in the arts and humanities, hard sciences, technical disciplines, professional studies, and interdisciplinary programs as well? To what extent does it exist only on the margins of the curriculum, or has it been allowed to penetrate to the institution's academic core?

8. *Community voice*: How deeply are community partners involved in determining their role in and contribution to community-based education, and to what degree can they shape institutional involvement to maximize its benefits to the community?

9. *Administrative and Academic Leadership:* Do the president, provost and trustees visibly support campus civic engagement, in both their words and deeds? To what degree have the president and academic leadership been in the forefront of institutional transformation that supports civic engagement? To what degree is the campus known as a positive partner in local community development efforts?

10. *Mission and purpose*: Does the college or university's mission explicitly articulate its commitment to the public purposes of higher education and higher education's civic responsibility to educate for democratic participation? Are these aspects of the mission openly valued and identified to reinforce the public activities of the campus? Are they viewed merely as rhetoric, or is there substantive reality to match such stated purposes?

EXAMPLES

What follows are concrete examples of the kinds of activities, policies, and organizational and administrative structures that indicate deepening engagement in local communities. For any of the indicators, the examples provided are not meant to suggest any kind of comprehensive overview but merely to provide specific examples of increasingly widespread practices.

Pedagogy and Epistemology

At the core of wider institutional engagement lies an academic commitment to the kind of teaching, learning, and knowledge creation that foster active civic engagement. Courses with a service-learning or community-based component signify adoption of an engaged pedagogy. Yet, embedded within such a curriculum is a reflective teaching methodology that de-centers the instructor, and in doing so, recognizes that the authority of knowledge in the classroom is shared among faculty members, students, and partners in the community. Since such a reconceptualization of authority necessitates multifaceted reflection upon all knowledge-producing activity, faculty need to develop and array of tools and effective means for encouraging deep reflection by students (Eyler and Giles, 1999).

At Portland State University in Oregon, the university's commitment to community-based public problem solving as part of its Land Grant mission creates a strong academic connection to the community. Students in their second and third years pursue clusters of inquiry dealing with a theme related to their major and relevant to the Portland community. Most of these courses involve some kind of service-learning or action research project. In the fourth year, seniors must complete a capstone experience, a project that uses a team of students from several different disciplines to address a community-based problem or issue. All undergraduate students must make a connection between their academic work and the surrounding community before they graduate (Campus Compact, 1999B).

At St. Joseph's College, a small Catholic, liberal arts college in Standish, Maine, over 25% of the full-time faculty embrace service-learning as a legitimate method of gaining knowledge. The College's Vice-President for Academic Affairs has included service-learning in his strategic plan for academic learning with the goal that all students will experience this method of learning during their undergraduate education. Further, he is working with the faculty to infuse service-learning in the core curriculum. At a very different institution, the University of San Diego, approximately sixty classes use service-learning during the academic year, including courses that are offered both semesters and those that have more than one section. Over fifty faculty members have incorporated service-learning into their courses and between 450 and 500 students participate in service-learning courses each semester. Courses are offered in the schools of business and education, and many arts and sciences departments. These include anthropology, biology, chemistry, communication studies, English, fine arts (music and studio arts), foreign languages (French, German, Italian, and Spanish), gender studies, history, philosophy, political science, psychology, and sociology. There are service-learning business courses in accounting, economics, information systems, marketing, and management.

Faculty Development

For community-based education to take hold on campus, faculty must have opportunities to develop new teaching skills. The traditional trajectory for faculty developing their teaching skills results in a lecture-based format that aims at the delivery of a certain content consisting of disciplinary knowledge. For faculty to confidently incorporate community-based learning into their courses, they will need curriculum development grants, reductions in teaching loads and to the opportunity to attend on-campus workshops and seminars, and/or support to attend regional and national institutes and conferences that will help them gain the skills they need to employ an engaged pedagogy. Faculty development must be taken seriously as a component of institutional engagement (Holland, 1999; Zlotkowski, 1998).

An increasingly common faculty development strategy provides faculty stipends to redesign their discipline-based courses to include a service-learning course. In this model, the stipend is accompanied by a commitment by the faculty member to attend a series of workshops on experiential learning theory, reflection, community partnerships, and other key elements of community-based education. Further, the participating faculty commit to teaching their redesigned courses at least twice. The assumptions behind this model are twofold. First, the initial teaching of the course is treated as an experiment and the faculty member is encouraged to reflect on the successes and challenges of the course and make needed adjustments. Second, faculty who develop the competencies of community-based education and realize the enhanced learning potential of such an approach will continue to teach service-learning courses.

Early in the development of service-learning, Indiana University-Purdue University, Indianapolis (IUPUI) adopted a model of offering course development stipends to faculty, a model that had been used successfully at University of Notre Dame. Faculty were offered stipends of $1,000 to support the creation, implementation, or improvement of service-learning courses. Faculty recipients agreed to participate in three campus workshops during the academic year of the award. At the University of San Diego, all faculty members interested in service-learning attend a one-day curriculum development workshop on the foundations and theory of service-learning facilitated by experienced faculty members. During the semester that faculty integrate service-learning for the first time, they attend a second workshop. Faculty members receive $250 for two days for participating in the workshops. They also receive $250 for revision of their curricula and $250 for writing evaluation reports. All beginners have an experienced faculty "facilitator" as a resource person who meets with them several times during the semester and is available for assistance. In this way, the university works toward the goal of building a critical mass of faculty committed to service-learning as a viable pedagogy.

At St. Joseph's College, faculty have been selected to receive course development grants and each semester a faculty development workshop has been offered. Topics have included an introduction to service-learning, reflection and academic integration, assessment of student learning outcomes, working with community partners, and discipline-specific approaches to service-learning. Grant funding was secured to bring in leading national service-learning practitioners and community partners to facilitate the workshops. Additionally, faculty have participated in the problem-based service-learning workshops offered each summer by the Maine Campus Compact, and the Vice President for Academic Affairs has participated in regional meetings of provosts to discuss service-learning and strategies for faculty development.

Enabling Mechanisms

The single most important enabling mechanism for community-based education is a centralized office that performs a wide variety of functions. Indeed, so important is this particular "mechanism" that there exist few, if any, genuinely engaged campuses that do not have one. However, both its location/configuration and functions vary enormously from campus to campus.

Although many schools have some kind of "volunteer center" operating out of student affairs, most schools that become serious about developing a comprehensive engagement profile find it highly advantageous to locate such a center on the faculty affairs side of the institution, or at least to establish formal links between a more traditionally located center and academic administrators. Indeed, the degree to which a center has succeeded in developing effective, widely respected programming linked to scholarship and the curriculum is one important indicator of its institution's commitment to the concept of an engaged campus. Almost every school profiled in *Successful Service-Learning Programs: New Models of Excellence in Higher Education* (Zlotkowski, 1998) features a center under the authority of the provost or academic dean. When a different arrangement is involved, as in the case of the University of Utah, it still features multiple links to those responsible for academic programming.

Aside from the actual location of such a center on the institution's organizational chart, its relationship to other offices responsible for assisting faculty and/or students is another important consideration. Most frequently, an office that facilitates service-learning and other forms of engaged scholarship also facilitates other forms of off-campus work; for example, traditional extra-curricular community service and/or traditional internships. The advantage of bringing together under the same roof different kinds of partnering efforts is that such an arrangement helps the institution better keep track of and coordinate its relations with the community. On other campuses, the office that facilitates academic partnering is linked with faculty development (Portland State University) or student career services (Michigan State University).

Naturally, the location and linkages that define a center also help define the kinds of services it provides. Clearly its single most common function is to serve as a clearinghouse for faculty-community collaborations. Examples of this function range from a relatively passive indexing of what is available in the off-campus community to providing assistance with transportation, orientation, and reflection to highly proactive attempts to build and sustain long term partnerships based equally on faculty and community needs. However, some centers also assist faculty in learning about what is being done in comparable academic programs at other institutions. An increasingly frequent and especially promising function of many centers is to locate and train students capable of serving as faculty-community intermediaries (University of San Diego and Miami-Dade Community College). Regardless of their specific functions, centers must develop the forms and procedures that allow them to organize and document their work.

Internal Resource Allocation

Nothing is more common than for a college or university to recognize the benefits of engagement — and to try to capitalize on those benefits — without making any substantive investment in the resources such engagement requires. Many potentially fine programs have been initiated with the help of grants, only to crumble away once their external source of funding has dried up. Few schools would consider trying to reap the benefits of corporate or alumni support without first investing in a development or alumni office, and yet, when it comes to community engagement, this is precisely what they often do. Internal institutional funding is, therefore, one significant measure of an institution's commitment to engagement.

This being said, it is important to note that internal resources come in many forms, not the least important of which is space. How much space and where on campus a school is willing to dedicate space to organizing its engagement activities often says more than any catalog copy about the real significance the school attaches to them. Another indication is its willingness to tap already existing resources to strengthen those activities. When Bentley College in Waltham, Massachusetts, first began developing a service-learning program in the early 1990s, its provost not only made it clear that summer scholarship funds should be used to support quality work in this new area, he also made it possible for the program to "employ" graduate students through a reallocation of graduate assistantships and undergraduates through a reorganization of community-focused work-study placements. While the program's operations and staff line items grew modestly over the course of several years, a redistribution of already budgeted resources made it possible for the program to accomplish far more than the growth in those line items would suggest.

External Resource Allocation

Investing resources off campus for community-building has a powerful effect in 1) demonstrating a commitment to the value of reciprocity in campus-community partnerships, and 2) recognizing the erosion of boundaries between the campus and community. The broader educational value of external resource allocation is that the institution, in its economic relations, models the values instilled in community-based academic study.

Increasingly, there are examples of campuses that are investing in their surrounding communities as a way of demonstrating their civic engagement and leveraging other resources for improving challenged communities. These investments are, in some cases, direct financial contributions that may be as large as the $20 million that Harvard has invested as seed funds for low and moderate income housing development in Cambridge, Massachusetts, or the $8 million that Trinity College in Connecticut has invested in a "learning corridor" adjacent to their campus, or as modest as the $150,000 in small business development funds pledged by the President, Theodore Long, of Elizabeth College in Pennsylvania, to the Elizabethtown Economic Development Corporation. Similarly, in 1995, Georgetown University in Washington, DC, purchased $1 million worth of stock in *City First Bank* of DC. In 1999, *City First* opened its doors to service Washington's low- and moderate-income neighborhoods, seeking to increase home ownership and establish stable, mixed-income communities, to provide a range of financing needed to upgrade housing stock and commercial centers, and to strengthen the base of local small businesses. In each of these cases, the campus serves as one of a variety of actors (public, corporate and non-profit) that are investing in community improvement.

Development of campus structures designed to serve both campus and community is another increasingly common strategy for external resource allocation. For example, Metropolitan State University in St. Paul, Minnesota, is developing a shared-use building that will be a joint community-university library to include a job resource center, a youth/adult study center, a children's reading room, and a community learning and meeting room. At DePaul University in Chicago, a downtown department store has been renovated into a mixed-use facility that includes city government office space, a retail mall, and campus classrooms and support facilities. Increasingly, campus athletic facilities are open to community use, particularly in the summer.

Other, more indirect ways in which campuses are extending resources to their communities come in the form of purchasing and hiring policies that favor local residents and businesses. The University of Illinois at Chicago has experimented both with neighborhood hiring and the use of local vendors. The University of Pennsylvania has sought, in all of its construction projects, to increase the participation of minority and female-owned firms.

Faculty Roles and Rewards.

Faculty are at the core of any higher education institution, and faculty roles and rewards are at the core of faculty life. No matter how genuine a school's commitment to engagement as articulated in its mission, that commitment will probably amount to little, at least in the long run, if the school is unwilling to address the specific ways in which it formally recognizes a faculty member's contribution to that commitment. Logistical and technical assistance is essential, as is the availability of other resources, but if, when it comes down to what the faculty as a body regard as valuable, community-based work is nowhere explicitly identified, faculty engagement will perforce remain a peripheral concern.

The last five years, in particular, have seen a recognition of this fact in the ever increasing number of schools that have adopted some variant of Boyer's expanded understanding of scholarship (Boyer, 1990). West Virginia University, for example, revised its promotion and tenure guidelines in 1998 to allow faculty to renegotiate their contracts. Faculty can now, with the agreement of their department chair and college dean, work to achieve excellence in teaching and service instead of teaching and research. To assess the degree to which this, and other programs on campus, are helping students develop civic competencies and habits, providing opportunities for faculty to engage in true civic partnerships, and encouraging faculty to engage in community-based teaching and action research, the university has begun an evaluation process that will gradually expand into a full civic assessment program (www.compact.org/model programs).

Portland State notes that "[s]cholarly accomplishments in the areas of research, teaching, and community outreach all enter into the evaluation of faculty performance" (Zlotkowski, 1998, G-7). IUPUI includes in its faculty annual report a category called "Volunteer Community Service" for which it stipulates "voluntary, civic responsibilities...deem[ed] relevant to [one's] professional work." Not to be included under this heading is "[s]ervice to the community as a citizen rather than as a professional whose work can be assessed by peers" (IUPUI Faculty and Librarian Annual Report).

Disciplines, Departments, Interdisciplinarity

No one would deny the importance of quality community-based work in nursing, teacher education, and sociology. However, institutions where the vast majority of engaged projects are located in areas like these can hardly be said to have made significant progress toward campus-wide engagement. While the fact that the anthropology department at the University of Pennsylvania boasts a demonstrated commitment to work in West Philadelphia is commendable, but the fact that the university's history department can also make such a claim probably tells us more about Penn's determination to become a truly engaged campus. Colleges and universities need to avail themselves of resources such as the American Association for Higher Education's 18-volume series on service-learning in the disciplines (1997-2000) and Driscoll and Lynton's *Making Outreach Visible: A Guide to Documenting Professional Service and Outreach* (1999) to ensure that community-based work is not seen as the concern only of a few "naturally appropriate" disciplines (Driscoll and Lynton, 1999).

Even more difficult to achieve is unit ownership of outreach efforts, regardless of the discipline or department involved. The Compact's newly launched "Institute on the Engaged Department" represents one of the few resources currently available to help transform engagement from something of interest only to individual faculty practitioners to a commitment made by an entire academic unit. But only when such a commitment has been made can students and community partners rely upon the availability of faculty to maintain the integrity of community-based programs. Although specially endowed units like the Feinstein Center for Public Service at Providence College have for years been able to make this commitment, schools like Calvin College, with its well established record of academically based service, are only now beginning to plan for such a commitment by a range of departments across the curriculum.

Institutionalization of this kind should also lay the foundation for more community-based academic work that draws upon several disciplines. As the AAHE series on service-learning in the disciplines makes clear, we already have many fine examples of community-based capstone experiences in which students are expected to use the natural interdisciplinarity of off-campus work as an opportunity to demonstrate their ability to integrate skills and concepts from different areas of their academic careers. Less common are programs such as Purdue's EPICS program (Engineering Projects in Community Service) which folds a variety of disciplinary perspectives into an engineering core. But as Boyer suggested in his now famous sketch of "The New American College" (1994), the engaged campus of the future will "organize cross-disciplinary institutes around pressing social issues" as a matter of course.

Community Voice

Establishing and maintaining meaningful community partnerships as part of a broader vision of civic engagement requires the development of trust, long-term commitments, and formal obligations on the part of all involved (Campus Compact, 2000; Holland and Gelmon, 1998). While partnerships take time to develop, there are certain initial strategies that can be implemented from the beginning to foster deeper, more lasting partnerships. A common starting point is the creation of an advisory committee with significant representation from the community. The make-up of such a committee typically includes faculty, administrators, the campus community service director, students, and community partners. The committee can function in such a way as to involve community partners in joint strategic planning and in fostering dialogue between the campus and community, particularly around mutual campus-community understanding. Community partners can also be invited to assist in curricula development and in course instruction.

At IUPUI, community partners have been involved in providing important guidance and feedback in the development and maintenance of the service-learning program. Community representatives have served on the Service Learning Advisory Committee, Service Learning in University College Advisory Committees, Community Service Scholars selection committee and the Universities as Citizens Summer Institute planning team. Agency personnel also work with individual faculty in the design, implementation, and administration of service-learning classes. At Providence College, community partners have played a significant role in strategic planning about community-based education and have been involved in curriculum development. Community partners have also been provided a stipend to team-teach service-learning courses with department faculty.

Similarly, at St. Joseph's College, community partners participate in needs assessment and evaluation meetings, meet with faculty as they have designed courses, supervise and evaluate students, and participate in several workshops offered for their learning on service-learning, effective supervision and partnerships, community asset-mapping, etc.. There are also opportunities for community partners to come into the classroom for orientation and discussion of particular topics, as well as to teach a course.

Administrative and Academic Leadership

Essential to accomplishing all of the indicators of engagement identified here is leadership from the top that actively endorses and supports engagement efforts. In the best of all possible worlds, the trustees, the president and the provost (or academic equivalent) would all be enthusiasts. The trustees and presidents can raise funds to support civic engagement and can provide a bully pulpit for fostering it. At Swarthmore College, a trustee committee on social responsibility was formed to reflect on the institutional mission to "prepare and motivate students to engage issues of social responsibility facing our communities and societies and to set their own paths as responsible citizens toward shaping a more inclusive, just and compassionate world." At Tufts University, President John DiBiaggio worked for 10 years to develop a "college" of public service and citizenship and raised $10 million from the E-Bay corporation to support it. At Alcorn State, Clinton Bristow leads a "communiversity" effort that is common in Historically Black Colleges. At the University of Vermont, Judith Ramaley is leading the effort to increase engagement (building on her experience in transforming Portland State) and has instituted such practices as an "Introduction to Vermont" for new faculty. At Miami-Dade Community College, Eduardo Padron has made real a commitment that his institution is indeed the "community's college" through such efforts as a technology learning center located in a local church. These presidents are only a few exemplars of many presidential leaders in every type of institution committed to the civic engagement of higher education. Nearly 400 presidents have signed the Presidents' Declaration on the Civic Responsibility of Higher Education (Campus Compact, 1999A).

Academic leadership is also key. At IUPUI, Provost William Plater has led the effort to create a promotion and tenure system that recognizes, documents and rewards the scholarship of engagement. At DePaul University, Richard Meister, Executive Vice President for Academic Affairs, has built community engagement into the university's five year strategic plan and reinforced and celebrated engagement at every opportunity (e.g. convocation addresses). Increasingly, development opportunities on civic engagement and the scholarship of engagement are being offered for chief academic officers, primarily by Campus Compact and its state affiliates. This is in recognition of the important role these leaders play in bringing engagement from the "margins to the mainstream" in the academy.

Mission and Purpose

There is hardly a campus in America that does not have a mission statement that speaks in some way to the role of higher education in providing education for civic engagement. In some cases, reference is made to producing leaders or socially useful graduates. For example, Harvard University expects "that the scholarship and collegiality it fosters in its students will lead them in their later lives to advance knowledge, to promote understanding, and to serve society." (Harry R. Lewis, Dean of Harvard College, 2/23/97 from http://www.harvard.edu/help/noframes/Faq110.nf. html). Georgetown University "educates women and men to be reflective lifelong learners, to be responsible and active participants in civic life, and to live generously in service to others" (http://www.georgetown.edu /admin/publicaffairs/factsheets/mission.html). Other campuses have mission statements that make it even more explicitly clear that engagement is a central enterprise. For example, at Antioch College "all programs...aim to develop students and graduates who grow in their commitment to contribute personally to improvement in the human condition through responsible leadership that fosters productive, democratic change in the institutions and communities in which they live and work. " At California State University, Monterey Bay, "The identity of the University will be framed by substantive commitment to a multilingual, multicultural, intellectual community distinguished by partnerships with existing institutions, both public and private, and by cooperative agreements which enable students, faculty and staff to cross institutional boundaries for innovative instruction, broadly defined scholarly and creative activity, and coordinated community service" (http://www monterey. edu/vision/).

The mere presence of a mission supporting civic engagement does not, of course, ensure that such a mission has a real and dynamic impact on the life of the college and the community. In many cases, colleges that wish to reassert their civic purpose undertake a review of their mission and foster widespread discussion of it. Some, like Olivet College in Michigan, devised an updated vision statement based on the school's founding principles (in this case 1844) and then sought adoption of the vision by key constituencies such as faculty and trustees.

SELF ASSESSMENT AS AN ENGAGEMENT STRATEGY

One of the first challenges facing a campus that wishes to undertake a major initiative to extend and deepen its civic engagement is to discover what already exists on campus. Adopting a conscious process of discovery can be, in itself, a very useful exercise; the process of self-assessment is as important as the product. If approached with care, this process can honor the faculty, staff and students who are already engaged in the community through volunteerism, service-learning, community-based research or other forms of civic outreach. Because of the decentralized nature of higher education, unearthing what is already going on is not always easy to do. It requires a significant commitment by the administration and time for department-by-department research. Further, any survey of faculty requires assiduous follow up. On a large campus it can take the better part of an academic year to find and document community engagement activities.

However, once a report has been compiled and published, it often causes other faculty, staff, and students to step forward because they do not want their course or program to be overlooked. This is particularly true if a sense of excitement and pride has been built on the campus regarding these activities. Increasingly campus inventories are becoming web-based documents that can be added to and changed. Once an inventory of engagement activities is created it an be employed as a valuable campus-wide catalyst for a dialogue about what engagement means and can mean to different constituencies within the institution.

Large universities like the University of Wisconsin, Madison, or the University of Maryland, College Park, or Harvard, each of which has recently done a full inventory of their outreach activities, have benefited from this process (See www.wisc.edu/wiscinfo/outreach, www.umd.edu/ academic/ partnerships.html, and http://www.hno.harvard.edu/community/). Each has found that it gives their institution a way to tell constituents — including board members, legislators, local community activists, and alumni — what the campus is contributing. It also makes clear how strategic or focused these activities are and how much they reflect the particular strengths and mission of the institution.

Two contrasting approaches to institutional self-assessment are those of the University of Wisconsin, Milwaukee and the University of Minnesota. At Wisconsin, a new Chancellor, Nancy Zimpher, challenged her entire staff and faculty to come up with a series of ways to assist the city of Milwaukee within a 100 days. She then sorted out those ideas and moved aggressively forward to implement the "Milwaukee idea" (based on the famous "Wisconsin idea" [1897] of the engaged campus). She also made herself available to meet with many organizations and leaders from the city to express her school's interest in participating.

The benefits of this approach are that her campus quickly gained a reputation in Wisconsin and across the nation for its interest in being of and for the city in which is located. This has brought funds, has increased student applicants, and has resulted in a range of exciting programs. It has energized both students and faculty. The down side is a concern that the effort has been too driven by publicity and might not last. However, there is presently a Milwaukee Idea office that is charged with broadening and deepening the effort. One specific result of this new commitment to civic engagement is a "Cultures and Communities" initiative to design foundation courses that will "connect students to the rich diversity of our urban communities through a variety of learning" (Cultures and Communities, ND). These courses will be part of an alternative general education option.

At the University of Minnesota, a self-examination of the institution's civic involvement has been modeled on an earlier examination of the need to address cultural diversity. In this model, the charge to the institution from the provost's office has been multi-faceted, including defining civic engagement as well as identifying communities to work with, ways to leverage current civic activities to take advantage of the teaching and research strengths of the university, criteria for strategic investments and practical suggestions for strengthening both undergraduate and graduate students' interest in civic engagement (Charge letter from Bob Bruininks, Exec. VP and Provost, 9/29/00, Web site p. 2). The leaders of this assessment believe that involving the campus broadly in a discussion of both the meaning of civic engagement and its manifestations is most likely to gain the attention of senior faculty.

More difficult than compiling an inventory of activities is undertaking an assessment of the quality and depth of its efforts. How can a campus think about the quality and depth of its civic engagement? What should a campus be considering: the student learning experience, the faculty research agenda, the community impact and the extent to which the community is determining what needs to be addressed? Several discovery and assessment tools have recently been developed that can help a campus start a conversation about its level and type of engagement as well as inventory and assess its activities (Bringle and Hatcher 1999; Holland, 1997). Campus Compact has devised a civic self-assessment instrument that is framed as a series of questions a campus can ask about the student experience, faculty and staff culture, presidential leadership and institutional engagement (Campus Compact, 1999A). Campuses that have used this instrument include the University of Maryland, College Park, and the University of Utah. While no two campuses will answer the questions posed in the civic self-assessment in the same way, the process will enable each campus to see their public role in a new light.

As institutions of higher education continue to shape their civic identities and define their public purposes, they will adopt strategies of engagement that will, to a greater or lesser degree, transform their campuses. An engaged campus is not a vague, amorphous idea that escapes concrete definition and form. Over the last decade, here have emerged clear indicators of civic engagement have been identified, and they are increasingly visible at colleges and universities around the country.[1]

REFERENCES

Alinsky, S. D. (1946). *Reveille for Radicals*. Chicago:University of Chicago Press.

Bender, T. (1993). *Intellect and Public Life: Essays on the Social History of Academic Intellectuals in the United States*. Baltimore: Johns Hopkins University Press.

Boyer, E. (1990). *Scholarship Reconsidered: Priorities of the Professoriate*. New York; The Carnegie Foundation for the Advancement of Teaching.

Boyer, E. (1994*)*. The New American College, *Chronicle of Higher Education*, A48.

Boyer, E. (1996). The Scholarship of Engagement, *The Journal of Public Service and Outreach*. 1:1, pp. 11-20.

[4] The authors would like to thank Erin Swezey, Richard Cone, and Keith Morton for their assistance in providing institutional examples of engagement activities. We are also grateful to Brooke Beaird and Kerri Heffernan for their critical insights and thoughtful reading of the essay.

Boyte, H. (2000). The Struggle Against Positivism, *Academe: Bulletin of the American Association of University Professors*, July August, 86:4, p. 46-51.

Bringle, R. & Hatcher, J. (1999). *Campus Assessment of the Scholarship of Engagement*, Center for Public Service and Leadership, Indiana University, Purdue University, Indianapolis.

Bruinicks, B. (2000). Charge letter from Bob Bruininks , Exec. VP and Provost, To the Civic Engagement Task Force, 9/29/00, Web site p. 2) www1.umn.edu/civic/index.html

Campus Compact.(2000). *Benchmarks for Campus/Community Partnerships*, Campus Compact, Providence, RI,.

Campus Compact (1999 A). *The Presidents' Declaration on the Civic Responsibility of Higher Education*, Providence, RI.

Campus Compact. (1999 B). *Service Matters: The Engaged Campus*, Campus Compact, Providence, RI,.

"Cultures and Communities: Learning for the New Century," University of Wisconsin, Milwaukee, ND: WWW.UWM.EDU/MILWAUKEEIDEA/CC

Damon, W. (1998). The Path to Civil Society Goes Through the University, *The Chronicle of Higher Education*. October *16*, B 4-5.

Dewey, John (1916). *Democracy and Education*. New York; The Free Press (1944).

Driscoll, A. & Lynton, E. (1999). *Making Outreach Visible: A Guide to Documenting Professional Service and Outreach*. Washington, DC: American Association for Higher Education.

Ehrlich, T., (Ed.) (2000). *Civic Responsibility and Higher Education*. Phoenix, Arizona; Orynx Press.

Eyler, J. & Giles, D. (1999). *Where's the Learning in Service-Learning?* San Francisco, CA: Jossey-Bass.

Freire, P. (1970). *Pedagogy of the Oppressed*. New York: Continuum.

Holland, B. (1997). Analyzing Institutional Commitment to Service: A Model of Key Organizational Factors. *Michigan Journal of Community Service Learning*. Fall, 30-41.

Holland, B. (1999). Factors and Strategies that Influence Faculty Involvement in Public Service, *The Journal of Public Service and Outreach, 41*, 37-43.

Holland, B. & Gelmon, S. (1998). The State of the 'Engaged Campus': What Have We Learned About Building and Sustaining University-Community Partnerships, *AAHE Bulletin*, October.

Indiana University – Purdue University at Indianapolis (2000). Faculty and Librarian Annual Report. N.P.

Hollander, E., & Saltmarsh, J. (2000). The Engaged University, *Academe: Bulletin of the American Association of University Professors*. July August, *86*(4), 29-31.

Jacoby, B. & Associates (1996). *Service-Learning in Higher Education: Concepts and Practices*. San Francisco, CA: Jossey-Bass.

Lynton, E. A. (1995). *Making the Case for Professional Service*. Washington, DC: American Association for Higher Education.

Mathews, D. (1998). Creating More Public Space in Higher Education, The Council on Public Policy Education.

Morton, K., and Troppe, M. (1996). From the Margins to the Mainstream: Campus Compact's Project on Integrating Service with Academic Study, *Journal of Business Ethics*, 15 (1).

National Commission on Civic Renewal (1998). *A Nation of Spectators: How Civic Disengagement Weakens America and What We Can Do About It*. University of Maryland, www.pauf.umd.edu/civicrenewal.

Rhoads, R., & Howard, J. (Eds.) (1998). *Academic Service-Learning: A Pedagogy of Action and Reflection*. New Directions for Teaching and Learning, San Francisco, CA: Jossey-Bass, (73), Spring.

Saltmarsh, J. A. (1996). Education for Critical Citizenship: John Dewey's Contribution to the Pedagogy of Service-Learning. *Michigan Journal of Service Learning, 3*, 13-21.

Stanton, T., Giles, D., & Cruz, N. (1999*). Service-Learning: A Movement's Pioneers Reflect on Its Origins, Practice and Future*. San Francisco, CA: Jossey-Bass.

Sullivan, W. M. (1995*). Work and Integrity: The Crisis and Promise of Professionalism in America*. New York: Harper Collins.

Walshok, M. L. (1995). *Knowledge Without Boundaries: What America's Research universities can do for the Economy, the Workplace, and the Community*. San Francisco, Jossey-Bass.

Zlotkowski, E. (1998). A Service Learning Approach to Faculty Development, in R. A Rhoads & J. Howard (Eds*). Academic Service Learning: A Pedagogy of Action and Reflection* (p. 81-90). San Francisco, Jossey-Bass.

Zlotkowski, E. (Ed.) (1998). *Successful Service-Learning Programs: New Models of Excellence in Higher Education*, Bolton, MA: Anker.

CHAPTER 4

THE CULTURE OF SERVICE AT ALVERNO COLLEGE

Stephen Sharkey
Russell Brooker
Judeen Schulte
Alverno College

INTRODUCTION

For more than a century, commitment to others through service has been a core value of Alverno College. In this paper we most fundamentally and urgently hope to show, first, how service remains at the center of our educational enterprise for both students and faculty through the operation of our curriculum and the norms and values guiding our daily life; and second, how we collectively judge whether we are succeeding. We say "fundamentally" because, from our experience, we are convinced that a service-learning program can work only if in some way it is located in the commons of the institution, where the curriculum and co-curriculum, the goals of students and the goals of faculty, intersect. And we say "urgently" because we share with the editors of this book the concern for the future of this country, and believe that effective service-learning programs in colleges can go far to help create the citizens we need to better our social order.

Alverno is a private, urban liberal arts and professional college for women located in Milwaukee, Wisconsin. The founders of the college, an order of Catholic women religious, thought it only natural to centrally position commitment to the social teachings of the Church in the framework of a liberal arts curriculum. This was so throughout the last century, when most graduates, both religious and lay, found careers in the helping professions, education, and the arts, defined their careers in terms of service, and pursued programs that supported such an outlook.

Today Alverno's approximately 1,900 students are of all ages, races, religions, and financial means. More than half are among the first generation in their families to attend college; 75 percent are age 23 or older (the average age is 30); many are employed, often full-time; and more than 90 percent qualify for need-based financial aid. In addition, 35 percent of students are women of color, the highest percentage of minority students for any four-year public or private college in Wisconsin. A key emphasis in the Alverno mission has always been to offer the advantages of a private liberal arts education to women who might not otherwise find it within their means. Thus our tuition is comparatively low, and we provide strong academic systems to support students with unrealized and perhaps unidentified college potential to make an effective transition to postsecondary learning.

In the early 1970s, Alverno undertook a radical re-visioning of its curriculum and approach to college teaching, articulating its core values in more explicit and precise terms as learning outcomes that students needed to achieve to become liberally educated. "Creating ties to the community" — both on campus and in the city — became one of the four pillars of the mission, and this was realized through a new "ability-based" curriculum and assessment process. To reach a wide range of students, in 1977 Alverno also inaugurated one curriculum in two time frames: a traditional weekday program for students mostly right out of high school, and a weekend program — one of the first in the country — with classes on alternate weekends targeted especially for adult students.

These factors and others give a distinctive shape and tone to our service-learning work: it is very broad, inclusive, and pervasive. In many institutions "service learning" applies to a special program in which some segment of the student body performs service for nonprofit organizations, social agencies, community groups, or needy individuals. At Alverno, service learning is infused throughout the curriculum; while there is a separate internship program, service learning is found at all levels of the curriculum and is integral to a wide variety of courses in all majors. When asked how many students and faculty are engaged in the service-learning "program," Alverno faculty correctly answer "all of them."

Despite such unique features, we think our method of integrating service learning into the life of the college can be instructive for educators at other institutions who seek to develop service learning in terms of what their students need to learn and need to be able to do in order to effectively learn as they serve their community. We understand service learning as an expression of certain *abilities* students can be taught and assessed for in any major and in general education. In a parallel fashion, the broader campus culture supports the service idea, and faculty performance is evaluated and rewarded in terms of how effectively faculty fashion the methods for developing those abilities in their students. Reading about our approach may stimulate colleagues on various types of campuses to consider service learning as a set of student abilities that cut across disciplines, the discussion and pursuit of which could knit faculty from various niches and contexts together in pursuit of a common, potentially transformative educational agenda.

ALVERNO'S ABILITY-BASED APPROACH TO COMMUNITY INVOLVEMENT AND SERVICE

Today the students, faculty, and staff of Alverno are engaged in the community in a variety of ways, through courses, internships, individual volunteering, and student organization projects. Our approach to civic involvement — our theory-in-use for creating the engaged campus — flows directly from our philosophy of education as embodied in the curriculum, developed over 30 years from our practice.

What distinguishes Alverno from most other American colleges is its ability-based curriculum and assessment process. Students are expected to acquire the knowledge traditionally associated with a specialized baccalaureate degree *and* to master eight core abilities needed to apply that knowledge effectively throughout their lives (see Alverno College Faculty, 1976/1992, for a fuller description of each ability). The abilities are:

- **Communication**
- **Problem solving**
- **Developing a global perspective**
- **Effective citizenship**
- **Analysis**
- **Valuing in decision making**
- **Social interaction**
- **Aesthetic engagement**

These eight abilities serve as the foundation for the curriculum and constitute the core of each student's learning sequence from start to finish. Thus faculty use them to shape all of their courses in general education and in the majors and minors, strongly emphasizing active, experiential learning in the process. We sustain the ongoing scholarly exploration of teaching and assessing these abilities in cross-disciplinary departments — one for each ability. These departments study the latest pedagogy in that domain, offer workshops to colleagues, help create special student learning opportunities related to the ability, network in the community, and have some responsibility for monitoring the curriculum for effectiveness in teaching and assessing the ability.

A key dimension of the ability-based curriculum is *assessment*. Faculty have developed systematic programs of performance-based assessment to accountably measure student demonstration of the abilities at progressively higher levels of sophistication within both general education and the disciplines. Student progress toward graduation is tracked simultaneously in terms of both course requirements and ability levels accomplished.

Assessments are *criterion-referenced*. That is, they are designed to reveal the level of each student's abilities in applying content knowledge in a performance, and they include explicit criteria for satisfactory achievement, which faculty use in their judgment and which students themselves use in a *self-assessment* of their performance — a critical part of the over-all assessment process (Alverno College Faculty, 1979/1994). Some assessments are conducted in class, while others are "external"; that is, they constitute outside validity checks on students' cumulative development in an area of study, often involving complex, real-life tasks such as independent research or simulations that are evaluated by community volunteers.

DEFINING THE HEART OF SERVICE LEARNING IN TERMS OF ABILITIES

We define "service" as using one's personal resources — time, talent, knowledge, and ability — to meet the needs of another individual, of a specific group, or of a broader community, as well as the needs of oneself (Wagner & Spore, 1995). The "learning" comes from applying disciplinary frameworks to analyze the experience and perform effectively in it, always including self-assessment as a key component. Service opportunities may be:

- linked to general education, the major or minor, or the co-curriculum;
- pursued for credit or no credit;
- mandatory or voluntary;
- initiated by the individual, a student group, or a course instructor.

The general outcomes of a service-learning experience are that the student:

- becomes a more informed, proactive citizen who understands her obligation to enhance the quality of others' lives and to meet the needs of her community;
- develops the specific citizenship skills and leadership abilities to provide service to others in personal, professional, and civic arenas (While the service activity itself may be humble or humbling, the student nevertheless can situate it in a broader political or spiritual context.);
- better integrates her values, abilities, and actions.

Four of Alverno's eight abilities relate very directly to the development of these outcomes through community involvement and service learning:

- In *effective citizenship*, students learn to function as effective citizens in society, through their knowledge of political and social issues and structures and through their ability to navigate social systems to accomplish worthy goals. In one aspect of this ability, students are required to perform service for a client who may be on or off campus. All students fulfill this requirement at least once, and some fulfill it several times. In discussing their understanding of this ability, many students have said that they believe it is impossible to spend more than a year at Alverno without beginning to feel a conscious sense of obligation to work to improve their communities, broadly construed. They come to believe that developing a personal moral ethic of obligation to one's community is essential for all people.

- In *valuing in decision making*, students learn to appreciate others' values, to explore value debates shaping a community's decisions about critical issues, and to apply their values to their own personal actions in concrete situations.
- In *developing a global perspective*, students learn about the perspectives of other cultures in a global context and to articulate their own perspectives about global connectedness.
- In *social interaction*, students learn to work effectively with others in small and larger groups in a variety of interpersonal and task-oriented situations.

Since all students must demonstrate proficiency in these four abilities regardless of their particular major, the base of students prepared for service-learning experiences is broader than the more typical groups in the social sciences, education, and nursing. In addition, since all disciplines must address student development of these abilities in some way within their major or minor, service-learning opportunities and assessments exist across the curriculum. This was our intention: to create a coherent curriculum with service learning as a key dimension, readily accessible to all students. Also required are general education courses dealing with the content of civic engagement, the meaning of the good society, and frameworks for social change that add specific content knowledge to all students' preparation for service and the integration of a service mindset with their field of study.

COLLABORATION: A SPECIAL CATALYST FOR SERVICE LEARNING

In addition to formally evaluating students' social interaction ability in certain key courses, the college places special emphasis on student teamwork and collaboration across the curriculum, from brief exercises to longer-term group projects. Students develop their ability to work with others effectively by frequent practice, and faculty evaluate their interaction ability using commonly agreed-upon criteria that become familiar to students because of their continuity. Social interaction experiences give students the skills to evaluate diverse group settings and help them make appropriate decisions when interacting in them. Because of the broad diversity of the college's population, students regularly learn to work with others from different backgrounds. They are actively encouraged to help each other. Faculty regularly discuss how best to accomplish this both formally and informally. Our assessment processes demonstrate that such frequent, criteria-oriented social interaction helps students succeed academically, to be sure, but a crucial, qualitative added value is the deepening of their capacity for empathy and collegiality.

Now, in order to teach and assess for these four abilities, and to build a campus culture that supports their development, *faculty and academic staff* must likewise actively, consistently interact across disciplinary boundaries to explore student performance in various contexts. They must cooperate to devise means to reinforce or complement lessons being learned in diverse courses to maximize curricular coherence and the benefits of synergy for students. A key way we concretely accomplish this is through the interdisciplinary ability departments, which have the status of standing college committees. Alverno has also set aside every Friday afternoon, plus three sets of several days at the beginning, middle, and end of the academic year, for meetings of the ability departments, other committees and work groups, and the faculty and staff as a whole. Helping to plan and implement these sessions is a regular part of professional responsibility and is rewarded positively in performance evaluations.

The details of this aspect of our campus life are beyond the scope of this paper. The point here is that faculty and staff live in a culture of collaboration and mutual assistance, which is prominent and visible to students and carries over into how students perceive what it means to be "from Alverno." This culture of collaboration is a major strength of the institution; it has enabled us to sustain an ongoing revolution in higher education theory and practice that has affected institutions across this country and abroad. But more important, it has created a tangible atmosphere in which service to others is "normal" and valued, and has influenced the way faculty design courses and treat students.

Thus both the structure of the curriculum *and* the character of faculty/staff work life combine to nourish a "culture of service" that shapes how student and faculty roles are played. Both student and faculty performance evaluations include explicit criteria related to collaboration and service, using in fact some of the same language. The benefits of a culture of collaboration to the institutionalization of service learning are simply profound. This reality is consistent with what Harry Boyte (2000) recently called a "public work philosophy" of service, which sees the civic value of daily work and institution building as perhaps more important than "volunteering," insofar as it is more sustained and more deeply connected to more aspects of an individual's identity. We believe we have built on campus a public work philosophy in which service is a central fact of our culture, a defining characteristic of our work, and is explicitly linked to our understanding of professional responsibility and roles. This said, we now consider some more specific details of the service-learning theory and practice on this campus.

SERVICE LEARNING FOR OUR DIVERSE STUDENT POPULATION

In addition to being diverse in terms of age and ethnicity, Alverno students come from a variety of socioeconomic groups. While the majority are from middle- to lower-income families, both ends of the economic spectrum are represented: very wealthy and very poor, including some who receive public assistance.

Furthermore, ongoing surveys show that almost all Alverno students work either full- or part-time, and they occupy nearly every level of corporate America. Some are officers in publicly held corporations; others occupy low-end service jobs. Some are intimately familiar with corporate culture; others have never worked in an office setting.

This diversity leads to an expanded vision — a more inclusive model — of service learning. First, because of their personal background, many Alverno students are well acquainted with the problems and challenges of modern urban life. They may live in neighborhoods "served" by service learning. Alverno therefore has somewhat less of a need than many colleges and universities to emphasize helping students overcome anxieties about entering low-income neighborhoods to work with the poor. Thus we can take advantage of many of our students' own local knowledge in building programs.

Second, many Alverno students are already involved in activities that would be classified as "service," and possibly "service learning." They work or volunteer in community organizations or assist the underserved in their neighborhoods. Still others are involved with their children's schools and in neighborhood churches. Commitment to service is already an integral part of their daily lives. We can therefore focus somewhat less on building the initial motivation for service and more on developing conceptual frameworks for analyzing their service experiences.

Third, because of the collaborative and cooperative nature of the Alverno curriculum, students of necessity *teach* each other. In classes, students of diverse backgrounds and abilities help each other understand the course material and apply it to their lives. More experienced students help those less experienced understand the curriculum, which enhances the classroom climate but also helps to form networks and cohorts that students draw upon after graduation for professional growth and community problem solving. Thus we can often frame service as an act of teaching from the heart.

And finally, while the literature on service learning does not identify specifically who must be served in service learning (Brooker, Engelmann, & Schulte, 1998), there seems to be a widespread assumption that the beneficiaries should be social service agencies or nonprofit organizations that work with the underserved (e.g., the poor, the elderly, the disabled). From this perspective, serving a successful corporation like IBM would not "count" as service learning. We do not make that assumption. We place our interns and volunteers in successful companies and government offices as well as in community organizations. We believe that if a student can successfully learn important skills in such a setting and bring something of the Alverno philosophy to colleagues or clients there, *we should support it as service learning.* Innumerable cases in which our students have taken what they have learned in such a venue and later applied it to a less re-source-rich organization also lend support to the merits of this approach. Their experience helps distribute human resources across the social spec-trum, which is a valuable means to achieving social justice.

IMPLEMENTING SERVICE LEARNING

During the mid-1990s faculty and staff became interested in examining our current theory and practice of service learning in a more systematic way, as part of Alverno's broader involvement in national discussions about how to better link college and community. Alverno has been very active in the American Association for Higher Education, Campus Com-pact, and other, regional networks of schools interested in emphasizing the role of service in student development, and in improving the organiza-tional structures and processes to support service learning in a more ex-plicit way.

We formed an interdisciplinary service-learning study group, which has attended national and regional conferences, studied the scholarly literature on service learning as a concept, and led on-campus workshops. This study group encouraged faculty to think about the topic in greater depth and to revise course syllabi and other learning experiences accordingly. It also conducted systematic quantitative and qualitative research on both the ex-tent of current service-learning opportunities in the curriculum, as well as the extent of student activism and volunteering both individually and within student organizations. This research confirmed for us that many opportunities did exist but that they could be made more explicit and could be linked to each other to highlight their prominence. Data also confirmed our perception that the large majority of our students — on the order of two-thirds — already volunteered in some fashion in their communities, for an average of about 20 hours per month. This from a student body in which 89 percent hold full- or part-time jobs! The main question then be-came how to enhance already solid support for service learning in both the curriculum and co-curriculum. While most improvements are coming through gradual revisions of the ability curriculum and increased efforts by key offices like the Internship Office and Student Services, we have also developed a new major whose focus is leadership and service.

In the ability arena, the Effective Citizenship Ability Department co-ordinates civic education and takes particular responsibility for maintain-ing and enhancing the ways in which civic education occurs across the curriculum, in courses from freshman through senior year (Schulte, 1996). The Valuing Ability Department has defined valuing to include "contrib-uting to forming the values of one's community" as a central criterion for student performance; the advanced level of this ability is typically required in the capstone courses and professional socialization experiences of many majors.

In the arena of majors, the following examples can illustrate how service is integrated. All professional communication majors and minors are required to take a course in which they work in teams to create public relations materials for a local not-for-profit agency. In the art education/art therapy curriculum, students forge ongoing relationships with community agencies as they move through a series of developmental field experiences. In capstone courses in business and computer studies, students are required to work as consultants to local small businesses or not-for-profit organizations. Over the years, they have designed a computer system, organized inventory control, and developed public relations campaigns.

That students can become thoroughly engaged in course-related projects and that these projects can result in a definite good for the client is demonstrated by the following example. A six-member team of students in the marketing research class recently worked on a project for the Milwaukee Symphony Orchestra. The team's goal was to develop a marketing plan that would enable the MSO to generate more revenue from merchandising. This is how one team member, a self-described "avid supporter of the arts," described her experience:

> *This project gave me the opportunity to work in a team environment where we had a common interest and goal....This was not just a class assignment, but a passion for the entire team. When we were invited to share our project with the marketing team at MSO, we considered it a great honor and a perfect conclusion to the hard work we had done. The presentation was scheduled for after the end of the semester, so there was no requirement to participate, and yet every team member was excited to give the extra time.*

The MSO used the Alverno team's plan as a springboard for new marketing initiatives, and this student's commitment to the arts remains strong. She went on to say, "We need to find ways to continue providing our society with the opportunity for aesthetic experiences."

All Alverno majors require some sort of extended practicum experience. Weekday students are required to spend eight to twelve hours per week for at least one semester in a field internship that is usually unpaid. (Student nurses and teachers have more extensive requirements.) In coordinating internships, Alverno's Internship Office, with a full-time staff of 1.5, matches community needs with student disciplinary backgrounds and interests. The office also provides logistical and instructional support for interdisciplinary and disciplinary seminars associated with internships. These required seminars prepare students for the internship, demand that they reflect on and analyze their experiences, and help them better integrate them into their overall learning (Grantz & Thanos, 1996).

Internship sites number in the hundreds and range from homeless shelters, community organizations, and church associations to government agencies and private companies large and small. The key point for present purposes is to signal the core value of interning and volunteering in all academic departments, and the crucial "enabling" role of the Internship Office, which is sufficiently familiar with the disciplines to effectively assist us to realize the college's service learning and community engagement goals.

In 1996, Alverno also introduced the Community Leadership and Development major specifically for women who wish to improve the quality of life in their community. A combination of business and social science courses, the program strongly emphasizes civic as well as political engagement, concentrating on how communities work and how the organizations that serve them can do a better job. The program continues to grow and now enrolls about 75 majors.

Outside the formal curriculum, many students find opportunities for service through student organizations, which are strongly encouraged by the Office of Student Life to include a service dimension in their charter. Science students have started a program to work with local middle school students on science activities; art education and art therapy students provide art experiences for the resident children of a local domestic-violence safehouse; the social science and history group sponsors an annual campus volunteer-recruitment fair. In addition, many of the organizations regularly sponsor food and clothing drives for the needy.

Finally, faculty, staff, and students provide service for organizations when needs arise that cannot be integrated into courses, internships, or student group planning. Again, these range from local activities to travel abroad to serve in missions or other volunteer centers.

Resources and Rewards for Service

The resources and rewards dimension is clearly critical to the success of our total campus approach. In addition to what departments and the Internship Office do to help students meet degree requirements, Alverno's Career Education Lab also makes information on service opportunities available to students. The lab maintains a notebook, regularly updated, that contains agency newsletters, volunteer opportunities, and information from Milwaukee's Volunteer Center. The Office of Student Services coordinates co-curricular activities, many of which involve activities that provide civic education.

Community service is also one criterion used to identify students who graduate with honors. Furthermore, in recent years several major scholarships have become available for incoming and continuing students who commit to serving the community in lieu of working to remain in college. In effect these scholarships enable especially moderate-income students to pursue their dream of community involvement without enduring the sidetrack of holding down a routine job to meet basic college expenses. Thus there are additional incentives to view service as a central aspect of college life and personal growth.

From a faculty perspective, service is strongly emphasized in annual performance evaluations and counts directly in career-advancement decisions. The meaning of service is described in our public criteria for assistant, associate, and full professor, and faculty use these criteria when they complete an annual self-assessment of their performance. This self-assessment, reviewed with their department chair, involves both identifying the sorts of service (on and off campus) they are engaged in and also analyzing how that service relates to their overall development as educators. Service is not given short shrift relative to research, as so often happens.

EVALUATING CIVIC INVOLVEMENT AND SERVICE LEARNING

Alverno faculty and staff have researched and evaluated the civic involvement of students extensively over the years. We approach the issue from two perspectives: 1) how service experiences have helped students develop specific abilities and increase their understanding of their disciplines while in school, and 2) how the Alverno curriculum affects the way Alverno graduates continue to learn, develop, and perform in work, personal, and civic life after leaving the college.

Student Learning in College

Like the rest of the curriculum, Alverno's internship program and other components of civic education are regularly assessed by faculty and staff and by clients served by the students. First, instructors assess students' learning in their courses — for service learning as well as for other course components. As part of ongoing course evaluation, each instructor evaluates the effectiveness of a course's service-learning aspect and assesses each student's performance. Instructors may use students' written reports, oral presentations, or project logs to assess their learning.

Second, each of the ability departments regularly gathers data about the teaching, learning, and assessment practices used to help students develop that particular ability and to integrate the abilities overall. These data are routinely analyzed to determine whether the intended outcomes are being achieved and to identify areas for change or improvement. The Effective Citizenship Ability Department and the Internship Office take primary responsibility for monitoring and improving the learning experiences related to civic involvement.

Third, faculty and staff maintain ongoing dialogue with students, clients, and mentors to ascertain their opinions of the service and to elicit suggestions for improving and enhancing it. For example, surveys are sent to clients at the completion of the student internship or project to gauge client satisfaction with the service, and mentors attend on-campus events for training and discussion of the program.

An example may help illustrate this process. In an applied research course in social science and in a marketing research course in business, students are required to help meet the research needs of real-life external clients. Instructors evaluate student learning by assessing students' secondary-research reports, both written and oral, as well as other materials like weekly logs. In addition, instructors stay in contact with clients to make sure they are well served, and evaluate the client-satisfaction surveys. Finally, instructors work with the Effective Citizenship Ability Department to analyze patterns in student work over time, to review assessment designs, and to forge collaborations with other instructors across campus working with similar issues.

Learning After College

We also have extensive data on how our students do after graduation. The Alverno Office of Educational Research and Evaluation has conducted research on the long-term effects of education for social responsibility. This research has taken place in the context of evaluating how the Alverno curriculum affects the way graduates continue to learn, develop, and perform after they have left the college.

First, in general, longitudinal interviews of students from entrance to Alverno to five years after graduation found that students came to value liberal education after experiencing its contribution to their competence as developing professionals (Much & Mentkowski, 1982). Students experienced growth in interpersonal abilities early in the curriculum and attributed this growth to the curriculum (Mentkowski & Associates, 2000; Mentkowski, Much, Kleinman, & Reisetter Hart, 1998).

Second, more specifically, we found that students identified a number of areas of growth that directly relate to civic education and that suggest how deeply and broadly their education affects them. For example, students often said they learned the value of listening to others and being sensitive to the values that others hold. Although a few students complained about group work, some students spontaneously described their progression toward what might be called a collaborative identity, where they came to value group goals as well as those they held as individuals. Curriculum experiences in self-assessment and valuing were linked to their development as learners, performers, and collaborative professionals. And curriculum experiences in engaging diverse approaches to learning and multiple perspectives led to development of self-direction and the appreciation of multiple perspectives.

We also used the Behavioral Event Interview to study alumnae performance in work, family, volunteer, and other settings (Mentkowski & Rogers, 1993; Rogers & Mentkowski, 1994). This research has clarified the multidimensional and complex abilities that support effective citizenship, particularly in the workplace, which is where three-quarters of Alverno alumnae say they spend most of their time and energy.

We used factor analysis to help us create a clearer picture of how our five-year alumnae contribute in the workplace (Mentkowski & Associates, 2000; Rogers, 1999). Alumnae demonstrate the following intriguing abilities:

- collaborative organizational thinking and action: a distinctive kind of participative leadership, in which alumnae took responsibility for collective effectiveness;
- balanced self-assessment and acting from values: the continued learning of alumnae remained connected to their active reflection on how their values and actions are linked;
- developing others and perspective taking: what might be called social skills;
- analytic thinking and action, which emphasizes independent contributions.

Finally, longitudinal data, both from questionnaires and a battery of human potential measures (Mentkowski & Associates, 2000), further clarified the causes of growth during and after college. These findings link the breadth of preparation in the Alverno curriculum to key qualities of civic participation: broad engagement and collaboration. In addition, we found that this kind of breadth helps explain why integrating service learning across the curriculum leads to personal growth. This is one way that service learning serves life-long learning.

OUR NEXT CHALLENGE: LINKING SERVICE AND CIVIC INVOLVEMENT MORE DIRECTLY TO POLITICAL LIFE

We believe that Alverno develops students who effectively serve their workplaces, families, churches, and communities, and who can learn to improve how they perform in future service roles. On the other hand, our women students tend to be less involved than men in political institutions, movements, and parties. We think our graduates ought to serve society more directly in the political arena. Thus we have recently embarked on a revision especially of our effective citizenship and global perspectives curricula and services to provide better political training and opportunities. To help fuel this work, we have recently joined the Kellogg Civic Learning Cluster Project, a network of innovative institutions dedicated to improving their students' contributions to civil society. Our project is entitled "Involving Women in Civic Life in New Ways." Specific activities include revising a required general education course to include more political content and projects, and building our network of political sites for internships and volunteerism.

But a more challenging concern is how to get students engaged within the context of very busy lives. Alverno students often juggle many responsibilities and demands on their time — school, job, marriage, children. They have little time "left over" for civic or political activity. Recent studies have shown that even traditional-age college freshmen feel extremely pressured for time. Alverno's goal in the coming years is to assist students to find ways — new ways along with the old — to become civically and politically engaged while they struggle with limited time. As a start, various committees are collaborating to build political information and opportunities into web-based resources.

And finally, we must continue to know as much as we can about our students' lives, values, and issues. Shortly we will begin a new quantitative and qualitative study of the social and political dimension of our students' experiences, involving both faculty and students as researchers.

CONCLUSIONS

What key lessons might our experience offer a campus seeking to improve its service-learning dimension? First, to ensure that there is documentable learning in the service activities, faculty and students must use an explicit framework of learning outcomes derived from their academic areas to frame and track student development. This gives backbone to the social commitments being encouraged. Faculty across fields should collaborate to create shared standards.

Second, the boundary between in-class, on-campus, and off-campus learning should be very porous: each should flow into the other. One implication is that classroom activities and assessments should include substantial experiential components linked to actual issues and problems facing the community, to model the lived, ongoing nature of college learning and its value in postcollege commitments.

Third, the curriculum itself needs to foreground, model, and explicitly reward what is required for service. A particular emphasis on collaborative learning is especially valuable in this regard — collaboration among students, reinforced by a culture of collaboration among faculty that is visible to the students. Collaboration and its embedded mindset can and should be taught, to provide students the tools they need to act effectively on their compassion. And faculty have to show in their daily modus operandi that they actually walk the talk of dedication to helping and community building that they propose to their students, lest their message of service be received with cynicism.

Fourth, the acceptable locations for service learning should be as inclusive as possible, since, in our view, what is at issue is student development of abilities that help build a better society. And are not such abilities, well-honed through practice, useful everywhere in our society?

REFERENCES

Alverno College Faculty. (1976/1992). *Liberal Learning at Alverno College.* Milwaukee, WI: Alverno College Institute. (Original work published 1976, revised 1981, 1985, 1989, and 1992).

Alverno College Faculty. (1979/1994). *Student assessment-as-learning at Alverno College.* Milwaukee, WI: Alverno College Institute. (Original work published 1979, revised 1985 and 1994).

Boyte, H. (2000). *Public engagement in a civic mission: A case study.* Washington, DC: Council on Public Policy Education.

Brooker, R., Engelmann, D., & Schulte, J. (1998). Service learning at Alverno College. Milwaukee, WI: Alverno College Institute.

Grantz, R. & Thanos, M. (1996). Internships: Academic learning outcomes. *NSEE Quarterly, 21,* (1), 10-27.

Mentkowski, M., & Associates. (2000). *Learning that lasts: Integrating learning, development and performance in college and beyond.* San Francisco: Jossey-Bass.

Mentkowski, M., Much, N., Kleinman, L., & Reisetter Hart, J. (1998). *Student and alumna learning in college and beyond: Perspectives from longitudinal interviews.* Milwaukee, WI: Alverno College Institute.

Mentkowski, M., & Rogers, G. (1993). Connecting education, work, and citizenship: How assessment can help. *Metropolitan Universities: An International Forum, 4,* (1), 34-46.

Much, N., & Mentkowski, M. (1982). *Student perspectives on liberal learning at Alverno College: Justifying learning as relevant to performance in personal and professional roles.* (Final Report to the National Institute of Education: Research Report No. 7). Milwaukee, WI: Alverno Productions. (ERIC Document Reproduction Service No. ED 239 563).

Rogers, G. (1999). *Ability factors for five-year alumnae: Defining criteria and illustrating outcomes.* Milwaukee, WI: Alverno College Institute.

Rogers, G., & Mentkowski, M. (1994). *Alverno faculty validation of abilities scored in five-year alumnae performance.* Milwaukee, WI: Alverno College Institute.

Schulte, J. (1996). *Alverno College: Effective citizenship and service learning.* Milwaukee, WI: Alverno College Institute.

Wagner, V., & Spore, M. (1995). Service learning at Alverno College: A report to the Wisconsin Association of Independent Colleges and Universities. Unpublished manuscript.

CHAPTER 5

CIVIC RESPONSIBILITY THROUGH MUTUAL TRANSFORMATION OF TOWN AND GOWN: SERVICE LEARNING AT ANDREWS UNIVERSITY

Niels-Erik Andreasen*
Andrews University

INTRODUCTION

In what follows I explain the commitment of Andrews University to service, then describe a sustained experience that this commitment prompted and, finally, share some of the tentative assessments that we have made of our service-related work.

COMMITMENT TO SERVICE

The founders of Andrews University believed that a community driven by a sense of purpose needed to be educated for at least two reasons. First, the very identity of any such community required that its members develop an informed understanding of their personal and social responsibilities. This is what Thomas Jefferson had in mind when he referred to the importance of education in a democratic society: only educated citizens could be trusted with political power. Without the education of its citizens democratic organizations would regress into dictatorship or dissolve into anarchy.

Motivated by this principle, the Seventh-day Adventist church established Battle Creek College (later Andrews University) in 1874, only eleven years after that small denomination of religious believers had organized, selected its name and adopted its mission (1863). The challenge of the new college was to ensure that its students would develop their physical, mental and spiritual attributes well enough to become active and responsible participants in their church and citizens in their community.

*I am pleased to acknowledge the considerable contribution of Professors Oystein LaBianca and Larry Ulery, both of Andrews University, to the preparation of this article. They are respectively the initiator and the current director of the project highlighted in this paper. My assistant, Gary M. Ross, helped with the editing.

Second, to carry out its purpose in a practical and sustained way, any community, or the nation as a whole, must fill its ranks with committed, skilled and competent professionals who can meet human needs and grasp the economic opportunities around them expertly and effectively. With that in mind, Andrews University from the beginning focused on preparing its students for the human services, especially teaching, ministry, other forms of religious work, and health care. The latter was done in collaboration with the then famous Battle Creek Sanatorium established in 1866 by Dr. John Harvey Kellogg.

These two educational principles, the development of responsible citizens and their preparation for professional service to church and society, heavily influenced the founders and early leaders of Andrews University. They spoke relentlessly of the holistic development of all the human potentials, body, spirit and mind, as well as of the importance to prepare oneself for devoted service to others through education of good quality. Education, the founders of Andrews University said, is a "harmonious development of the physical, the mental and the spiritual powers" that "prepares the students for the joy of service in this world and for the higher joy of wider service in the world to come." (E.G. White, *Education*, 1903, p. 13). From this early beginning in urban Battle Creek, the college moved to a much larger rural campus near Berrien Springs, Michigan in 1901. After adding a graduate school and a school of theology, it became Andrews University in 1959. But change did not preempt the principles of its founders. The three Latin words, *mens, spiritus, corpus* on the university seal are a visible reminder of that fact.

Through time three developments, together with their appropriate institutional responses, came to characterize the current involvement by Andrews University in service learning and civic responsibility.

Service, responsibility and the curriculum

Andrews students have long been taught the virtue and responsibility of meeting needs in the world around them. Traditionally, they would organize into helping bands during their free hours and bring cheer or support to children in the community, the aged in senior care facilities, and inmates in prison. When they could have carried regular paying jobs instead, they would volunteer a summer or even a whole year to teach English abroad, or serve as church volunteers or as counselors at summer camp. Students who volunteered for these activities repeatedly expressed the life-changing effect of their volunteer activities: their own lives were enriched and at times even redirected to unanticipated educational goals or life work.

During the past two decades Andrews University has become far more deliberate about providing students with service opportunities. The introduction of the Community Service Assistantship Program (CSAP) led the way. As we will see, it provided students with work-study experience in local agencies, institutions and services — real-life, hands-on experiences that met documented needs of the local community under the supervision of professionals.

Recognizing how this enhanced the students' education, the university redesigned its general education curriculum to include a required course in the philosophy of service, followed by a required service learning activity designed by each student in collaboration with a service-learning coordinator. During their senior year the students must evaluate how their service experience contributed to their chosen specialization or profession.

Behind these opportunities and reinforcements lies the premise that community service and civic responsibility, like other human traits, are acquired most effectively not through a course of study, but rather through repeated reinforcements that lead to habits of service. Effective service learning is not unlike what religious people call a conversion, or life-changing experience. Just as a literate person is someone who not only knows how to read, but reads widely and frequently, so also, according to the founders of Andrews University, the desirable kind of service learning continues throughout life, changes a persons's character, and touches every aspect of the human experience.

Diversity and International Perspectives

During the past two or three decades Andrews University has become increasingly diverse in terms of its student body, faculty and staff. At present around 50% of the student body of 3000 is represented by various minorities, and about 25% are international students representing over 100 nations. Observers now identify Andrews University as one of the most diverse universities in the nation.

This development has placed service learning and civic responsibility in an entirely new light. For example, the university is awash with strongly held views on nearly every international crisis, development, or relationship reported on the evening news. The Kosova crisis, peace in the Middle East, the border clashes between India and Pakistan, the Somali-Ethiopian confrontation, internal unrest in Sierra Leone, Rwanda, Zimbabwe and Sri Lanka, and the AIDS crisis in sub- Sahara Africa, have special and even personal meanings for some of our students, staff and faculty. And, of course, involvements by the United States, the UN, the World Bank, the European Union or Russia, are matters of discussion and debate. Old loyalties, tribalism, family connections, language affiliations, religious and cultural traditions, all play a part in this debate. What does service learning and civic responsibility mean in such an environment?

We have barely begun to address such questions, even as we acknowledge their importance. Because representatives from over 100 national groups live and study together in this university and conduct their ordinary affairs in our community, the large international issues are played out in microcosmic, but nevertheless real, ways on our campus and in our community. We have unparalleled opportunities to address these matters and enormous resources at our disposal to gain understanding of them.

This is a particularly important project for the university in the new century. For it is now clear that community service and civic responsibility that just a few decades ago directed a citizen's responsibility toward an ethnically and economically diverse local community, must now add an international perspective in order to be effective. Economics, trade, travel and communication have no national borders, yet play an important role in our daily life and thus directly impact our response to civic responsibility at home. Even American military engagements internationally are no longer designed simply to maintain the integrity of our borders and the borders of our allies, but rather to restore internal stability in other nations, or to maintain the integrity of borders between other nations. As a result international relationships are more complex than in the past, and the international perspective on civic responsibility, within the United States, has become correspondingly complex.

In the fall of 1998 the Ford Foundation funded a public opinion poll on diversity and concluded that in the next century (the current one) we will all have to learn and to live with people who are different from ourselves. The responsibility for such learning falls in large part on colleges and universities. Such learning implies that although community service and civil responsibility may focus the immediate attention of our graduates upon their local communities, their state and their nation, they will not be able to respond effectively without understanding the issues of diversity not only in our nation but also in the international community of which we are a living part. When one sets out to serve one cannot always control WHOM one will be serving, and our experience with diversity prepares us for this reality.

A Mutually Transforming Experience

Andrews University's experience with service learning suggests a mutual transformation. By this we mean two things. First, service learning not only benefits the external community but also — perhaps in more subtle ways — benefits the university community. Both university and community become changed. I will be illustrating below how this happens. Second, service learning implies that the university teaches students to serve willingly and effectively in the community, but service also becomes a teacher. Students who serve become changed in their outlook, attitude, understanding and values. During my six-year tenure as president of Andrews University, I have been informed repeatedly by community leaders that before the introduction of the service component in our educational programs a virtual fire wall existed between campus and village, but that now, after decades of community involvement by students and faculty, gaping holes have appeared in that wall. And a remarkable thing has happened: We have discovered that as the community needs us, so we need the community. That awareness will do much, perhaps more than all our programs put together, to make community service and civic responsibility a habit-forming reality.

CASE IN POINT: BENTON HARBOR

A small urban community (4.2 sq. miles) of approximately 12,000 people, and once an area with a strong manufacturing base and high employment rates, the city of Benton Harbor experienced a severe economic decline from which it may be recovering now in small but fairly consistent strides. Not having benefited from the country's recent economic good times, it struggles mightily with the problems common to larger urban centers in the United States. In June, 1988 the *Wall Street Journal* put Benton Harbor alongside the inner city neighborhoods of New York, Chicago, and Los Angeles in terms of per capita unemployment, arson, crime rates, high infant mortality, single-parent households, substandard housing conditions, and the education levels of its students.

In the past decade the city has received state and national attention for the dubious distinctions of having the highest per capita murder rate in one year; making *Money Magazine*'s top ten worst cities to live in; and for having a high state per capita level of various forms of sexually transmitted diseases and births out of wedlock. In 1998 Alex Kotlowitz's book, *The Other Side of the River*, highlighted the racial tension that can develop between Benton Harbor and geographically adjacent communities. More recently, the state of Michigan has considered a take-over of the Benton Harbor public school system because of its poor achievement test scores, high drop out and absenteeism rates, low graduation rates and a deteriorating infrastructure. Additionally, a high turnover in city mayors, managers, police chiefs, and city commissioners afflicts the city. As one resident remarked, "the problems of Benton Harbor have resulted in the rise of a generation with reduced aspirations and expectations and too many uneducated and unskilled people living in one area."

Andrews University, some fifteen miles from Benton Harbor, launched its Community Service Assistantship Program (CSAP) against this backdrop. It is a story worth telling because it addresses something that predates Michigan Campus Compact (MCC) and that has operated over many years. A behavioral science professor and his colleagues decided that rather than simply learning and theorizing about social challenges and problems, our students should become part of the local solution for them. At that moment the mission became and remains to affirm the work of community service organizations and non-profit agencies/institutions and to help these entities meet their goals and objectives.

We set out to accomplish this mission by enlisting and deploying the energies and talents of the Andrews University faculty, staff, and students. Because of the high cost of a private education and our students' need for gainful employment, the decision was made to recompense the students for their efforts on the assumption that they would serve beyond their paid time if possible and would, in any case, serve their community in some manner when they left the university and relocated. The initial activity was launched in the 1986/1987 academic year when Andrews University partnered with a Benton Harbor community activist organization, the Neighborhood Information and Sharing Exchange, on the basis of a start-up grant from the McGreggor Foundation in Detroit. A handful of students went door to door to ascertain how Benton Harbor residents could make their city a better place in which to live and work. While this was not the first or only Andrews University initiative to partner with our neighbors to the north, it was meaningful in terms of growth, achievements, challenges, and impact.

Within a few years of the inaugural launch of CSAP, the number of students involved, the agencies and institutions partnered with, and the hours served, markedly increased. Work-study was the hallmark, and the effort was funded and supported by soft money from such sources as Andrews University administration; federal, national, and local foundations; corporations; individuals; and church denominations. In 1991/1992 the program was institutionalized when CSAP became part of the formal Andrews University budget and planning process and acquired a full-time director. This meant that hard money earmarked for community service would form the foundation of the program, supplemented with monies from the above-mentioned sources. Each succeeding year of CSAP has resulted in varied kinds of growth opportunities, new paths to pioneer, and a re-energized vision of service.

How CSAP Works: Venues of Engagement

Organizationally, CSAP is part of the academic program of Andrews University. It is housed in the Department of Behavioral Sciences, and its director reports to the chair of that department. As noted above, salary and benefits of the director and funding for the general operating expenses of the CSAP office and its staff are contributed by the university.

The director of CSAP and his support staff facilitate and mobilize student engagement in the wider community. At least five different venues of engagement are offered to students: work-study, volunteerism, service-learning, practicum, and fieldwork.

Work-study is a student employment program supervised by the CSAP office that places students in various agencies in Benton Harbor and elsewhere in Southwestern Michigan and Northern Indiana. Funding for the program is provided through federal work-study dollars, through student aid funds provided by the university, and through donations to this program by local churches, corporations, foundations and individuals. Students work 10-15 hours per week in positions maintained by local inner city schools, human service agencies, churches, and various private voluntary organizations. CSAP staff and the local employer provide the supervision.

Volunteerism offers experiential learning opportunities in community service for students who come to the CSAP office and request such opportunities. Sometimes encouraged by teachers, the student is often the initiator. Students in this program may work side-by-side with students in any of the other programs, although, typically, they contribute fewer hours per week.

Supervision is provided by CSAP staff and the agency providing the volunteering opportunity.

Service-learning happens in various classes and departments across the university. Presently some twenty professors include service out-reach as a requirement for their courses. Academic divisions offering such courses include agriculture, architecture, behavioral sciences, biology, business, communication, history and political science, and nursing. Supervision of students in these programs is primarily the responsibility of the individual instructors.

Practicum and fieldwork offer pre-professional experience for majors in such fields as social work, family studies, nutrition, nursing, public health, education, political science, law, music, and ministry. Students in these programs must meet the standards established by their major department and are normally supervised by a professor in that department in addition to the coordination provided by CSAP staff.

How the service experience arising from these various venues of community engagement links to student learning varies greatly. While it is probably fair to say that a "reflection component" is built into every one of these venues, the extent to which the student is guided and supported in undertaking such reflection is generally greater in the case of venues where faculty members are directly involved, as in the case of service learning, practicum and fieldwork.

Highlights of the CSAP

- The number of agencies/ institutions partnered with over the years has increased (close to 150 different ones) and the types of programs, agencies, and institutions worked with include a varied and diverse spectrum of non-profits.
- The geographic area served has been expanded (by demand) to include most of Berrien County and other areas of Southwest Michigan, but the area of strongest concentration remains Benton Harbor.
- A ten-year interface with MCC has helped keep us abreast of changes, trends, opportunities, and ideas related to service and civic responsibility/civic engagement. This relationship has resulted in grant monies, action related to curriculum and service learning, and awards and recognition for faculty and students. Networking with other MCC Community Service Coordinators has been invaluable.
- A 1992/1993 Research Project involving current and past CSAP students disclosed that the CSAP experience had positively affected the willingness to volunteer (90% of respondents) and that CSAP had helped participants choose their academic majors and careers.
- CSAP has participated in an increasing number and variety of national, state, and local events related to service or social issues. These include United Way "Day of Caring," "Make A Difference Day," "Mentoring

Week," Martin Luther King Day, Special Olympics, and campus blood drives–just to name a few.

- In 1996 a $90,000 grant ($30,000 a year for three years) from the Frederick S. Upton Foundation enabled thirty teachers to receive financial assistance for redesigning their classes to include service learning. CSAP served as a facilitator for this grant as well as liaison resource.
- As noted earlier, the success, results, and influence of CSAP were a major factor in the overhaul of Andrews University's general education requirements to include a Philosophy of Service class and Fieldwork Placement for all undergraduates. These requirements began with the 1996/1997 academic year and continue to the present. The CSAP director teaches sections of the service class and assists with evaluations and revisions of the course. For the latter endeavors the director of CSAP received a Campus Compact "Scholarship of Engagement" grant for 1999-2000. CSAP also facilitates and coordinates the required Fieldwork Placement.
- Student-initiated and student-led service projects and activities (one of our primary goals) have increased in the past five years and CSAP has promoted, supported, and helped fund them where possible.
- Local funding of the CSAP program by foundations, corporations and banks has been increasing and has the potential to increase even more.
- After graduating from Andrews University some students have chosen to move to Benton Harbor in order to work there and at the same time continue the activities begun while students at Andrews.
- Students reaching out to Benton Harbor sought and obtained funds from denominational laypersons (Adventist Services and Industries Group-ASI) to purchase a van for their service-related transportation needs.

Some Things We have Learned

In the 1980's, the university considered the purchase of a YMCA building in downtown Benton Harbor to house community programs, activities and events, but then–correctly we believe–decided to work and partner with existing non-profit agencies and community activist organizations. We have observed other universities entering Benton Harbor with great fanfare and establishing a presence downtown, only to falter when funding, the politics, and the long-term challenge took their toll.

While we know that benefits accrue and transformation occurs, what we believe and feel about the community effects of our endeavors are conjectural and anecdotal. Serious research is called for on the benefits and impact from the communities' perspective.

It may be time to take the next step, the "great leap" in our service journey, to further bridge the divide between campus and community by performing service that goes beyond the partnering stage, service that is focused on "doing with" rather than "doing for" the community. This implies service aligned with social change and social justice, not just charity. In effect, identifying root causes and solutions is now the challenge. And while we focus on the urban city several miles away, we must not overlook the village in our own backyard. This too faces problems that we must address together.

REGARDING CSAP'S IMPACT ON TOWN AND GOWN

A question to which we would return is whether, indeed, Andrews University's experience with service learning — especially as operationalized through our CSAP program — has transformed both the town and the gown.

That it has had a transforming impact on the university is certain. Measures of this impact include 1) the existence for the past ten years of a full-time service learning coordinator who is also the director of CSAP; 2) the steady accumulation of work-study hours by Andrews students in various community agencies — 250,000 hours to date; 3) the addition of service-learning as an integral part of the general education program at Andrews; 4) the addition of some twenty "service-learning courses" to the curricular offerings of over a dozen different academic departments on campus; and 5) the marked increase in student-initiated outreach programs in the community over the past ten years.

To these direct impacts can be added some "spin-offs" attributable to the institutionalization of service-learning. One would be the creation in 1987 of the GENESIS Single Parent program, a package of services that enable single parents to undertake a university education at Andrews. Not only has this program led dozens of young women to a bachelor's degree and gainful employment; it has also benefited their children with enriching schooling and warm friendships in a university environment.

Another significant side-effect is the Community Partnership Initiative (CPI) by means of which Andrews students are sponsored by a coalition of community partners — with the student's home church as the base — to carry out community service in their home towns during their summer vacations. This initiative in effect "exports" the idea of "service-learning" to dozens of local communities throughout Michigan, the Great Lakes regions, and beyond. It has also turned out to be a valuable retention and recruitment tool for the university!

Yet another example is the addition of two new graduate programs over the past decade — the Master of Science in International and Community Development and the Master of Science in Social Work. Whereas the former program was added to provide interdisciplinary graduate level training in sustainable community development concepts and methods, the latter was added to enrich the standard curriculum of the social work profession with the worldview of Seventh-day Adventists. The demand for these two programs, and the community resources needed to mount them, were a direct result of CSAP experience with service-learning. Both programs are serving to heighten awareness among Seventh-day Adventists of more effective ways to partner with local organizations and civic groups for the betterment of communities both in the United States and internationally.

A much more difficult question to answer is what impact, if any, this program has had on the local community — and in particular, on nearby Benton Harbor where the vast majority of Andrews' efforts have been directed.

Of course, one can point to the fact that over the past 15 years, Andrews students have contributed nearly a quarter of a million hours of "free labor" to some 150 agencies — well over half of them in Benton Harbor. In accordance with the CSAP motto — "to be the hands and feet of the community's grass-roots leaders" — these students have added manpower to existing community agencies. The fact that these agencies request help from Andrews year after year suggests that the students are helping them fulfill their various missions.

In the case of some agencies, our CSAP's students and other volunteers have made a remarkable difference. For agencies reliant on large numbers of volunteers, our Andrews program has provided a dependable source of personnel — a core group of persons, many of them with considerable talent and initiative, around which new programs can be built and mounted. From this perspective, everyone wins! The agency gains respect and legitimacy as it expands its offerings; students gain valuable experience, discover their talents and professional interests, and build their curriculum vitae.

But what impact has our service learning program had on the community of Benton Harbor taken as a whole, particularly when the public ranking of the city's appeal has not appreciably changed?

In coming to grips with this disappointing reality, the first thing to note is that Andrews' involvement in Benton Harbor through CSAP and other programs has been nonpolitical from the outset and thus quite beyond the reach of opinion surveys. Although some students were assigned to city-hall to help with various clerical jobs, the vast majority of student hours have been poured into tutoring programs, mentoring programs for high-school youth, and a host of other programs targeting single parents, at-risk teenage girls, the jobless, and the aged.

One notable exception would be a project undertaken by a grass-roots organization called Neighborhood Information and Service Exchange (NISE). Its director utilized an Andrews student to gather data on patterns of reinvestment in the city by banks located inside the city limits. The research revealed unwitting non-compliance with state regulations on the part of several banks. On learning of this, the banks quickly mobilized to create loan programs that would enable larger numbers of city residents to become home owners. Indeed, the director himself was later hired by one of the banks to be in charge of such a program.

By and large, however, Andrews' students have touched individual lives, in particular the lives of young people. It is impossible to accurately gauge the impact of these innumerable relationships, although stories abound of children being helped with their school work; of teenagers opting to stay another year in school; of single moms getting more involved with their kids' education; of shut-ins gaining access to more services.

What has been the long-term impact of these encounters? Unfortunately, little data can be pointed to. A possible source of information, however, may be found among our GENESIS single parent students. As at least 10% of these 250 students over the past ten years have come from Benton Harbor, they present a possible line of information to follow up on.

Among our GENESIS students we have examples of mothers on welfare who, upon graduating from Andrews with a bachelor's degree, returned to work in the city — usually for the schools or a human service agency. We also have examples of families who, by means of the GENESIS program, extricated themselves from the hopelessness of their previous Benton Harbor neighborhoods and moved onward with their lives as successful families in new locations where work and family life could be pursued more satisfactorily.

There is reason to believe that the latter outcome may be more common than the former — that is, that through our various interventions in Benton Harbor we facilitate emigration of individuals and families from Benton Harbor to other communities where the possibilities of an improved quality of life are greater! From the point of view of these individuals and families, this is a good thing. But what of Benton Harbor?

The possibilities for realizing mutual transformation of town and gown are today better than ever for Andrews University and Benton Harbor. Over the past fourteen years, we have come to know each other — there is a foundation of trust and understanding. On this we can build. The challenge ahead is to discover ways to work within the leadership of the city so that as individuals are given a hand up, they will chose to stay in the city rather than take the first opportunity to leave it.

In an important sense, the university today has a heightened obligation to pursue such a partnership. This is because the transformations that have occurred within the university — such as the addition of an MSW program and an MSA in International and Community Development — have strengthened the university's ability to provide capacity-building opportunities for city officials and grass-roots leaders in the city. Over the next few years, this is clearly our mandate.

CHAPTER 6

A GREAT LABOR: DEVELOPING KNOWLEDGE IN SERVICE TO OTHERS AT BOSTON COLLEGE

James J. Fleming
Mary Brabeck
Lynch School of Education
Boston College

INTRODUCTION

University mission statements have their objectives in the world beyond the campus walls. They represent vision statements that, along with focusing the work of individuals on making the university a better place to learn, also focus the concerted efforts of all its members on the shared task of making the world a better place. Through an historical process of encouraging its members to articulate their deepest desires, educational organizations "institutionalize" these desires in the form of mission statements that offer a widely-understood and compelling vision for realizing these shared aspirations (Holland, 1999). It is erroneous to think that mission statements at modern American institutions of higher education are aimed only at meeting the self-serving needs of the university itself. Rather, these statements also aim to meet the needs of the modern world in which these institutions exist.

Our modern world has, in some places, experienced an explosion of knowledge without a corresponding growth in understanding. Ours is a world that lacks trust in its leaders and has little faith in its institutions. It is a world that has developed technologies that link continents and planets but isolate humans. Many men and women are weary and dispirited, feeling distant from moral purpose, uncertain about knowledge or the very worth of human endeavors. Amidst these confusing and dangerous disconnections, universities like Boston College (BC), are called by their institutional missions to serve, among others, their students, their local communities, the greater world by developing knowledge in service to others.

Boston College is uniquely capable of answering the call to generate new knowledge in service to others. Because it is a university, BC offers the power, vigor, and authority of knowledge. Because it is a Jesuit and Catholic university, it also offers wisdom, hope, and faith, as well as the strength of a time-tested spiritual and intellectual tradition (Leahy, 1999). The Mission Statement of Boston College plays a central role in determining the nature and scope of the University's activities. The mission is embodied in the work of its students and faculty, administration and staff, trustees and alumni. The University's Mission Statement influences the extent of the institutional commitment to aspects of the ongoing intellectual enterprise. The aim of this chapter is to offer insights into how the service learning activities at BC are in line with, inform, and are informed by the University's mission (Fleming, 1999).

Focused, as a great university must be, on the world outside its walls, Boston College stands firmly on a foundation with an impressive 500-year heritage of Jesuit education. Graduates of Boston College understand that their alma mater explicitly embodies the fundamental human desire to know, to bring critical intelligence to bear on the longings and struggles of all women and men, and to achieve a world that affirms human dignity.

The tradition reflected in BC's mission, however, is not simply handed-down from one successive generation of scholars to another. Those who currently labor in this complex intellectual enterprise are not called simply to repeat what the founders did in order to carry forward the tradition (Kolvenbach, 2000, Santa Clara). Rather, today's scholars must do what the founders would do if they were here today living with the complexities of contemporary society (Kolvenbach, 2000, Loyola). As T. S. Eliot said in his influential essay *Tradition and the Individual Talent* (1919)

> *If the only form of handing down, consisted in following the ways of the immediate generation before us in a blind or timid adherence to its successes, 'tradition' should positively be discouraged...Tradition is a matter of much wider significance. It cannot be inherited, and if you want it you must attain it by great labor. (quoted in West, 1993, p. 9)*

Service learning is one form of this "great labor" that is capable of creating an institutional culture that can achieve an overarching mission to educate our students while enveloping and enriching the world outside the university's gates. It is a "great labor" predicated on a Catholic and Jesuit tradition and guided by Boston College's mission, both of which direct us to service to the world.

OVERVIEW OF THIS CHAPTER

In this chapter, we will briefly consider the various historical purposes of the American university, the variety of forms of relationships between universities and their local communities, the philosophical and historical foundation for Boston College's mission, and the current place of service learning activities in the University's self-understanding. To illustrate the way in which these concepts influence university policies and programs, we will discuss two types of academically-based programs that are supported by the mission of Boston College in service to others:

1) academic programs offered by individual departments, research centers and schools;
2) community-oriented inquiry supported by the University's research institutes, centers, and individual scholars.

Within each of these two types of university activities, we will highlight one case from which lessons can be learned through the consideration of:

a) the role of the mission of the university in support of the particular activities;
b) the learning that results from these activities; and
c) the challenges posed by such mission-supported, community-focused activities at a modern American university.

In conclusion, we will reflect on the ways in which service learning is consistent with and mutually reinforcing to the Boston College mission.

MISSION AND PURPOSE IN AMERICAN HIGHER EDUCATION

American higher education has never followed any single uniform pattern nor has it had any one single purpose (Brubacher & Rudy 1976; Greiner, 1994; Kerr, 1991; Levine, 1986; Shils, 1995; Skivington, 1998; Veysey, 1965; Westmeyer, 1997). Early American colleges, forebearers of our current universities, were formed through a long process of selective choices which allowed those who ran them to create hybrid institutions. The separation of church and state along with the powerful American suspicion of centralized power combined to yield amazing educational diversity (Brubacher & Rudy, 1976; Leahy, 1991). The purposes of American universities, their organizational structures, are multiple, co-existent, and often contradictory. As society made new demands and changed over time, most existing goals were maintained in some form and subsumed into the newer ones. The fact that some of these out-moded aspirations never completely disappeared, added to the institutional complexity. The multiple purposes of institutions of higher education paradoxically co-exist both in harmony and in tension. In fact, if a university were to focus exclusively on one purpose over all others, it would be considered a radical and historically new form of institution (Greiner, 1994).

The original implicit institutional self-understanding of the early American college persisted for nearly two hundred years before any widely accepted explicit statement of an underlying philosophy was publicly circulated and agreed upon (Brubacher & Rudy, 1976; Jencks & Riesman, 1968). By the mid-nineteenth century, the moral and cultural goals of the early American four-year undergraduate liberal arts college had been relegated to a secondary position. These purposes were uneasily joined together with the dominant utilitarian and research purposes of the evolving research universities. The university's eclectic character "is testified to by the fact that while democratic and utilitarian values inevitably gave tone to the entire structure, other out-looks, such as those of pure research and liberal culture, continued to exist (in somewhat modified form) within the framework and were totally assimilated to the dominant ethos" (Brubacher & Rudy, 1976, p. 400).

In 1876, when Daniel Coit Gilman was inaugurated as the president of Johns Hopkins, he called upon institutions of higher education to "make for less misery among the poor, less ignorance in the schools, less bigotry in the temple, less suffering in the hospital, less fraud in business, [and] less folly in politics" (Long, 1992, p. 123). The purposes of the university, by the turn of the twentieth century, could be seen as multiple, including but not limited to: improving the moral fiber of America's youth, educating well-rounded indi-viduals, training for a profession, preserving and transmitting knowledge, sharing useful knowledge with the populace at large, providing service as an agent of social change, being a vehicle of disinterested inquiry, offering re-sources for industrial and commercial growth, and generating new knowledge. Within this larger historical context of higher education in the United States, Boston College has articulated its unique mission, in response to the commu-nity context within which it resides.

UNIVERSITIES AND THEIR COMMUNITIES

The idea that an American university would serve the needs of the greater society is as old as the earliest colonial colleges and was formally captured in *The Wisconsin Idea*. *The Wisconsin Idea* (from the early days of the Land Grant College in the state of Wisconsin) proclaimed that "the boundaries of the University are the boundaries of the State" — highlighting the notion that the university's faculty served the citizens of the state.

Recent essays by such authors as Derek Bok, Ernest Boyer, and Ernest Lynton, as well as studies funded by the Pew Higher Education Research Pro-gram and other foundations have called for a return to the role that universi-ties historically played in contributing to the critical issues facing society (Lerner, 1999; Lerner & Simon, 1998). These authors call for a clearer ar-ticulation on the part of universities and colleges regarding how their missions link their research, teaching and service to the world around them. The uni-versity is one of the central social institutions, which historically has linked the great cities of the world to the outstanding achievements of civilization (Buckley, 1998; Marsden, 1994; Mumford, 1938). The revival of the cities in medieval Europe and the birth of the university were coincident; the city and the university share a common history (Bender, 1988). Many faculty and staff at American universities embrace their local communities and play active and productive roles as good neighbors. However, just as readily, as some on university campuses face-up to urban problems, many others find support for the "exercise of urban denial" (Hollinger, 1988, p. 250).

In 1985, the presidents of three universities (Brown, Georgetown, and Stanford) met to discuss the commitment of institutions of higher education to service, service learning and university-community partnerships. The result of this meeting was the Campus Compact, of which Boston College is a member. The Campus Compact is emblematic of the increasing engagement by universities in local communities' needs. Now, sixteen years after its inception, the Campus Compact boasts of more than five hundred member institutions. To assure that its research, teaching, and service are not far removed from the "conversation of the city", Boston College's students, faculty, staff, and alumni devote thousands of hours in service to the community each year (*Community Impact*, 1999; Leahy, 2000).

Universities and the local communities of which they are a part have many reasons to work together. One or both may be motivated out of the fear of decline or the desire to survive. Universities' institutional self-interests are tied closely to the success of their efforts in their local communities (Benson, 1996). Many have offered a moral argument for such partnerships. These arguments tend to reflect the altruistic side of our institutions. A university, the moral argument goes, should take an active role in the well being of the community in which it resides for the sake of society (Giamatti, 1981; Greiner, 1994; Kerr, 1991). Others tie this civic duty directly to the idea of a university (Checkoway, 1997; Cisneros, 1995).

While universities may take pride in their history of community involvement and their encouragement of students to become active community members and good citizens, institutions of higher education themselves are frequently unsuccessful change agents (Innes, 1996; Szantan, 1981) and often bad citizens. During the 1960s and 1970s, local, state and federal governments asked universities to help them solve their more intractable and interconnected complex social problems. Failure on the part of the universities to come up with satisfactory solutions caused many to become disenchanted with higher education (Cardozier, 1987). In the majority of cases, urban universities have widened rather than narrowed the gap between themselves and their surrounding communities (Kerr, 1991). At many universities and colleges across the country, there is a culture that supports the response of contemporary university leaders "to the current social pressures for greater, value-added contributions of higher education to the matters of everyday life affecting the communities within which they are embedded." (Lerner, 2000, p. 47) At Boston College our tradition and mission require us to strive to close that gap.

ASPECTS OF THE PHILOSOPHICAL HERITAGE OF BC WHICH SUPPORT SERVICE LEARNING

As a Jesuit University, Boston College is particularly committed to the application of knowledge to solve the problems of today's world and to prepare students to "serve others." Service learning is in accord with this commitment because of its potential to impact student's spiritual and moral formation. As Ignacio Martin-Baro, S.J., one of the Jesuit faculty members who was martyred at the University of Central America wrote, "The more active, critical, community-oriented, and dialectical that a pedagogical method is, the greater chance it will have of being able to affect consciousness" (Martin-Baro, 1991). Active learning, in service to the community is more likely to have a positive effect on the growing moral conscience of college students than learning which is distant or removed from the real world. This is in no way suggesting that there should be a softening of the demand for excellence in the liberal arts and sciences. Peter H. Kolvenbach, the international Jesuit Superior said in Vienna in 1987: "You would not attract outstanding, talented young people [to Jesuit Universities] if you did not offer them the prospect of academic excellence. But you would not respond to their deepest, though often poorly verbalized, aspirations if you did not carry them beyond academic excellence. The meaning and purpose of education is justice itself. Human dignity is its premise. Human freedom is its goal" (Kavanaugh, 1989). Service learning both maintains and extends academic excellence.

Education at Boston College will always challenge students' preconceived notions and encourage them to re-think their long-held conceptions of the world and to actively engage in learning. Service learning offers a potent and engaging pedagogy that is consonant with the underlying principles of the University's mission. Service learning is consistent with Boston College's aspiration "ever to excel" (the University's motto) by grounding academic excellence in the real world. As Dr. Johnson once remarked to Boswell: A great city is, to be sure, the school for studying life (quoted in Lawton, 2000).

Service learning offers the community as a setting not only for the application of knowledge but also for its generation. The idea of service learning grows out of a concept of learning "that takes fuller account of the competence practitioners sometimes display in situations of uncertainty, complexity, uniqueness, and conflict" (Schon, 1983, p. 18). Theory and practice meet; what students read in class is contemplated in light of the experience they have in the community. For Jesuits, contemplation flows into action regularly and we realize, to some extent, our ideal of being contemplatives in-action. This concept of contemplation in action also has its parallel in the world of general education. It is found in Donald A. Schon's (1983; 1995) idea of "reflective practice". Action, not solutions, is at the heart of reflective practice.

Certainty is replaced by critical questions. Knowledge deepens with action and is intimately joined to it (Tremmel, 1993).

The American educational philosopher, John Dewey offered one of the clearest articulations of active reflection on experience.

> *In unfamiliar cases, we cannot tell just what the consequences of observed conditions will be unless we go over past experiences in our mind, unless we reflect upon them and by seeing what is similar in them to those now present, go on to form a judgment of what may be expected in the present situation (Dewey, 1938, p. 68).*

This active reflection may take place in seconds, or it may proceed in leisurely fashion over the course of several weeks or months. It may even ebb and flow for years. Shon notes that, "the pace and duration of episodes of reflection-in-action vary with the pace and the situations of practice" (Schon, 1983, p. 62). Students come to understand by doing, by being involved in the activity, and by reflecting on their experience in light of the readings used by the professor and the class discussions. Reflection on experience has always been basic to Jesuit pedagogy. The *Ratio Studiorum,* (discussed in greater detail in the next section of this chapter), a document that has been central to the tradition of Jesuit education since the 1600's, offers a pedagogy that moves students through experience to reflection, to articulation, to interpreting and deciding, to doing (Letson & Higgins, 1995).

ASPECTS OF THE HISTORICAL ORIGINS OF BC WHICH SUPPORT SERVICE LEARNING

Boston College's institutional self-understanding emerges from a mission that not only offers a strong philosophical framework for service learning but also honors nearly half a millennium of educational theory that is inextricably joined through reflection with real-world practice and therefore supports service learning activities. The current Jesuit universities can be seen as having inherited the foundation of their pedagogical theory and rationale from the *Constitutions of the Society of Jesus* which were written in 1540. The source of their pedagogical methods can be traced back to two documents: the *Spiritual Exercises of St. Ignatius,* which were first published in 1548 and the *Ratio atque Institutio Studiorum Societatis Jesu* which was written in 1599. The mission of Boston College is, in large part, formed and informed by these three documents written nearly five centuries ago.

Throughout the nearly 500 year involvement in education, Jesuit schools around the world have selected useful pedagogical techniques from the contemporary array available. In 1599, the *Ratio*, the traditional handbook of Jesuit curriculum, brought about the first organized system of education in the Western world (Letson & Higgins, 1995). The *Ratio* still plays a central role in the contemporary Jesuit commitment to integrate service and learning into the university curriculum. Today, 3,000 Jesuits work at 191 higher education institutions in 46 countries, in which there are more than 500,000 students. Boston College is just one of the 28 U.S. Jesuit colleges and universities that are continuing their fidelity to the tradition of achieving educational excellence by integrating service and learning into the curriculum through action or "the doing" (Fleming, 2000).

The Center for Child, Family and Community Partnerships is located at BC. Creighton University has the Center for Service and Justice. At Georgetown University, several academically-based courses and research-related projects are housed in the Volunteer and Public Service Center. Loyola University, Chicago, has a well-funded Center for Urban Research and Learning. In fact, each of the 28 colleges and universities has a service learning or volunteer program, many housed within research centers. Also like BC, these Jesuit institutions of higher education articulate the need for these types of programs in their respective mission statements. Repeated throughout the 28 mission statements are clear desires to "serve the community and the world" (Canisius College); to be "responsible and active participants in civic life and to live generously in service to others" (Georgetown University); to develop a "concern for others especially for those most in need" in the local and regional community (LeMoyne College); to "dedicate their lives to the service of others, actively entering into the struggle for a more just society" (Marquette University); and to "prepare students who can help build, through service, a just and peaceful community" (Seattle University).

These pedagogical and curricular choices are predicated on the belief that the ultimate worth of the human person is not measured by what she knows, but rather by what she freely does, a belief that is interwoven into both the "Principle and Foundation" of the *Spiritual Exercises* and found in the Jesuit *Constitutions* (IV, 16). The *Ratio* offers several different pedagogical techniques such as lectures, classroom activities, laboratories, or case studies (as understood at that time) which, depending on the subject matter taught, may be more appropriate for a particular academic goal.

Students at Boston College are challenged to both learn "the good" and do "the good" through action in service to others. The virtue of this practical knowledge (knowledge through practice) is oriented toward action to such a degree that the measure of one's knowledge of the good is only "knowable" to the extent that one does the good. In Greek, the word "excellences", as in the Boston College motto "Ever to Excel," and "virtue" have the same root. When viewed in this dual meaning the familiar school motto takes on profound and complex meaning. In the Aristotelian sense, virtue, that is, excellences, are acquired, not from books, classroom teaching, and laboratories alone, but from doing; from engagement in the world, from *praxis*. Teaching students to serve others, to be honest, courageous, and generous in their pursuit of social justice, in short, teaching students to excel, in the sense of "Ever to Practice Virtue" requires the practice, the doing, in order to achieve excellence. Through practice, service learning, Boston College promotes the development of virtue and the formation of men and women for others.

Service learning activities at BC, along with many other programs, embody these ancient ideas and hurtle them into contemporary service and scholarship. Boston College has the highest standards of teaching and research in undergraduate, graduate, and professional programs and is committed to the pursuit of a just society through the work of its faculty and staff, and the achievements of its graduates. BC pursues this through its distinctive university mission of "fostering the rigorous intellectual development, the ethical and personal formation of its undergraduate, graduate, and professional students in order to prepare them for citizenship, service, and leadership in a global society; by producing nationally and internationally significant research that advances insight and understanding, thereby both enriching culture and addressing important societal needs" (Boston College. 1996, p. 3).

These efforts are supported in *Advancing the Legacy*, the University Academic Planning Council's current 10-year plan, which states that "[F]aculty, throughout their careers, should be engaged in the creation of new knowledge, and, where appropriate, in discovering how their research can contribute to a more just society" (Boston College, 1996, p. 16). In this way, and in line with the collective aspirations articulated in the University's mission statement, research and teaching can be of service to others. Present day service to the local community that can yield near-term measurable social change however, often is not viewed as a proper goal of a university. As Shils notes, "It would be very misleading to think about universities as local institutions in the way that municipal governments or a civic association is a local institution. It is imperative that [universities] attend to local affairs, but they would not amount to much as universities if they attended largely to them. Universities are intellectual institutions, and intellectual activities have their objects everywhere in the world and beyond the world of time and space" (Shils, 1995, 210). Jesuit universities, and Boston College in particular, offer a potent pedagogy for the possibility of exponential change, a multiplier effect, a learning activity which is not only appropriate to the nature of teaching, research and service in a Jesuit university, but actually essential to it if we are to stay faithful to our philosophical and historical heritage.

BOSTON COLLEGE IN SERVICE TO OTHERS

The idea of service learning has been a part of American campus life for more than 30 years. At the University of Pennsylvania, it is called "academically-based community service;" at Portland State University it is called, "community-based scholarship;" at Santa Clara University its closest parallel is the Eastside Project which was begun more than 15 years ago as a pedagogical tool aimed at fostering "a paradigm shift in the minds of the [SCU] students" to yield a "significantly altered world view" (Sholander, 1994, 4-5). Boston College does not call its programs "service learning," but there are several programs in which research, critical reflection, pedagogy, and practical experience in service to others are connected in the kind of informed action that prepares our students to bring about a society where all men and women benefit from human interaction (Boston College Jesuit Community, 1994). These activities at BC fit into the definition of service learning as defined in 1990 by the Corporation for National Service:

> *Service learning is a method under which students learn and develop through active participation in thoughtfully organized service experiences that meet actual community needs, that are integrated into the students' academic curricula, and provide structured time for reflection while enhancing what is taught in school by extending student learning beyond the classroom and into the community.* (www.cns.org)

The character of Boston College is both determinant of and determined by those who make up the Boston College community: students, faculty, alumni, trustees, administration and friends. The mission of the university extends from the "questions that its research will entertain, to its evaluation of the knowledge most worth having, to the habits it inculcates as part of the education of its students, and to the common life, spirit and atmosphere it fosters" (Buckley, 1998, 21).

What started out as a Boston College Neighborhood Beautification Project, one-day Sports Camps, and holiday charity drives, has grown through rich and trust-building organic changes into effective partnerships between Boston College faculty/students and community agencies/schools. Undergraduate philosophy students serve soup to the homeless and read books to urban school children; university nursing faculty and their students assist community health professionals; law students help families that are new to the community navigate through the social service network; and student teachers are mentored by local school teachers. The outreach-research, of which this institution and its partners have been successful, has added greater force to prior individual civic efforts. Students at BC are challenged to view the world through another person's eyes, while they are given an academic structure in which reflection and action are integrated. They are encouraged to focus both theory and practice on questions of justice in service to others. At Boston College, this focus on justice in service to others takes several programmatic forms, two of which are the remaining focus of this chapter.

The Mission in Action at Boston College: An Undergraduate Academic Program

There are academic programs sponsored by individual departments or schools that explicitly address values or religious formation, such as: the *PULSE* Program; the *Perspectives* Program; the *Capstone Courses*; the

Faith/Peach/ Justice Undergraduate Minor; the Holmes Partnership collaboration with urban schools in the Lynch School of Education; the required freshman business ethics course in the Carroll School of Management; and programs in the Law School that integrate the study and discussion of ethics, jurisprudence, and service to the poor.

In the College of Arts and Sciences, the *PULSE* Program, a year-long academic program that can be used to meet four course requirements in the core curriculum, provides students with the opportunity to combine supervised social service or social advocacy fieldwork with the study of philosophy, theology, and other disciplines. Using lenses provided by classical philosophical and theological texts, *PULSE* students examine the relationship between self and society, the nature of community, the mystery of suffering, and the practical difficulties of developing a just society. *PULSE*, which requires 10 hours of service in the community each week for an entire academic year regularly has a waiting list for its 350 seats. The program is 30 years old, and a first of its kind in the country. Throughout the years, the relationship between fieldwork and classroom study has evoked rich conversations (Byrne, 1995). Students address basic life questions when they act as a companion to a handicapped adult, tutor an adolescent in a lock-up facility, extend a sympathetic ear to a suicidal person over a telephone line, or feed a homeless person on a cold winter night. Students are guided through these experiences by a leader/facilitator teacher and the classical texts. What follows is a discussion of the role of the mission of the university in supporting *PULSE* activities; the learning that results from these activities; and the challenges posed by such mission-supported, community-focused activities at a modern American university.

In a very real way, *PULSE* supported the current Boston College mission statement before *it* supported *PULSE*. The student-founder of this academically-based service learning program (now a professor of philosophy at the University) remembers that 30 years ago when he was involved in setting up *PULSE*, he repeatedly heard the words, "Service learning doesn't belong in an academic curriculum" (Byrne, 1995, p. 5). Now, as the university is happy to bask in the bright success of *PULSE*'s 30 years of accomplishment, the Academic Planning Council can speak openly about fostering rigorous intellectual development that prepares its students for citizenship and service through addressing important social needs.

Patrick Byrne describes the particular type of learning that takes place for the students of the *PULSE* program as a unique combination of service, *praxis* and academic reflection. As one of the *PULSE* students put it, "It's not that an idea taught in a classroom cannot be as profound [as learning through an experience]; it is simply that when you live by the principles discussed in class, they become imprinted in your life" (Byrne, 1995, p. 5). This application of principles to the larger life experience of the students is one of the particular aspects of *PULSE* that occurs more smoothly than other service learning programs that have a "pre-professional" training focus. *PULSE* is part of the core offerings for Boston College students and is located in the philosophy department and therefore not necessarily associated with any single future career or profession. Byrne has written extensively and spoken to national audiences on the topic of reflective practice. He points out that, the *PULSE* program is rooted in the liberal arts, which are at the academic heart of the university. Combined with the basic conviction that "appropriately structured forms of *praxis* can add depth to the comprehension of theoretical issues", the *PULSE* program is aligned with the long tradition of "reflective-practice" associated with Boston College's academic traditions (Byrne, 1995, p. 6).

Much has changed since its inception, but the basic challenges of reflective action remain the same. However, the greatest single dilemma that the *PULSE* program continues to face is the tension between rigor and relevance. This dilemma emanates from a particularly limited epistemology built into the modern American university that sees the legitimate discovery of new knowledge to be the province of theoreticians, removed from the world. The underlying epistemology of the *PULSE* program turns this concept on its head and proposes thinking about practice as a setting not only for the application of knowledge but for its generation as well (Schon, 1995). Since a critical mass of Boston College faculty espouse a *PULSE*-friendly conception of what counts for legitimate knowledge, a once marginalized program has become central to the university. Our tradition and now our explicit mission continue to reinforce this centrality.

The Mission in Action at Boston College: A Research Institute

In a similar, yet distinctive way, the work of research institutes and centers direct their investigation to questions of how values intersect with contemporary culture. Boston College has a number of such centers. *The Social Welfare Research Institute*, founded in 1970, is a multidisciplinary research center, which investigates issues related to economic prosperity and philanthropy, the motivations for charitable involvement, and the underlying meaning of practice and care. *The Center for Religion and American Public Life* engages in research related to questions of religion as they bear on issues of public policy in America and outreach activities that contribute to a more robust public discussion of critical issues. *The Center for Work and Family* in the Carroll School of Management, engages in research, policy initiatives, and university-employer partnerships that help promote both employer and community responsiveness to families. *The Center for Corporate Citizenship* also in the Carroll School works towards the advancement of the understanding of and creating new strategies for the practice of corporate citizenship aimed at achieving healthy, sustainable communities in which to live, work, and do business. *The Institute for the Study and Promotion of Race and Culture* is housed in the Lynch School of Education. It supports research and practice that address the societal conflicts associated with race and culture. *The Jesuit*

Institute is a university-wide research institute, which works in cooperation with Boston College faculty, schools, and programs, and faculty from outside the university in an intellectual exchange on those issues that emerge at the intersection of faith and culture.

The Center for Child, Family, and Community Partnerships (*CCFCP*), located in the Lynch School of Education draws from all the professional schools on campus. It was established in the early 1990s to foster comprehensive university-community initiatives aimed at improving the quality of life for children and families in Metropolitan Boston (Brabeck *et al.*, 1998). The aim of the *CCFCP* is to bring together faculty from across the university and community practitioners from the fields of health care, social service, law, economic development, and education. Faculty and students collaborate in the generation of useful research, the improvement of urban practice, and the development of new professionals who will work collaboratively in addressing the needs of children and families.

Central to the work of this research center is the generation of new knowledge — knowledge informed by the latest research in the field and grounded in the work of the faculty/researchers, students and community practitioners who are associated with the *CCFCP*. In the spring of 2000, the staff of the Center produced a bibliography of the published works written by faculty and community partners who are considered CCFCP associates. That bibliography, available from the CCFCP office in the Lynch School of Education at BC, has more than 125 entries. Many of these works have received full consideration in the tenure and promotion process for these faculty members. Much of this research also has informed the professional practice of those involved (Brabeck *et al.,*1998; Brabeck, Walsh, Kenny, & Comilang, 1997; Walsh & Buckley, 1994) as well as classroom teaching (Mooney *et al.,*1999).

One of the *CCFCP's* most successful community-based research projects has been the *Gardner Extended Services School (GESS)*. Community practitioners along with students, faculty, and university researchers from the Lynch School of Education, the Nursing and Law schools, and the Graduate School of Social Work have worked as co-learners. They have collaborated as an interprofessional team to form a partnership which has led to a deepened understanding on the part of both the university and community regarding the research-practice relationship (Walsh, Brabeck, Howard, Sherman, Montes & Garvin, 2000). The *GESS* project melds research with practice to address educational legal, health, and social barriers to learning.

Several lessons can be learned from the consideration of three particular aspects of the research conducted by the members of the *Center for Child, Family, and Community Partnerships* at the *Gardner Extended Services School*. What follows is a discussion of: the role of the mission of the university in supporting *CCFCP* activities; the generation of new knowledge that results from these activities; and the challenges posed by such mission-supported, community-focused research at a modern American university.

Unlike the aforementioned *PULSE* program, the *GESS* project originated from the graduate professional schools at Boston College. Because of this, there was a natural predisposition to join research and outreach in the minds of many at the university who were involved. Almost all professional school programs have some form of required "internship" program and refocusing that "internship" to include community-based research was not difficult. The missions of each of the schools involved in the project supported the work. The University's overall mission of encouraging the faculty and researchers to engage in the creation of new knowledge that can contribute to a more just society further aided recruitment of other faculty and researchers. In its effort "ever to excel" as a world-class university, Boston College offered assistance, both financial and organizational, to the *Center for Child, Family, and Community Partnerships*. The CCFCP served as a point of access for both the University faculty and the community practitioners. The *GESS* project provided "research-based inquiry on questions of importance to the community and opportunities for community-based practice" (Walsh et al., 2000, p. 14).

Although service learning is more often written about as a way of meeting the moral/civic goals at American universities, it can, as is the case with the *GESS* project at Boston College, be a useful way of generating new knowledge and helping students better understand this "real world" based knowledge (Eyler, Giles & Braxton, 1997; Waterman, 1997; Zlotkowski, 1998). The ongoing integration of theory with practice and visa-versa helps dispel the idea that one thinks in the laboratory, nurtures thinking in the classroom, and, then practices the learned professional knowledge in the real world. Community-based research such as that which is being conducted through the *GESS* project demonstrates that theory, created in the crucible of practice, is then informed and reformed by the cycle of application and reflection so that (in the process) new knowledge is generated. The systematic separation of theory and practice excludes many more ideas than it includes and distances most ideas from the critical reflection necessary for real learning to take place. This exclusion, either one that is unintentionally reinforced or one that is intentionally created, denies "the power of liberatory education for critical consciousness" (hooks, 1994, pp.18-19). This liberatory education connects the will to know with the will to become and the inclusion of the will in the learning process makes the experience an ontological one in which the learner is changed by the learning that is taking place. Universities learn that when they work in "the real world" the professional education changes and students are better prepared to enter that world.

Finding professional support for community-based outreach and providing integrated services are both challenging endeavors. As Walsh and colleagues write, "Although Boston College faculty have always engaged in some interdisciplinary collaborative work, particularly around curriculum development, there is and has always been a tension among academic departments that must compete for resources and retain independence and autonomy in accounting for productivity" (Walsh *et al.*, 2000, p. 10). Attaining funding for this form of research is also a challenge. Relationships, once established with community partners can weaken if funding for the research-related activities in which they are involved is cut. Tensions arise when the funding agency must be determined and schools, the university, and community agencies must share the resources. Both professional respect and ongoing funding depend on the ability of the researchers involved to turn their community-based research into publishable articles, book chapters and books. The development and maintenance of trusting relationships, essential for this work, takes time; untenured faculty who are racing against a short tenure clock, often do not have enough time to engage in work in schools and communities (Kline & Brabeck, 1999). Tenured faculty who have avoided the time consuming work in community and schools have been rewarded with tenure for conducting research that is separate from the community. Recruiting and sustaining committed faculty for action/reflection, service/learning, practice/research is a challenge. Often the work is relegated to part-time or adjunct faculty, eroding the status and long-term commitment of the institution (Tourse & Mooney, 1999).

CONCLUSION: THE MISSION OF BOSTON COLLEGE IN SERVICE TO OTHERS

Three aspects of the "fit" between the University's mission and these service learning activities have been raised by the discussion in this chapter. Service learning is rooted in the foundational ideas from which the Mission Statement of Boston College has grown and this "rootedness" facilitates the integration of these activities into the University's self-understanding. Service learning is compatible with the ideals articulated in the Mission Statement and, therefore, these two (Mission Statement and service learning activities) can become mutually reinforcing. Service learning offers one viable method to achieve the mission and this viability offers the hope that service learning will become a self-sustainable aspect of the educational project of BC.

Boston College, like other American universities, can be a vehicle for change in the world; commitment to education at all levels can be a very effective way to help reform social structures to be more just. We can not simply expect justice to happen, we must work for it and teach it. Our hope is not that people simply understand justice, but that they live justly. The history of Jesuit education, while connected with the scholastic method, is also intimately tied to the humanistic ideal that "education was to prepare the individual for the 'active life' of service to the common good of society" (O'Malley, 1989, p. 15). At the same time, we have learned that service learning changes the research questions that we ask, because those questions become situated in the realities of the lives of the people with whom we collaborate. It changes the way we teach and the curricula that we develop because we are confronted "in the real world" with the challenges professionals face when they leave the university. In this iterative manner, service informs teaching and scholarship and scholarship informs teaching and service.

At Boston College, we have learned, through practice, the same lesson that experience taught Newman, Dewey, the presidents of great universities and many others who have gone before us: "all substantial or permanent changes in a culture result from institutions" guided by their mission (Buckley, 1998, p. 63; Marsden, 1994). At Boston College our great labor is to develop knowledge that improves the lives of others, and to develop men and women who excel in service to and with others.

REFERENCES

Bender, T. (1988). *The university and the city*. Oxford: Oxford University Press.

Benson, L. , J. Puckett & I. Harkavy, (1996). Communal participatory action research as a strategy for improving universities and the social sciences: Penn's work with the West Philadelphia Improvement Corps as a case study. *Educational Policy,* 10 (2), 202-222.

Bok, D. (1990). *Universities and the future of America* Durham, NC: Duke University Press.

Boston College (1996). *Advancing the legacy: The final report of the Boston College University Academic Planning Committee,* Boston College.

Boston College Jesuit Community (1994) Boston College Jesuit Community Web Page. (http://fmwww.bc.edu/sj/)

Boyer, E. (1990). *Scholarship reconsidered: Priorities for the professoriate.* Princeton, New Jersey: The Carnegie Foundation for the Advancement of Teaching.

Brabeck, M. M., Cawthorne, J., Gaspard, N., Hurd-Green, C., Kenny, M., Krawczyk, R., Lowery, C., Lykes, M. B., Mooney, J.,O'Keefe, J., Ross, C., Savage, J., Soifer, A., Smyer, M., Sparks, E., Tourse, R., Sandra Waddock, & Zollers, N. (1998). Changing the Culture of the University to Engage in Outreach Scholarship. In R. M. Lerner & L. A. K. Simon (Eds.), *University-Community Collaborations for the Twenty-First Century: Outreach Scholarship for Youth and Families* (pp. 335-364). New York: Garland Publishing.

Brabeck, M.M., Walsh, M.E., Kenny, M. & Comilang, K. (1997). Interprofessional collaboration for children and families: Opportunities for counseling psychology in the 21st century. *The Counseling Psychologist,* 25 (4), 615-636.

Brubacher, J & W. Rudy (1976). *Higher Education in transition: A history of American colleges and universities, 1636-1976.* NY: Harper & Row.

Buckley, M. (1998). *The Catholic university as promise and project.* Washington: Georgetown Press.

Byrne, P. (1995). Paradigms of justice and love. *Conversations,* Spring, 1995, pp. 5-17.

Cardozier, V. (1987). *American higher education: An international perspective.* Aldershot, U.K,: Gower Pub. Co.

Checkoway, B, (1997). Reinventing the research university for public service. *Journal of Planning Literature,* 11 (3), 307-322.

Cisneros, H. (1995). *The university and the urban challenge.* Rockville, MD: Aspen Systems Corporation.

Community Impact (1999). A report compiled by the Boston College Office of Community Affairs.

*Corporation for National Service (1990).*http://www.nationalservice.org/about/Index.html.

Dewey, J. (1938). *Experience and education.* New York: MacMillan.

Eyler, J., Giles, D.E., & Braxton, J. (1997). The impact of service-learning on college students. *Michigan Journal of Community Service Learning,* 4, 5-15.

Fleming, J. (2000). Unpublished compilation of the programs that exist at all 28 Jesuit colleges and universities. Available from the author.

Fleming, J. (1999). The emerging role of service learning at Jesuit universities. *Explore Bannan Institute for Jesuit Education and Christian Values.* 6-10.

Giamatti, A. B. (1981). *The University and the public interest.* NY: Athenaeum Press.

Greiner, W. (1994). In the total of all these acts: How can American universities address the urban agenda?" *Teachers College Record* 95 (3) 305-323.

Holland, B. (1999). From murky to meaningful: the role of mission in institutional change. In *Colleges and Universities as Citizens.* R. Bringle, R. Games & E. Malloy (Eds.). Boston: Allyn & Bacon.

Hollinger, D. (1988). Two NYU's and the obligations of universities to the social order in the great depression. In T. Bender (Ed.). *The University and the City: From Medieval Origins to the Present* (pp. 249-266). Oxford: Oxford University Press.

hooks, B. (1994). *Teaching to Transgress.* New York: Routledge.

Innes, J. (1996). *Indicators for collective learning and action: Rethinking planning for complex systems.* Unpublished paper prepared for delivery at the University of Newcastle, Department of Town and Country Planning, 50th Anniversary Conference.

Jencks, C. & D. Riesman D. (1968). *The academic revolution.* New York: Doubleday.

Kavanaugh, J. (1989). Jesuit education and social justice in theory and practice. In R. E. Bonachea (Ed.) *Jesuit Higher Education* (pp. 172-173). Pittsburgh, PN: Duquesne University Press.

Kerr, C. (1991). T*he great transformation in higher education.* Cambridge, MA: Harvard University Press.

Kline, P., & Brabeck, M. (1999). Ethics and collaborative practice in public schools. In. R.W.C. Tourse and J.F. Mooney (Eds.) *Collaborative Practice* (pp. 285-298). Westport, CT: Praeger.

Kolvenbach, P. H. (2000). Creative fidelity in mission, Paper presented at Loyola, Spain, 2000.

Kolvenbach, P.H. (1989). Address to the Teachers at Kalksburg College. Vienna: April 1987.

Kolvenbach, P. H. (2000) The service of faith and the promotion of justice in American Jesuit higher education. Paper presented at *Commitment to Justice in Higher Education Conference*, Santa Clara University, October 6, 2000.

Lawton, R. (2000) *University president's inaugural address.* Los Angeles, CA: Loyola Marymount University, Oct. 5th.

Leahy, W. (1991). *Adapting to America.* Washington: Georgetown University Press.

Leahy, W. (1999). *The Critical Movement is Now.* Speech given at Boston College, November.

Leahy, W. (2000). Paper presented to the Boston Chambers of Commerce, Spring.

Lerner, R.M. (1999). University-Community collaborations: A view of the issues. *Applied Developmental Science,* 3(4), 194-197.

Lerner, R. (2000). Transforming universities to sustain outreach scholarship: A communiqué from the front. F. Sherman & W. Torbert (Eds). *Transforming Social Inquiry, Transforming Social Action* (pp. 37-56). Boston: Kluwer.

Lerner, R.M. & Simon, L.A. (1998). *University-Community collaborations for the twenty-first century.* N.Y.: Garland.

Letson, D. & Higgins, M. (1995). *The Jesuit mystique.* Chicago: Loyola Press.

Levine, D. (1986). *The American college and the culture of aspiration 1915-1940.* Ithaca, NY: Cornell University Press.

Long, E. L. (1992). *Higher education as a moral enterprise.* Washington, DC: Georgetown University Press.

Lyton, E.A. (1996). Reversing the telescope: viewing individual activities within a collective context. *Metropolitan Universities,* Winter, 41-55.

Marsden, G. (1994). *The soul of the American University.* Oxford: Oxford University Press.

Martin-Baro, I. (1991). Developing a critical consciousness through the University curriculum. In J. Hassett & H. Lacey (Eds.), *Towards A Society that serves its people: The intellectual contribution of El Salvador's murdered Jesuits* (pp. 236-237). Washington: Georgetown University Press.

Mooney, J., Kline, P. & Davoren, J. (1999). Collaborative interventions: Promoting psychological competence and academic achievement. In J. Mooney and R. Tourse (Eds.) *Interprofessional collaboration: school and human service partnership* (pp. 105-136). Westport, CN: Greenwood.

Mumford, L. (1938). *The culture of cities.* New York: Harcourt, Brace.

O'Malley, J. (1989). The Jesuit Educational Enterprise in Historical Perspective. In R.E. Bonachea (Ed.) *Jesuit Higher Education.* (pp. 1-32) Pittsburgh, PN: Duquesne University Press.

Schon, D. (1983). *The reflective practitioner.* New York: Basic Books.

Schon, D. (1995). Knowing-in-action: The new scholarship requires a new epistemology. *Change* Nov./Dec., 27-34.

Shils, E. (1995). The university, the city, and the world: Chicago and the University of Chicago. In T. Bender (Ed.) *The University and the city.* (pp. 210-230). Oxford, England: Oxford University Press.

Sholander, T. (1994). Am I my brother's keeper? *The Bridge Newsletter*, 4-6.

Skivington, K.D (1998). Positioning a university outreach center: strategies for support and continuation. *Metropolitan Universities*, Spring, 37-50.

Szantan, P. (1981). *Not well advised.* NY: Russell Sage Foundation.

Tourse, R.W.C. & Mooney, J.F. (Eds.). (1999*). Collaborative Practice: School and Human Service Partnerships.* Westport, CT: Praeger.

Tremmel, R. (1993). Zen and the art of reflective practice in teacher education. *Harvard Educational Review, 63* (4) 437-438.

Veysey, L.(1965). *The emergence of the American university.* Chicago: University of Chicago Press.

Walsh, M., Brabeck, M.M., Howard, K.A., Sherman, F.T., Montes, C. & Garvin, T.J. (2000). The Boston College-Allston/Brighton partnership:Description and challenges. *Peabody Journal of Education, 75* (3), 6-32.

Walsh, M. & Buckley, M. (1994). Children's experience of homelessness: Implications for school counselors. *Elementary School Guidance and Counseling, 29* (1), 4-15.

Waterman, A. (1997). An overview of service-learning and the role of research and evaluation in service-learning Programs. In A. Waterman (Ed.) *Service-learning: Applications from the research.* (pp. 1-11). Mahwah, NJ: Lawrence Erlbaum Associates, Publishers.

West, C. (1993) *Keeping faith.* New York: Routledge.

Westmeyer, P. (1997). *An analytical history of American higher education.* Springfield, IL: Charles C. Thomas Pub. Co.

Zlotkowski, E. (Ed.). (1998). *Successful service-learning programs. New models of excellence in higher education.* Bolton, MA: Anker Publishing Company.

CHAPTER 7

HISTORICAL BASE, EVOLUTION AND FUTURE DIRECTIONS OF CIVIC ENGAGEMENT AND SERVICE LEARNING AT CORNELL UNIVERSITY

Hunter R. Rawlings, III
Francille M. Firebaugh
Susan H. Murphy
Scott Peters[1]
Cornell University

INTRODUCTION

Cornell University occupies a unique niche in the landscape of American higher education. Founded as the land grant university for the State of New York, it has from its beginning also been a private university. Its founder, Ezra Cornell, was a New York State assemblyman at the time of the passage of the Morrill Land Grant Act. Not formally educated, he had secured, lost and earned again a fortune as an entrepreneur. By the mid 1860's, he had amassed considerable wealth from exploitation of a device he invented for the purpose of stringing the telegraph wires for Samuel Morse.

Ezra Cornell envisioned an institution of higher education that would "combine practical with liberal education, which shall fit the youth of our country for the professions, the farm, the mines, the manufactories, for the investigation of science and for mastering all the practical questions of life with success and honor" (Bishop, 1962, p. 88). His goal was to "qualif(y) (students) to serve their fellow men better, prepar(e) them to serve society better, train them to be more useful in their relations to the state" (Ibid.). Cornell combined that vision with the dreams of Andrew Dickson White, a fellow New York State assemblyman, much younger and better educated than he. White promoted classical education, but he too wished to contemporize it through a structure that would allow students considerable choice in designing their own curricula of study. In White's

---

[1] The authors greatly benefited from the substantive suggestions of Cornell City and Regional Planning Professors John Forester, Kenneth Reardon, and Stuart Stein in the formative stage of the chapter.

words, "students would come, not to be made, but to make themselves" (Account of the Inauguration Proceedings, 1869).

Cornell and White lobbied successfully to secure the Land Grant Act funds for New York State and combined them with Cornell's gift of his farm and $500,000 to create, in 1865, Cornell University. Thus, from its inception, Cornell has had a commitment to the combination of the "practical with the liberal education" (Ibid.). The University continues its interest in and commitment to engage students from all walks of life in the academic enterprise, grounded in both the classical liberal tradition and in the practical applications of the disciplines to people and to societal issues. Today, Cornell is known as a private university with a public mission.

In widely varied and sometimes disparate paths, Cornell's public mission has evolved to include students, faculty, and staff, and the broader community. Steadily broadening its civic mission and cultivating a public service ethos in its students (Boyte & Kari, 2000), Cornell has developed a statewide system of cooperative extension, created programs to promote student leadership and offered community-oriented courses that include service learning opportunities. Cornell seeks to attain a sustainable community-university partnership for public service and scholarship that is conducive to cooperative problem solving, community building and regional development. Community-based service learning is a major contribution toward the larger goal.

The University's engagement with the community emanates from the formative years, with the early leadership of Professor of Agriculture, Issac P. Roberts, and the arrival of Liberty Hyde Bailey in 1888 (Colman, 1963). A professor of practical and experimental horticulture, Bailey believed that the College of Agriculture should reach the farmer through bulletins, lectures, demonstrations and even farm visits, since farmers could rarely come to the campus (Dorf, 1956). Bailey's work defined the direction of the developing Extension movement and set in place important principles used today in service learning. In 1903, he became the second dean of the College of Agriculture at Cornell and oversaw, during the ensuing decade, a dramatic transformation and expansion of the civic mission and purpose of the College. At the dedication of new college buildings in 1907, Bailey declared that agricultural colleges have "now taken on a much larger scope and must deal also with the farm as a part of the community and consider farming interests with reference to the welfare and the weal of the commonwealth" (Bailey, 1907, p. 39).

Curricular offerings expanded during Bailey's tenure and more opportunities arose to connect the college with the farming community. Bailey believed that the home deserved as much attention from extension workers as the farm. "The whole range of household subjects must be taught, and if so, there must be specialization in food, sanitation, nursing, house building, house furnishing and similar subjects" (Dorf, 1956, p. 137). From that belief developed a curricular concept directed at young women which would come to be known as home economics. Early in the 20th century, Martha Van Rensselaer's bold work advanced the concept to spawn in turn a department and a separate college which became today's College of Human Ecology (Rose, Stocks & Whittier, 1969).

Today through the Colleges of Human Ecology and Agriculture and Life Sciences, the Cornell Cooperative Extension mobilizes research and scholarly expertise for the benefit of New York State while bringing the issues and concerns of the people of New York State to the campus and designing research in response to them. Apart from its research bases, the extension system builds on experiences of practitioners and participants to enable people and communities to improve their situations. The concept of public scholarship, where scholars collaborate with the public to identify, debate and act on public issues, is deepened and refined through the continuing interaction that the extension system nurtures.

BACKGROUND OF CORNELL TRADITION PROGRAM

Ezra Cornell had the bold and enduring idea of combining work and study. In the first prospectus offered by the university in 1868, Cornell and White indicated that students unable to pay their way could obtain manual work to support their academic endeavors. Throughout its history, Cornell University has provided work opportunities for its students, attaining for years one of the largest federal work-study allocations. Long before the federal requirement, Cornell allocated part of the work study money for students who wished to work in community service rather than on campus. The service aspect of student work gave rise in the 1980's to the student fellowship program known as the Cornell Tradition.

At its creation, several goals were set for the Cornell Tradition. One was to encourage students to assume greater responsibility for educational costs through participation in work. A second was to reduce the accumulated indebtedness upon graduation. With a lower debt load, graduates could chose to pursue graduate study or relatively lower-paid community and public service careers (Murphy & Mulugetta, 1994).

Finally, Cornell Tradition fellows have been encouraged to develop a philosophy of "giving back" to their alma mater through future service or financial contributions. Tradition program fellows are cultivated as future active and engaged citizens, with expectations and opportunities for service. Since the inception of the Tradition program, research has been conducted comparing the Tradition fellows with their peers, and tracking their commitments during the years since graduation. Consistently, Tradition fellows have been more involved in their communities and more generous to their alma mater than their peers (Mulugetta, Nash & Murphy, 1999).

DEVELOPMENT OF THE PUBLIC SERVICE CENTER

As the Tradition program grew over the years, so too did interest in formalizing the university's support of the service mission for students. For decades, students have been encouraged to volunteer and to use work/study time in the community through the outreach efforts of Cornell United Religious Work known as CIVITAS. Each year, scores if not hundreds of students were referred to or matched with volunteer opportunities in the Ithaca Community. Moreover, many fraternities and sororities undertook philanthropic projects, while some living units (especially theme-based residence halls) interacted with community organizations. Such disparate activates, however, lacked an integrated effort to link community experiences with the academic, research or extension missions of the university.

This gap was addressed in 1991 with the creation of the Public Service Center at Cornell. Designed to bring together several existing programs on campus and to create a locus of effort, especially for students, the Center was founded to "champion the conviction that the Cornell University experience confirms service as essential to active citizenship." Through planned and responsive service initiatives, the Center enhances learning and strengthens the community in several ways. The Center broadens the academic experience by:

- engaging students in active citizenship through the integration of academic learning with practical applications in community settings;
- promoting a safe and supportive environment for students to explore ideas and seek solutions to social problems;
- supporting a faculty network to share experiences and develop service learning initiatives.

The Center promotes student development through:

- providing community-based experiences that develop knowledge, skills, career exploration and civic engagement;
- creating opportunities for personal growth and value clarification while acquiring and applying leadership skills in a public service context;
- supporting and encouraging student-initiated efforts for social change.

The Public Service Center fosters a sense of community by:

- bringing together students from different cultures, genders, studies and interests to work together for positive social change;

- facilitating collaboration among faculty, students, staff and the community by encouraging the sharing and confronting of ideas in a public service context;
- supporting and integrating Cornell alumni in their ongoing commitment to service.

The Center furthers an ethos of social responsibility by:

- recognizing community input as an integral component of the service learning universe;
- directing available resources to enhance the capacity of communities for positive social change;
- structuring relationships inside and outside the university to promote principles of mutuality and reciprocity.

Student programs and leadership programs are organized along a continuum of service that meets students at their level of service commitment: "Into the Streets," a one-day exploratory service event; a Leadership Fellows program that encourages social responsibility through the development of leadership skills (as outlined in the Astin model of leadership for social change); and the Community Fund Board which provides funding for community based student-led projects. Undergirding this work is a fundamental commitment to a broad application of the principles of service learning.

EVOLUTION OF SERVICE LEARNING AT CORNELL

The current model of service learning at Cornell builds on the institutional history and mission of service as well as a long tradition of experiential education at the university. From at least the mid-1930s, students carried out projects and conducted research for academic credit within the surrounding community. Faculty closely monitored the projects and research. For example, Ella Cushman and her students designed kitchens for individual families in the Ithaca area to meet special family needs. Cushman reported her own follow up and evaluation after the actual renovation or construction (Cushman, 1952).

In 1969, a group of Cornell faculty from across the university designed the Human Affairs Program (HAP), with undergraduate and graduate students joining faculty in HAP-approved programs. Initial support by the University president was supplemented by external funding and later by cooperating colleges. The purposes of HAP included linking "the human resources of the university with the concerns of community groups and organizations, as they seek to solve their human problems and improve the conditions of their lives" (Whyte, 1971). Poor and disadvantaged members of the community received special attention.

While the program remained active for several years, challenges developing as early as 1971 contributed to its eventual demise: difficulties of collaboration with community agencies and individuals; competing time demands on students; difficulties in evaluating student work; and uncertain appropriateness of the role of the university in particular community organizations and movements. A governing document notes that "... no HAP project takes, or should take, a direct part in partisan politics" (White, 1971, p. 36). By 1975 an "implicit adversary position" assumed by some of the HAP participants was cited as the major reason for its discontinuance (Barlow, 1975).

The College of Human Ecology was among the cooperating colleges actively participating in HAP. Parallel with HAP, following from a 1971 study, the College opened a Field Study Office in 1972. The study delineated levels of field experience, all involving academic credit: directed observation, participation, and field study usually involving living off-campus near the site (Rivers, 1971). The director of the Field Study Office (Knitzer, 1972) offered a five year plan for "Human Ecology in the Field." The plan included preparation for the cognitive demands of field study, the on-site demands of field study, an enriched field process, and post-field-related needs of students. Early on, the location of the office outside departmental aegis fostered tensions between the field study program and departmental faculty on such issues as support for departmental field programs and concerns that the field study programs were "not substantive" (Annual Report, 1973-74).

In 1975-76, a faculty committee and the field study staff agreed on the need to develop closer working relationships between the Field Study Office and departmental faculty. The program enjoyed close ties with business and it was thought that business and industry would provide much of the support for the Field Study program (Evans, 1977), an expectation that was only partially met.

By the end of the fifth year of the Field Study Office, various concerns had developed: a) separation of field study staff from curriculum development and from face-to-face student advising; b) deteriorating departmental collegiality; c) the question of sustainability of funding through the Dean's discretionary budget; d) perceived competition between Field Study Office and departments; and e) the administrative costs of maintaining a separate unit.

During the expansive decade of 1978-1988, a number of noteworthy pioneers in service learning were involved in the Human Ecology program at Cornell (Stanton, Giles & Cruz, 1999). Timothy K. Stanton, Michelle Whitham, Dwight E. Giles, Jr., and Kenneth Reardon led the interdisciplinary experiential learning program for undergraduates interested in organizational development, community problem-solving and social change. Participating students complemented their classroom-based education with one or more semesters of field-based learning through internship placements and community-based research projects offered by the five full-time lecturers in the Field Study program.

Kenneth Reardon, (personal communication, 2000) who taught the field study course in New York City, recalls the structured program as a highly effective, developmentally based model that began with a pre-field preparation course to introduce students to the basic principles and methods of experiential learning, ethnographic methods and urban ecology. Field Study students developed learning contracts and identified the learning goals, objectives and outcomes they hoped to achieve during their upcoming field-based learning semester. Students pursued their learning objectives by completing internships and/or community-based research projects in Ithaca, New York City or more remote sites across the U.S. Students could earn up to fifteen academic credits in recognition of the new knowledge and skills they had acquired.

The students documented a series of capstone projects in a portfolio and had the opportunity to participate in weekly reflective seminars that applied basic ethnographic research, organizational behavior, and urban ecology principles and methods to issues they were confronting at their placements.

In the mid-1980s, the increasing career focus of many of the Cornell students in the New York City component of the Field Study program resulted in considerable interest in investment banking on Wall Street. Accompanying the increased interest was a reluctance to reflect critically on the policies and activities of the firms where students were placed. Reardon reduced the number of days in corporate placements and required participation in community-based research in low-income areas of the city. The students balked at this involuntary community service-learning requirement, but the experience became a highly valued aspect of the field study as evidenced by the student evaluations of the course.

An international development emphasis was added to the program in the College of Human Ecology in the 1980s and the name of the unit changed to Field and International Study Program. A new faculty member developed a parallel set of pre-field preparation, field-based learning and post-placement reflection seminars for students engaging in experiential learning activities abroad.

The program as a whole was popular with students who even today readily identify the experience as being particularly meaningful to them. The program challenged students to develop a critical perspective on the causes of social inequality through a systematic integration of theory and action.

Beginning in the late 1980s, College support for the Field and International Study program declined as: 1) the College experienced a continuing succession of budget cuts from the state and, as they accumulated, decisions were made to distribute scarce resources to programs that were core to the mission of the college; 2) the lack of integration of the field study program within departments resulted in limited support when competition for funding increased; and 3) the labor-intensity of the program made costs disproportionately high in comparison with other social science-based programs in the College; 4) the attrition of field and international study faculty who held non-tenure track term appointments increased as they had opportunities (often tenure track appointments) in other universities.

Over time, the issue of evaluation of learning through field work continued to arise. The field and international study program was reduced in scope and size of faculty; eventually, only the component in New York City remained in the formal program. That program today, the Urban Semester, includes internships and placements in health care, financial, educational and social service organizations. Weekly seminars continue, staffed by a single faculty member who also oversees the internship placements. The program attracts 30-35 students per semester and has a strong multi-cultural focus.

INTRODUCTION OF FACULTY FELLOWS IN SERVICE PROGRAM

Across the Cornell campus, in 1990, special funds dedicated to Innovations in Undergraduate Education were used to launch a three-year pilot program involving faculty and undergraduate students in public service and service learning more particularly. The Faculty Fellows in Service program resulted and continues to encourage and facilitate vigorous service-learning efforts across the university. Stated program goals follow:

1. to strengthen Cornell's commitment to community service;
2. to broaden the university's involvement at the local, state, national and international levels;
3. to focus primarily on undergraduate students, and to involve them in community service activities;
4. to identify community service as an integral part of liberal arts and professional education; and
5. to encourage more faculty members to work with undergraduate students in community service activities.

Over the ten-year history of the program, more than 110 faculty from all of Cornell's seven undergraduate colleges have been involved in service-learning activities. Projects have ranged across many arenas, including work in public schools, development of a community science center and a community playground, aid to environmental groups, work with Harlem literacy, construction of a pedestrian bridge across a flood channel and far more. The program seeks to enrich students' disciplinary and interdisciplinary education, and to strengthen their values related to citizenship, community, and diversity, while advancing their career goals.

Interest in the local community as a partner with the university has grown with the increased participation in and recognition of the Faculty Fellows in Service program. Interest from the community is heightened as the local volunteer pool is strained and budgets are tight. The university's commitment is to expand hands-on service learning opportunities to more students and faculty and to collaborate with the community for the betterment of the welfare of the citizenry.

A Governance Committee composed of faculty from each of the undergraduate colleges administers a modest grant program to cover developmental project expenses of the Faculty Fellows in Service program. It further maintains a peer support network for faculty interested in developing service learning initiatives and sponsors an annual symposium to stimulate interest in and exchange of ideas about service learning (Bounous, 1997; O'Connor & Vargas-Mendez, 1999). The program combines academic integration with student leadership development; strengthened critical thinking skills and reflection on the meaning of the combined service and learning experiences; and attention to needs identified by the community (Bounous, 1997).

While a focus on undergraduate students has dominated Cornell's commitment to service learning, a number of graduate students have benefited from the leadership role of Cornell faculty in action research in conjunction with the local community (Greenwood & Levin, 1998). The Cornell Participatory Action Research Network (CPARN) (see http://www.parnet.org) brings together faculty, staff, undergraduate and graduate students who respect and advocate partnerships between the academy and society. Also, through the Graduate Student Outreach Project, graduate students conduct mini-courses in local schools based on their scholarly research and academic interests.

FUTURE DIRECTIONS IN SERVICE-LEARNING AT CORNELL

As a signatory of the Presidents' Fourth of July Declaration on the Civic Responsibility of Higher Education (Ehrlich & Hollander, 1999), Cornell is committed to reinvigorating its public purpose and civic mission and supporting a national movement devoted to strengthening higher education's role as a "vital agent and architect of a flourishing democracy." Service learning is an important part of pursuing a robust civic mission. Yet, as the university explores ways to deepen and intensify its civic engagement, the effort must be undertaken with the reality that not all parts of the institution can be or will be involved. The large size of the institution, the range of disciplines, the emphasis on discovery and research, and the scale of the local community define the limitations.

Nationally, Sullivan (2000) has argued that much of higher education suffers from a lack of clarity and coherence in civic identity and mission. While a large number of inspiring and effective examples of academic-community partnerships that include service learning have been developed over the past decade, often they are not well coordinated or connected within specific institutions.

Such a description could apply to Cornell today. The accomplishments of the past decade through the Cornell Tradition, the Faculty Fellows in Service, the Public Service Center, the Urban Semester and the Participatory Action Research efforts remain largely uncoordinated. Moreover, manifold initiatives at the university are known only to the individual faculty, office, or department involved. Defining the institutional mission in the context of a multi-college, research university paradigm remains a challenge. It is particularly so given the focus on the large scale basic sciences and rapidly evolving technology that is the dominant reality of a university like Cornell.

Historically, the ideals of liberal education, around which the university has structured undergraduate education, made preparing all students for the responsible exercise of citizenship a fundamental objective. Research university leaders face the difficulty of extending basic, theoretical scholarship into practical applications in society at large and in the public interest, with the faculty's preoccupation with specialized research and the students' technology driven professional aspirations. What level of priority should be given to service learning in the contemporary research university? How should faculty responsibilities for organizing, supervising, and assessing such experiences be distributed? For how many students should such applied approaches to learning be provided? Or required?

Faculty and administrators at Cornell are differentially concerned about a number of other related service-learning issues: How are the outcomes of service learning to be effectively assessed? What constitutes good supervision of student experiences? How critical is social change in service learning? How can the interest in service learning be increased in the biological, physical, and environmental sciences? How can we combine service learning ideals with transmitting conventional disciplinary knowledge? (Lounsbury & Routt, 2000). What should be the limits for academic credit for service learning programs in relation to total academic credits? Indeed, some faculty believe that the service aspect of learning should be a wholly voluntary enrichment without academic credit.

While recognizing these and other concerns, Cornell can nonetheless strengthen the importance of community engagement in academic programs. Building on experiences in service and experiential learning more broadly at Cornell, on recent evaluations of service learning, (Astin et al., 2000) (Gray et al., 2000) and on Cornell's commitment to foster a sense of civic responsibility among its graduates, the university proposes the following actions:

1. to integrate further "the cognitive with the affective domain, theory-with practice, and knowledge with context" in service learning (Duffy & Bringle, 1999, p. 4);
2. to examine the financial and administrative support available to faculty involved in service learning and define what is necessary to stimulate more participation;
3. to encourage the integration of service learning into appropriate academic majors (Astin et al., 2000), combining professional development with community service;
4. to engage the community in defining the needs toward which student and faculty energies are directed;
5. to increase the opportunities for student participation in research that is directed toward community issues and problems (Hinck & Brandell, 2000), including the design and analysis of action research in the community (Greenwood & Levin, 1998, Porpora, 1999) and opportunities to work in action research with Cornell Cooperative Extension staff;
6. to increase the participation of underrepresented racial minority students in service learning; and
7. to foster student's reflections on and analyses of community service, through use of personal journals, presentations involving community partners, and electronic means (see Bringle & Hatcher,1999).

Campus discussions are underway about the meaning and implications of an engaged university with an increased role of service learning as an important component. The University administration has demonstrated a commitment to civic engagement of students, faculty and staff through the appointment of a Director of Special Projects in the Offices of the President and Provost, with responsibilities for encouraging community outreach, partnerships and civic engagement. A review of the Public Service Center has strongly recommended increasing the role of tenured or tenure-track faculty in the leadership of the Center. Each of these actions is associated with the institutionalization of service learning in higher education (Bringle & Hatcher, 2000), and with Cornell's efforts to increasingly have "curricular-integrated" service learning (Pollack, 1997).

REFERENCES

Account of the proceedings at the inauguration October 7, 1868 (1869). Ithaca, NY: Cornell University Press.

Annual Report. (1973-74). Field Study Office, College of Human Ecology. Unpublished. Ithaca, NY: Cornell University.

Astin, A.W.,Vogelgesang, L. J., Ikeda, E. K. & Yee, J.A. (2000). *How service learning affects students*, (Executive Summary). Los Angeles: Higher Education Research Institute, University of California.

Bailey, L.H. (1907). The outlook for the college of agriculture. In *Addresses at the dedication of the buildings of the New York State College of Agriculture*. Ithaca, NY: Cornell University.

Barlow, Jr., M. (1975). Letter to William A. Lyons, Chairman, NYSEG Corporation, Cornell University.

Bishop, M. (1962). *The history of Cornell*, Ithaca, NY: Cornell University Press.

Bounous, R. M. (Ed.) (1997). New directions: Teaching and research. *Working papers series on service learning 1*, Ithaca, NY: Cornell University.

Boyte, H. C. & Kari, N. N. (2000). Renewing the democratic spirit in American colleges and universities. In T. Ehrlich (Ed.). *Civic responsibility in higher education* (pp. 37-59). Phoenix, AZ: American Council on Education/The Oryx Press.

Bringle, R. G. & Hatcher, J.A. (1999). Reflection in service learning: Making meaning of experience. *Educational Horizons, 77* (4), 179-185.

Bringle, R. G. & Hatcher, J.A. (2000). Institutionalization of service learning in higher education. *The Journal of Higher Education, 71* (3), 273-290.

Colman, G.P. (1963). *Education and agriculture: A history of the New York State College of Agriculture at Cornell University*. Ithaca: Cornell University Press.

Cushman, E. M. (1952). Faculty Annual Report, College of Home Economics (unpublished). Ithaca, NY: Cornell University.

Dorf, P. (1956). *Liberty Hyde Bailey, an informal biography*. Ithaca, NY:Cornell University Press.

Duffy, D. K. & Bringle, R. G. (1998). Collaborating with the community: Psychology and service-learning. In R. G Bringle. & , D. K.Duffy (Vol. Eds.), E. Zlotkowski (Series Ed.) *With service in mind, concepts and models for service-learning in psychology* (pp.1-17). Washington, D.C.: American Association for Higher Education.

Ehrlich, T. & Hollander, E. (1999). Presidents' declaration on the civic responsibility of higher education. Providence RI: Campus Compact.

Evans, K. (1977). Annual Report of the Fifth year of the Field Study Office, College of Human Ecology. (Unpublished). Ithaca, NY: Cornell University.

Gray, M. J., Ondaatje, E. H., Fricker, Jr.,R. D. & Geschwind, S. A. (2000). Assessing service-learning. *Change 32* (2), 31-39.

Greenwood, D. & Levin, M. (1998). *Introduction to action research: Social research for social change*. Thousand Oaks, CA.: Sage Publications.

Hinck, S. S. & Brandell, M.E. (2000).The relationship between institutional support and campus acceptance of academic service learning. *American Behavioral Scientist, 43* (5), 868-881.

Knitzer, Jane E. (1972). Human ecology in the field, a five year plan. New York State College of Human Ecology. (Unpublished) Ithaca, NY: Cornell University.

Lounsbury, M. & Routt, D. (2000). Negotiating course boundaries: Service-learning as critical engagement. (Draft) Service-Learning Symposium, January 21, 2000. Ithaca, NY: Cornell University.

Mulugetta, Y., Nash, S. & Murphy, S.H. (1999). What makes a difference: Evaluating the Cornell tradition program. In , J. Pettit & L. Litten (Eds.) *A new era of alumni research: Improving institutional performance and better serving alumni* (pp. 61-80). San Francisco: Jossey-Bass Publishers.

Murphy, S. H. & Mulugetta, Y. (1994). Making a difference: The Cornell tradition. *College Board Review 173*, 22-28.

O'Connor, T. & Vargas-Mendez, L. (Eds.). (1999) Service learning partnerships: Developing and defining the roles of university and community. *Working paper series on service learning 2*, Ithaca, NY: Cornell University.

Pollack, S. S. (1997). Three decades of service-learning in higher education (1966-1996): The contested emergence of an organizational field. Unpublished doctoral dissertation. Palo Alto, CA: Stanford University.

Porpora, D. V. (1999). Action research: The highest stage of service-learning? In J. Ostrow, G. Hesser & S. Enos. (Vol. Eds.) E. Zlotkowski (Series Ed.). *Cultivating the sociological imagination: Concepts and models for service-learning in sociology* (pp. 121-133). Washington, D.C.: American Association for Higher Education.

Rivers, J. (1971). Report of the Ad Hoc Committee to Develop Guidelines for Field Experience, New York State College of Human Ecology. Unpublished. Ithaca, NY: Cornell University.

Rose, F., Stocks, E.H. & Whittier, M. W. (1969). *A growing college: Home economics at Cornell University*. Ithaca, NY: New York State College of Human Ecology.

Stanton, T. K., Giles, Jr., D.E. & Cruz, N.I. (1999). *Service-learning, a movement's pioneers reflect on its origins, practice, and future*. San Francisco: Jossey-Bass.

Sullivan, W. M. (2000). The university as citizen: Institutional identity and social responsibility. In T. Ehrlich (Ed.) *Civic responsibility in higher education* (pp. 19-36). Phoenix, AZ: American Council on Education/The Oryx Press.

Whyte, W. F. (1971). Report of the Educational Policy Board. Unpublished. Ithaca, NY: Cornell University.

CHAPTER 8

WEAVING A WEB OF SERVICE: ACADEMIC AND CIVIC LIFE AT FLORIDA STATE UNIVERSITY

Sandy D'Alemberte
Peter Easton
Florida State University

INTRODUCTION

The roots of service learning at Florida State University reach back several decades. They have begun to bear institutional fruit over the last ten years. The model that has evolved — a web of service opportunities surrounding students and faculty with multiple avenues for relating university and community — took shape over this period through a mixture of administrative intention and individual initiative. Despite real successes, the program is still undergoing decided growing pains that are rich in lessons learned.

THE SETTING

Florida State University is the second oldest public higher education facility in the State, a Research I institution that currently caters to over 34,000 students — undergraduate and graduate students — in 16 colleges and schools and over 200 different academic programs. FSU is located in the State capital of Tallahassee: a small city environment within the predominantly agricultural northern tier of Florida. It is a context in some ways more related culturally and historically to the Deep South than to the peninsular portions of the State, though the University draws students from every one of Florida's counties, as well as all 49 other States and 138 foreign countries. Tallahassee is in fact home to three institutions of higher education — including Florida Agricultural and Mechanical University and Tallahassee Community College in addition to FSU. Its economy is tightly interwoven with public service, higher education and state government — a pattern typical of many university towns and state capitals. Like most of them, the City of Tallahassee and the surrounding county have been attempting, with mixed success, to diversify their economic base and attract clean industry, but the labor market remains dominated by clerical, public service and academic positions.

FSU emerged from a series of predecessor institutions. It was initially established as the Seminary West of the Suwanee River or "West Florida Seminary" in 1851 to serve as a normal school for males and females, a school of husbandry, mechanical arts and agricultural science. The Seminary opened its doors in 1857 and became a College in the 1880s, gradually focusing its program exclusively on higher education. By 1901 it was a four-year institution chartered as the Florida State College. In 1905, however, the legislature reorganized higher education in Florida and segregated the sexes. The institution in Tallahassee was made "Florida Female College" to serve the aspiring young women of the State, then renamed the Florida State College for Women in 1909.

So it remained until the aftermath of World War II, when the flood of returning GIs seeking a diploma and anticipated increases in immigration from the North convinced State leaders that they needed to reinforce Florida's higher education infrastructure. In 1947 FCSW was therefore restored to co-ed status and endowed with graduate programs, becoming Florida State University.

ROOTS OF SERVICE LEARNING

The Florida State College for Women had a strong academic record and produced classes that played a key role in women's history in Florida. It was scarcely a center for service learning and active college-community interchange, however, simply because the culture of southern women's educational institutions at the time did not allow or provide for students leaving campus or mixing to a great extent in local life. As Parr (2000) points out, these influences colored for a while the character of the new University as well.

> *Because of its long history as a southern women's college, FSU entered the 1960s as a great bastion of in loco parentis. Social regulations at Florida State College for Women [had been] typical of regulations at other women's colleges in the North and South... Travel into town was limited to one visit per week and had to be carefully chaperoned... After the college became coeducational in 1947, ... the rules regarding female student life stayed on the books but the punishments were somewhat moderated... These social regulations did not apply to males, but the men unofficially adhered to and imposed on each other ... conservative dress codes. (pp. 60-61).*

A Decade of Ferment

Things began to change in earnest, however, in the 1960s. The impetus really came from Florida Agricultural and Mechanical University (FAMU), the black higher education institution in Tallahassee, now a co-equal branch of the State University System catering as well to a minority of white students interested in various of its specialties. FAMU students and local African-American clergy became very active in the civil rights movement and staged nonviolent sit-ins and a bus boycott that put Tallahassee on the map of civil rights history. Though FSU was not to admit its first black student until 1962 and experienced its own internal struggle over desegregation through the middle years of the decade, a vocal minority of students and faculty organized support for the civil rights effort and the issues that it raised transfixed the campus.

The spirit of involvement carried over to the latter part of the decade, when the causes of peace, students' rights, and environmental activism hit home. A series of vocal struggles between student groups, the University administration and the local constabulary gave FSU a new nickname: "the Berkeley of the South." Students fanned out to play an active role in lobbying, demonstrating and varieties of community action. A "free university" – the Center for Participant Education — was founded on campus by and for students to sponsor classes in social action themes and a variety of alternate lifestyle topics that lay well outside the official university curriculum. It exists to this day and has constituted one local prototype for relating service and civic action to learning.

Though attitudes were changing on campus, a poll conducted by Louis Harris and Associates in 1970 reveals a split between student and faculty perspectives that prefigured some of the problems a service learning movement would face:

> By a wide 67 to 20 percent margin, undergraduates favor ... student involvement [in the surrounding community]. Graduate students also support it by 58 to 30 percent. Administrators take the same position by 49 to 43 percent. The faculty and the alumni, however, ...prefer that FSU courses ...emphasize learning, not social action – the faculty by 43 to 36 percent and the alumni by 51 to 48 percent. Among full professors the margin is a substantial 53 to 23 percent for learning over community involvement. (p. 13)

This faculty sentiment is likely a reflection of reactions to perceived excesses in radical activism on campus and concern to preserve an academic climate and image. As a relative newcomer on the scholarly block from a Sunbelt state, the University community has typically been concerned to establish its scholarly bona fides and reputation as a major research institution. Where a Berkeley or Harvard can arguably afford sieges of student — and faculty — activism with minimal threat to individual and collective academic reputations, a new university with high scholarly ambitions is understandably a bit more sensitive.

Converging Currents

Whatever, in any case, the divergence in reactions to events in those two decades, Florida State emerged a very different place in 1980 than it had been in the mid-1950s: larger, more diverse and more open to a variety of means for civic involvement. four currents converged in the following years to give birth to the service learning movement on campus: individual creativity, student organization, departmental initiative and growing administrative support. Examples of each will illustrate the flavor and dynamics of the FSU movement in its early years.

Individual creativity

Beginning in the late 1980s, a handful of students became actively involved in health delivery and social service work in Gadsden County, a rural area adjacent to Tallahassee with a majority African-American population and a growing contingent of Hispanic farmworkers. One of these pioneers, an Hispanic pre-med student, developed volunteer work in rural health clinics – and later returned, as a doctor, to lead whole cohorts of pre-med and nursing students in a broader extension of the effort. A trio of others began English language courses for farmworkers. And an Education graduate student recently returned from overseas voluntary service helped develop weekend enrichment programs for children in the public housing neighborhoods of the county seat. Efforts like these coalesced by the early 1990s into a joint undertaking for student volunteering in Gadsden County, dubbed "Project Amistades" (Spanish for "friendship"). It received some logistic and funding support from the University Office for Community Partnerships and progressively transformed itself into a key element of CCES programming.

There was notable creativity on the faculty side too, well before service learning became a recognized and campus-wide program. Throughout the 1980s, ways of involving students in service applications of knowledge were devised by individual professors in fields from Anthropology and Special Education to Statistics (where the pioneer faculty member decided his mission was "to transform statistics from a stumbling block into a stepping stone" toward greater community involvement). By the latter years of the decade, a campus minister had started actively recruiting faculty to offer students in some of their classes an option between traditional papers and reflective service in satisfaction of academic requirements – and allies from sociology and public administration signed on.

Student Organization

Such efforts began concurrently to take institutional form. In 1987, students in the FSU Law School undertook a movement to make "pro bono" work mandatory for all law degree candidates. They succeeded in persuading Law School Student Government to support them, despite some reticence from faculty who didn't necessarily want to be held to the same standard. The mechanism adopted was that students could affiliate with a local attorney, since all members of the Tallahassee Bar Association were required to engage in pro bono work, or come up with a proposal of their own. Some law students affiliated with Project Amistades to provide rural legal services, while others undertook work with human service organizations or helped in death penalty post-conviction cases.

Volunteer initiatives had spread far enough across campus by 1990 that the University student government decided to establish a program for matching volunteers with community agencies and programs interested in their services. In that same year, FSU students took the lead in lobbying the Florida Legislature to fund a "Florida Office of Campus Volunteerism".

Departmental Initiatives

The Department of Urban and Regional Planning in the University's College of Social Sciences adopted in 1987 a "studio" formula for part of its graduate own program. A "planner in residence" — i.e., a practicing professional with live experience in community development processes – was engaged as adjunct faculty for a three- to five-year period with the assignment of generating and coordinating projects by which students could carry out community service and gain experience in local planning problems. Early work focused on efforts to help Florida communities develop comprehensive plans, as mandated by the State; but the undertaking gradually took on more of a social service and community development tenor. The effort led to a lasting involvement with the redevelopment needs of a low-income neighborhood adjacent to the University.

In addition, Departments in many of the University's professional schools maintained a variety of linkages with community settings where interns or apprentice students might apply their skills; and these relationships often became incubators for wider service involvement. Thus, for example, the College of Education regularly sent its students into area schools for practice teaching and instructional support, creating "bridges" that proved critical when campus-wide initiatives to assist low-income neighborhoods developed in subsequent years.

Administrative Support

To underwrite trends like these, the University administration joined Campus Compact in 1987 and set in motion a series of exploratory efforts to develop and recognize linkages between academic life and community service. The following year, the Associate Vice-President for Student Affairs spearheaded establishment of a residential unit focused on service activities and creation of a "Humanitarian Award" to recognize exemplary public service by undergraduates.

By the early 1990s, a sufficient mass of activity was underway to motivate thinking about a University umbrella structure that could serve to coordinate and support them. In 1991 the Division of Student Affairs set up a Campus-Community Partnership Office to begin performing these functions. The following academic year, then-President Dale Lick chaired the Florida Campus Compact and appointed a Task Force on Community

Service and Service Learning to study options for enhancing these activities, and it came up with 29 recommendations, divided into three categories: those designed to encourage faculty involvement; those targeted at increasing student participation; and those focusing on means for institutionalizing community service and service learning at FSU. Prime among the latter was the development of "a centralized ... [support] structure jointly administered by Academic Affairs and Student Affairs."

THE DEVELOPMENT OF A CAMPUS-WIDE PROGRAM

Currents like these interwove over the late 1980s and early 1990s to create a climate for implementation of at least a good number of the Commission's recommendations. In addition, the Dean of the Florida State Law School who had supported the "pro bono" initiatives among law students assumed the duties of University President in 1994 and turned increased focus on new avenues for town-gown relations and the civic involvement of the institution. By Fall of that year, the most important of the Commission's institutional recommendations had been achieved: the creation of a Center for Civic Education and Service (CCES) with responsibility for coordinating support for the whole set of service learning and social involvement programs that had begun to take shape around the campus.

In the seven years since its creation, CCES has become the hub of a varied web of civic education and service. Brief sketches of the principal ones will convey an idea of the environment for service learning that has taken form.

Service Learning And ServScript

CCES serves as a support and fulcrum point for service learning courses and community service throughout the University, though these remain quite decentralized. The Center develops affiliations with service agencies throughout the Tallahassee region and has a databank of placements and contacts. The University adopted in Fall 1995 a system of "ServScript" to certify students' service involvements and officially register them on their transcripts. ServScript has become a desirable form of reference and accreditation in its own right. Students must work at least 20 certified hours in a semester to quality. Guidelines disseminated regarding ServScript are reproduced in Figure 1 hereafter.

ServScript only represents a portion of student investment in service, since many take part without necessarily signing up for the program; but hours logged and numbers of participants have nonetheless increased steadily over the last five years, as indicated in Table 1.

At the same time, the Center for Civic Education and Service provides support to faculty throughout the University who are interested in launching or upgrading service learning offerings in their own Departments, and — within limitations of its personnel — keeps approximate tabs on courses of this type offered. A census carried out in 1995 revealed over 200 offerings described by their instructors as service learning courses, ranging from a Seminar in Small Business Assistance and Analysis in the College of Business to a Music Therapy class in the School of Music, a Food and Beverage Management course in Hospitality Administration and Aquatic Pollution Biology in the College of Arts and Sciences. There is, though, no standard set of requirements for qualifying a course as a

GUIDELINES FOR ServScript REGISTRATION

You must perform a minimum of 20 hours of service per term to qualify for ServScript.
All forms must contain an agency supervisor's signature for each service activity and your signature. Service hours from a previous term will not be accepted. All forms must be turned in to the Center for Civic Education and Service no later than the Wednesday before final exam week of the current term.

Service Activities to be Considered for ServScript include:
- Service at a not-for-profit agency (e.g. Boys and Girls Clubs).
- Service at a for-profit organization whose mission involves meeting social service needs of the community (e.g. nursing homes and hospitals).
- Church sponsored service where the goal is meeting secular needs (e.g. church soup kitchen).
- Government sponsored service at the federal, state and local level (e.g. county school program)
- Independent service projects in areas where human needs exist (special proof required).
- The coordination of fundraising activities with direct interaction with a not-for-profit beneficiary.
- Work in non-partisan political organizations and campaigns.

Service Activities NOT to be Considered for ServScript:
- Participation in fundraising activities (e.g. car washes, walk-a-thons and benefits).
- Work at any organization where you obtain a wage or stipend (exemption: scholarships).

Figure 1: Florida State University ServScript Guidelines

Academic Year	Participation (numbers of student-semesters)[*]	Total number of semester service hours	Average number of semester hours per student
1995-1996	313	22,697	72.5
1996-1997	978	45,128	46.1
1997-1998	1,224	60,499	49.4
1998-1999	1,562	68,137	43.6
1999-2000	2,114	113,120	53.5
TOTAL	6,191	315,772	51.0

Table 1: Data on ServScript participation, 1995-2000

"service learning" offering nor any system for tracking enrollments and activities. In addition, a considerable number of students engage in service

---

[*] Note that yearly figures represent totals of students participating each semester. Individual participants may therefore be counted more than once, but the data do accurately represent the "volume" of student participation.

as what are termed "co-curricular" participants — that is, people who call in to CCES or come by on their own to find a service assignment, without necessarily being involved in any related coursework.The Center handles, in fact, a considerable amount of daily "traffic" of this sort and facilitates placements for many students who have learned of the opportunities in student publications, through friends or on the CCES website (http://www.fsu.edu/~service). In 1997, the Adult Education graduate program in the College of Education developed an undergraduate course – entitled "Learning in the Community" — to offer co-curricular students the opportunity to get academic credit for their volunteer work while engaging with others similarly involved in reflection of what could be learned from the experience and how lessons might be applied to the rest of their University experience; but the bulk of co-curricular participants do not take part in any structured learning activities related to their service.

Though there are as yet limited means for tracking the size, composition or "longevity" of the groups engaged in these different types of service (and those described below), best estimates indicate that somewhere between 3000 and 5000 students presently participate each semester.

Service/Outreach Projects

Individual student volunteers and service learning participants may only be able to engage in these activities irregularly or for semester-long periods of time, but CCES knows full well — as any organization involved in facilitating volunteer placement learns — that the programmatic affiliations with community agencies that make successful placement possible must be nurtured over a much longer period of time and carried out more consistently. A framework is then created into which student participants can fit.

In this spirit, the Center maintains a series of ongoing collaborations and projects with community service organizations who offer regular volunteer opportunities to students. These include at the present time:

- *The Boys' and Girls' Club of the Big Bend, Incorporated*: Students have for several years worked here as volunteers tutoring, mentoring, and coordinating arts and crafts and sports activities with children and young people from low income neighborhoods of the city.
- *Gadsden County ESL*: Gadsden County is a predominantly rural area northwest of Tallahassee, where the migrant (and largely Hispanic) population involved in farm labor has increased rapidly in recent years. Students interested in these opportunities are trained in English as a Second Language programming and techniques and assist ESL teachers with one-on-one or small group instruction. Other students work with the children of the ESL adult students providing educational and recreational support.

- *The Johnson-Brinson Project*: This activity is sponsored and organized in conjunction with the Johnson-Brinson Community Center
in Madison County, another largely rural area to the northeast on
the Georgia border. Student volunteers work primarily with middle
school students (though actual ages range from 5-18 years old),
serving as mentors and companions and sharing special skills special skills they may have in music, art, computers and sports. The
objective is to reduce school dropout among the participating
young people, increase academic performance and build self-
esteem.

- *Project Friendship*: Another undertaking in Gadsden County, coordinated by its school board and dedicated to fostering a positive
living and learning climate by the provision of tutoring, mentoring
and recreational support for at-risk elementary and middle school
students.

- *America Reads*: An FSU affiliate of the national organization
trains and supports students in providing assistance in elementary
and middle schools to students reading below grade level.

- *FSU Mentoring Initiative*: A program initiated in response to an
appeal but Florida's governor to all State workers involves faculty
and (particularly) staff of the University in personally mentoring
K-12 students in local schools.

Student Service Organizations

The Center also serves as headquarters for several service-oriented student organizations that develop related programming on their own, often
through affiliation with national networks. These include at present:

- *The Alternative Break Corps*: ABC is a local affiliate of the nation-
ally-recognized organization "Break Away" (http://www. alterna-
tivebreaks.com) now, in fact, hosted by Florida State University —
and, like the larger organization, is dedicated to offering students
opportunities to engage in challenging service projects during their
Spring and Summer breaks from the University in locations around
the world.

- *Service Corps* : The FSU Service Corps is an association created by
students themselves to promote volunteering and service learning
across the campus and to provide input to University administration on related programs and practices. It organizes a Fall and a
Spring Volunteer Fair every year, sponsors a week of Hunger
Awareness and carries out a number of other campus events and forums in pursuit of its goals.

- *International Medical Outreach*: This organization of pre-med students sponsors projects devoted to bringing medical care to areas of
the world that have been deprived of it. Nine participants visited

Haiti in 1999, for example, serving some villages who had not seen a doctor or nurse in 20 years.

- *FSU Chapter of Habitat for Humanity*: The Chapter organizes students to participate in improving substandard housing in Tallahassee and takes part each year in a collaborative "build" with parallel organizations from five or six other campuses in the region.

Statewide Initiatives

At the same time, the Center for Civic Education and Service is the site of a series of programs devoted to developing different aspects of volunteerism throughout the state of Florida. Their activities further expand the outreach of FSU's web of service beyond campus boundaries. They include:

- The *Florida Office of Collegiate Volunteerism*: Founded by FSU students and those of other State universities in 1990, FOCV links service learning coordinators on higher education campuses around the state, provides networking and resource services to those involved in the field, and offers workshops and study tours to develop capacity in volunteer management and retention.
- *Florida Campus Compact*: The offices of the Florida branch of nationwide Campus Compact, an affiliation of administrations of higher education institutions supportive of service learning and devoted to creating community partnerships and policy coalitions to further it, is located in CCES.
- *Florida Learn and Serve K-12*: Learn & Serve awards grants to schools and school districts throughout Florida to engage K-12 students in service learning, or service that is both a means and an application of learning. Funds for this project are derived from the Corporation for National Service as part of the National Service Initiative.
- *VISTA and Peace Corps*: Both of these national organizations maintain local recruiting offices in the Center. In addition, the University hosts a VISTA project with 18 volunteers who work on promoting service learning around the entire state of Florida.

Parallel Ventures

Two related activities of note are headquartered elsewhere in the University but carried out in close alliance with CCES. The first is Florida State's campuswide K-12 initiative — a concentrated effort to enlist faculty and students from all the different Colleges and Schools of the institution in providing volunteer support and technical services to schools in the lower income neighborhoods on the southern side of Tallahassee and in needy areas throughout surrounding counties.

The program is coordinated out of the Office of the Provost by the former principal of a southside middle school on sabbatical leave to handle these responsibilities, and it enlists faculty and students from Florida Agricultural and Mechanical University as well. It has had an appreciable impact, already partly reflected in improved test score results and has developed into a dense network of programs, described in more than twenty webpages (http://www.fsu.edu/~k12/leonprograms.html#stride class=). They vary from "Science Students Together Reaching Instructional Diversity and Excellence" (SSTRIDE), a program of premedical students devoted to raising levels and interests of students at risk in science, to the School of Music's "Strings in Schools" initiative and the Saturday-at-the-Sea Program of the FSU Marine Lab.

A second service-relevant initiative has been undertaken in the course of the last year in cooperation with the national Society for Values in Higher Education, which chose Florida State University as one of a handful of sites nationwide to test procedures for campus-wide inquiry into "academic and civic integrity." The inquiry is coordinated by a President's Task Force composed of faculty, staff and students from across the University and is housed in the FSU Foundation. The Task Force maintains close relations with the Center for Civic Education and Service and is examining the forms of the University's civic commitment — including its service learning performance — during its mandate.

Awards and Scholarships

Finally, the Center handles attribution of a number of University-wide awards and scholarships designed to recognize and motivate exemplary service in the student-body. These include the FSU Service Scholar Program, which awards scholarships each year to a dozen incoming freshman who have demonstrated exemplary patterns of service in their high school years; the President's Undergraduate Humanitarian of the Year Award that spotlights campus volunteers who exhibit tremendous commitment to a cause; and the Ben Rosenbloom Memorial Service Scholarship, awarded each year to an undergraduate student already at FSU and designed both to recognize students with an outstanding record of service and to foster their commitment to a lifetime of service.

AN INTERIM BALANCE SHEET:
RESULTS AND IMPACT OF AN EMERGING PROGRAM

Florida State University has thus created around the hub of the CCES – but not authoritatively controlled by it – an increasingly substantial "web" of service opportunities that manage both to provide students and faculty with avenues for community involvement and create new links with the community at different levels. Though the myriad of activities undertaken in recent years was in some sense spearheaded and promoted by the report of the President's Commission, it has not followed a "master plan" and is not tightly organized. Like any dynamic phenomenon that grows — with significant administrative support — on the periphery of the official business of an institution, the civic service and service learning movement at Florida State has genuine strengths and weaknesses, and many lessons of experience are embodied in them.

Strengths

A prime virtue of Florida State University's civic service and service learning program is its decentralization. Though the efforts are supported and facilitated in important ways by the Center for Civic Education and Service, they are no one's exclusive property and are not subject to doctrinal control. As a consequence, initiatives have sprung up in all sectors of the institution and from all stakeholder groups: students, faculty, administrators, parents and alumni.

Along with that decentralization goes a healthy dose of creativity. The fuel firing the growth of the movement is as much the variety and imaginative quality of the activities undertaken as any other single factor. Nursing candidates came up with a clinic for poorly served Hispanic farmworkers in rural north Florida, while students and faculty in the School of Visual Arts and Dance found support to bring in the New York dance troupe "Urban Bush Women" and engage their entire Department in offering live workshops to residents of local Tallahassee neighborhoods. By a policy of accretion and openness to innovation, the program has thus become quite comprehensive.

The movement has likewise benefited — up to a point, at least — from very strong administrative support. The establishment and maintenance of a full-time and well-housed facility like the Center for Civic Education and Service to anchor, backstop and "resource" service learning activities throughout the campus and beyond has been extremely instrumental in strengthening offerings and recruiting students. Central FSU administration has sponsored a number of events stressing the importance of the service vocation of the institution, including regular efforts to improve "town-gown" collaboration, convocations with noted scholars and spokespeople in the field, and a pattern of engaging the FSU delegation to all bowl games in a day of service in the host city.

Weaknesses

For all its virtue, the FSU model is distinctly stronger on community service and civic commitment than it is on service learning *per se*. In short, while a rich variety of options are in place, the University has not yet entirely faced up to the question of *how to integrate the academic and service dimensions of the phenomenon*. Though the original report from the President's Commission recommended that CCES be set up under the joint administration of Academic Affairs and Student Affairs, it is in fact attached only to the latter and service learning tends to be treated as a student affairs issue much more than an academic one.

The problem is particularly evident at the level of faculty, though it manifests itself in the student body as well. Teaching personnel at Florida State, like most of their colleagues in Universities across the nation, are subject to heightened competition for tenure and increased emphasis on research, grants and publications. Their official "assignment of responsibility" specifies three areas of duty — teaching, research and service. In practice, however, University academic authorities place heavy emphasis on research, whereas the State legislature is most concerned with volume teaching, given budgetary restrictions and the number of students in the pipeline statewide. The result is that service just does not count for much in the balance sheet that determines tenure and promotion. Lynton's (1995) agenda for developing "professional service" remains a goal to be achieved.

As for students, interest in service is on the rise, but so is pressure to complete courses of study as expeditiously as possible. University administration has in fact trumpeted a motto — "Don't Delay Your Dream: Take Fifteen" — to encourage undergraduates to enroll in fifteen hours of coursework per semester and conceivably complete their degree within three years. When this is added to concerns for employability, the natural consequence is that students feel less latitude to pursue service options as part of their learning experience than they otherwise might.

Overall the situation is one then of multiple options but few policies that give service learning full status in academe — and a general unwillingness to bite this particular bullet. The Center for Civic Education and Service, despite many achievements and valuable work, has not yet been able to accomplish its prime mission — linking academic affairs and community service. Proposals have been made for appointment to CCES of personnel with faculty status who could act as the "glue," but to date they remain proposals. The struggle to "institutionalize" service learning analyzed by Bringle and Hatcher (2000) is underway.

A second area of weakness, also symptomatic of under-institutionalization, is the lack of careful monitoring and evaluation. The movement at FSU faces a triple challenge in this realm:

1. There are few data on just what is happening in service activities, or just what can be considered true "service learning" – which makes it more difficult to certify the phenomenon.
2. We continue to lack convincing measures of performance and of the impact of service experience.
3. And there has consequently been little critical or university-wide analysis of the "yield" of programs or the policy implications and conditions for better integrating them into academic life, at least since the President's Commission. Assessments have tended to be inventories of the variety of involvements

rather than critical analyses of problems and measures of accomplishment.

In short, University service learning itself not yet a "learning organization" at Florida State University. There are, of course, real obstacles to overcome. The legislative and political climate on which a public institution like FSU depends to underwrite innovative policy has not been very favorable in recent years, and legislators — themselves under pressure in times of slim public budgets and increasing educational demand — seem principally interested in moving young people through the system. Increased accountability of academic departments and greater emphasis on faculty performance measures, while defensible in their own right, have undermined some of the motivation for the kind of commitment service learning requires, because service learning itself does not register as certifiable faculty performance. And an atmosphere of downsizing, mixed with the uncertainties of competition from distance learning and private sector education, make even the administration skittish about fulfilling promises or living up to rhetoric.

WHITHER?

The Florida State University experience offers some examples of the rich potential of service as an environment for higher education, but also illustrates the obstacles yet to be surmounted in a major university environment. In a number of respects, the institution has made major progress toward achieving the goals set in the Wingspread Declaration (Boyte & Hollander, 1999). In others, the heart of the issue remains to be jointed. Truly yoking service with *diplomaed* learning — the stock and trade of a higher education institution — and with its institutional derivatives like tenure and accreditation constitutes the underlying challenge. It is inevitably a bit more difficult for a relatively new university with ambitions of breaking into the elite of Research I institutions to accept the risks and costs than for a school enjoying a long history of high status. At the same time, the absence of constraining tradition also grants a degree of freedom, and the kinds of practical community involvement characteristic of a public institution in a growing state provide a rich environment. Will the University be as creative in meeting these challenges as it has been in getting to them? We have every confidence.

REFERENCES

Boyte, H., & Hollander, E. (1999). Wingspread Declaration on Renewing the Civic Mission of the American Research University. (Final report of the Wingspread Conference). Providence, RI: Brown University.

Bringle, R., & Hatcher, J. A. (2000). Institutionalization of service learning in higher education. *Journal of Higher Education.* Vol. 71 No. 3 (May-June), pp. 273-290.

Harris, L., & Associates (1970). *A study prepared for Florida State University.* Study No. 1959. Tallahassee, FL: Florida State University

Lynton, E., & Hirsch, D. (1995). Bridging two worlds: Professional service and service learning. *ERIC Document ED 3943777.* Rockville, MD: Educational Resources Information Center.

Parr, S. E. (2000). *The forgotten radicals: The New Left in the Deep South, Florida State University, 1960-1972.* Dissertation. Tallahassee, FL: Florida State University.

CHAPTER 9

SERVICE LEARNING AT FORDHAM UNIVERSITY

Joseph A. O'Hare, S.J.
Fordham University

The role of service learning in the formal academic programs of Fordham University remains modest, if growing. Community service, however, as an extracurricular activity of both undergraduate and graduate and professional students has been a distinctive emphasis at Fordham for the past 25 years, inspired by Fordham's Jesuit tradition of education and the University's location at two different campuses in New York City, Rose Hill, its original 85-acre campus in the Bronx, and Lincoln Center in Manhattan.

Public service has always been an important tradition at Fordham, as the large number of alumni and alumnae in such professions as law, education, social service, and church ministry demonstrate. In the mid-1970's, however, what the President of the United States had called, a few years earlier, the "crisis of American cities" challenged the University to take a more active role in its surrounding communities.

This was particularly true at Rose Hill, located in the Bronx, a part of New York City that had become by the mid-1970's a metaphor for urban decay. The Bronx was burning in a literal sense at that time as frustrated property owners turned to arson as a means of recouping their investment. The response of the University to this challenge of the 1970's planted the seeds of the interest in community service that became a defining theme of the Fordham undergraduate experience in the 1980's and 1990's. A word about this institutional response to urgent community needs will help set the context for the development of a tradition of service learning, both formal and informal, at Fordham.

Under the leadership of its President, the late Rev. James C. Finlay, S.J., the University established an office of Urban Affairs that worked with the Northwest Bronx Catholic Clergy Conference to develop a broader organization of community groups that became the Northwest Bronx Community and Clergy Coalition. Over the next 25 years, the Coalition helped reverse the tide of abandonment and arson and worked to secure the funding and the volunteer participation needed to rehabilitate buildings and restore embattled neighborhoods. Fordham students, both graduate and undergraduate, joined in this effort. Today, many of the present generation of Fordham undergraduates volunteer to work with the community organizations that were first born in the 1970's and now, in may instances, are led by Fordham alumni of that era.

While Fordham did not have the financial resources to fund in any substantial way important urban renewal initiatives, it did serve as a convenor of community groups and provide research assistance. These efforts were institutionalized by the establishment of the Bronx Urban Resource Center, which continues to develop important data to support the efforts of local activist groups, and the University Housing Program, which sought public and private funding for the restoration and creation of housing for lower- and middle-class families in the borough. University representatives continue to serve on the boards of these organizations, and opportunities for students to participate in the work of these organizations are included in the broad range of community service programs now available for student volunteers.

By 1985, Fordham students, some of them working in projects connected with the Office of Campus Ministry, were involved in a number of disparate community service initiatives, but there was no central University office to coordinate these efforts. In the belief that these individual efforts would expand if they were more widely publicized, the Community Service Program was officially inaugurated and its first Director appointed. The expectation that more students would volunteer for community service if more opportunities were brought to their attention has been confirmed by the experience of the past 15 years.

In its report for the 1998-1999 school year, the Director of Community Service Program could report that 876 volunteer opportunities had been filled by 659 student volunteers. These volunteers participated in a wide range of programs that included care for AIDS victims (delivering noon-time meals to home-bound patients) and the elderly (visiting senior citizens in a residence sponsored by the University and located at the edge of campus), various projects protecting the environment (like the Bainbridge Urban Garden where students worked with local residents to turn an abandoned lot into a neighborhood garden), supporting the work of local shelters and soup kitchens for the homeless, including a local shelter for homeless mothers and their children, tutoring and mentoring students at local public and parochial schools, and serving as surrogate family for young people associated with a mental health organization located in the South Bronx that serves a predominantly Hispanic population.

In addition to these year-long programs, Fordham's community service volunteers also participate in special projects during the year, including special food and toy drives at Thanksgiving and Christmas, working with local residents in removing graffiti from neighborhood buildings, sponsoring an Oxfam Hunger Banquet, where over 200 students, administrators and faculty participate in a meal designed to demonstrate the differences in the diets of people in the First and Third Worlds, and Urban Plunge, a program designed to introduce incoming freshmen to the experience of community service in the Bronx.

In the summer of 1999, Fordham's Community Service Program was asked to work with St. Rita's Immigrant and Refugee Center, located in a local Catholic parish, to develop a summer camp for Kosovar children who were refugees from the NATO bombing in Kosova. Student volunteers drew on University resources to provide instruction in English, athletic facilities for recreational sports, and supervised trips to Yankee Stadium, the Bronx Zoo and the Brooklyn Aquarium. The responses of the campers illustrate how the experience was a learning experience for all involved, the Kosovar youngsters and their Fordham student mentors.

"In Fordham University, I found friends and a teacher who helped me to cure my wounded heart for my country and my grandfather whose fate I don't know," wrote one young girl. The students enjoyed the campus and liked America, but one wrote of a deeper loneliness, "I feel very lonely even if I am with my friends. I laugh when something's funny, but I don't laugh from deep in my soul because deep in there I feel very, very sad." But another was more optimistic than international events might warrant, "Goodbye to all of you and I wish you a very happy life here in America. I have to go back to Kosovar to spend a happy life there, too, in a free Kosova, in my country."

The close association with refugees from the war in the Balkans was an unusual experience for student volunteers in Fordham's Community Service Program, but the recognition that their service is a learning experience has been a constant refrain of generations of student volunteers. Students from other parts of the country and from the suburbs of the Northeast come to Fordham's Rose Hill campus conditioned by stereotypes of the Bronx made popular by movies like *Bonfire of the Vanities* and earlier, *Ford Apache*. It is understandable that they first venture out into the neighboring communities with some apprehension.

Invariably, these initial misgivings are overcome and stereotypes are put to flight when a typical suburban college student gets a lesson in authentic multiculturalism by tutoring a Hispanic high school freshman from the South Bronx. These and other insights emerge as students are encouraged to reflect on their community service experience as part of the Urban Reflections Forum, which meets monthly so that students, who wish to do so, can exchange views on the implications of their service projects. More formal possibilities for reflection on experience, a process that Jesuit spirituality calls discernment, are provided by faculty members who have made service learning a component of their course.

During the 1999–2000 school year the following courses provided an opportunity for students to incorporate volunteer service with their academic course work, so that they could discuss in an academic environment their community service experiences and critically reflect on that experience: Dr. Mark Niason's course in Action Research in the Urban Community, Dr. Katherine Combellick's course in Business Communication, Dr. Mary Procidano's course in Community Psychology, Dr. Jay Mancini's course in Environmental Physics, the Rev. Donald Moore's course in Faith and Critical Reasoning, and Dr. Mark Warren's courses in The Modern City and Urban Schools in Crisis and Renewal.

Beginning in the Spring semester of 2000-2001, a Service-Learning Credit Program for Fordham undergraduates, under the direction of Dr. Mark Warren of Fordham's Department of Sociology and Anthropology and in collaboration with the office of the Community Service Program, was inaugurated with the purpose of encouraging other faculty to engage their students in reflection on their experience in community service projects in New York City. Students will be able to earn one extra credit for community service after receiving formal approval from the course instructor, the community service site supervisor, and Dr. Warren, the director of the program.

Faculty members have been asked to designate which of their courses would be appropriate for service learning. Students can apply for an extra credit in these courses by accepting a service learning agreement that will require 40 hours of community service during the semester, two written essays reflecting on the experience gained in community service, participating in a mid-semester seminar with other students in the Service-Learning Credit program, and any other requirements stipulated by the instructor of the course.

While community service is defined as "student activity that provides assistance or advocacy benefiting a poor, disadvantaged or marginalized community," the credit is earned for the learning experience not the service itself. Dr. Warren, as director of the program, will assign the two reflective essays, but the course instructor will grade the essays, as well as any other work the instructor assigns in connection with the student's community service. The instructor will then integrate these grades with an assessment of the student's performance in other course requirements. Workshops will be offered for faculty interested in learning more about service learning and the possibilities of including service learning in their courses.

Students will be able to earn only one extra credit for service learning in a semester and a total of only three credits for their entire undergraduate program. Interestingly enough, the rationale given for these limits is that "the benefit to the student (should be) set high enough to encourage participation, but not so high as to lead students to do community service for the sole purpose of gaining the credit (and thereby) undermine the essentially voluntary nature of community service." Over the years, students involved in community service have usually argued against proposals that would make some community service a requirement for graduation. In their view, the voluntary nature of their community service was an essential ingredient of their experience.

From its founding as St. John's College in 1841 by John Hughes, the first Archbishop of New York, to serve an immigrant population, Fordham University has always been engaged in the life of New York City and in service to its changing population. Over the last three decades, that engagement has been largely focused on the social challenges that constitute what some have called the crisis of American cities. For hundreds of Fordham students, at both of our urban campuses in Manhattan and the Bronx, community service has provided an opportunity to participate in this contemporary struggle and to learn from the experience. It is our hope that the new Service-Learning Credit Program will provide new opportunities for faculty and students to work and learn together in the City that is both classroom and laboratory.

CHAPTER 10

EQUAL TO THE DEMANDS OF JUSTICE IN THE WORLD

Leo J. O'Donovan, S.J.[1]
Georgetown University

INTRODUCTION

In welcoming freshman classes to Georgetown University, I have more than once, after introducing them to the defining traditions of Jesuit education, posed the following series of questions:

> *When you have reached your Georgetown journey's end, where will you find yourselves? You will, of course, be 'educated,' as your diplomas will attest. But what will that mean? Will you have shaped for yourself growing habits of inquiry and reflection? Will you understand responsibility? Will you recognize suffering and work to lessen it? Will you be, in the words of a great Jesuit who explored the whole world of late 20th century experience, 'men and women for others'?*

To be educated at Georgetown in the Jesuit tradition, I tell these new students, means to take the store of knowledge that they gain as undergraduates – and to which they will add actively throughout their lives – and use it to assume their place as leaders capable of bringing about change in a world longing for justice, compassion and peace. This is no small charge for a freshman to digest and no small responsibility for a university and its faculty to fulfill. The project demands that the university community constantly renew its commitment to its fundamental mission of education in service to God, constantly evaluate its success in that respect and constantly imagine anew how to fulfill that mission.

EDUCATION, SERVICE AND THE PROMOTION OF JUSTICE

Like many other colleges and universities in the United States, Georgetown University was founded to be of service to the nation. In 1789, John Carroll, the first Catholic bishop in the United States, established what

---

[1] Leo J. O'Donovan, S.J. is President Emeritus of Georgetown University.

would become the nation's first Catholic and Jesuit university. He envisioned Georgetown as an academy dedicated to educating the citizens who would be responsible for leading and sustaining the new Republic and the Catholic church in pluralistic American society. Carroll knew that with the rights of freedom came responsibility for justice, equality and opportunity. He wanted young people to learn to lead, and through their leadership to strive toward those ends – preparing themselves to work, as the Jesuits say, "*ad majorem Dei gloriam inque hominum salutem,*" as well as "*ad civitatis utilitatem.*"[2]

In adapting its defining Jesuit traditions to meet contemporary needs, Georgetown has been buoyed by the leadership of two Superior Generals of the Society of Jesus, the late Pedro Arrupe, S.J., and his successor, Peter-Hans Kolvenbach, S.J. In 1973, at an International Congress of Jesuit Alumni of Europe, Fr. Arrupe delivered what was then termed a "radical" address. He stressed "education for justice" as a chief concern of the Church and establishing the formation of "men-for-others" as the "prime educational objective" of Jesuit institutions. Fr. Arrupe insisted that the Society "make sure that in the future the education imparted in Jesuit schools will be equal to the demands of justice in the world." (Arrupe).

In the 30 years since Fr. Arrupe established this agenda for Jesuit education, the Society has held robust discussions on the subject and has crafted strong statements to guide its work.[3] Most recently, in October 2000, the 28 Jesuit colleges and universities in the United States convened at Santa Clara University for a conference on the "Commitment to Justice in Jesuit Higher Education." There Fr. Kolvenbach renewed the call to educate "men and women for others" (as Fr. Arrupe's phrase has been updated), making explicit the critical link between the "promotion of justice" and the mission of serving faith. In the conference's keynote address, Fr. Kolvenbach affirmed what those in the academy who are dedicated to service learning have long believed:

When the heart is touched by direct experience, the mind may be challenged to change. Personal involvement with innocent suffering, with the injustice others suffer, is the catalyst for solidarity that then gives rise to intellectual inquiry and moral reflection.

Students, in the course of their formation, must let the gritty reality of this world into their lives, so they can learn to feel it, think about it critically, respond to its suffering and engage it constructively. They

---

[2] The first phrase, "for the greater glory of God and the welfare of humankind," is the motto chosen by Ignatius Loyola for the Society of Jesus. The second phrase translates "for the advantage of the citizenry."

[3] See, for example, "The Characteristics of Jesuit Education, the International Commission on the Apostolate of Jesuit Education," 1986 and Peter-Hans Kolvenbach, S.J., "Themes of Jesuit University Education," Assembly '89: Jesuit Ministry in Higher Education, Georgetown University, 7 June 1989.

should learn to perceive, think, judge, choose and act for the rights of others, especially the disadvantaged and the oppressed (Kolvenbach).

This powerful and remarkably succinct statement suggests why service programs, and service learning in particular, are an essential element of educating young people to become reflective, principled and active citizens. But a critical question remains: how does a university secure a central place for service in the academic enterprise?

This chapter, while not proposing Georgetown's as a model program, describes our own recent work as a student-centered research university to ensure that we offer students direct experience with those in need and equally important opportunities to combine that experience with intellectual inquiry and moral reflection. I will concentrate exclusively on Georgetown's integration of service into undergraduate education and the relationship of that integration to the research of faculty teaching in our undergraduate schools. The chapter therefore does not discuss the nationally recognized public interest and clinical programs of the Georgetown University Law Center, the considerable work done with and for the city by the Graduate School's Public Policy Institute or the significant community involvement of the Medical Center's School of Medicine and School of Nursing and Health Studies. It is inarguably the case, however, that these programs have helped to shape and sustain a culture of service across the entire university, facilitating our progress in incorporating the ethos of service into undergraduate intellectual life.

The chapter will focus on work to institutionalize experience, inquiry and reflection as a central part of undergraduate life and campus culture. I hope that these observations about Georgetown's experience will be of value to colleagues at other institutions seeking to secure a more central place for service amidst the research and teaching on their own campuses. I should note, too, that the scope of Georgetown's service programs is a reflection of the University's location in Washington, DC – a city whose considerable needs beckon the University community to engage with the broader community on all manner of educational and social issues.

THE SERVICE, TEACHING AND RESEARCH CONTINUUM

As the phrase "Catholic and Jesuit student-centered research university," taken from Georgetown's mission statement, makes clear, the educational development of students is the center of Georgetown's work as it fulfills its responsibilities related to the Church and society through the advancement of human knowledge. Accordingly, concern for student development serves well as the organizing principle for our efforts to answer our Catholic and Jesuit calling to advance social justice. It likewise strongly influences our teaching faculty's community-based scholarship and research projects.

The development of Georgetown's contemporary service mission consists of three major phases: 1) the introduction of a comprehensive set of direct community service opportunities into student life as a means of fostering our students' fuller development and their sense of their capacities as citizens; 2) an increasing emphasis on enhancing that development by combining service with critical analysis and reflection through the service learning curriculum in order to educate men and women interiorly committed to service and capable of effecting change; and 3) service learning instruction's acting as a catalyst for faculty research and scholarship in collaboration with community partners. Progress on this continuum in recent years has brought Georgetown to a defining moment in terms of securing the prominent place of service in the promotion of justice within undergraduate education, an opportunity to which I will return below.

Throughout the late 1960s and early 1970s, a variety of service initiatives were launched on campus, primarily by students. Various mechanisms for coordinating the programs evolved before the establishment in Student Affairs of the Office of Community Involvement Programs (OCIP) with a full-time professional director. As Georgetown's service mission continued to develop, OCIP in 1987 became known as the Volunteer and Public Service Center (VPS), institutionalizing an impressive array of student-led initiatives and claiming a more visible role in University life for service efforts. Today VPS supports 21 student-led service organizations engaged in such activities as tutoring, mentoring, building homes, staffing soup kitchens and homeless shelters and teaching violence prevention and conflict resolution. In addition, the professional VPS staff administers three service programs, including D.C. Reads, the local implementation of the *America Reads* program, which directs federal work-study funds to hire students as literacy tutors for elementary school children. VPS supports these programs by providing training, orientation and reflection opportunities for student volunteers; maintaining a fleet of vehicles to transport the student volunteers to their service sites; fund raising; offering leadership training and development opportunities for student leaders; and evaluating the quality of service delivered.

VPS has for many years also administered Georgetown's Service Learning Credit program, which was among the first of its kind in the country when it was established in 1980. This linking of service directly to the curriculum was a natural development as the university increased emphasis on its service mission, and so this experiential learning initiative found its first home alongside the university's direct service initiatives. The program offers undergraduates the opportunity to earn one extra course credit by linking a minimum of 40 hours of community-based work in a semester to an academic course in which they are enrolled. VPS assists students in identifying organizations to which they can contribute their service, provides the training they need to serve effectively, and ensures appropriate opportunities for students' structured analysis of and reflection on their service work. Originally, the program was designed to allow students themselves to initiate the integration of service into coursework, and indeed they have successfully and creatively applied the Service Learning Credit in nearly every academic discipline of undergraduate study. It has grown increasingly common, however, for the course instructor to establish a service dimension as a formal part of the course.

In the early 1990s, VPS began to offer faculty development initiatives to generate additional faculty interest in service learning through such programs as the week-long "Faculty Institute on Integrating Service into the Curriculum" and seminars on advanced practices in service learning, which explored topics such as evaluation, reflection, national models of service learning, building effective community partnerships and constructing a community oriented research agenda. It became evident, however, that the faculty-focused efforts would be better based in the academic arena than within Student Affairs, and so in 1997 the Center for Urban Research and Teaching (CURT) was established by our Provost to shepherd greater integration of service into undergraduate intellectual life. While VPS continues to support service learning by providing training, transportation and opportunities for guided reflection, CURT works among faculty to promote the integration of community service activities and the undergraduate curriculum with an emphasis on development of academically rigorous courses and expansion of service learning courses to academic departments where they are not now represented. Among CURT's aims is to develop an academic minor or certificate program in community or public service. CURT also assists in the promotion and development of faculty and student research projects that are responsive to the needs of the community, cultivating the relationship between service learning teaching and community-based research and outreach scholarship. Five of the 30 courses that constitute the service learning curriculum at Georgetown are community-based research courses.

To illustrate the synergistic relationship between service learning and community-based research and outreach scholarship, I will offer a recent example in which service learning teaching led directly to unanticipated scholarly writing and another in which a research project naturally encompassed course development. Both cases also demonstrate the importance of institutional support for service learning and community-based research. The productive course and research initiative were both launched by university grants that were designed to bolster the service learning curriculum and university-based efforts in the community. In 1997, on the recommendation of a task force that had assessed the state of the university's mission of service, I appropriated resources for competitive grants to fund new service learning courses and other university-based efforts in the community. The course development grants have resulted directly to date in the introduction of seven new service learning courses involving 10 faculty and representing disciplines ranging from Hispanic literature and African studies to languages and nursing. The other grants have funded four major community-based research initiatives and assistance efforts.

In 1997, Estelle Irizarry, professor of Spanish and Portuguese, received a modest service learning course development grant to create a 400-level symposium on "Charity and Community Service in Hispanic Literature: Readings/Praxis."[4] In her evaluation of the course, she noted numerous constructive consequences of the course's implementation. Among these were achieving the standard service learning objectives of cultivating in students the habits of heart and mind and the seriousness of purpose needed to advance the common good. For example, one student who came to the course with no previous involvement in community service became deeply engaged in service as a result of the course. Others have written moving letters reporting to Prof. Irizarry that the course had led them to re-evaluate and alter their career objectives to focus more on service to others.

The course's direct influences on the instructor's scholarship were likewise notable. Her observation of the significant differences between students' reaction to assigned texts when the course's primary focus was altruism and service and the reactions she had seen among students considering the same readings absent a focus on service led to the publication of a monograph on service learning pedagogy (Irizarry, "Altruism and Community Service"). Her own differing reactions and interpretations within the context of the service learning course structure led to the publication of a book (her 25th!) on the concept of altruism and literature in her primary field of Spanish literature (Irizarry, *Altruismo y literatura*). It is worth noting that the originally low enrollment in this experimental and ultimately remarkably productive course nearly led to its cancellation – a compelling reminder of the importance of perseverance and departmental support for service learning courses in their developmental phases.

In 1998, the grant fund to bolster further Georgetown's work in the community provided seed money for the innovative year-long pilot seminar of Partners in Urban Research and Service Learning (PURS), which brought 10 Georgetown faculty from several disciplines together with 10 local community leaders to exchange knowledge about pressing social issues, to develop research projects that address real and immediate needs in two of Washington's most under-served communities and to plan new Georgetown courses, or adapt existing ones, with faculty and community partners serving as co-instructors.

The service component of these courses is often the students' active engagement in a community-based research initiative. For example, among PURS's first collaborative projects was assisting the Council of Latino Agencies (CLA), an association of 32 community-based organizations that serve the Washington Metropolitan area's large Latino population, in the production of a report on "The State of Latino DC." The report was an effort to produce and compile original research about the condition of

---

[4] The course description follows: "Guided by László's social-cognitive approach to literature, students will read Spanish and Spanish-American works by St. Ignatius of Loyola, Saint Teresa of Avila, Cervantes, Galdós, Concepción Arenal, Unamuno, and contemporary writers in the context of community service as theme and as praxis. Service learning will integrate regular participation in community projects with discussion and reflection activities enhanced by an experiential appreciation of readings."

various dimensions of Latino life. It documented where services and resources are inadequate, thereby allowing agencies to identify the greatest areas of need and to offer compelling evidence in seeking resources to address those needs. The scope of the project was unmanageable for CLA alone, given its skeletal staff, but students from Georgetown's "Project DC" course were able to take on an essential role in the project's completion.[5] The students processed and analyzed specific data sets pertaining to Latino health, education, housing and employment. One student examined health care statistics compiled from national and local health agencies and community non-profit health care providers and analyzed data from a CLA health consumer survey. Another student examined national and local education statistics and interviewed teachers and counselors to compare educational opportunities and barriers for Latino students to those of the general population. Opportunities such as those this course and PURS provide help students to put their knowledge into action – and to understand that knowledge that is not somehow active is spurious.

Within a year of the university's initial investment in the program, PURS won a $400,000 grant from the Department of Housing and Urban Development to establish a permanent community outreach and partnership center that will help the university and community partners to address a number of community priorities, including violence and crime reduction among adolescents, community planning and organization and economic development. As with the service learning courses, this investment of institutional resources in this community-based initiative has yielded a handsome reward. Indeed, this project's multi-faceted approach to engaging the university community in partnership with and in service to its neighbors provides important opportunities for the works of justice that are essential to a genuine conversion to justice.

CENTER FOR SOCIAL JUSTICE RESEARCH, TEACHING AND SERVICE

To expand initiatives such as our student-led direct service programs, Prof. Irizarry's seminar, and the PURS project, Georgetown in January 2001 established under our Provost a new Center for Social Justice Research, Teaching and Service. This Center brings together Georgetown's direct service programs, service learning curriculum and community-based

---

[5] Taught by Associate Professor of Sociology Sam Marullo, who is also the former Director of the Volunteer and Public Service Center, "Project DC" is a 400-level year-long course designed to enable students to undertake policy-oriented research while working as paid interns in city government agencies or nonprofit organizations. Students focus on urban issues such as health care, housing, economic development, education and violence prevention. The course begins with a brief overview of the problem areas, methods of research and potential sites. Students produce policy option/position papers, conduct research and arrange workshops for policy-makers, academics and interested community partners and work eight to 12 hours per week in the internship, which can serve as a work-study assignment.

research and outreach scholarship efforts. It intends to institutionalize those activities as a core component of university culture. It will also serve as an umbrella for the work now undertaken by VPS and the curriculum and faculty development initiatives currently spearheaded by CURT, ensuring maximum opportunities for collaboration among faculty and students and fostering productive synergy among direct service, service learning teaching and community-based research and scholarship for the benefit of the university community and the larger community of which it is part.

Our most pressing priority in establishing the Center was to recruit an imaginative, effective and energetic leader for it, and we have been very fortunate in that respect. Kathleen Maas Weigert, Ph.D., joined Georgetown's faculty this year as founding director of the Center for Social Justice; she will also serve as research professor in sociology and the interdisciplinary Program on Justice and Peace. Dr. Weigert comes to Georgetown from Notre Dame's Center for Social Concerns, where she was associate director of academic affairs and research. She also held appointments as associate professor of American studies and fellow at the Joan B. Kroc Institute for International Peace Studies. Dr. Weigert has published on such topics as experiential and service learning education, nonviolence and education for justice and peace, co-editing or co-authoring several books on those topics, including *Teaching for Justice: Concepts and Models for Service learning in Peace Studies*; *The Search for Common Ground: What Unites and Divides Catholic Americans*, which received the 1998 Award for Excellence in Research from the National Conference of Catechetical Leaders; and *America's Working Poor*.

Dr. Weigert is working in earnest with the Provost and faculty and staff colleagues to develop a strategic plan for the Center's first five years. It is already clear that one of the first focuses of the Center will be faculty. We hope to offer faculty development programs which will 1) bolster involvement in service learning teaching and community-based research, 2) support the work of those faculty already deeply engaged in the community, and 3) foster opportunities for interdisciplinary and cross-campus collaboration in ways that will bring a range of scholarly expertise to bear on pressing problems of the day. Dr. Weigert will also work closely with our University Chaplain to strengthen further the bonds between Georgetown's service mission and its religious character. She likewise looks forward to collaborating with sister Catholic and Jesuit colleges and universities to advance our common social justice concerns, with special attention to exploring ways in which schools located in the Washington metropolitan area can work together to enhance the benefits of the academy's work in the community.

While plans for the Center's first five years are in the formative stages, it is clear that to achieve almost any immediate or long-term goal, Georgetown must dedicate appropriate resources to the project. The Provost has allocated start-up funding for the Center, and its constituent programs (such as VPS) will retain their existing funding. The increase last fall in Georgetown's Third Century Campaign goal from $750 million to $1 billion brought with it an opportunity to dream boldly about the future of the Center. We have established a working goal of $10 million for initiatives relating to Georgetown's service mission. One of the chief priorities of this fund-raising effort will be endowing the Center directorship and establishing an endowed program fund for the Center. The $10 million goal also reflects, of course, funding priorities relating to faculty (such as endowed professorships, curriculum development funds and community-based research funds) and students (such as financial aid vehicles and a loan forgiveness fund to assist young graduates who pursue careers of direct service with non-profit or government organizations). We are confident that this fund-raising effort will capture the imagination of the university's alumni and friends who prize the university's service mission and will ensure an enduring and central place for that mission in Georgetown's third century.

The idea of a Center for Social Justice emerged from a comprehensive self-study that Georgetown undertook in preparation for the Jesuit colleges and universities conference on the "Commitment to Justice in Jesuit Higher Education." The self-study was part of Georgetown's regular evaluation of our success in fulfilling Georgetown's mission of education "for the greater glory of God and the welfare of humankind." We anticipate that the Center will be a leading participant in our ongoing process of self-evaluation and renewal of our commitment to social justice. It will regularly pose important and challenging questions, encouraging our faculty to ask themselves what Fr. Kolvenbach urged all faculty to ask: "When researching and teaching, where and with whom is my heart?" (Kolvenbach, 2000) Placing a new and powerful emphasis on the indispensable role of service and service learning in the intellectual and moral formation of our undergraduate students, the Center for Social Justice will help the university to live out its commitment to educate "men and women for others" and to become ever more truly "equal to the demands of justice in the world."

REFERENCES

Arrupe, S.J., P. (July, 1973). Men for Others: Training Agents of Change for the Promotion of Justice. International Congress of Jesuit Alumni in Europe. Valencia, Spain.

Irizarry, E. (1999). Altruism and Community Service in Hispanic Literature: Readings and Praxis. In J. Hellebrandt & L. T. Varona (Eds). *Construyendo Puentes (Building Bridges): Concepts and Models for Service Learning*. Washington: American Association of Higher Education,.

Irizarry, E. (1999). *Altruismo y literatura: Odón Betanzos Palacios.* Rociana del Condado: Fundación Odón Betanzos Palacios and Fundacion El Monte (Collección Investigación).

Kolvenbach, P. H., S.J. (Oct. 2000). The Service of Faith and the Promotion of Justice in American Jesuit Higher Education. Commitment to Justice in Jesuit Higher Education Conference. Santa Clara University.

Weigert, K. M., & Crews, R. J. (1999) (Eds.) *Teaching for Justice: Concepts and Models for Service Learning in Peace Studies*. Service learning in the Disciplines Series. Washington: American Association of Higher Education.

Weigert, K. M., Davidson, J. M., et al. (1997). *The Search for Common Ground: What Unites and Divides Catholic Americans*. Huntington, IN: Our Sunday Visitor.

Weigert, K. M., & Swartz, T. R. (1995). (Eds.) *America's Working Poor*. Notre Dame: University of Notre Dame Press.

CHAPTER 11

LIBERAL ARTS COLLEGE FACULTY REFLECT ON SERVICE-LEARNING: STEPS ON A TRANSFORMATIVE JOURNEY

Joan Burton[1]
Laurie Kaplan[2]
Judy Jolley Mohraz[3]
Lawrence Kay Munns[4]
Barbara Roswell[5]
Carol Weinberg[6]
Goucher College

INTRODUCTION

In the early twentieth century Jane Addams counseled college students to "keep one foot in the library and one in the streets." This philosophy of learning linked to community engagement characterized not only higher education in the Progressive Era but is also a hallmark of liberal arts education today. The connection between education and civic action naturally grew out of the mission of liberal arts institutions, historically committed to educating the whole person through a broad ranging curriculum. Intellectual inquiry and academic competency have served as one pillar of the liberal arts experience, while informed moral action represents another. Each is ultimately directed toward a shared goal: Preparing students for lifelong learning and joyful, humane lives.

Liberal arts institutions are ideal "petri dishes" for learning integrated with community involvement thanks not only to their wide-ranging holistic curriculum but also to their size, residential setting, and engaged pedagogy. Goucher College offers an excellent case study of the confluence of these factors and the resulting environment where service-learning flourishes. A student body of 1200 undergraduates allows each student to experience the

---

[1] Associate Professor of Sociology
[2] Professor of English and Director of the Honors Program
[3] Former President
[4] Professor of Political Science
[5] Assistant Professor of English
[6] France-Merrick Professor of Service-Learning and Assistant Professor of Education

power of the individual. With ease students design their own majors, introduce new student organizations, and voice their views through shared governance. Additionally, since 75% of the students live on campus, students have the opportunity to learn civic responsibility simply through their interaction twenty-four hours a day with classmates. Perhaps most importantly, since three-fourths of the classes enroll twenty or fewer students, discussion drives the classes. There are no back rows that allow students to become invisible. As a result, students are constantly called upon to engage actively in class discussions and course projects. Learning by doing realizes John Dewey's vision on a daily basis.

Service-learning at Goucher also stands as a compelling calling for students and faculty alike because of the school's proximity to Baltimore City, an urban center confronting the challenges of poverty and a weakened civic fabric. Although Goucher enjoys the idyllic setting of 287 acres in Towson, eight miles from the downtown area, the College has always recognized its responsibilities in Baltimore. An isolated island of woods and tranquility hardly prepares students for the world they will enter, and students as well as faculty traditionally have understood the need to connect with Baltimore City and the mutual benefits that can accrue. As Goucher has cultivated these connections, we have discovered the complexities and advantages of genuinely building reciprocal partnerships. The City has become the laboratory for learning and application in a variety of disciplines, and the strength of this focus has prompted philanthropists and alumni to underwrite the service-learning infrastructure and programs. A recent one million dollar grant from the France-Merrick Foundation, for example, has endowed a faculty chair in service-learning. Students who participate in community-based courses almost universally report that they would take another such course and would recommend such courses to other students. The felt need for service-learning in higher education and the impact college-community partnerships can have are as apparent today as they were a century ago when Jane Addams and John Dewey first called for learning to be linked to civic action.

PHILOSOPHY AND MODELS OF SERVICE-LEARNING AT GOUCHER COLLEGE

What is democratic citizenship and how can a liberal arts education help nurture it? Many of us at Goucher share the assumption that democratic citizenship requires an appreciation of our common humanity. Acknowledging this interdependency is the first step in becoming democratic citizens. As John Dewey argued, the next step is to interact with diverse others to work towards shared goals. We must create a learning environment in which our students experience that interaction, personally feel the interdependence, and thus become equipped to contribute as democratic citizens to the larger public when they leave Goucher.

Across disciplines, the goal of all faculty at Goucher involved in service-learning is to enable students to learn what can only be learned by experience beyond the classroom—to see theory and concepts in real life contexts, to challenge themselves and their education, and to explore what their responsibilities are as engaged members of the larger community. College students should be able to apply their skills, knowledge and interests in ways that improve the communities around them, while also learning from and appreciating the people with whom they work.

Service-learning models at Goucher have expanded since they began in 1994 with the *service credit option.* This option allows faculty to offer students the opportunity to receive an additional credit (graded Pass/No Pass) for doing 30 hours of service at a site related to the course and completing integrative assignments such as journals, papers, or oral presentations. While this option was a good way to introduce service-learning into the curriculum, it met with mixed success.

Kay Munns was one of the first faculty members to offer the service credit option. He recalls, "Although the students did do useful community service, the connections between what they were doing and the course subject matter was never made clear...either by them or by me. The add-on was just that — something added — without clear articulation of the purposes of the add-on, the relationship of the community service to the course, or what the student was to learn and how the work was to be evaluated. In my rush to do service-learning, I had not really spent the time necessary to figure out just what that meant in terms of my own responsibilities and those of the students and the community organizations as well."

Barbara Roswell offered the option in women's studies and peace studies classes. She reports, "Over time, I became increasingly critical of what I began to view as an 'entrepreneur' model of service. This optional experience required significant vision and assertiveness on the part of the students who pursued it, making it frustrating for some students. There were also many missed opportunities. Students did not benefit from regular conversation about their work in the community with other members of the class, their experiences never fully became part of the resources of the course as a whole, and community members with whom students worked remained essentially 'silent' in our classroom dialogue."

As faculty committed to service-learning recognized the limitations of the service credit option, they took steps to improve on the situation. One sociology professor who had offered the option in her Domestic Violence seminar, for example, revised her three-credit course which had a research assignment into a four-credit course where all students performed their research with and for local domestic violence agencies. Other faculty moved from the 30-hour add-on option to a *service component*, with varying degrees of choice and hours of service. In some classes (such as Barbara Roswell's writing class described below), all students are expected to work in the community and reflect on that work. In other classes (such as Joan Burton's and Laurie Kaplan's freshman seminars) students may choose to do service and an integrative as-signment or opt for a non-service alternative. Laurie Kaplan has found that the ideal class is one that has all students participating in the service. She re-flects, "During the fall semester, I was rather apologetic that I was incorpo-rating an extra couple of hours a week into the students' schedules and made the service-learning an option that would provide five extra points toward the final grade. During the spring semester, however, as I became more comfort-able with the procedures, I made the experience a requirement that would be 10% of the final grade. Over this year, I've learned that service-learning should NOT be optional for the Honors Program students."

Several faculty have also developed *full service-learning courses* in which the service work is the centerpiece of the course for all students. In most of these, the class works together on a single project. Kay Munns' Sur-vey Research class described below is an example of a full service-learning course. Goucher's unique senior course, *Making Connections: An Interdisci-plinary Service-Learning Liberal Arts Capstone*, is another example. The Capstone challenges graduating seniors to collaborate on a community project (e.g., interviewing residents in a Baltimore neighborhood and developing a brochure and web page to preserve the strengths and history of the commu-nity) while using that experience and related readings to reflect on the impact of a liberal arts education.

The nature of the service experience varies on multiple levels. For first year students, direct contact with different communities that offers them new perspectives and brings course material to life seems most appropriate. For more advanced students, opportunities to apply specialized skills and knowl-edge (as researchers, writers, technicians) to community and agency-defined needs have been especially effective for students and community partners alike. According to Jen Langdon, former Associate Director of ACTS, an or-ganization providing transitional services for women and children who are homeless as a result of domestic violence, "With the help of Goucher volun-teers, we were able to develop and implement a psychosocial history tool, as well as a program evaluation survey. These important additions would not have been possible without the help of the very capable and enthusiastic vol-unteers."

The flexibility of Goucher's service-learning models is consistent with more general traditions and climate at the college. Hallmarks of our academic program have been to offer students options, to make service attractive rather than required, and to encourage student initiative. All this is facilitated by the good communication among the cadre of committed faculty and students, the support of the Shriver Center Higher Education Consortium, and the Col-lege's commitment of some professional development funds and strategic planning grants.

Flexibility is balanced with focus. Our service-learning program (and our parallel efforts in student-led volunteer service) is rooted in a number of on-going partnerships with particular service agencies, public schools, and neighborhoods in Baltimore City and County. Often our relationships with particular schools and neighborhoods are facilitated by service agencies and umbrella associations such as Baltimore Reads, Civic Works and the HARBEL Community Organization. As these partnerships have developed, we have sought to break down the walls between the Goucher campus and the off-campus community. Instead of only having students go "to the community," we also have the community join us on campus. Increasingly, we've invited people from the community to speak to us as experts, hear presentations of final projects, and take advantage of our facilities (computer labs, etc.), thereby helping expand participants'—especially children's—vision for the future. In other words, we've tried increasingly to consider what reciprocity entails, and what structures we need to create to support and nurture it.

Since 1994 a remarkable one-third of the Goucher faculty have experimented with service-learning in their courses. Over 15 have made community-based work central to their pedagogy and scholarship. As faculty have taken their first steps into service-learning and found it to be an exciting academic experience, they have enthusiastically re-designed existing courses and developed new ones that more fully integrate service-learning. The remainder of this chapter presents the reflections of four faculty members as they have navigated this process. As each recounts their personal journey, certain patterns emerge: from service option to integration, from individual to systemic perspectives, and from more narrow visions of service to reciprocal relationships.

FACULTY REFLECTIONS
Laurie Kaplan – First Year Honors Program

The Honors Program at Goucher College offers exceptionally prepared students a chance to challenge themselves in a series of six interdisciplinary courses that culminate in a General Honors Degree. The Program is composed of students from all majors across the campus, but as the students take these courses together, they form a learning community that extends beyond the classroom and into the life of the College.

Over the past two semesters I have tried to show that, in my mind, service is simply an implicit value of being a member of the Honors Program, that it is up to students in the Honors Program to give back to the community, and that it is the responsibility of all students in this program to examine for themselves the meaning of their educations and to participate in what we hope will become a life-long dedication to volunteer work and good citizenship. Many students report that high school service projects changed their lives, and it was my goal to make service in college equally meaningful. Service-learning is now required in three courses in the Honors Program, and we hope that the service-learning component will have programmatic as well as individual dividends.

The theme of the Honors section of the freshman seminar was *Passports: Crossing Frontiers*, and under this rubric we focused on issues of cultural diversity that affect our everyday lives in the United States. As we explored the historical context for patterns of immigration to the U.S., we discussed such themes as the myth of the American Dream; race, class, and gender stereotypes; the idea of education as a "passport to success"; and the making of multicultural societies. The service component for the course was arranged through the Goucher Community Service Office with the Baltimore Reads Program. Students assisted in classrooms in one Baltimore City elementary school an hour a week over the course of the semester. Fifteen of the 20 students enrolled in the course took advantage of the opportunity. During the spring semester, in *The Modern Condition*, the first course in the Honors sequence, service-learning was a course requirement. Out of an enrollment of 17, 12 had taken the *Passports* course, and most of them were enthusiastic about seeing "their" children again. Only one student could not fit the tutoring project into her schedule, and she performed an alternate service assignment. The year-long experience provided continuity not only for the Goucher students but for the children as well.

The Web Board

Key to student reflection and learning was the use of a Web board to provide a forum for student conversation. This format produced a certain freedom for the students in terms of what they felt they could and wanted to reveal about themselves. For example, they admitted such "honest" feelings as "I didn't want to tutor again. I am NOT on the same wavelength as kindergartners and have no small difficulty communicating with them . . . . But I will continue my duty and hope to be a small inspiration to even the laziest ones in the class . . . ." A comment such as this would elicit responses about motivation, inspiration, role models, aspirations, etc. The web board extended the community: students who did not ordinarily interact with each other in the classroom had give-and-take sessions on the web. They were polite but firm; they had opinions that they valued and wanted to communicate. They also shared observations and results. At times the Goucher students praised each other, and they meant it.

Course Structure

Two of the course goals were "To introduce students to works by authors of diverse cultural backgrounds" and "To engage in dialogue that tolerates others' views." Getting out into the community seemed to be a way to get our students to mix and interact with more diverse people—to break the Goucher bubble, as the students say—and to begin to understand what real tolerance entails. Simultaneously, under the umbrella of "passports" to success, we examined the opportunities offered by education, asking: "What is education for?" To explore these ideas the class read several essays collected in *Re-reading America,* including "From *Report of the French Commission on American Education, 1879,*" Malcolm X's "Learning to Read," Maxine Hong Kingston's "Silence," Rose's "I Just Want to be Average," and Cheney's "Politics of the Schoolroom."

A primary focus throughout the course was the question of what motivates people to succeed—to cross a frontier—and we talked about how internal/external motivation sets us on the road to change and to success. It was at the time we began to discuss this topic that the students began to tutor, so a major part of our conversation focused on how education could transform people. The Goucher students worried about the conditions in crowded classrooms and their own influence on the expectations and lives of the students they were tutoring.

As a final assignment, we read Athol Fugard's *My Children! My Africa!,* a play which addresses some of the same moral dilemmas and issues the class had been discussing all semester. The play worked well to conclude the course as well as the tutoring experience.

Impact on Students

From the web board and the classroom discussions, I could see that the students in both courses recognized very quickly that they had the power and ability to change other people's lives. They saw that they could give a lot of themselves in just one hour away from Goucher; they discovered that for the youngsters there is real joy—as well as real frustration—in "learning how to learn"; and they were amazed that the children "needed" them so much. An hour away from campus working with the children liberated them from the role of "student," and they felt free to try do things their own way. As one student put it, "I'm extremely grateful for the opportunity that this experience offered me . . . I feel that they [the children] helped me more than I could have ever helped them." Interaction with the children, with the other students who shared rides, and on the web board grounded the honors students, making them see more clearly the value of their own educational experiences and leading to various outcomes. These outcomes included:

- *changing students' ideas and challenging expectations*: One student who initially resented the added "duty" of tutoring writes: "Little did I know, but my experiences . . . would prove to be most enjoyable. I learned much about respect and authority from the children."
- *making their own discoveries about what works in terms of external/internal motivations*: The tutors found that using incentives worked with the children, so they began to create their own incentive systems.
- *providing personal attention for the students and learning the limitations of what they could accomplish during the time they were with the children*: A typical comment reads as follows: "While academically I might

night not have helped the kids that much, as a friend and as a kind of mentor/counselor/all-around-helper, they benefited from me as much as I did from them."

- *learning the lesson that "tutoring" had multiple meanings*: The students found that they actually provided "a positive and supportive educational experience" for children who may be at risk in an educational environment that is less than ideal.
- *discovering that they can make a difference in other people's lives simply by being themselves and answering children's questions about themselves*: The students in my courses found that they were acting as role models for students whose vision of the future often does not include college: "One child, who was withdrawn and did not seem to enjoy school, wrote that because he saw that I was able to do it he is going to work 'really hard,' go to college, and try to get a scholarship himself."
- *breaking what the students refer to as "the Goucher bubble" and e*n*couraging them to "think outside the box" in terms of what education means*: "It was exciting to watch these children grow and have first hand experience on how we as humans learn and absorb information. I think it reminded me that learning is a constant process, and that it is okay to be naive at times and to make mistakes—in the college world you forget to allow yourself the luxury of being wrong."
- *developing ideas about educational realities:* Students were shocked at the overcrowded conditions in the classroom, and repeatedly they noted how easily a child can be overlooked when so many students are clamoring for attention and the teacher's nerves are frazzled. They were a little overwhelmed by what they perceived as the "chaos" in the classroom. Focusing on individuals rather than systems, they almost universally "blamed" the chaos on the teacher and the teacher's methods.

Interdisciplinary in nature, the course encouraged students to make connections between what they were reading, what they were experiencing, and what they were learning in other classes. In the long run, this combination has made students more thoughtful and critical not only about people and communities different from their own but also about their own education in the liberal arts.

Joan Burton – Sociology Courses

For the past two years, I've offered a service-learning option in three classes: the freshman seminar (*Remaking America: Race, Ethnicity, and the Immigrant Experience*), *The Sociological Imagination*, and *Women and Work: A Global Perspective*. Students who chose this option devoted a minimum of 10 to 12 hours attending conversation classes for immigrant women at the Greater Homewood Community Corporation's Literacy Program in Baltimore City. The on-site literacy classes, supervised by a Greater Homewood Vista volunteer, were designed to provide Greater Homewood (GH) students with an opportunity to improve their reading and conversation skills by discussing American culture and the immigrant experience with Goucher students. As a framework for their weekly discussions, Goucher and GH students chose topics from texts on American culture, the Amish way of life, and cross-cultural variations in the lives of women. Goucher students kept a journal describing the topics discussed and wrote a paper applying the theories about culture, work, race, ethnicity, and immigration covered in the assigned texts to what the GH students told them about their experiences as immigrants. Because the conversation class was small, the Goucher and GH students quickly became comfortable with each other, creating an environment that allowed each group to explore their pre-existing stereotypes. Both groups were enthusiastic about what they learned from their meetings.

Design of Project and Evaluation of Assignments

The Commission on National and Community Service defines service-learning as a method "under which students learn through active participation in organized service experiences that meet actual community needs and that are coordinated in collaboration with the school and community" (Waterman, 1997, p.2). I designed the service-learning option in my courses with this definition in mind. The first semester I offered the option I participated regularly in the GH literacy classes for the first several weeks of the semester. My participation enabled me to better understand what the students were experiencing and to provide them with guidance and feedback on what was expected from them. Because the service-learning option was closely related to all other course assignments, it was relatively easy to integrate structured opportunities for reflections on the students' experience at GH into class discussions of assigned readings. During these discussions, Goucher students re-examined the connections between what they had learned from the GH conversation classes and the analyses of the immigrant experience raised in the texts we were studying in class. For example, all students were impressed by Richard Rodriguez's memories of the personal costs he suffered to become accepted by white American society, but his assimilation experiences were especially meaningful to the service-learning students who witnessed the immigrant parents they met at Greater Homewood facing a similar dilemma. One Goucher student described looking out the door of the GH classroom and watching the daughters of a GH student studying English and playing computer games. She wrote in her journal, "Unbeknownst to her, Ameena's (a fictitious name) two little girls have been swimming in the Melting Pot. In time, she will have American children." Another student observed that "we expect that immigrants will assimilate, because it inconveniences us if they don't. After their culture is lost we say, it must not have been that important, if it was so easy to lose."

Most of the students were impressed by the stories written by immigrants describing how difficult it was to leave their homeland and their loved ones not knowing what they faced in a new world. Immigrant stories became very real to the service-learning students who heard them first hand. They developed deep respect for the courage of the women they met at GH and an understanding of the immigrant experience that went beyond what the texts provided. In the words of one student, "Attending the GH classes showed me for the first time how America would appear to an immigrant living here in this day and age." She reevaluated the American life style that she thought she knew so well and began to contemplate what she might do to influence policies that affect immigrants. Another student questioned what she came to see as her "individualistic" views on life and observed:

> *I found myself much more concerned with money than some of the other women were. Even more disturbing, I found myself feeling that my whole world was not as close as it should be. Most of these women had very loving and caring families that supported each other. Not that my family doesn't care, but in the spirit of being American, we all tend to do what we want without considering other people's feelings.*

As I had hoped, getting out of the classroom and participating in a program that provides service to the community had a positive effect on the learning experience of the Goucher students. Most students in my classes understood how our readings about the significance of cultural differences related to their discussions with women from countries as varied as China, Romania, and Brazil. However, regular meetings with women from other cultures did not automatically reveal the link between the service-learning project and other significant aspects of the course, especially the segments on class and race inequalities. The service-learning students knew that the women attending the GH classes were well educated and sufficiently affluent to give up their jobs and travel to the United States with their husbands. Nevertheless, in their self reflections, not one student suggested that the comfortable relationships they quickly developed with the GH women might be due, in part, to class similarities that allowed them to overcome racial and ethnic differences. They failed to see that their conversations focused almost exclusively on topics of cultural significance, such as food differences or wedding practices, rather than on the problems of economic survival faced by many immigrants. None of the Goucher students referred to the evidence in the assigned readings that, unlike the GH students, many immigrants come to this country specifically to find work so they can support their families back home.

Seminar with Greater Homewood Students

Each semester I invite the Greater Homewood students to attend class at Goucher on the day the service-learning students present summaries of their papers. On each occasion, the joint seminar reinforced the commitment of Goucher and GH students to the project. Students who did not participate in the service-learning option wrote in their journals that they wished they had. Students who did participate were pleased by how interested the GH women were in what they had to say. Goucher students were proud of the GH students for their willingness to voice their opinions in front of a large group and share their experiences with students they did not know.

Although the seminar was always a success, a few problems did emerge. Unfortunately, some of the Goucher students who had not participated in the service-learning experience made sweeping generalizations about immigrants based on just one meeting with the GH women. One student commented in a journal entry, "these women had no self esteem while a woman with equal education and knowledge [born in the United States] would have a lot of esteem." Because the GH women seemed quiet and demure, this student concluded that they were "uneducated" and "dragged" to America by their husbands. Though rare, such comments convinced me that I need to provide an opportunity before the semester ends to respond to students' reactions to the joint seminar.

Concluding Thoughts

As I reflected on my experience with service-learning, I was pleased with the outcome of the projects, but I realized that I couldn't easily separate what worked from what didn't work. I could detect personal growth and maturity in the students' journal reflections on their experience, and I was impressed with the sophisticated level of analysis some students demonstrated in their final papers. In some instances, however, students' papers revealed problems with integrating experiential and classroom learning. In a freshman seminar, for example, first year students had difficulty understanding how the findings of scholarly research on immigration and the points made in the stories we read about immigration were linked to the experiences described by the Greater Homewood students. Goucher students drew conclusions about the ways in which race, ethnicity, class, and/or gender can influence the immigrant experience that are not supported by either the social science research or the personal stories written by immigrants. For example, a small minority of students defined the middle class immigrant women they met at GH as the only immigrants who brought something positive to American life, concluding that poor immigrants were always illegal "aliens" who came to America just to receive welfare benefits. For these students the service-learning experience reinforced stereotypes and prejudices rather than enhanced their understanding of the immigrant experience.

As Waterman (1997, p. 7) observed, "connections spontaneously made by the students between educational concepts from the classroom and participation in the service project are likely to be haphazard and incomplete." Achieving the academic goals of the project, in particular, depends on careful monitoring of students' analyses of the link between the concepts studied in class and their application to the service-learning experience. I also share the concern of Kerry Strand (1999, p. 32) that we "avoid the pitfall of prioritizing individual experience over systemic analysis in understanding social life." Strand observes that "students should recognize that their personal experience is only one source—and not a terribly valid or reliable one—for understanding the world." I discovered evidence of the pitfalls described by Waterman and Strand in my students' written work and realized that their misinterpretations of the sociological significance of community service were due, in part, to the design of the course. In the future, consistently integrating students' service learning experiences into class discussions, responding more systematically to self reflections in journals, and requiring earlier drafts of final papers, will make the relationship of learning in class to learning through community service clearer and more meaningful.

Lawrence (Kay) Munns – Political Science

The most successful experience for me in integrating service into my classes has been a new political science course developed in 1998-99: *Practicum in Survey Research*. This course replaced a required research methods course in political science which students often felt lacked relevance.

As a result of the mixed response to the course, I began searching around for a substitute. At the outset, I had three principal goals in mind: somehow combine theory and practice; make it a hands-on course; emphasize experiential learning. Of course, these three goals are really just different ways of saying the same thing. I had a long- term interest in survey research and had always wanted to put my knowledge to some useful purpose. It struck me then that a practicum in survey research would be a perfect way of fulfilling my goals. The course design was clear: students would do a survey from start to finish. In this course, the art and science of doing surveys would unfold naturally as students confronted the different phases of survey research, from meeting with the client, writing questions, designing and pre-testing the questionnaire, to conducting the survey, analyzing the results and writing and presenting a report.

The final piece of the puzzle came into play when I began to envision as a client a non-profit organization in the Baltimore area that had the need for data but no resources to conduct a survey on its own. The idea of finding such a client was at first intimidating until I realized that Goucher's Coordinator of

Community Service would likely have ideas and contacts for me, which of course turned out to be the case.

If successful, the course would teach students survey research in a hands-on experiential way, thus combining theory, practice and service by engaging with the larger community. The most exciting aspect of the course, however, was that all these goals would be achieved SEAMLESSLY. The goals were so interconnected that one didn't have to say or think: today we are going to do community service, or today we are going to do a survey, or today we are going to join the theory we have learned with the practice of survey research. Everyday, in every way, simply by doing the survey, all the goals were being accomplished.

At this point, the course has been offered twice: first in 1998-99 and again in 1999-2000. In the first instance, the class did a survey for the HARBEL Community Organization in Northeast Baltimore City. HARBEL had been running a substance abuse program for some time but had never had the re-sources to conduct an evaluation of the program. Working with HARBEL, the class completed a survey of individuals who had participated in the substance abuse program in an effort to find out what, if any, impact the program had had on their lives. The course culminated in a written report and an oral, PowerPoint presentation to HARBEL officials. HARBEL has told us that the report has been very useful to them and they will be able to use it in future grant-writing activities. The second time around, the client was the Active Coalition for Transitional Services (ACTS), an organization which provides services for victims of domestic violence. ACTS was interested in seeking funding for expanded services to clients in Baltimore County, but at the same time needed research to demonstrate that such services were needed. The class once again did a survey, this time primarily of church leaders in Balti-more County, and presented a written report as well as a PowerPoint oral presentation to leaders of ACTS. The staff of ACTS assured us that the report will be very helpful to them as they proceed with efforts to develop new pro-grams. Indeed, one of the students in the class is now working as a summer intern with ACTS in an effort to implement some of the recommendations made in the report.

In a spin-off from developing this course, two students and I put in a pro-posal to the Strategic Planning Committee of the College for funds to support a Survey Research Group on campus. Patterned after the course, the Group was funded to conduct surveys for non-profit organizations in the Baltimore area. In this instance, however, rather than receiving credit, students who have completed the survey research course are hired to work with me in conducting the surveys. This provides the students with the opportunity to further develop their understanding of survey research as they address community needs.

I see five major ways my survey research classroom is different from other courses I teach.

1. Students *learn to do*. The ultimate tangible goal of the course is to produce a report—both oral and written—to be presented to the client. They must DO in order to accomplish this tangible goal.

2. Students *learn by doing*. The project can be completed only by doing survey research, only by getting one's hands dirty by writing questions, entering data into the computer, analyzing the data, writing the report, making recommendations based on the data, etc.

3. Students *learn by being part of a team*. Most social science research, and certainly survey research, is not done by one person. Instead, research is done collaboratively and involves working with others, sharing one's work, being open to constructive suggestions from other members of the team. The final product will only be as good as the team that does it. Students learn all important interaction skills as they learn to work together and to share the responsibility for the final product.

4. Students *learn through interaction with others — in the classroom and in the larger community*. This is I think service-learning at its best, where students come to realize that they are not simply a lone researcher or a lone person, but realize that they are part of a larger community, that they are in part defined by that larger community.

5. Students *learn through the seamlessness of learning, doing, teamwork, and being part of the college and larger communities*. In many ways, the virtue of this approach is that the process is so natural, there is nothing contrived about it.

Barbara Roswell – First Year Writing Class

For the past two years, I have taught a second-semester freshman writing course that incorporates a required service component. Because this is a significant commitment from students, we have taken several steps to ensure that students both know about the service component in this required course (listing it in the course schedule) and have the opportunity to take a different "section" of academic writing during the same time period.

Course Structure

Bruce Herzberg, in his often quoted "Community Service and Critical Pedagogy" (1994), raises the important concern that community service can, paradoxically, leave students more complacent about inequality, can reinforce stereotypes, and can distract students from larger systems of inequality and their role within these systems. To use the language of Peggy Macintosh, service-learning experiences run the risk that students will analyze poverty without reflecting on their own privilege or will valorize "bandaid" treatments in place of more sustained, systemic analysis of issues in their full complexity.

To address these concerns, I've organized my course around the theme "So How Did I Get Here?" – a question I take from the title of a 1992 *New York Times Magazine* essay by Rosemary Bray. Throughout the semester, students ask this question of themselves, and listen to how others answer this question, in increasingly sophisticated ways. I open the course by asking students to write an essay answering this question about their own lives. Students read their essays aloud the second day of class. After each student reads, other members of the class (including me) simply repeat or "echo" those words, phrases and images which resonate for us. From this class onward, students have begun to know each and trust each other, to listen attentively without judging, and to have affirmed that their ideas matter and that they will be "heard."

We next read Bray's essay (reflecting on her experience growing up "on welfare") as well as several other pieces concerning poverty and welfare policy. As part of our inquiry, we also record our monthly expenses and research Maryland welfare and food stamp allowances in order to create a plan that would allow us to live within budget. Since several of my students work at a home for people living with late stage AIDS, we next read several pieces that reflect the ways that AIDS has been conceptualized over the last two decades – again, attending to how each writer answers questions of "How Did I Get Here?" Bringle and Velo's analysis of attribution theory and how it applies to helping situations (1998) then provides a theoretical framework with which students consider how different authors (including themselves) answer "why" questions in their lives. This sequence of assignments is deliberately recursive, inviting closer and closer scrutiny of a set of questions from multiple perspectives. It also aims to create a conversation in which service recipients, published writers, and my students are all participants.

Rather than having the service component "added on," an examination of the notion of "service," itself, is central to the course. In recent years, writing courses that examine literacy and involve students in a tutoring program have become well established on a number of campuses. I have drawn on their model, but have broadened the concern from literacy to more general questions of poverty and privilege. I have also come to believe, as do such thinkers as Ivan Illich, Benjamin Barber, Robert Woodson, Neil Postman, and John McKnight, that the notions of "service" and of "community," far from being simple and straightforward, themselves demand examination, critique from multiple perspectives, and inquiry.

Essays by these and other theorists—often quite dense and difficult—provide students the opportunity to sharpen their critical reading, synthesis, and academic writing skills (all mandates of the course), in addition to providing material from which I invite students to take a position on some question over which there is disagreement or debate. This central process of familiarizing oneself with the scholarly conversation and then identifying a meaningful question in response to which one supports an informed view is central to what I hope my students learn in this academic writing course.

Guided Reflection

Perhaps most successful has been what I would call the "guided reflection" that students do each week in response to their work in the community. As Chris Anson has pointed out, too often students' reflections remain at the level of reportage, cycling back through a series of observations, routines, or complaints, without achieving the "critical examination of ideas, or the sort of consciousness-raising reflection, that is the mark of highly successful learning" (1997, p. 169). Below I list and annotate some of the questions I pose to students. These generally proceed from observation and reportage to analysis and inquiry, at the same time supporting each student in his or her work to "show, not tell," and to develop a distinctive voice as an academic writer.

- *Articulation of expectations*: Before you visit your service site, write a few paragraphs about your expectations (about the agency, clients, yourself, etc.).
- *Observation of site*: "Take us" to the place where you are doing your community service. You may choose to describe the physical setting (sights, smells, sounds; what your eye sees as it travels across the room; analogies with other places; etc.), the mood of the place, and/or the social setting.
- *Questions about site–getting to know the organization:* Fill out the "questionnaire" about your agency (addressing such questions as Where does the agency get its funding? Who determines funding levels, staffing, involvement of volunteers? Who are the clients? If the agency did not exist, what other services would be available to clients?).
- *How do you plan to use your time?:* After consulting with clients and staff, write a few paragraphs proposing how you think you can best contribute to the organization. In this piece, you should shift from "just joining in" to pro-actively planning how you will spend your time.
- *An experience or moment that stands out:* Name something you've witnessed at your community service site that you find striking. What beliefs or assumptions seem to be behind this phenomenon (on the part of clients, staff, etc.)? Do you share these beliefs and assumptions? How might you respond to such a moment in the future?
- *Analysis of model of "service" operational in your organization*: What model seems to be operational in your agency? What are the assumed relationships among staff, clients, and volunteers? How are "help" and "community" defined and enacted? Who makes knowledge, sets priorities, determines policy? What do you find effective or problematic about the model you observe?

- *Analysis of problem:* Name a problem you've noticed in your community service work. What are the sources of that problem? What could you, the agency or the clients do to address the problem? What legislation or public agency or official might have an impact on this problem?
- *Portrait/ Interior monologue*: Read two brief portraits from Sandra Cisneros, *The House on Mango Street* and consider what contributes to the effectiveness of these short, concentrated pieces? Create a brief portrait of one of the clients with whom you work. If you prefer, assume the voice of one of your clients, and write an interior monologue from his or her perspective about yourself, your community service site, or someone whom that client knows.

Following these shorter assignments, the last portion of the semester is devoted to students researching a question that has emerged from their service experiences.

Classroom Discussions

Of course, what happens in class matters, too. I usually devote about 10 minutes of my twice-weekly 75-minute class to students' updates, queries, brainstorming, etc. For example, several students in my class worked at an after-school Police Athletic League center. Early in the semester, they recognized that they could organize an ongoing project that—ideally—would support the children's literacy skills; make good use of their own particular interests; create a lasting project (that might even be of help in securing additional funds for the center); and help the children build self-confidence. Together, the class brainstormed ideas, which eventually took the shape of a "literary magazine" that would enable students to write "all about me" and "all about PAL." Other students who worked at an assisted living facility for the elderly were quick to adapt this idea to their setting, thinking about ways to work with residents to create and anthologize informal oral histories.

Concluding Thoughts

My reflections on the successes and shortcomings of this course have prompted me to ask, Where am I asking students to travel in this course? What losses must they grieve as they leave familiar ways of understanding the world? An initial answer is that I invite students to think and know and learn relationally. To do this, students must give up the home of authority and expertise as they have come to know them—and perhaps as other disciplines are asking them to know them. They must give up their innocence of privilege. They must give up their faith in objectivism—and they must cultivate a new home. It is a home where they listen differently, where the language is contextual and situated, where different things "count." It is a home where new rules are constantly being negotiated, crowded with people who a few short weeks ago would never have even been admitted to the neighborhood, much less invited to pull up a chair and tell their stories. In this home personal experience matters, but careful observation and theoretically based inquiry do, too.

But I have come to appreciate, also, what I can't do in this course. In fourteen weeks, I can't build this house with my students and also dismantle it to build a new one more focused on political analysis and public action. For second semester freshmen, I've come to believe, it's enough to dwell here. Students' development of critical consciousness–much like students' development as writers—cannot be fully achieved in a single semester. When I look through the lenses offered by scholars who study intellectual development, I see that students' development as knowers may be slower than I would have hoped when I first designed the course—but that it cannot be artificially sped up. I hope I can respect the work students are doing, stay with their losses, and celebrate their transformations with them, and I hope I can develop the patience and foresight to think about community-based writing as an ongoing process in which my course is just the first step.

Impact on Faculty

As faculty, we are usually so focused on the impact of our practices on our students that we rarely reflect on our own changing perspectives—both personally and professionally. We have been grateful for this opportunity to reflect and share our thoughts with one another. This process has confirmed for us that what we ask of our students—engagement with community and sustained conversation about that engagement—is indeed transformative.

After only one year of experience with service-learning, Laurie Kaplan writes, "What I found was that service is the practicum or the reality that brings together so many of the essays that I choose to teach. My involvement with this project has allowed me to meld theory and practice in such a way as to make my courses and the Honors Program in general a unified whole. This experience has solidified my feeling that service to others should simply be part of a person's life. The more a person has—and the students in the Honors Program have plenty—the more a person should give back."

Joan Burton reflects, "I know that becoming actively involved in community service will have long term effects on how I live my life, professionally and personally. I suspect the same is true for students. As part of my research agenda, I plan to trace the outcomes for students and community members who participate in projects sponsored by agencies where my students are placed. Once I would have used a qualitative model of research that attempts to replicate quantitative research in its search for what Carol Stack has called 'the singularity of truth.' As a result of my experience with service-learning combined with reading the most recent literature on standpoint theories and field research (summarized in Denzin, 1997), I have shifted to a qualitative model that attempts to authentically capture reality as it is experienced by those I would once have called 'subjects.' In other words, I plan to use a methodology that includes students and community members as active partners in each stage of the research process. I have also re-examined my philosophy of teaching and begun a long-term process of dramatically changing the methods I use to accomplish my goals in the classroom. Specifically, I've replaced the 'student as passive, empty vessel' or 'banking model' of teaching with an approach that defines learning as a reciprocal process and that engages students directly in defining and implementing the goals of the course. Giving up much of the control of the classroom involves risks and uncertainties for teachers and students. I am finding that the initial discomfort and the time commitment involved in making these changes is overcome by the enthusiasm for learning and the sense of agency that result.

Perhaps the most surprising personal outcome of   service-learning is my discovery of a whole new world beyond the academic community that I previously saw as peripheral to my daily life. Through volunteering my time to community agencies, I've observed the contribution made by those whose work directly affects the quality of living for individuals and minimizes the impact of institutions that reinforce structural inequities at the local, neighborhood, national, and international levels. I've become acutely aware of how significant the ideas of 'community' and 'service' are to all our lives and to our future. Somehow it never occurred to me that my share of the benefits of service-learning would have such a significant impact on my work and my life."

Kay Munns notes appreciatively, "The value of this approach is that I am able to accomplish something I have always wanted: to make my regular work on a daily basis serve not only the immediate needs of the students and the college but also to make some modest contribution to the larger society that sustains us. Too often political science has taken the approach that we, as political scientists, must remain neutral and objective as we approach problems in the larger society, that we should produce knowledge for its own sake. I have never really accepted that position. I have always believed that political science, and the other social sciences as well, should be engaged in the larger community, to try to ameliorate human suffering, as Richard Rorty says. This course and my survey research group are very satisfying to me as a human being, political scientist, teacher and researcher as I try to engage the larger community as I use the resources made available to me by the College to help those who are helping others. This has been a profoundly satisfying experience for me."

Finally, Barbara Roswell concludes, "Like many of my colleagues, I have found that my involvement with service-learning has re-invigorated both my teaching and my scholarship. Some of this is a result of the very active and thoughtful communities of service-learning professionals and scholars with whom I work – across disciplines here at my own school, within the larger Baltimore area, and in various disciplinary organizations. It is within the professional conversations about service-learning that I now find the energy, curiosity, political consciousness and deep interest in and respect for students as learners that first drew me to the field of composition two decades ago."

Like many other faculty who teach at liberal arts colleges and are committed to social justice, over the years I have often questioned my professional choices and sought ways to connect my research and teaching with my political commitments and beliefs. Community-based learning, I have found, changes my role dramatically, as students themselves raise questions about inequality and as the situations they confront compel them to seek explanations and solutions. Instead of experiencing a "split" between the mandates of the curriculum and "extra-curricular" commitments that render one or the other marginal, students, faculty, and ultimately the institution itself re-envisions academic expertise as a way to leverage our capacity to create change. While individual faculty, I think, are often aware of how they are transformed by participation in service-learning, this impact on the institution is more subtle and gradual. Nevertheless, faculty (and students) who meet regularly with community partners and think substantively about community needs and capacities bring different perspectives not only to their classrooms but also to the many formal and informal interactions that weave the fabric of an academic community. It is this more subtle, institutional transformation that I ultimately find most exciting."

FUTURE DIRECTIONS: WHERE WE STILL NEED TO GO

Out of our distinct experiences, a shared vision for the future emerges. Simply put, we would like to see service-learning become a more central part of the Goucher culture, but the challenge remains how to achieve this goal. We are a small campus, and faculty already assume many roles – not only as teachers and researchers but also in advising, committee work and college governance. It would be unfortunate if participation in outreach scholarship were to be perceived as "added on" to faculty responsibilities as one more competing demand. Just as we have begun to understand the many changes needed to make service-learning integral to teaching and learning, we must begin to ask the same of our work as researchers and scholars.

As Joan Burton and Kay Munns have already begun to discover, community collaborations can provide faculty with a venue for conducting innovative research and the community with the opportunity to use research results to meet their needs. Yet, despite the "high profile" recognition of community-based work in several important public settings (for example re-instituting the alumni association community service award and featuring public service initiatives in the alumni magazine), Goucher has yet to explicitly recognize civic engagement as a value in the formal reward structures for faculty. Part of our challenge is to build upon our success with service-learning pedagogy in order to rethink our work as scholars and researchers, as well. Ideally, such a change would take several forms, including revising tenure criteria to encompass "outreach scholarship," considering venues other than peer-reviewed journals as appropriate means through which knowledge can legitimately be made and shared, and instituting conversations about outreach scholarship in orientations for new faculty to signal the importance of this work to the institution. Without these changes, service-learning will continue to reinvigorate mid-career faculty without becoming central to the agendas of junior faculty, short-circuiting its potential to transform the work of the college as a whole.

Some of the challenges lie closer to home. As we have explored the ways to link students' work in the community to the traditional curriculum we teach, each of us has begun to rethink our own relationships to our own training and professionalism, as well. We attend to how knowledge in our fields is made, shared and legitimated, to the self-concepts we have developed as scholars, to commitments to "objectivity," and to the obstacles that definitions of disciplinary expertise may pose for civic engagement. Perhaps one of hardest questions we each ask is how our own disciplines and the assumptions on which they are founded may help to maintain exclusion or inequality and the ways that our expertise builds walls instead of the bridges we seek.

As part of this rethinking, we also hope to do more to honor and nurture our community partners as scholars and producers of knowledge, and to include them more fully in the reflection, research and sharing of knowledge that constitutes our professional lives. We still tend to identify our course objectives and design our syllabi independently, and only then to talk with community leaders about how work with them might "fit in." As our partnerships mature, we intend to more fully involve our community partners in the design and evaluation of our courses and projects. These initiatives take time and require resources on the part of both the college and the community partner. For faculty, it requires courage to break from the norm and run the risks emanating from the uncertainties associated with service-learning as the classroom becomes more permeable to outside forces and pressures. Time, commitment, tolerance for risk—these are all things that have to be developed and encouraged, valued and rewarded, if service-learning is to become an even more integral part of the Goucher curriculum.

Apparent to all of us is how much we can learn from one another. We intend to institutionalize regular meetings to share our ideas and practices and make better use of the various disciplinary perspectives we each bring to the integration of community and classroom. These meetings can enable us to introduce additional faculty to the practice of service-learning while creating a new forum for more general discussions about teaching and learning. We also need to become more deliberate about how we assess the impact of service-learning. We DON'T need to reinvent the wheel. We do, however, need to draw on what we know about cognitive and social development to better understand how to design and sequence service-learning experiences so they have the greatest impact.

Among our challenges, however, is to take the next step and empower students as leaders. We find a distinction between students' interest in providing direct community service (serving meals in a homeless shelter) and their aspiration to leadership roles, such as organizing homeless people for more affordable housing or arguing for particular housing policies before the state legislature or in other public forums. This distinction shouldn't surprise us, however, since we tend to reflect this same dichotomy. We, as faculty, are informed and aware, yet our interventions tend to be private, focusing on improving individual situations more than making systemic changes. Thus, we are not yet modeling for our students the roles we hope they will assume. Perhaps we need to challenge ourselves to consider what we expect of our students, and to try to create conditions in which we too can begin to meet these very high goals.

Students' experience with service-learning has made privilege visible to them, has engaged them in sustained conversations about the responsibilities that come with privilege, and empowered them to begin to address the inequities they see. Put simply, service-learning works to disrupt complacency. This disruption of complacency has been of special value to students who arrive at Goucher somewhat disaffected or directionless. Many students talk about becoming more intentional about their own educations in response to what they see and experience in communities. At the same time, service-learning initiatives have made public service and community-based work compelling for many of our most talented and able students. Service often "lights them up" and sets them on a path toward putting their knowledge, skill and passions to work to help communities to thrive.

We are motivated to confront the challenges ahead of us. A recent example has been a pilot program on leadership and civic engagement initiated by Goucher colleagues in student life, the administration, several faculty, and a Goucher parent actively involved in the community. This pilot pairs selected Goucher students with adult mentors from the planning group, offers them reflective opportunities to explore their current choices and experiences in leadership and civic engagement with an eye towards selecting future experiences that would best develop their skills and talents, and introduces them to community leaders who have made commitments to bettering the world around them. We are about to enter the second year of this pilot, with the hope that it will expand in years to come, providing Goucher students with a leadership/civic engagement thread to intentionally weave throughout their educational experience.

Goucher is perfectly positioned to bring together students, faculty, and community participants to engage in what Sandra Enos (1999, p. 71) has called a "deep dialogue" about community work. Encouraging a commitment to service-learning among our faculty directly addresses our mission as a liberal arts college to educate the whole person in preparation for lifelong learning linked to civic action. Those of us who have already followed this path can testify to the deep satisfactions experienced by all involved.

REFERENCES

Anson, C. (1997). On reflection: The role of logs and journals in service-learning courses. In L. Adler-Kassner, R. Crooks, & A. Watters (Eds.), *Writing the Community: Concepts and Models for Service-Learning in Composition* (pp. 167-180). Washington, DC: AAHE/NCTE.

Bray, R. (1992, November 8). "So how did I get here?" *New York Times Magazine*.

Bringle, R.G. & Velo, P.M. (1998). Attributions about misery: A social psychological analysis. In R. Bringle & D. Duffy (Eds.), *With service in mind: Concepts and models for service-learning in psychology* (pp. 51-67). Washington, DC: AAHE.

Denzin, N.K. (1997). Standpoint epistemologies. In N. Denzin, *Interpretive ethnography: Ethnographic practices for the 21st century.* Thousand Oaks, CA: Sage Publications

Enos, S. (1999). A multicultural and critical perspective on teaching through community: A dialogue with Jose Calderon of Pitzer College. In J. Ostrow, G. Hesser, and S. Enos (Eds.), *Cultivating the sociological imagination: Concepts and models for service-learning in sociology.* Washington, DC: American Association for Higher Education.

Herzberg, B. (1994, October). Community service and critical teaching. *College Composition and Communication, 45* (3), 307-19.

Strand, K.J. (1999). Sociology and service-learning: A critical look. In J. Ostrow, G. Hesser, and S. Enos (Eds.), *Cultivating the sociological imagination: concepts and models for service-learning in sociology.* Washington, DC: American Association for Higher Education.

Waterman, A.S. (1997). An overview of service-learning and the role of research and evaluation in service-learning programs. In A.S. Waterman (Ed.), *Service-learning: Applications from the research.* Mahwah, NJ: Lawrence Erlbaum.

CHAPTER 12

SERVICE LEARNING AT KANSAS STATE UNIVERSITY: EDUCATING CITIZENS FOR THE FUTURE

Carol A. Peak
Kansas State University

INTRODUCTION

> *"...the democratic compact: Freedom and responsibility, liberty and duty, that's the deal[1].."* (Gardner, quoted in O'Connell, 1999, p. 126).

John Gardner's words describe the fundamental principles of service learning at Kansas State University. Since its beginning on October 1, 1987, the K-State Community Service Program (CSP) has been based on the belief that citizens *must* be full participants in the communities in which they live and work and that higher education has an important role to play in preparing students for their citizenship responsibility in our democratic system and global society. The learning laboratories are the communities of rural Kansas and the world, communities that are often on the cusp of either continued survival or decline as they struggle to meet the economic, social, and educational needs of their citizens and to maintain a healthy environment. In Kansas, their struggle is reflected in the decline in population and the erosion of quality of life and services for citizens. In the international communities where we serve, meeting the practical needs of sufficient and healthy food and water, safe housing, and education for families and children is a daily challenge. The leadership and experience of community leaders combined with the talent and enthusiasm of K-State students participating in the Community Service Program has produced visible results both for students and for communities.

The stories told by communities and students illustrate the impact of service learning. The rural Kansas community of Sterling, like many small communities, is working hard to enhance the quality of life for all its citizens. An important part of this quality is the vitality of its downtown. The director of the community's Chamber of Commerce, Genifer Campbell, heard about the student and faculty assistance available through the Kansas

---

[1] Gardner, quoted in O'Connell, 1999, p. 126.

State University Community Service Program (CSP). The community visioning sessions, the quality and feasibility of design work, and the involvement of the community made the CSP Team a success. The work of that team has been highlighted by the State of Kansas through the Kansas Mainstreet Program.

Students have also made a difference in Almena, Kansas. In 1994 a CSP Summer Team helped to establish a volunteer newspaper in this small town. Becky Madden says that before the project, community members were feeling isolated but having their own town newspaper brought the people of Almena together. The *Prairie Dog Press* continues to be published and has increased its circulation to 438 subscribers. The students, Becky says, "have helped give the community back a sense of identity."

A sense of optimism was inspired by a 1988 CSP Summer Team in Wallace County. Students helped to renovate the historic livery stable in Weskan to be used as a museum. They catalogued and designed exhibits for the museum and prepared a brochure for a self-guided historic tour of the entire county. Stephanie Brock of Wallace County says, "the work students have done gives us a spurt of new hope that life cannot only survive in rural communities, but can prosper."

Shante Moore, an international relations major, had his first international experience through the Community Service Program. As a member of a team in Paraguay, Shante worked in a small rural community to assist in re-establishing the community market. Following his summer service experience, Shante returned to Paraguay on a Fulbright scholarship and later won a Truman scholarship for his graduate study. He will pursue a career in foreign service. Shante has maintained contact with his host community in Paraguay and now assists the Community Service Program in organizing new projects there.

Since the CSP was founded in 1987, these experiences have been repeated with more than125 community development/service-learning projects in Kansas and international communities, providing more than 150,000 hours of service. In addition,

- over 1,000 students have provided academic assistance as CSP and America Reads tutors;
- more than 1,000 students have participated in course-based service learning experiences;
- 150 faculty have facilitated service projects or adopted service learning as a teaching tool; and
- students and faculty have partnered with community agencies to provide thousands of hours of volunteer service.

SERVICE LEARNING AND THE LAND GRANT MISSION OF KANSAS STATE UNIVERSITY

Kansas State University, founded February 16, 1863 under the Morrill Act, is a comprehensive research, land grant institution serving students and the people of Kansas, and also the nation and the world. K-State is committed to providing the highest quality programs and to creating an institution that is responsive to a rapidly changing world and the aspirations of an increasingly diverse society. As one of the six universities governed by the Kansas Board of Regents, K-State shares responsibilities for developing human potential, expanding knowledge, enriching cultural expression, and extending its expertise to individuals, business, education, and government. To meet these intentions, the institution dedicates itself to providing academic and extracurricular learning experiences that promote and value both excellence and cultural diversity.

All public colleges and universities are accountable to the communities in which they reside. But the land grant institution was created with service in mind. In the mid 1980's, we heard from our rural communities that our traditional commitments to extension and outreach, teaching, and research were not meeting their needs. We realized we were using yesterday's tools to solve today's problems. At the same time, we were hearing that our young people, the students we were educating, were using their college education as an escape from their rural roots and that they cared little about the communities from which they came. They were reportedly self-interested and disconnected from their responsibilities as citizens. It appeared that in spite of our history, our record of service and outreach, the loyalty of thousands of alumni, and our reputation for unequaled research in several areas, a new commitment to our land grant mission was called for.

The response at K-State was to recognize that the demand for change represented an opportunity to enhance our service to communities and students alike. An interdisciplinary group of faculty, with the support of our President and Provost, joined forces to create a new vision of the land grant mission at K-State. This vision engaged the entire university in service to communities rather than isolated departments and programs or selected faculty. Further, it was recognized that our institutional responsibility to our students included not only educating excellent professionals but also educating excellent citizens. We could not fault our students for their disengagement if we did not provide the opportunities for them to participate and demonstrate their concern. Our communities were not benefiting from our greatest resource — student talent and energy — and our university was not including students in our land grant obligation Our renewed commitment is expressed in the December 1991 mission statement that describes our intent to "prepare...students to be informed, productive and responsible citizens who participate actively in advancing cultural, education, economic, scientific, and socio-political undertakings."

The K-State Community Service Program was born out of the recognition that the connection between service and learning is the true expression of our land grant mission. It is this understanding that has lead us to develop a unique model of community service and service learning that draws upon the strengths of the land grant institution, the art and practice of community development, the ethic of service for the common good, and the values of citizenship in a democratic society.

WHAT DO WE MEAN BY SERVICE LEARNING AT K-STATE?

Service learning at K-State directly engages students and faculty in critical and challenging social issues and then facilitates structured reflection to gain a deeper, more substantive understanding of these issues. We have consciously identified a set of values and civic skills that are at the core of our model of service learning.

At K-State, service learning starts with community voice. We do not believe that the university is the keeper of all knowledge and wisdom. Communities are the experts on their needs and on appropriate solutions. It is not our exclusive role to diagnose and prescribe. Our role as a university is to help communities define their core issues, ask the critical questions, collaborate in problem solving and, with the consultation of community leaders, design appropriate solutions.

Service learning at K-State is a reciprocal process. We have as much to learn as we have to teach. But it means we must listen. Communities can inform our teaching and our research. Communities are the best models of citizenship for our students. They are also the best classrooms for demonstrating the relevance of important theories and the reality of critical social, political and economic issues. Community based learning requires that we relinquish control of the delivery of information and thus empower the learning process.

Service learning at K-State emphasizes the duties of citizenship as well as the privileges. We believe educated citizens have a moral and ethical responsibility to be active in community life. The current trend in higher education is to encourage community service as a tool to teach community involvement. While volunteerism is commendable, it is not sufficient for teaching civic and social responsibility. We ask the question "service learning for what?" We are more interested in developing effective and involved citizens for the future than in creating more and better donors. Citizens have a responsibility to seek solutions to the complex social issues we face, not merely address the symptoms through "feel good experiences."

Service learning at K-State goes beyond educating citizens for political participation to engaging citizens in social change. There is no doubt that the political alienation of our citizenry, particularly college students, demands attention. Civically competent citizens are also socially responsible citizens. They are connected to their communities and society at large and they take ownership in critical societal issues. We often illustrate the need for interconnection between the individual and community by using the analogy of "passengers in a first class cabin on the Titanic." It is impossible for responsible citizens to isolate their lives and personal well-being from the social and economic issues around them.

Service learning at K-State also means educating students about working with people who are different from themselves. We live in a diverse world that requires an increasing level of intercultural competence. Knowledge, skills, and behaviors to effectively contribute to a multicultural environment are essential. Scholarship related to defining diversity, transforming curricula, and understanding the relationship between diversity and learning must be part of the educational experience.

Our meaning of service learning is value-laden. The CSP at K-State operates from moral and ethical principles that emphasize justice, equality, tolerance, and integrity. We believe these basic values are fundamental to citizenship in a democratic society. We also assume that there is a set of civic skills at the root of practicing citizenship that can and should be both modeled and taught in higher education institutions.

Communication. Citizen communication involves more than talking. While it is critical for citizens to be able to articulate the issues, they must also be able to listen and understand. Citizens must be willing to actively engage in dialogue and mutual inquiry with diverse populations. Each of these communication skills is essential for meaningful civic conversations.

Civic thinking. Citizens must think both individually and interactively. They must be able to thoughtfully consider a broad spectrum of problems and issues as critical thinkers, applying both logic and reason. At the same time, they must be compassionate thinkers, possessing the ability to empathize with other perspectives and represent those whose voices may not otherwise be heard. It is this type of civic thinking that makes citizens feel connected to the larger world and consider issues in more inclusive ways.

Judgment. Civic judgment is the ability to be comfortable with ambiguity yet still discerning, and to see the simplicity on the other side of complexity. Citizens must be able to define and solve problems by balancing the common interest against the available choices.

Imagination. Citizens need the ability to imagine how the world could be different. From simple improvements in local communities to bold new visions for the world, citizens must be able to envision change. Exposing students to diverse perspectives, personalities, and ideas stimulates this creativity.

Courage to act. Responsible citizens must take action. The other citizenship skills are worthless without it. Citizens become engaged in their communities through informed, active, and sustained participation. They act because they believe they can make a difference.

Design Components

Because we are firmly committed to providing the highest quality experience possible for communities, students, and faculty, service learning activities through the K-State Community Service Program are carefully structured and implemented. Five critical design components provide the framework.

Important Community-Identified Need

The CSP believes that communities are the experts on their needs. Our role is to assist in developing responses and focused action plans. We do not do projects *for* communities or *to* communities but *with* communities.

Adequate Preparation Prior To Service

We go to communities having done our homework. Students and faculty, in partnership with community or agency leaders, study the critical issues, become acquainted with the context, culture and traditions, and clearly identify the work to be done and the goals to be accomplished. Each community is unique and requires an appropriate response that fits its circumstances. The CSP provides preparation for students through a combination of coursework, community research and guidance from faculty.

Meaningful Service/Citizenship

The CSP believes that citizenship is a full-time job requiring not only the use of academic training but involvement in the total life of a community. All citizens, including students serving through the CSP, must apply not only the skills they have gained through their education, but also their life experiences and their commitment to others in order to maintain healthy communities. We want to make a difference--both in the lives of the students who participate and for the communities and agencies who act as hosts for our service learning activities. The work we do must have value. It must contribute to the students' learning and it must directly benefit communities. It must bring students into contact with critical community issues where they can contribute to solutions. It must demonstrate the importance of citizenship participation and democratic principles.

Reflection after Service

The CSP believes that all experiences provide opportunities to learn many valuable lessons--about oneself, about community, and about our democratic society. Structured student reflection following a community service experience, guided by experienced CSP staff and faculty, ensures this learning. We help students make meaning of their service. We want students to go beyond retelling the stories and remembering events to critically analyzing and making connections through structured reflection.

Evaluation

The CSP believes that evaluation by all participants is essential for program improvement and continuation. Each community project offers new opportunities for program improvement. We want to constantly adapt and improve our activities using feedback from host communities and agencies and from students and faculty. We always have more to learn and we insist on the highest quality possible.

The issues facing communities are not easily resolved, especially for rural or low resource communities that face significant barriers. They require interdisciplinary solutions and technical knowledge brought by our students and faculty. Our work stresses building capacity at the local level to empower the community to take charge. Further, we believe that the community focus provides the best citizenship lesson available for our students. Students learn that what they do both on and off the job has important community impacts and those impacts are grounded in connectedness with others in the community.

THE CHALLENGE OF INTEGRATING SERVICE LEARNING AT K-STATE

Although the link between service and learning is now widely accepted at K-State, integration of the ethic and methodology of service learning has not been without challenges. We face many of the typical institutional barriers to change in higher education. Our culture and our reward system have perpetuated disincentives among faculty to community involvement in their teaching and research. And although our university has embraced community service through student organizations and more recently through the introduction of service learning into the curriculum, this service still more often takes the form of charitable volunteerism rather than true service learning. The inclusion of service learning in teaching, research and outreach has been hindered by the scarcity of resources, further impeding full institutionalization of the Community Service Program. However, we value our land grant mission and thanks to the leadership of our President and Provost, we are actively working to encourage new ways of teaching and acting that connect the resources of our campus to our communities. We are also fortunate at our university to have student leadership that has put service at the top of the agenda. Our Student Body Presidents for the past two years have provided leadership on our campus resulting in a resolution endorsing our membership in Campus Compact.

Several ongoing planning initiatives from the Provost's office are encouraging an environment that supports and integrates service learning into teaching and research and are helping to redefine service as scholarship.

- The Provost has been leading a major effort to revise the criteria used in faculty promotion and tenure reviews. The adoption of an individualized, criterion-based approach to using faculty time and talent is a giant step forward in making the best use of our limited resources. The results of this initiative have been a featured presentation in 1999 and 2000 at the American Academy of Higher Education Conference on Faculty Roles and Rewards.
- Through the Center for the Advancement of Teaching and Learning, the Faculty Exchange for Teaching Excellence workshop series has been conducted for the past four years. These workshops have focused on active learning strategies for academic faculty.
- Service learning contributes significantly to five of the strategic themes in he recently completed Strategic Plan for 2000-2005; (1) Support Recruitment, Retention, and Professional Development of High Quality Faculty, (2) Strengthen the Learning and Teaching Environment, (3) Enhance a Diverse and Multicultural Environment, (4) Enhance International Emphases, and (5) Contribute to the State's Economic Development and Environmental Health.

While these are highly visible and successful examples of our commitment to civic learning, it is important to recognize that much of the dedication is less visible. The everyday commitment of our institution is demonstrated by the work of individual faculty members who incorporate community-based learning projects into their courses on a regular basis and provide the technical assistance and consultation to communities, non-profit organizations, and small businesses, the applied research that benefits communities, the educational programs that are designed to meet workforce development needs, and the reorganization of our Cooperative Extension Service to be more flexible and responsive.

SERVICE LEARNING ACTIVITIES AT K-STATE

The Community Service Program was initiated in the first round of community service funding from the Fund for the Improvement of Post Secondary Education (U.S. Dept. of Education). Since its inception, the K-State CSP has carefully designed service learning experiences providing students with preparation through academic course work, meaningful service experience that addresses expressed community needs, and structured reflection following service. Although the CSP is primarily organized to provide students with service learning opportunities, the activities directly involve faculty so that the ultimate outcome is community involvement at multiple levels of the university. At K-State, students and faculty play a major role in project development and program administration. The CSP acts as a facilitator and provides support for project implementation. The CSP not only supports the community service activities of students and organizations throughout campus but is also the home of a full range of service learning activities supported by five academic courses.

CSP Administration and Leadership

The structure of the CSP is designed to promote interdisciplinary interaction and team work among students and faculty. The program is managed by a full-time director reporting directly to the Provost of the university. Although initially organized through the administrative office supporting student services, the move to the Provost's Office in 1994 was a direct result of our growing experience in the field of service learning and the evolution of our internal understanding of our service learning and citizenship education mission. This adminstrative arrangement has also served to promote the interdisciplinary nature of our program activities and has facilitated contact with all academic units of the university.

All CSP activities are administered on a daily basis by our highly skilled Student Coordinators, chosen from participants in our program activities. These students are the true leaders of service learning on our campus. They shoulder high levels of responsibility for program implementation and interact with faculty and community leaders as well as their peers. As they graduate from the university and our program, they train their successors.

Throughout its history, the CSP has promoted shared ownership of the program. During the crucial initiation phase, a group of faculty and the Director met weekly to discuss all aspects of program implementation. Many of these faculty remain active on one or more of the multiple advisory groups for the program. As the CSP has evolved, we continue to rely heavily on the direct involvement and leadership of Deans, Department heads, and faculty in a variety of ways.

- A group of ten faculty and administrators appointed by the Provostmeets monthly with the CSP Director to provide feedback and advice on CSP activities.
- Each year, faculty serve as mentors for students participating in one of the major CSP activities, the Kansas teams. This group of faculty also serves as the advisory group specifically for this service learning activity. During our history, more than eighty faculty representing all academic colleges have served as mentors, many more than once.
- A group of five faculty and administrators serve as the support and advisory group for the International teams. These faculty members meet monthly and are currently assisting in designing and adapting our CSP seminars to be included in at least two academic secondary majors. In addition, they contribute significant time and expertise in support of students selected for service abroad.

CSP Program Activities

The CSP offers a variety of opportunities to incorporate service learning into the education experience at K-State.

Kansas Summer Teams

The Kansas Summer Teams was the core activity of the CSP in its beginning and continues to be the flagship program activity. This model of co-curricular service learning has remained constant throughout the history of the program and has become well-known as a resource for communities in Kansas.

In response to invitations from Kansas communities, the CSP organizes interdisciplinary team of four to five K-State students. Each team of students spends eight weeks during the summer living and working in the host community, applying their academic skills to identified community issues. The project is conceived and designed by the host community in consultation with the CSP staff and K-State faculty. The faculty provide the teams with assistance in preparation, technical expertise regarding the project during the summer, and consultation to the community.

The student team members, chosen from numerous applicants, come from across the entire campus. The members of each team, most of whom are completing their junior year of college, bring a wide variety of skills and experiences to their projects. Among the students who have participated are Truman, Marshall and Rhodes scholars, leaders in student government and campus organizations, and top scholars from many academic disciplines. The student team members are carefully chosen, not only for their talents, but also for their commitment to service. Jennifer Johnson of Winfield, Kansas applied for participation because she wanted "to be a part of an exciting moving force in our battle to preserve the soul of the community." CSP Summer Teams are such a force.

The students work through the spring semester in a three credit hour seminar specifically designed to prepare them for their summer experience and to help them become acquainted with their host communities. Their preparation includes a study of rural community development, discussions of issues specific to each host community, and background research on the requested project. In addition, the students visit their host community and read the community newspaper throughout the semester.

Students live and work in host communities during the summer months, completing the project and participating in the life of the community. Students are housed with families, providing a first-hand opportunity to become involved in community activities. Supervision is provided by an identified community contact, the faculty mentor, and the CSP staff.

The commitment to providing learning experiences for all participants continues through the fall semester following service when students participate in a Reflection Seminar on the K-State campus. Under the guidance of faculty and CSP staff, students explore the impact of their experience at many different levels. The goal is to assist students in recognizing the important social and community issues which underlie projects and to understand the role of citizens in effectively addressing these issues.

Although the CSP has been fielding Kansas Teams since its beginning, the nature of this service learning activity is dynamic and changing. Each group of students is different, each community is unique and the interaction of faculty, student team and community input and involvement presents new challenges constantly. The indicators that are used to define success in a Kansas Team project include:

- A tangible product that demonstrates community ownership in the project and meets the agreed upon community expectations;
- A positive relationship among team members and between team members and the faculty mentor for the team;
- Community involvement of student team members beyond the project and evidence that the students are "known" in the community; and
- Implementation of the project by the community after the student team leaves.

CSP International Teams

The CSP International Teams follow the Kansas Team model in an international setting. In the summer 2001, teams will serve in China, Bosnia, Jordan, Mexico, Paraguay, and Belize. Selected students follow the same preparation, service and reflection plan. Criteria for participation also include demonstrated proficiency in the language of the host country. Host sites are developed through K-State faculty and are asked to commit to a long-term relationship with the CSP. Similar to the Kansas Summer Teams, the students serving in an international setting apply their academic skills as well as their life experiences.

CSP Tutors and American Reads/Counts Tutors.

CSP Tutors and America Reads Tutors provide academic assistance in area schools and non profit organizations. Tutors receive training and participate in ongoing reflection activities. Academic credit is available for CSP Tutors.

Community Action through Learning and Leadership (CALL)

Although the primary function of the CSP is service learning, the program continues to support students and campus organizations in volunteer activities. This need has become more critical as community service has become more visible and as the desire and motivation for participation has increased among students. The CSP maintains a listing of volunteer opportunities for use by students and faculty and provides support for student groups wishing to organize service activities. The Director and student coordinators are frequently invited to speak to classes and student organizations about the benefits of service. Our primary goal on these occasions is to help students learn to organize high quality service projects.

In addition, the Student Coordinator for CALL has provided leadership for the organization of several campus-wide service events.

- The Jon and Ruth Ann Wefald Day of Service (named after our President and his wife who are exemplary leaders for community service) and K-State Community Service Week engage Leadership Studies students and the campus at-large in service to the Manhattan community during the fall semester each year.
- The Martin Luther King Jr. Day of Service brings together community and campus volunteers to serve agencies in the community on the Martin Luther King "A Day On — Not A Day Off" holiday observance during January.
- National Youth Service Day celebrates the contributions of young people throughout the community and places student volunteers with community agencies during National Volunteer Week in April.
- Alternative Spring Breaks are organized to provide K-State students with the opportunity to provide service in a multicultural setting.

Learn and Serve America at K-State.

The CSP was one of five programs funded by the Corporation for National Service in the 1997 Innovative Campus Based Program Awards. Through that project, faculty from K-State and eight partner community colleges have incorporated service learning into their existing courses through mini grants and logistical support from the CSP. In 2000, the CSP received a second award from the Corporation for National Service to build a higher education consortium for service-learning in Kansas. This project is continuing to expand faculty expertise and is developing leadership in service-learning across the state.

Our Learn & Serve America project experience has expanded service learning on our campus and extended our experience to the higher education community in Kansas. Our success in this partnership has created a strong core of committed faculty, administrators and students who believe that service learning is a critical part of higher education. Faculty at these colleges are incorporating service learning into their courses, developing new service learning courses, or establishing organizations to support service learning on their campuses. In addition, our President is leading the formation of the Kansas Campus Compact.

Student and Community Outcomes

The ultimate value of incorporating service learning into higher education must be measured in the outcomes. Data gathered from the K-State CSP indicate that service learning provides positive outcomes for students, faculty and the communities served.

Student Outcomes

Expected cognitive and affective outcomes from CSP program activities are outlined in course syllabi and guidelines for faculty involvement. They include:

- Developing an awareness and appreciation for the principles of service learning;
- Learning the ethics and principles of community development;
- Developing cultural awareness and sensitivity and cross cultural communication skills;
- Understanding the culture, history and current situation of the host site;
- Learning and applying project-specific skills and planning for project work; and
- Learning leadership and interpersonal skills.

Because the activities are academically-based, assessment of student performance and course evaluation by students occurs systematically. In addition, ongoing evaluation activities provide feedback for program improvement, measure affective outcomes and provide rich qualitative data that document program impact.

Students participating in the CSP Kansas and International Team activities are selected through a competitive process that includes criteria such as grade point average and upper level academic standing. It is not surprising that these students perform at a very high level. With few exceptions, they are predisposed to participate in service and are highly motivated.

Students participating in service learning in academic classes through the CSP represent the more general student population at K-State These students complete pre- and post- service surveys assessing the impact of the service learning experience on their attitudes toward community involvement, and their understanding of community issues. Outcomes from this survey are consistent with those of Astin and Sax (p. 255), Giles and Eyler and the RAND Corporation report for the Corporation for National Service that document positive impact on students' academic development, life skill development, and sense of civic responsibility. The CSP post test showed an increase from 54% to 64% of students surveyed who believed becoming involved in a program to improve their community was important and an increase from 17% to 41% of students who believed community involvement and volunteering was essential.

Reflective judgment analysis, adapted by Giles and Eyler from the earlier work of King and Kitchener (1985/1996) for use as a service learning reflection tool, is used with the CSP International teams as a reflection tool and a measurement of intellectual development of student participants. Prior to the service experience, students are asked to respond to an unstructured problem or key social issue by addressing a series of questions designed to reveal their ability for complex problem solving. Following the service experience, the assignment is repeated. Comparing the students' performance to the prototypic Descriptions of Beliefs and Reasoning Patterns assesses their advancement in cognitive development. CSP students who have participated in international service experience consistently show advances in their ability for complex problem solving and in their integrated understanding of multidimensional social issues.

CSP evaluation activities include focus groups and personal interviews with K-State and community college faculty to provide feedback for program improvement and to assess the impact of the service experience on students, communities and faculty. The data show positive support for service learning among participating faculty but also point to the need for continued support and faculty development activities. Faculty also expressed a need for stronger emphasis on the importance of service.

Community Benefits and Outcomes

Host communities provide evaluative feedback through personal interviews with key community leaders and written surveys. In addition, the CSP staff and faculty mentors receive ongoing comment through frequent contact and site visits to host communities. Our Kansas communities report many significant benefits resulting from the summer service learning projects.

Relevant Projects. Because the CSP addresses needs that the community itself identifies as being important, projects represent significant accomplishments for the community. The host community selection process requires documentation of broad based community support for the project and conformance with long-term community goals.

Quality. Based upon the results of the past fourteen years, we estimate that communities receive a minimum 1,200 hours of direct service during the eight weeks they host the student team. The synergy and motivation of high caliber students working as a team combined with the experience and expertise of the program staff and K-State faculty result in high quality work for communities.

Ownership of the Project. By involving the community in the design and implementation of the project, the CSP fosters a sense of community ownership in the development project. In addition, the host community is asked to organize an advisory committee that advises the team throughout the project and leads implementation after the students have completed their part of the project. In many cases, this process results in increased community capacity and the development of new community based leadership.

Tangible Results. The CSP helps to bridge the gap between ideas and action. Host communities and projects are selected not merely to have students involved in a planning process but based on the feasibility of project implementation. Further, many projects continue to provide long-term benefits to the community by strengthening local capacity for continued community development. Further, communities have reported that "spin-off" projects frequently result from CSP involvement. We often see unanticipated outcomes several years after a team project or a community may request a follow-up team to assist with further implementation or new ideas that develop.

Personal Benefits. Families who have hosted team members in their homes often develop strong bonds with the students. For many students, life in a Kansas community is a unique and special life experience. Students have reported experiences such as seeing wheat in the field for the first time, learning new recreational activities, participating in the county fair, or playing and coaching softball, to name a few. Many lifelong friendships are established. For example, recently the CSP learned that a student serving on a 1988 team in Washington, KS is still writing regularly to his host family. Results such as these may not be measurable, but they provide important insight into the benefits of this program to both students and communities.

Empowerment. Among the intangible but very important benefits communities receive is empowerment. Excitement about the project spreads, a sense of community identity is strengthened, and new learning opportunities arise. In this way, CSP projects help communities build its capacity to address its needs.

The Future of Rural Communities. The past success and continued expansion of the program provides ample evidence of the willingness and desire of college students to respond to the needs of communities. One participant, Tandy Trost, returned from her CSP experience in WaKeeney eager to know how she could redesign her major to emphasize community development as a career. She is now employed as an Extension Agent in North Central Kansas. Clearly, the partnerships formed between young people and community leaders through our program will be a valuable resource for the future of rural Kansas.

THE FUTURE OF SERVICE LEARNING AT K-STATE

The vision for service learning at K-State is ambitious and positive. Under the leadership of President Jon Wefald and Provost James Coffman, faculty and administrators are supporting new initiatives and creative strategies to expand and institutionalize service learning. There is a significant commitment to engage the entire campus in building closer connections with the communities we serve. Two exemplary programs are partnering with the CSP to lead a project that will embed civic learning in the curriculum. During the next year, the CSP, Leadership Studies and Programs, and American Ethnic Studies will collaborate on the development of a secondary major in Leadership and Community Service. This program will complement the existing Leadership minor and its service learning component and will serve as the academic home for the CSP.

Even with our long and successful history, significant barriers in institutionalizing service learning exist at K-State. Many of the issues we face are persistant and pervasive in higher education, i.e. faculty reward structures, funding issues, questions about academic rigor, and misunderstanding of service learning. These challenges are addressed not only within the institution but through the network of universities facing similar challenges. Our membership in Campus Compact will be a major resource for information and faculty development in these areas.

Although we share many issues with other institutions, two challenges unique to our environment and circumstances deserve special mention. K-State is a major public institution with an enrollment of approximately 22,000 students located in a community of 45,000. Our students have a great deal of desire and a range of motivations to be involved in service and volunteerism in a community that is overwhelmed with volunteers wishing to do good work. Further, this small community, while not isolated, does not face many of the pressing social and economic issues with the same intensity as larger urban areas. Our students who are taught the ethic of social responsibility become frustrated by the lack of opportunity for them to take action near the campus. And for many of these students, rural service learning and volunteerism lacks the magnetism and excitement, and even romanticized self sacrifice often portrayed in the news media. Placing students from a large university in meaningful service experiences in a small town calls for a great deal of education, a broad definition of service, and a cooperative and encouraging community.

A second unique challenge to institutionalizing service learning at K-State is the successful history of the CSP itself. As our program has evolved and demonstrated high productivity and success, the expectation of the university has been to continue that successful model. We have enjoyed a good record of extramural support and we are known to provide exceptional learning experiences for students. However, in many ways our success and our long history have become barriers as well. There is resistance against changing what has operated successfully for fourteen years. And generating new excitement among our faculty and administration becomes more challenging with each year.

Service learning can transform institutions of higher education into energized, exciting learning environments that are fully utilizing resources to prepare students for civic responsibility. At K-State we are fully committed to that goal. We are working to transform our university to create a flexible and responsive institution for students, faculty and communities with service learning as a central component of this effort. The integration of teaching, research and outreach with service learning and university/community partnerships will result in a truly "engaged" university that more effectively meets the needs of communities and prepares students to be the productive and participating citizens essential in a democratic system and our global society.

REFERENCES

Astin, A. W. & Sax, L. J. (1988). How undergraduates are affected by service participation. *Journal of College Student Development, 39*(3), 255.

Eyler, J., Giles, D., Lynch, C., & Gray, C. (October, 1997). Reflection skills workshop. Paper presented at the annual conference of the National Society for Experiential Education, Kansas City.

Giles, D. E. & Eyler, J. (1999). *Where is the learning in service learning.* San Francisco: Jossey Bass.

Grace, B.. (2001). *Ethical leadership In pursuit of the common good.* Seattle, WA: Center for Ethical Leadership.

Gray, M. J., et. al. (1999). *Combining service and learning in higher education: Evaluation of the Learn and Service America, Higher Education Program.* Santa Monica, CA: RAND. (MR-998-EDU).

Kitchener, K. S. & King, P. M. (1985/96). *Reflective judgement scoring manual with examples.*

O'Connell, B. (1999). *Civil society.* Hanover, NH: University Press of New England.

CHAPTER 13

HISTORY OF COMMUNITY COLLEGES

Mark Drummond
Los Angeles Community College District

INTRODUCTION

The idea of placing the lower division general education study in a "junior college" is credited to Henry Tappan, president of the University of Michigan in 1851. Numerous other educators including William Rainey Harper of the University of Chicago and David Starr Jordan of Stanford suggested following a modified European model wherein the universities would offer the higher-order scholarship and "junior college" would offer lower level academic and vocational education. Harper was involved in the formulation of the first public two year college which was opened in 1901 in Joliet, Illinois[1].

The motivation for beginning two-year colleges or "post secondary schools" in California was somewhat different from that in Illinois. California, at that time, was a largely agricultural state with great distances between rural communities and the few state universities. In the early years of the twentieth century the State Legislature passed legislation enabling school districts to offer grades 13 and 14, and thus, the foundation for the California Community College system of today was established.

Early years of post high school study in California mostly centered in coursework that would better prepare students for jobs in local communities. Many years of public and political debate over the "proper" role of the junior college followed, often led by presidents of major public and private universities. By the 1960's, junior colleges had been renamed community colleges and offered a broad spectrum of job related and lower division academic coursework. The tradition of blending job related coursework with practical experience through apprenticeships and cooperative education started in the 1940's and became widespread and commonplace by the 1960's.

---

[1] Eells, W.C. (1941). Present Status of College Terminal Education. Washington, D.C.: American Association of Junior Colleges.

THE SERVICE-LEARNING MISSION IN CALIFORNIA COMMUNITY COLLEGES

Because research is not part of the formal mission of the California Community Colleges, the idea of "community based scholarship" is foreign to these institutions. On the other hand, the reason for calling the institutions "community colleges" stems, in part, from the tradition of local governance and from the important role the institutions play in many aspects of community life.

Volunteer service ranging from help with community cleanup to elder care has long been part of the community college tradition. The blending of coursework with practical experience ranging from carpentry to nursing has also been a key component of community college history. Therefore, the idea of students working in the community for credit or non-credit and having this work coordinated by the institution is not new to California Community Colleges. What is new is an attempt to link community need with courses (both academic and vocational) in a way that makes volunteer or work experience an integral component of a college-level course.

Service-Learning in the California Community College would ideally have these characteristics:

- Some type of field-based work experience linked conceptually to an approved college course offering;
- Coordination between what happens in the field with what is being studied in the linked course;
- A formal structure for tracking and feedback from the field-based work;
- An evaluation component linked to field-based work;
- A symbiotic relationship between the field-based agency or entity and the college offering the Service-Learning experience; and
- Credit or a definite component of a non-credit course dependent upon the outcome of the field-based experience.

Myth versus Reality

The university Service-Learning experience is likely to have a value-laden aspect which links conceptual learning with hands-on experience. This linkage may be present in some community college Service-Learning programs, but most often, the community college experience will have a largely practical aspect making it difficult to find the line between strictly career-based apprenticeship and more "pure" Service-Learning. This blurring of Service-Learning and on-the-job training has been further complicated by the fact that there has been no financial incentive for colleges to mount Service-Learning efforts that would require a coordinating structure to be put in place. The California Community Colleges are funded, on a per-student basis, significantly below the national average. For this reason, colleges have put scarce resources into the classroom and other on-campus needs. Although a minority of colleges in the state have significant community service programs funded through performing arts centers or other notable community-linked agencies, the availability of such funding is the exception rather than the rule. The 2001-2002 State Chancellor's Budget Proposal to the Governor will include funding for Service-Learning enabling up to 40 community college districts to establish pilot programs that would include coordination and oversight of Service-Learning. Unless such funding is provided, Service-Learning will continue to be an often overlooked function in the California Community Colleges.

The Context in California

The founding of Campus Compact in 1985 by the presidents of Brown, Georgetown, and Stanford Universities, together with the president of the Education Commission of the States, signaled and legitimized the call for the full scale involvement of the higher education community in the pursuit of public and community service. The involvement of the president of Stanford University brought heightened attention to the effort in California and the Western States. In 1988, the California Campus Compact was formed and shortly after that, in 1990, the Campus Compact National Center for Community Colleges opened at Mesa Community College located in Phoenix, Arizona. Campus Compact has helped spread the word and develop methodologies to legitimize and integrate Service-Learning into the college curriculum. Early advances were mostly in the domain of private institutions who stressed service as an integral part of their mission.

After nearly a decade of experimentation and implementation of Service-Learning in California's public post secondary institutions, the Governor of California formally called for the inclusion of Service-Learning in the curriculum of the state's public colleges and universities. In a letter to University of California President, Richard C. Atkinson, dated July 15, 1999, Governor Gray Davis said, "I strongly support community service and believe that a service ethic should be taught and reinforced as a lasting value in California". He went on to ask that the three segments of public higher education in California "join him in his call to service."

In February 2000, State Senator Tom Hayden introduced a bill into the legislature (SB 1737) that would create a statewide Service-Learning and Community Service Center for the purpose of administering a grants program to establish Service-Learning and community service centers on the campuses of individual public and private colleges and universities. Although this bill proceeded successfully through the 2000 legislative session, it was not signed into law by the Governor.

However, the fact that the Governor publicly supported the inclusion of Service-Learning in the educational mission of the state's colleges and universities prompted the Chancellor of the California Community Colleges to include in the 2001 budget request a proposed $10 million dollar pilot program that would establish or expand Service-Learning programs in 25-40 campuses. Specifically the proposed budget language states, "Our state continues to face enormous unmet human needs and social challenges including undereducated children, increasing illiteracy, teenage parenting, environmental contamination, homelessness, school dropout, and growing elder care. Access to the privilege of attending the community colleges is made possible for many by our state's tradition of keeping fees low. The California community colleges are charged with the duty of maintaining a tradition of public service as well as teaching. Community service and Service-Learning are activities of extreme importance to the mission of the California community colleges, the student's development of a life-long ethic of service to the community, and the ability of policymakers to find creative and cost-effective solutions, including increased efforts for community and student public service." During the upcoming months of political activity the Governor and Legislature will have an opportunity to press their call for more involvement in Service-Learning by California's community college system.

THE LOS ANGELES COMMUNITY COLLEGE DISTRICT

History

The origins of the Los Angeles Community Colleges are found in the early years of the nineteenth century when schools in the Los Angeles High School District began offering a few post-graduate courses. Although this effort was curtailed during World War I, from 1929 on the junior colleges in Los Angeles grew rapidly. The Los Angeles City Board of Education founded and administered the junior colleges from 1929 to 1969. The formal separation of the junior colleges and the establishment of the renamed Los Angeles Community College District in 1969, made the district one of the last to separate from K-12 systems in the state and made it the largest community college district in the nation today.

Like many other junior colleges across the country the Los Angeles junior colleges expanded their vocational and adult education programs rapidly, leading to heated competition between junior colleges and adult schools. Through the years many attempts have been made to legislate and/or administer the two systems in a way that would reduce duplication of effort. But to a large extent the overlap between adult education, as offered by the K-12 school system, and many offerings of the community college continues to exist with differences largely sorted out by the marketplace.

Demographics

The Los Angeles Community College District is the largest community college district in the country, comprised of [2]:

- 9 colleges and 120,000 students;
- 6 million District residents from the City of Los Angeles plus a number of surrounding communities and un-incorporated areas including East Los Angeles and South-Central Los Angeles;
- 10% of all California community college enrollment; and
- 7% of all public undergraduate enrollment in California.

The Los Angeles Community College District's service area is densely urban with similar issues confronting many urban cities across the nation as reflected by the following statistics:

- 18% of the District's residents live below the poverty level in 1990 compared to 11% for Los Angeles County and 13% for the state of California and 13% for the nation[3];
- The median household income and per capita income for Los Angeles residents in 1989 falls below the state median rates at $30,925 and $16,188 respectively[4];
- 38% of the District's residents (in 1990) are foreign born as compared to 22% of California and 8% of U.S. residents respectively; more than half of the District's residents over the age of 18 are not native English speaking; and 19% of residents over the age of 25 possess less than a 9th grade education[5].

The figures above reflect an abundant potential for the students of the Los Angeles Community College District to make a substantial impact on issues confronting urban Los Angeles through Service-Learning activities.

Decentralization

Community colleges throughout California were shaken in their paths toward expansion by the passing of the Jarvis-Gann Initiative known as Proposition 13 on June 6, 1978. Community college funding had been over 80%

---

[2] Los Angeles Community College District (2000). Los Angeles Community Colleges Fact Sheet. Los Angeles, CA: Office of Institutional Research and Information.
[3] Los Angeles Community College District (2000). Los Angeles Community Colleges Fact Sheet. Los Angeles, CA: Office of Institutional Research and Information.
[4] City of Los Angeles, (1999). Poverty Demographics of the City of Los Angeles, Los Angeles Almanac. Los Angeles, CA.
[5] Los Angeles Community Colleges Fact Sheet; Office of Institutional Research and Information

based on local property taxes. Upon the implementation of Proposition 13 this portion of funding dropped to around 10%. The gap was partially filled by emergency state funding but it took many years of financial crisis at the colleges to bring about a patchwork state funding formula that exists to this day. State funding was closely tied to enrollment--so the rules for enrolling students and counting attendance became paramount in the affairs of colleges. The neglect of urban centers and race-based flight to the suburbs further eroded the financial capacity of inner-city community colleges through the 1970's and 1980's. Faced with continuing funding shortfalls and enrollment declines, the Los Angeles Community Colleges regrouped time after time, cutting programs and expenses. Central administration was increasingly ineffective in providing either support or solutions to local college problems-- resulting in a Board action in 1998 that effectively decentralized both academic and administrative operations except those necessary to coordinate funding, programs, and state reporting requirements. Thus, the Los Angeles Community College began a transition from a highly centralized system to a rather loose confederation of colleges each with an independent mission and organizational structure.

Because Service-Learning is an "add on" for California community colleges it was not seriously pursued during the years of financial turmoil that followed Proposition 13. And only one of the nine colleges in the Los Angeles Community College District, Valley College, has pursued a formal Service-Learning component that includes a separate administrative office with coordination and oversight responsibilities, which are also linked to institutional research. The other eight colleges in the district all provide some Service-Learning opportunities for students, which are reported later in this chapter. Of course all nine colleges provide traditional work experience training that, as mentioned previously, is difficult to sort out from Service-Learning given the practical aspect of the community college mission. The difference is that the programs at Valley College are developed using the design components mentioned above resulting in Service-Learning programs that are easier to identity as such.

The District (central administration) role in Service-Learning is primarily focused on leadership aspects. The Chancellor and the President's Cabinet have formally stated that the provision of Service-Learning is a priority for the district. Attempts have been made to link community college Service-Learning programs of the District with those of several local universities that have recognized Service-Learning programs. Although specific funding for Service-Learning programs must be determined through the budgeting process at each college (since college funding is enrollment driven and each college "earns it keep"), there is emphasis in the goal setting process for presidents and other administrators to include Service-Learning as an ingredient of their intentions. The other role that the District plays in the provision of Service-Learning is that of lobbyist to the Governor and Legislature. The Governor has publicly, stated support for Service-Learning programs at all three levels of higher education in the state (community colleges, state universities, and University of California). The Chancellor of the Los Angeles Community College District is an advocate of funding for the programs and for clear definition and evaluation of Service-Learning program outcomes.

Current Service-Learning Activities

Over 4,300 students throughout the Los Angeles Community College District participate in Service-Learning activities. Students are performing community Service-Learning activities in a variety of settings and courses such as "pure volunteerism", course-related fieldwork, practicum, cooperative education, and state- and federal-supported volunteer programs (i.e., Americorps, Welfare Reform, etc.). Because the Los Angeles Community College District is comprised of nine decentralized colleges there is little, if any, similarity across the district in the way Service-Learning activities and programs are administered, implemented, and results reported. This is reflected in the table below, summarizing student and faculty participation in Service-Learning. This is further reflected in the brief descriptions of Service-Learning activities at each of the District's colleges that follows.

College	Volunteerism	Internships/ Cooperative Ed	Total Students	Faculty	Courses	Disciplines And/or Departments (unduplicated)
Pierce	65	26	91	3	6	4
City	20	385	405			19
Valley	200		200	65		29
East	700	156	856			
Trade Tech	296	33	329		21	6
West		115	115			
South-west		1,897	1,897			11
Mission	300	15	315	3	3	3
Harbor	87	33	120	5	5	4
TOTALS	1,668	2,660	4,328	65	21	76

Los Angeles Pierce College

Service-Learning Program. Pierce College currently has a two-part Service-Learning Program. Service-Learning 1 is an in-class, one unit course, which educates students on the importance of responsible community action with an emphasis on the "common good". Service-Learning 2 is a one-unit fieldwork course that engages students in a Service-Learning activity related to their major area of study. Both Service-Learning 1 and 2 are articulated with the California State University system.

The Service-Learning Program at Pierce College is designed to give faculty and students an opportunity to experience Service-Learning by participating in various community service activities related to student and faculty members' field of study. The instructor and the student collaborate to design the responsibilities of each person and organization involved and match the Service-Learning experience and service needs through a process that recognizes how the experience is tied to the students' and instructors' academic curriculum.

One Service-Learning opportunity as part of the Service-Learning 2 course has been made possible through the Teacher and Reading Development Partnership Grant. Pierce college students participating in this program provide tutoring to local K-6 school students in the Los Angeles Unified School District. In conjunction with the tutoring experience, in-class curriculum includes examining issues in education, campus protocol, report laws, the need for teachers, and state-of-the-art reading instructional techniques.

Los Angeles City College (LA City College)

Union Rescue Mission Program. In partnership with the University of Southern California (USC) Dental School, both LA City College and USC dental students volunteer their services to residents of the Union Rescue Mission in downtown Los Angeles. Each LA City College dental student is required to complete internships in dental offices and work six unpaid hours per week for the last two semesters of their program. This program provides approximately twenty-four students with both practical work and direct clinical experiences.

Hollywood Beautification Team. Under this program, LA City College is providing approximately 20 interns to work on a variety of projects including environment, cinema, and art projects. LA City College provides students with tutors in the environmental curriculum that has been developed by the Hollywood Beautification Team with students in local elementary and middle schools. LA City College is also providing art students to work on the school mural project. Six Hollywood Beautification staff artists teach art workshops in selected Los Angeles Unified School District schools and then implement a mural project. High school youth are employed, college level interns assist the artists or have their own projects. Currently the Adams Middle School mural is under construction, and art students from Occidental College, UCLA, East Los Angeles Community College, and LA City College students are working as unpaid interns. LA City College students in turn receive 1-4 units credit in the cooperative education program for participating in the program.

The Hollywood Team Community Project. A project funded by a grant from the California Wellness Foundation under the direction of the Children's Hospital and Unite LA. The Hollywood Team Community Project partners with LA City College to establish mentoring between academically achieving college students and high school students. LA City College students from varying academic disciplines are given cooperative education credits based on the number of hours of participation.

Community Tutoring. Students enrolled in Child Development children's literature courses or tutor training, offered as part of the Learning Skills Department, provide tutoring to elementary and middle school youth during the summer. The tutoring experience is provided through a community partnership with the Cahuenga Branch Library and focuses on instilling a love for reading in youth.

Applied Office Practice. Approximately 80 students meet requirements for this Service-Learning course by completing three hours of practical work in offices on or off campus. This course is required of all students completing a certificate in Computer Office Application Technologies. Students earn two units of credit.

Cooperative Education. Under this program approximately 280 students may receive 1-4 units of credit a semester for paid or volunteer work experience within nineteen disciplines such as: child development, english, math, computer technology, music, political science, business, psychology, sociology, education, and law to name a few.

Los Angeles Valley College (Valley College)

In two short years the Service-Learning program at Valley College has grown to include more than 250 students, 65 faculty, 29 academic departments, and 107 non-profit agencies. The following are a few examples of the Service-Learning programs at Valley College.

Student Success. In response to President Clinton's America Reads Initiative, tutors from the Early Childhood Education classes work individually with children and in groups focusing on improving reading skills and enhancing self-esteem at 13 elementary schools in the San Fernando Valley.

Los Angeles Police Department Jeopardy Program. Students enrolled in Administration of Justice courses volunteer their time to support a gang prevention/intervention program for students aged 8 to 17 identified by local schools, social, and law enforcement agencies as needing extra help. Valley College Service-Learning students tutor youth within their own areas of expertise, help them complete their homework, and jointly participate in extra-curricular activities such as sports, crafts, drama, cooking, computers, dance, and story-telling.

Junior Achievement. Accounting 2 students teach elementary students basic business and economics concepts through age-appropriate curricula provided by Junior Achievement.

Building Up. Through this program, Valley College students serve as academic mentors at local elementary and middle schools participating in Building Up Los Angeles, San Fernando Valley, and in the HOSTS (Help One Student to Succeed) pull-out reading program. Students provide one-on-one tutoring to youth who have been identified as needing extra help with reading skills. This program also provides tutoring and homework assistance after school.

Gene Autry Museum. Valley College students volunteer time in the Hands-On Discovery Gallery at the Gene Autry Museum. Students assist elementary school children in the gallery with creative, hands-on learning experiences combined with factual knowledge and interpretation of museum artifacts. In addition, students assist Autry Museum research staff with the organization of library collections in order to make them readily available for patrons.

East Los Angeles College

Although the East Los Angeles College has no formal Service-Learning Program, there are three Service-Learning related activities transpiring with 856 students participating. These activities are described below.

Courses with Service-Learning Components. Approximately 447 Child Development, Administration of Justice, and Psychology students are assigned to work at community agencies, complete and community service project, and work in a community mental health facility respectively.

Cooperative Education. Under this program approximately 156 students may receive 1 credit for work experience at community service agencies within the following disciplines: child development, administration of justice, law, accounting, and office administration.

Volunteer Activities. Over 253 students participate in volunteer activities organized by 21 chartered Associated Student Union clubs at East Los Angeles College.

Los Angeles Trade Technical College (Trade Tech)

Los Angeles Trade Technical College has been formally participating in Service-Learning activities for many years. The college orientation to the trades area creates a natural opportunity for students to learn and serve. Over 371 students participate in internships or cooperative education activities and 296 students in volunteer activities through enrolling in 21 Service-Learning related courses. The following are examples of Service-Learning activities at Trade Tech.

Operation School Bell. Fashion Design instructor, Joyce Gale, was inspired to visit Operation School Bell after reading an article in the Los Angeles Times that described the operation. Many Los Angeles Unified School District students do not attend school because of a lack of clothing. Therefore, volunteers collect clothing for the Operation School Bell "store" which is distributed through a "Back to School" giveaway. As such, over 200 students design and donate 300 dresses to the program.

Christmas Dinner Party. Three instructors and 40 students donated their time to assist with the venue and to prepare and serve food at a holiday dinner for more than 500 school-aged emancipated youth (wards of the court due to a irreconcilable family circumstances).

Habitat for Humanity. Each semester approximately 30 students in carpentry programs volunteer in building homes for low-income families. In addition, 30 to 40 students from the Culinary Department coordinate food donations and prepare meals for Habitat volunteers.

Santa's Workshop. Approximately 25 students in the carpentry program built a "Santa's Workshop" for a local orthopedic hospital.

West Los Angeles College

Service-Learning activities at West Los Angeles College have been limited to two programs, the Americorps/Vista Literacy Project and the Los Angeles County Child Care Training Project. Both projects are administered through the Workforce Development Center at the college and both projects award cash grants for the completion of volunteer hours and course work in childcare. Over 115 students participate in these programs annually.

Los Angeles Southwest College

Students are performing community Service-Learning in a variety of settings and courses at Los Angeles Southwest College. The Service-Learning activities are identified as fieldwork, practicum, and cooperative education. An estimated 1,897 students participate in these activities within various disciplines including: administration of justice, business administration, child development, journalism, nursing, physics, accounting, law, office administration, economics, and real estate. Currently there are no volunteer-related activities formally arranged by the college for students.

Los Angeles Mission College (Mission College)

Los Angeles Mission College, during the fall semester 2000, initiated a minimal Service-Learning initiative. Over 240 students from 8 political science classes volunteered as part of the course work for the presidential elections and voter registration. In addition, 15 students enrolled in Co-Operative Education completed internships at a local high school in collaboration with the Liaison Citizen Program and Unite LA. And 60 students from the business department volunteer in the community preparing tax returns for senior citizens.

Mission College plans to implement additional Service-Learning programs in the coming academic year including tutoring youth in elementary and middle schools in collaboration with California State University at Northridge and the Gear-Up program.

Los Angeles Harbor College (Harbor College)

SIFE Program. Eighteen students in the SIFE (Students In Free Enter-prise) program participate in national contests involving community projects related to business such as Make a Difference Week, Teach a Child About Business, etc.

Math 230. As part of the course requirements, students make presentations and teach math exercises to local K-12 schools. Approximately 33 students participate in this Service-Learning activity.

Theatre Arts Program. Harbor College students (approximately 15) per-form plays at local schools related to anti-gang and anti-drug campaigns.

In addition, in Spring 2000, students from all disciplines are invited to volunteer for foster youth mentorships and early childhood literacy programs as part of the Americorps Project coordinated through the college's Job De-velopment Center.

Recently, Harbor College was awarded a Title V grant and as a result over $200,000 will be used to start a Service-Learning Center at the college.

Lessons Learned

The history of the Los Angeles Community Colleges is most likely not radically different from the majority of two-year colleges across the country. The initial mission of the colleges was two-fold. Post high school instruction was offered to local residents who were in need of job-related skill training and lower division college instruction was offered to those who--for reasons of distance, finances, or other personal circumstances--were unable to begin their college studies at a four-year institution. Over the years response to community needs brought recreation and "life long learning" opportunities to the community college curriculum. But many of these developments were abruptly interrupted by the passage of Proposition 13 in 1978. Tough financial times for the community colleges in California meant a focus on the primary mission and Service-Learning other than the traditional on-the-job training aspects of vocational education were not a priority.

Awareness of the need to more methodically involve college students in the affairs of the community in an organized and academically linked way was heightened by the national Campus Compact movement. The California Compact was founded in 1988 and is currently housed on the campus of San Francisco State University. It is telling that all 20 of the California State Uni-versities belong, seven of the nine campuses of the University of California belong, and only 8 of the 107 California Community Colleges are currently members of the California Compact. This could be attributed to the fact that Campus Compact was originally focused on private colleges and universities and that both private and public four-year schools are more likely to have funding sources for community services. Although it seems ironic that the colleges with "community" in their name have not been funded for community service this is, indeed, the case in California.

Because of the close articulation with the four-year institutions and the growing awareness in the national educational community of the importance of Service-Learning as a component of the educational experience, it is likely there will be significant growth of Service-Learning within community colleges in the near future. In California, community colleges enroll more than five times the total number of students in the State University and University of California systems. Therefore, the opportunity for broad-based Service-Learning is much greater within the community college system than elsewhere.

The obstacles to growth for Service-Learning continue to be lack of specific funding and lack of priority within faculties and administrations. Community college leadership will need to fill the awareness gap about Service-Learning (what it is; how it works; why it is important) so that the priority of Service-Learning programs will be heightened. Because California community colleges are highly organized and work conditions are determined through collective bargaining, it will also be necessary for leadership to make necessary accommodations to faculty contracts to recognize Service-Learning activities as components of faculty workload in a way that will reward desired activity and program growth.

The somewhat blurred distinctions between Service-Learning and career-based, on-the-job training should not hamper efforts to advance Service-Learning efforts at the community college. Once a statement of criteria for Service-Learning programs is agreed upon and faculty contracts are made to recognize this as legitimate work with workload credit, then it should not really matter which side of the "work experience" line an activity seems to fall on. Lucky for community colleges the research component of evaluation for tenure and retention is absent.

While the four year institutions must balance the need to engage faculty in Service-Learning with the need to require legitimate research accepted by peers, this is not necessary at the community colleges and the faculty contract is the only hurdle to full recognition of Service-Learning-related faculty work.

The most obvious lesson learned at the Los Angeles Community Colleges is that without pressure from District and college leaders, and without seed funding and the willingness to engage organized labor in the Service-Learning discussion, not much will happen. These issues are being rapidly addressed in Los Angeles and it is likely that in the near future Service-Learning will become a notable and key component to the teaching-learning experience in all of the District's nine colleges to a much greater extent than is presently the case.

CHAPTER 14

FULFILLING OUR MISSION: SERVICE-LEARNING AT MIAMI-DADE COMMUNITY COLLEGE

Eduardo J. Padrón
Miami-Dade Community College

"We [higher education] educate a large proportion of the citizens who bother to vote, not to mention most of the politicians, journalists, and news commentators. We also educate all the school administrators and teachers, who in turn educate everyone at the pre-college level. And we do much to shape the pre-college curriculum through what we require of our college applicants. In short, not only have we helped create the problems that plague American democracy, but we are also in a position to begin doing something about them. If higher education doesn't start giving citizenship and democracy much greater priority, who will?"[1]

OUR COMMITMENT TO PRESERVING DEMOCRACY

If you were to ask what Miami-Dade Community College does, I would reply that our fundamental purpose is to preserve democracy. We make it possible for thousands of people to gain a college education, people who would otherwise be excluded from higher education, and their education makes it possible for them to become active, committed, and productive citizens. Miami-Dade Community College maintains an open door policy to all who want to further their education, buttressed by a firm belief in every student's right to succeed. We believe that we are the "people's college," and that we play a vital role in preserving our American way of life, our democracy, and the individual visions of freedom that our country's name evokes for so many. We believe that every single individual who wants to attend college should have the opportunity to do so, and we couple that with a commitment to providing them the guidance and structure they need to not only attend but to also succeed.

If one has any doubt that America remains a place seen by many throughout the world as "the place," we invite you to sit in on one of our classes where 15 countries are represented in a class of 30 students. Come

---

[1] Alexander Astin, professor and director of the Higher Education Research Institute at UCLA on the unparalleled power higher education has to strengthen American Democracy *(The Chronicle of Higher Education*, October 1995).

and hear these students describe their personal dreams for the future or listen to their stories of family sacrifice that make it possible for them to be here studying at our American college. Freedom and democracy take on a very different meaning when we are confronted with the realities presented by stories such as these. In short, we take our responsibility for "preserving democracy" very seriously, and this may partially explain the development of service-learning over the last six years. This chapter will provide an overview of how Miami-Dade Community College developed one of the largest and most successful service-learning programs in the nation — including sharing our lessons learned, challenges, and successes so that others may build upon our experience.

History and Philosophical Underpinnings

M-DCC is a large, multi-campus, urban community college with six campuses, more than 130,000 students (credit and non-credit), and nearly 800 full-time faculty members. Miami-Dade County provides a rich and diverse setting for the college. More than fifty distinct ethnic groups can be found in the county, and the campuses range from the urban Medical Center Campus that specializes in health career education to the Homestead Campus — a rural campus in far south Miami-Dade County. The sizes of the campuses range from several thousand to more than fifty thousand students. The student body is diverse (84 percent minority), almost 70 percent attend on a part-time basis, and approximately 80 percent of incoming freshman must take at least one remedial course. The challenges facing our faculty members and students are many. However, M-DCC is known as an institution of higher education committed to innovative teaching with a high priority placed on student learning. In short, M-DCC believes in doing what's right to further the education of its students.

Six years ago service-learning was relatively unknown and undeveloped at M-DCC. Although individual faculty members at Miami-Dade Community College had used community service experiences to enhance their courses for more than twenty years without calling it service-learning, these efforts were not the norm and occurred with little fanfare and without the benefit of a supportive infrastructure. This began to dramatically change in 1994 when the college formally initiated a service-learning program. Starting with just a handful of faculty, students, and community partners, we have, over the last six years, created an internally-funded, college-wide infrastructure that includes three comprehensive "Centers for Community Involvement," a district director, three campus coordinators, faculty coordinators, part-time coordinators, 12 community service Federal Work Study student assistants, student ambassadors, more than 150 community partners, thousands of students and hundreds of faculty, and myriad other community engagement projects. In fact, during this period, more than 200 M-DCC faculty have utilized service-learning, involving more than 13,000 students in course-related service projects. These students have contributed more than 280,000 hours of service to approximately 500 agencies in South Florida. It has been a truly amazing journey that mirrors the growth and acceptance of service-learning on a national level.

This journey began when M-DCC sent a team to a Campus Compact Service-Learning Institute at Brown University in the summer of 1994. The institute, facilitated by leaders of the service-learning movement from around the nation, inspired the M-DCC team's desire and commitment to make service-learning part of the college. Upon their return, they worked with college leaders to prepare and submit a three-year grant to the Corporation for National Service designed to help the college build a sustainable service-learning program. This grant was one of 65 funded by the Corporation for 1994-1997. When this first three-year cycle of grant funding ended, M-DCC received another three-year grant from the Corporation that ended in August 2000. This support from the Corporation for National Service, coupled with significant cash and in-kind college resources, helped M-DCC build a foundation for service-learning.

The first challenge M-DCC faced was to define what we meant by service-learning. Our *Faculty Guide to Service-Learning*, defines service-learning as "...the process of integrating volunteer community service combined with active guided reflection into the curriculum to enhance and enrich student learning of course material." The faculty member uses service as the vehicle for students to reach their academic objectives by integrating teaching/learning objectives with community needs. We also made a conscious decision to focus on three areas as we developed our program. First, service-learning demands sound academically anchored partnerships. The nature of the partnership between the college and any community agency must be based on a shared commitment to the student's education. Second, service-learning requires that the service assignment be driven by community needs. It is essential for community agencies to identify the needs of their constituents and the service opportunities for students. Third, service-learning must include a faculty-led reflection component. It is essential that the faculty member develop the skills necessary to teach students to harvest the learning available through their service experience. In fact, the most important aspect of a service-learning course is the reflection component.

Reflection has been defined as the intentional, systematic processing of the service experience to accomplish rational harmony. Rational harmony is the result of the individual cognitive development of each student. The developmental psychologist William Perry labels the acquisition of new information either "assimilation" or "accommodation." He purports that assimilation occurs when one simply places new information into his or her knowledge base without processing it. The information does not result in any change in the individual's thinking or actions. On the other hand, accommodation requires the operation of consciously processing new information to fit into one's present thinking. This almost always results in individual change. Without this process, we run the risk of the student never truly learning from the experience. In short, true cognitive development and learning occur only when accommodation takes place, and reflection greatly enhances the probability for this to happen.

In fact, since community service experiences often produce conflicting emotions and cognitive dissonance in our students, faculty members are presented with rich opportunities to foster student learning. Rogers (1980) writes, "If a person's attitudes toward, reactions to, and feelings about the challenge s/he has experienced are facilitated with support, feedback, and integration, then the probability of achieving accommodation is increased." The key is the support the student receives which integrates the experience into the course constructs. With the faculty member's help, each student begins to realize the benefits of service-learning as he or she resolves internal conflicts regarding the personal and community issues brought out by the service-learning experience. Furthermore, the student begins to comprehend his or her place in the context of community responsibility. For as Silcox (1995) writes, "Meaningful service is not about doing good to someone, it is about the dignity and growth of the giver and receiver." To sum up, M-DCC requires an active involvement in the learning process from faculty, student, and community members as we connect real-life issues with course theory and context.

DESCRIPTION OF M-DCC'S PROGRAM

Figure 1 shows the organizational structure of M-DCC's Center for Community Involvement. The Center oversees all service-learning and America Reads activities, and coordinates myriad community outreach initiatives. The Center for Community Involvement is housed in the Academic Affairs side of the college with the academic deans providing primary direction and support. Each of our three largest campuses has a Center for Community Involvement that is staffed by a full-time professional staff member and a host of part-time employees. These Centers provide outreach to M-DCC's other three campuses so that all six campuses are involved in service-learning, America Reads, and other Center activities. Some of the key service-learning activities of these Centers include:

- *Faculty development and support*: the role of the Center is to recruit, train, and support faculty. The Center offers regular workshops and follow-up sessions for faculty (service-learning 101, reflection techniques, service-learning and civic responsibility, faculty discussion sessions, etc.), and handles all logistics related to service-learning — class presentations, agency partnerships, student placements and monitoring, problem solving, recognition (certificates and thank you letters), data gathering, reporting, and evaluation. In essence, the role of the Center is to take care of the many logistics associated with service-learning so that faculty can focus their energies on connecting students' service experiences with course content.

- *Faculty leadership.* Our Academic Deans each provide a small stipend to a "Service-learning Faculty Coordinator." This faculty member serves as an advocate of service-learning with other faculty and administration, guards academic integrity by helping faculty develop and implement service-learning in their classes, and serves as an advisor to the Center.

- *Agency partnerships.* The Center builds and maintains partnerships with approximately 150 community agencies that serve as "approved service-learning placements" for M-DCC students. Detailed information about these agencies and the service-learning opportunities they offer are maintained in a listing that is updated and disseminated each semester. In order to be included in this list of approved agency placements, the contact person must attend a 2.5 hour agency supervisor workshop and complete a "Letter of Understanding." The Center also visits agencies, contacts them regularly concerning student status, helps them solve problems they encounter (i.e., a student who is not showing up), evaluates their satisfaction, and invites agency partners on campus each term for a Service-Learning Fair.

- *Program coordination.* In addition to the College-wide Director and a full-time Coordinator, each Center is also staffed by a part-time campus coordinator and a number of Community Service Federal Work Study (FWS) student assistants. The Center coordinates every aspect of service-learning to ensure efficient and effective operation. These activities range from preparing the agency lists, to distributing and collecting student forms (application, placement confirmation, hour log, and evaluation questionnaire), to maintaining a database of all student and faculty involvement, to sending thank you letters and certificates, to counseling students about which agency to choose, and many other activities.

- *Forums on Civic Responsibility.* Each semester the Center organizes several campus-wide Forums on Civic Responsibility that bring students and faculty together to examine the meaning of civic responsibility and how it relates to service-learning and their role as citizens in a democratic society. We have found this to be a very effective means of more purposefully fostering this essential goal of service-learning.

- *Taste of Service events.* Each semester the Center organizes several college-wide service projects that provide faculty and staff the opportunity to enjoy the fellowship and goodwill that comes from service. Taste of Service events are held on a Saturday morning and include lunch and a group reflection session. Habitat for Humanity, coastal cleanups, and nursing home visits are examples of the kinds of projects selected.

- *Student Ambassadors.* Students who excel in service-learning are given the opportunity to apply to be student ambassadors. These students volunteer several hours a week helping coordinate service-learning activities and providing direct support to faculty and students. For example, ambassadors make class presentations, call students to check-in, present at workshops, and help advocate for service-learning on their campus. Each student receives a $250 stipend for their efforts.

FROM UNFAMILIARITY TO A FULLY FUNDED COLLEGE-WIDE PROGRAM—KEY COMPONENTS & LESSONS LEARNED

So how did Miami-Dade Community College move from no service-learning program at all in 1994 to a sustained, comprehensive college-wide infrastructure that supports hundreds of faculty and thousands of students each year? Some of the most significant factors that led to our success are described below.

- *Administrative Support and Leadership*: Obviously, the approval and encouragement of the college administration are critical for an initiative of this type to succeed. From the beginning, the college provided significant cash and in-kind resources to support service-learning, including money to hire program coordinators, space to establish the Centers, and encouragement to forge ahead.
- *Support from the Corporation for National Service*: This support, beginning in 1994 gave us the opportunity to experiment and the impetus to strategically work to create an institutionalized service-learning program. Corporation support also connected M-DCC to the national service-learning movement and all the experience and resources it had to offer.
- *Support from Campus Compact and the American Association of Community Colleges (AACC)*: Campus Compact, from the beginning of our program, has provided a national voice, encouragement, resources, and powerful advocacy for the service-learning movement. They also have regularly hosted service-learning conferences and workshops that helped create a cadre of service-learning experts at M-DCC. AACC has also been an invaluable resource for M-DCC's service-learning efforts by very effectively advocating for service-learning in community colleges and by working tirelessly to demonstrate service-learning's effectiveness and by disseminating a host of resource materials.
- *Visionary leadership from a core of committed faculty and administrators*: Success often results when a small group of committed individuals set their minds on a goal and work to make their dream a reality. The original M-DCC team that went to the Campus Compact Service-Learning Institute in 1994 included a dynamic administrator and a highly-respected faculty member who returned to the

college and dedicated themselves and their talents to making service-learning a part of the college—grant writing, faculty recruitment and training, advocacy, strategic planning—they did it all.

Since our formal program began in 1994, some 13,000 student and 200 faculty participants later, we have learned a great deal about developing and sustaining service-learning at an institution of higher education. Some of the most important of these lessons include the following:

- *Set and maintain standards* – clearly differentiate service-learning from volunteerism and internships and emphasize academic rigor—academic credit for demonstrated learning, not for hours of service provided—faculty must very purposefully and rigorously use reflective assignments to guide and assess learning,
- *Reflection, reflection, reflection* – without reflection, there is no service-learning, when reflection is understood and utilized, service-learning is successful,
- *Faculty coordinator/leadership* – faculty listen to other faculty — having a respected, knowledgeable faculty member to champion service-learning is invaluable in recruiting and supporting others,
- *Faculty training/workshops/support* – faculty need training in the pedagogy of service-learning so they can understand what it is and how to use it effectively, and they need support to handle the logistics of placing and monitoring students in service-learning projects,
- *Customer service* – the Service-Learning Center must provide outstanding customer service to all stakeholders to be successful—faculty, students, and agency partners alike,
- *Infrastructure is key* – in order for service-learning to become a widely utilized teaching strategy, there must be space and staff allocated to coordinate and administer the program,
- *Student leadership/student ambassadors* – there is nothing more powerful than student voices; utilize students as leaders, coordinators, and advocates for service-learning,
- *Utilize Community Service FWS to help coordinate program* – 7% of all Federal Work Study funds must be utilized for "community service" — coordinating a college's service-learning program is an approved use for these students. Student assistants can handle much of the logistics involved with placing and supporting service-learners,
- *Document and evaluate* – gather data on all program activities to demonstrate accomplishments and to constantly improve program,
- *Quality vs. quantity* – it is more effective to start small and maintain program quality than to grow too quickly,
- *Market, celebrate, and recognize* – say thanks to all program participants for their hard work and let college administrators and the

community know the excellent services being provided,

- *Hold mandatory agency workshops* – agency supervisors generally are unfamiliar with service-learning and require training to ensure that they help students both serve and learn,
- *Foster support of administration* – administrative support is required to make service-learning work. Administrators need to be consulted and involved from the beginning.

CHALLENGES

Certainly, there have been and continue to be challenges associated with building and sustaining a service-learning program. Helping faculty understand the service-learning pedagogy and the concept of reflective teaching takes much hard work and constant support. Managing the complex logistics and workload of a service-learning program can be labor intensive. Maintaining partnerships with large numbers of community agencies is difficult because of the high turnover among volunteer coordinators. Each semester a significant number of our service-learning contacts change, making our regular agency workshops and placement list revisions very important. Another challenge is finding resources to fund the program in an age of competing demands and limited funding. At Miami-Dade Community College we have worked hard to overcome challenges like these to the greatest extent possible, and our program continues to evolve and improve as we gain even more experience and expertise.

CONCLUSIONS

Miami-Dade Community College is proud of our commitment to service-learning and of the fact that we are part of an extremely important national educational movement that has been proven effective and is here to stay. Alexander Astin's challenge to higher education to introduce a renewed focus on democracy and citizenship is one that must be acted upon. In South Florida, and certainly in many communities around the nation, we are facing a worrisome decline in civic participation. There is less of a sense of common identity, less commitment to a collective vision that is centered in civic or political purposes, and our communities are faced with unprecedented challenges. Higher education is uniquely positioned to effectively and significantly respond to our society's need for civic and democratic renewal—and we have an obligation to do so. Fulfilling this obligation is in our own best interests, as well as the best interests of our students and of the society that supports us.

As with almost every higher education institution in this country, M-DCC's mission statement and goals prominently mention producing productive citizens and serving the community, yet too often not enough is done to bring these goals to life. Our students need to be ready and able to take up lives of informed citizenship. They should have an understanding of the idea of public good and a sustained desire to work toward achieving common ground and the common good. We know that a combination of practical and theoretical knowledge enhances the learning of students, and we know that our institution—our faculty, students, staff, and resources—has tremendous capacity to help build stronger communities. Service learning is an invaluable strategy that helps us bring life to our mission and goals. It also moves us along the path of being a truly engaged campus—one that builds and maintains genuine, on-going, meaningful partnerships with our community.

Service-learning at Miami-Dade Community College is but one of the examples of how the college is committed to its students and community. It does, however, provide the most striking example of M-DCC's commitment to make a difference in the lives of our students and community by focusing on the development of civic literacy. In the context of cognitive development theory, higher education is very good at moving students from the stage of dualism where knowledge is perceived as either white or black to that of relativism where varying opinions and points of view are acknowledged. We in higher education have become quite adept at challenging students' biases, prejudices, and pre-formed values. We can move students along the cognitive development road to the point that they do acknowledge the existence of many questions. What we have failed to do very well is support the students' movement on to the highest level of cognitive development where they make a moral commitment to values and beliefs which are truly the result of their own thinking and processing of multiple information. The ability to be completely devoted to one's own values and principles and yet demonstrate tolerance of others with differing values only comes with higher order cognitive development, and service-learning provides an extremely effective teaching strategy for this to occur. We at Miami-Dade Community College agree with Martin Luther King, Jr.'s comments in *On Being a Good Neighbor* when he said, "One of the great tragedies of man's long trek along the highway of history has been the limiting of neighborly concern to tribe, race, class, or nation." We are doing everything we can with our service-learning activities to extend our concern beyond the traditional limits of an academic institution.

M-DCC Center for Community Involvement – Organizational Chart

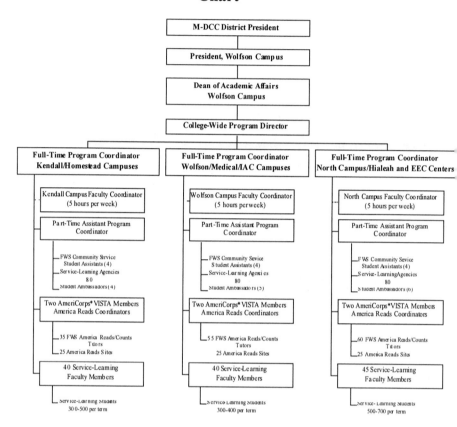

* Faculty Coordinator has no reporting relationship to the program coordinator.
** AmeriCorps*VISTA members work full-time and are paid by the Corporation for National Service.

REFERENCES

Astin, A. (1995). *The Chronicle of Higher Education.*

Perry, W.G. (1970). *Intellectual and Ethical Development in the College Years.* New York, NY: Holt, Rinehart and Winston.

Rodgers, R.F. (1980). Theories underlying student development. *Student Development in Higher Education.* ACPA, Student Personnel Series, *27*, 10-95.

Silcox, H.C. (1995) *Motivational Elements in Service-Learning: Meaningfulness, Recognition, Celebration, and Reflection.* (p. 11). Philadelphia, PA: Brighton.

"On being a good neighbor," by Martin Luther King, Jr. Quoted in Albert, Gail, ed. (1994) *Service-Learning Reader: Reflections and Perspectives on Service.* Raleigh, North Carolina: National Society for Experiential Education, p. 198.

CHAPTER 15

REAL-WORLD, PRACTICAL LEARNING: DEVELOPING A COMPREHENSIVE MODEL IN THE LAND-GRANT TRADITION

Peter McPherson
Diane L. Zimmerman
with Nancy H. Pogel and Robert L. Church
Michigan State University

INTRODUCTION

In *The Engaged Institution*, the Kellogg Commission on the Future of State and Land-Grant Institutions posits that "one of the best ways to prepare students for the challenges life will place before them lies in integrating the community with their academic experiences" (February 1999, p. viii).

In this chapter we make the case that, because of its founding mission and commitment to real-world, practical education, the land-grant university is in a unique position to achieve a renewed sense of civic engagement. The land-grant university has been permeated, from its very founding, with a spirit of commitment to serving the community by engaging its faculty and its students in applied research and service projects. The institution's rich, historical tradition of engagement, diversity, and research power serve as a base for building a comprehensive 21st century model that couples community service with research and teaching in global as well as local communities.

BLENDING RESEARCH AND SERVICE: THE LAND-GRANT MISSION

At the opening convocation on the first day of classes in 1857 at what is now Michigan State University, President Joseph Williams clearly set forth the ideals and mission of what, a few years later under the Morrill Act, would be called the land-grant university. The new educational experiment would go beyond the then-existing liberal studies model of the American university to "the application of modern science to the practical business of life" (Kuhn, 1955, p. 20). The emphasis on the scientific and practical, Williams insisted, would be combined with liberal learning and the duties of citizenship. The new institution was built and sustained by a strong practical vision that saw higher education as useful as well as liberal, excellent as well as equitable and accessible.

That strong practical vision was clearly evident during the early days of the institution. Faculty confirmed what was learned in classrooms and textbooks as they practiced alongside students on the experimental farm and the forests that were the school's first laboratories. Their early research findings had real world applications, such as protecting fruit orchards from insect damage, discovering and publicizing the danger in wallpaper tinted with paris green (arsenic), studying plant germination in experiments that eventually led to hybridizing corn. Much of their research was broadly disseminated in journals that reached farmers across Michigan and beyond.

Mission and Experiential Learning

Students of the contemporary service-learning movement (a subset of experiential learning) assert that, where it is most effective, service learning is tied to the mission and the type of institution (Holland, 1997). Across the numerous studies of service learning, "there is a growing understanding of the importance of institutional mission and infrastructure to the success and sustainability of community service and service-learning" (Holland, 1997, p. 31). Holland points out that Zlotkowski, a key promoter, "believes that institutional service-learning strategies must be distinctive and appropriate to the individual institution and its contexts if the commitment is to be realized and sustained" (Holland, 1995, p. 130).

Interestingly, the conventional wisdom is that the missions of small liberal arts and religious colleges make them most suited to adopting and institutionalizing service-learning activities (Holland, 1995). The literature seems to focus on these smaller institutions because their missions are more specialized and focused. There have been numerous studies of the institutionalization of service learning as it is conducted among the wide diversity of American colleges and universities. None of them has focused specifically on the issues related to the large land-grant university.[1] And yet, the very mis-

---

[1]Barbara Holland used "data from 23 case studies conducted between 1994 and 1997 to prepare a matrix of levels of commitment to service" (Holland, 1997). The matrix identifies four levels of commitment and seven key organizational factors, including leadership. The matrix is a helpful way for an institution to understand its commitment to service learning, particularly when coupled with the institution's understanding of its own mission and role in American higher education. And yet, since these case studies were drawn from across the spectrum of American higher education institutions, no conclusions can be drawn about service learning as implemented at a large, research-intensive, land-grant university of international scope. In another study, Bringle administered a survey that utilized the model of institutional change called Comprehensive Action Plan for Service Learning (CAPSL). Of the 179 respondents, 26 percent identified themselves as "Ph.D. granting," but these are not necessarily public research institutions. Mary Kay Schneider, reporting on a study of 27 colleges and universities conducted by AAHE, Campus Compact, and the National Society for Experiential Education, concluded that "institutional type may drive the focus of the program" (Schneider, 1998), but the data are not correlated with the type or mission of the institution.

sion of such institutions has been to imbue their students with a sense of civic responsibility through a variety of real-world, practical learning experiences. While service learning has, indeed, flourished in small liberal arts and religious colleges, we believe it may have its greatest potential for application in the research-intensive, land-grant university.

Mission and Model at Michigan State University

Starting with the assumption that the mission of an institution drives its model of experiential learning, what might such a model look like at a large university? [2] The comprehensive model would tie service learning both to the teaching and the research functions of faculty who engage in work in (and with) communities.

From its founding in 1855, Michigan State University has modeled this blend of research and service with student learning and civic engagement. As a member of the AAU community of research universities, MSU commits the work of its faculty to generating new knowledge. Faculty members are expected to engage in individual and/or collaborative scholarship of distinction. As a member of the community of land-grant universities, MSU is dedicated to translating knowledge into language and action useful for addressing quality of life and economic competitiveness concerns in community organizations and agencies. Through its Extension service, MSU disseminates information to the local community and throughout the state of Michigan. Engagement cuts across all the work of the university and is the responsibility of the entire university community – faculty, staff, and students – locally, statewide, nationally, and globally.

This integrated model flows out of the mission statement updated and approved by the Board of Trustees in 1982:

> *[Michigan State University] is committed to intellectual leadership and to excellence in both developing new knowledge and conveying that knowledge to its students and to the public. And as a pioneer land-grant institution, Michigan State University strives to discover practical uses for theoretical knowledge, and to speed the diffusion of information to residents of the state, the nation, and the world. In*

---

[2] Others have made the attempt to devise a comprehensive model. Bringle, Games, and Malloy have created a model of intersecting circles to reflect the interaction of the engagement of faculty work in the community with the tripartite mission of the university. The circles are teaching, research, service, and community. Their model places service learning as a form of engagement at the intersection of the circles of teaching, service, and community. The model places participatory action research at the convergence of the circles of research, service, and community (Bringle, Games, Malloy, 1999, p. 5). This is a laudable attempt to visualize the multiple roles of faculty in fulfilling the tripartite mission of the university through engaging communities. Nonetheless, it separates service learning from applied research and, we believe, does not go far enough to reflect integration across the mission.

*fostering both research and its application, this university will con-
tinue to be a catalyst for positive intellectual, social, and technological change.*

This commitment to research for the public good is also reflected in the
teaching mission.

This comprehensive model has become the basis for the institution's
planning to advance its legacy and make the transition into this new century.
After campus-wide conversations, this model was disseminated as "The Guiding Principles." The Guiding Principles promote six areas for accomplishing
the university's goals:

- Improve ACCESS TO QUALITY education and expert knowledge
- Achieve more ACTIVE LEARNING
- Generate new KNOWLEDGE AND SCHOLARSHIP across the mis-
  sion
- Promote PROBLEM SOLVING to address society's needs
- Advance DIVERSITY WITHIN COMMUNITY
- Make PEOPLE MATTER

Although divided into six areas to enable the university to develop implementation steps and better gauge its progress, the Guiding Principles are
meant to be interrelated. The description of "Active Learning" illustrates the
interrelationship of the six principles:

*At MSU, teaching and learning are connected to students' personal
and professional goals and to faculty expertise and scholarship.
Teaching and learning are also relevant to state, national and international concerns.*

While active learning is a shared responsibility of faculty and students, it
is demonstrated not only in the classroom and student life but also in application to community concerns. In a "Final Report Developed by the Implementation Task Group: Involving Students in Outreach," task group members
stated that "involving students in outreach[3] related to curriculum represents
a practical, innovative initiative to operationalize the Guiding Principles of
MSU." The Report calls on the university to "invest . . . resources to effec-

---

[3] MSU continues to use the language of "outreach" as well as "engagement," but
the word does not imply a one-way delivery of expertise. In the MSU model, outreach
is collaborative and reciprocal.

tively expand student involvement in outreach and to integrate this form of active-learning with faculty scholarship" (Michigan State University, 1995, March 2, p. 2).

The comprehensive model, thus, not only exhibits the tripartite mission of the university – research, teaching, and service – but promotes their inter-relationship for the benefit of the students, the faculty, and the community-at-large. This model was clearly stated in 1999 as the "MSU Promise," a re-statement and refocusing of The Guiding Principles. Attention to undergraduate education in this model is among the goals we have set ourselves, as an international, engaged institution, to achieve by our 150th anniversary cele-bration in 2005:

- MSU will offer one of the best undergraduate educations available by providing the advantages of intellectual inquiry at a major research university and practical learning in the land grant tradition.
- MSU will be a great global university serving Michigan and the World.
- MSU will be an exemplary "engaged university."

The following section looks at the various types of experiential learning, discusses their relationship to a broadened, more inclusive model, and cites examples from Michigan State University.

SEEING THE COMPREHENSIVE MODEL IN PRACTICE: EXAMPLES FROM MSU

The advocates of service learning carefully place it under the overall um-brella of active learning, or experiential learning. Under the umbrella they also include such experiences as internships, practica, learning, field experi-ence, clinical service, and student teaching. These advocates maintain, how-ever, that service learning differs from other forms of experiential learning in three ways: (1) it is course and credit-based, (2) it is an organized service activity that meets community needs, and (3) it requires students to reflect on the service activity "in such a way as to gain further understanding of course content, a broader appreciation of the discipline, and an enhanced sense of civic responsibility" (Bringle and Hatcher, 1995, p. 112). Other forms of experiential learning are, they point out, focused on career devel-opment and skill building (Bringle and Hatcher, 1999) "and do not empha-size, either explicitly or tacitly, the importance of service within the community and lessons of civic responsibility" (Bringle and Hatcher, 1996, p. 222).

We contend that in the research university, particularly within the land-grant tradition, many forms of experiential learning carry the benefits that Bringle and Hatcher attribute exclusively to service learning. At MSU en-gagement may be course-based, as defined by Bringle and Hatcher. It may also be program-based, as in internships, practica, and clinical service. It may also be research-based, as in undergraduate involvement in faculty/community research projects. In addition, of course, many students volunteer to do community service activities not connected to their curriculum. As Bringle and Hatcher observe, many forms of experiential learning have an explicit focus on the student's career objectives rather than on civic contribution or commitment. But that does not mean that these experiences do not also involve students in learning about and reflecting on, for example, the elementary teacher's commitment to social good through helping his students exercise their minds or the molecular geneticist's commitment to improving the lives of people through expanding our understanding of the inheritableness of disease. Indeed, the essence of the land-grant tradition is preparing students for careers that serve the public good. Thus, by definition, experiential learning related to one's eventual career promotes both engagement and skill building. We think it is a mistake to confine "service learning" to a single form of course experience that separates it from all the other forms of experiential learning. That separation restricts engagement to a small place in the curriculum when it should, and does, pervade it all.

Michigan State supports numerous examples of various forms of experiential learning. Because of its size and the diversity of its programs, MSU accommodates and encourages multiple variations, from traditional to innovative, from single course or volunteer activity to longer-term field research and community partnerships.

The Service-Learning Center

The Service Learning Center was established as the Office of Volunteer Programs in 1967 and renamed the SLC in 1987 to reflect the integration of active learning through career and civic development. The mission of the SLC is expressed in its motto: "Linking Education with Service and Experience." Approximately 4,000 students took advantage of 1,000 local area opportunities to provide sustained service during the 1999-2000 year. Approximately 5,000 volunteered for one-day service activities. Students report that service experience increases their motivation to learn, to succeed in pursuit of their dreams, and to engage in civic endeavors.

Young Spartans

The Young Spartan Program is a university-community partnership promoting academic achievement and career awareness for students through experiential learning opportunities. The program provides MSU students with hands-on experience in nine K-5 schools in the Lansing School District. Under the guidance of professors from diverse disciplines, students serve as classroom assistants or facilitators, recreation leaders, tutors, foreign language instructors, speech coaches, writing consultants, student council advisers, science club facilitators, pen-pals, and mentors. Several local businesses and local government agencies are partners in this effort.

The Service-Learning Writing Project

The SLWP is a joint endeavor of MSU's College of Arts and Letters, the Department of American Thought and Language, the Service-Learning Center, and the Writing Center. The course unites challenging intellectual content centered on public culture studies, effective writing instruction, and community-based service-learning assignments into an innovative educational experience in academic and field learning. Teams of students are matched with community organizations to prepare written materials for the organization. Based on research they conduct, the students write grant proposals, pamphlets, reports to the Board, policy papers, or other organizational written pieces. The product fulfills a class assignment.

Public Policy Field Experience

One of MSU's 14 colleges, James Madison College provides liberal education in public affairs for undergraduates. A Madison education focuses on the application of knowledge and analysis to public issues, concerns, and events, as well as on theoretical approaches to social science. During the junior or senior year, students spend at least one semester in an internship with an agency, organization, business, or legislative office. The field experience is designed to help students make the transition from classroom learning to professional careers *and* lives of public service. At the end of the experience, students are required to reflect on their experiences in two concurrent courses designed for that purpose.

Residential Initiative on the Study of the Environment

RISE is a residential program for undergraduate students interested in the environment. The residential experience may also be coupled with a Specialization in Environmental Studies (equivalent to a "minor" at other institutions). An important feature of the experience is involvement in community projects. Applying their learning to real life problems, RISE students worked alongside soil scientists to develop plant communities that can be used to stop soil erosion, analyzed records of groundwater wells to map contamination from a local Superfund toxic site, used beetles to save Michigan wetlands from being overwhelmed by invasive purple loosestrife and lobbied state legislators to pass a bill keeping garbage from other states out of Michigan landfills.

Applied Developmental Science Graduate Specialization

ADS@MSU is a cross-departmental, multidisciplinary program designed for graduate students examining the problems of individuals and communities across the life span. The specialization requires 18 credits of course work as well as field research experience. The field research experience is based on the principle that models for community intervention must be tested in the community setting in full collaboration with community partners. Partnerships address community-defined concerns and help solve problems, generate new knowledge, and build community capacity for self-sufficiency. ADS nurtures 15-20 partnerships concurrently, involving over 30 faculty and staff as well as numerous graduate and undergraduate students. One of the projects, Project HELP, trains groups of African-American males as peer educators on health issues that affect the choices, lives, and personal development of young males. This project is an outstanding example of the integrated model: An MSU undergraduate initiated the project through MSU's Summer Research Opportunities for Minority Students; a group of MSU faculty and staff were involved in the planning, research, and implementation phases; an MSU graduate student continues to provide leadership; and young men in Michigan cities are learning leadership skills that should help them to effect changes in attitudes toward drugs and violence among their peers.

The Bailey Scholars Program

The Liberty Hyde Bailey Scholars Program in MSU's College of Agriculture and Natural Resources is a distinctive form of learning community. It is a 21-credit specialization available to all ANR undergraduate students and a learning laboratory for faculty members across the college and beyond. In operation since January 1998, the program has been recognized as a best practice by the National Association of State Universities and Land Grant Colleges and is featured in the John Templeton Foundation's national publication, *Colleges with Character.* In this program, faculty members assume the role of co-learners, not experts, and engage with undergraduate students in collaborative learning. Through dialogue, students and faculty decide what to learn, when, how, and where. Some learning experiences are offered through courses connected with Bailey's 21-credit specialization. Other learning experiences are undertaken as co-curricular opportunities involving in-reach to Michigan State or outreach to society. Organizations and community groups across the state and around the world have asked Bailey Scholars to work with them. For example, they have worked on a peace and reconciliation project in Ireland. Twenty-five community development practitioners from Northern Ireland and the Republic of Ireland attended a two-day conference, held in Derry, Northern Ireland, in late June 1999. The Congregation of Religious of Ireland and the Northern Ireland Community Development Agency co-sponsored the event. The conference was funded by the Office of Peace and Reconciliation, European Union, and was designed and organized by Bailey Scholars Program faculty and students.

University-Community Collaboration to Reduce Woman Battering

Discovering new ways to define, create, and share resources became the theme for the ongoing university-community collaboration to identify and link resources of MSU and its three surrounding counties to improve services for battered women. The project was conceptualized and carried out by faculty and students participating in the Women's Studies Research and Scholarship Initiative. The project involved identifying and mapping MSU resources, especially information, expertise, and connections with relevant community groups and change agents. It also assessed the needs of both university and community for information from and dialogue with each other and developed linkages and a collaborative process. Finally, the project evaluated particular strategies for tapping and coordinating resources of the community and the university to address identified needs. As a result of the project, numerous linkages now exist among university faculty, students, and staff and community agencies, advocates, and service providers. Together they actively work to meet the needs and reduce the incidence of woman battering. These collaborative relationships are facilitating additional research and outreach activities and building permanent mechanisms for university and community communication and cooperation in the area of domestic violence.

As these examples illustrate, student involvement with service and civic engagement occurs at MSU in a wide array of forms – in volunteer community service, course-based service learning, field experiences related to the student's profession or discipline, community-based and applied research studies, or multidisciplinary combinations. Unique to the research-intensive, land-grant university is the blended, comprehensive model that integrates service with teaching and research and encourages students to participate with faculty and community agencies in collaborative, applied scholarship. The experience informs the students' studies, teaches them research skills, helps them value the contribution of the community's knowledge in scholarly work, provides a setting in which they reflect on the work, and imbues in them a sense of civic responsibility.

CHALLENGES FACING THE COMPREHENSIVE MODEL IN THE 21ST CENTURY

In order to move large universities toward this broadened, more inclusive model of real-world, practical learning for the 21st century, higher educators must address a number of challenges: the scope of the community, faculty development, measuring outcomes and impacts, and competing demands on student and faculty time.

The Scope of the Community

Unlike small liberal arts colleges or even large urban universities, research-intensive, land-grant universities are national and international in scope. To what extent can the comprehensive model of civic engagement work in a larger geographic context? There are three issues we need to consider. First, we need to involve our students in the collaborations we are forming among universities and with business and industry to address issues of state and national importance. MSU is working with the other research institutions and businesses in the Michigan Life Sciences Corridor.

Second, the comprehensive model we are describing here relies on the campus environment and its spirit of service and on face-to-face interaction between faculty and students. For that part of our student body that receives our programs through the Internet or by other technologies, we need to design ways not only to build community among the students and faculty but also to encourage and help them to engage in program-based civic activities in their own local communities.

Third, as we open up national and international study opportunities to our campus-based students, we need to ensure that those opportunities incorporate experiential learning activities. MSU has designed two programs to address this issue of engaging students in civic activity when they elect to study overseas or in other parts of the nation.

Michigan Life Sciences Corridor. A statewide research opportunity for students at Michigan's research universities is the result of Michigan's share of the tobacco settlement. In July 1999 Governor John Engler signed legislation creating the Michigan Life Sciences Corridor. The MLSC links MSU, Wayne State University, the University of Michigan, and the Van Andel Institute in Grand Rapids. The goal of the MLSC is to enhance research in the life sciences through collaborative efforts among Michigan universities, research institutions, and industry. The funds are intended for new ventures that are collaborations among colleagues at different institutions as well as in the private sector. Qualifying research and development fields include genomics; animal models and comparative medicine; aging; chronic disease, particularly diabetes; neuroscience; bioengineering; and other areas related to health and the life sciences. We believe this Corridor will provide both faculty and students opportunities for basic and applied research, working in collaboration with communities, industry, and other educators, and will prepare students for leading roles as they come to understand the place of scientific research in sustaining economic competitiveness.

Semester Study in Washington, D.C. To give students a national learning and service experience, MSU's Institute for Public Policy and Social Research implemented, in 1998, an exciting new program that provides an opportunity for students to live and work in our nation's capital while maintaining a full program of academic study. The Semester Study Program in Washington, D.C., includes a policy seminar, a work assignment, and directed study. The work assignment, to which participants devote approximately 32 hours per week, is in one of Washington's wide range of government agencies, not-for-profit organizations, or corporations. Students are expected to interact as entry-level professionals while taking responsibility for assignments such as research, participating in meetings and special events, preparing reports and correspondence, and developing briefings. The directed study component invites analytical as well as creative and visionary thinking. The student is required to compose a paper that integrates coursework and internship experiences. Some students produce a narrative on the conclusions they derived after participating in and studying the policy-making process. Other students elect to use a case study approach that follows a particular bill or policy proposal as it is dealt with by lobbyists, the media, and policy makers. This program is a creative example of the comprehensive model of service and learning, combined with an off-campus, national experience around public policy.

Study Abroad. Internationally, MSU's Study Abroad program has expanded dramatically and is now one of the largest in the country. Last year, 1.3 percent of all students in the U.S. who studied abroad came from Michigan State. We now have over 150 programs in over 60 countries. International academic internships are proving to be an excellent way to apply ideas, concepts, theories, and principles acquired in an academic program to the professional world. MSU's longest running international internship offering, CIC/AESOP internships in Australia, have been administered since 1993. This program offers qualified students an opportunity to blend work experience with specific learning objectives and structured reflection. Placement options are available in Australian national and state parliaments, government agencies, print and electronic mass media, public relations agencies, and criminal justice. One specific internship opportunity in Australia offers undergraduate seniors and graduate students an opportunity to work on a project or field-work assignment with the New South Wales Police Service. Limited placements are also available in banking and finance, marine biology, and wildlife.

The focus of service learning, as currently being practiced, seems to be the residential, undergraduate student. Given that the Internet allows, and globalization requires, that many of our students spend an increasing amount of time away from the main campus, higher educators must consider innovative means of providing opportunities for them to engage in experiential learning that both enhances their career preparation and stimulates their spirit of service.

Faculty Development

Faculty development is of primary importance, of course, if we are to move our institutions toward community engagement. Faculty need to review examples of setting objectives, of implementing service-learning activities in their classrooms and field work in their research, of measuring student outcomes, and the like. In the comprehensive model we are presenting here, faculty development activities must also include help in working in a reciprocal relationship with community and ways of incorporating undergraduate students in research programs.

A 1995 survey of full-time, tenure-track MSU faculty revealed that 85 percent of the 1,000 respondents have been involved in an outreach project of some type. The survey report concluded that the "most important determinant of outreach involvement is having contacts with the community." Two points stood out in the report: (1) faculty value outreach work but need assistance in working with community partners and (2) the greater their involvement with community, the more likely faculty are to engage in outreach (Michigan State University, Fall 1995). One of the advantages of a land-grant institution is its extension service, which hires and trains special-ists who have built-in linkages with communities. With or without an exten-sion service, however, universities can form other community-oriented units that appoint people with experience in the real world – in community-based organizations or government agencies, for example – to accomplish similar functions.

Measuring Outcomes and Impacts

Vernon and Ward point out that the existing literature on service learn-ing focuses on pedagogy – that is, the impact on student learning. They state that "overwhelmingly, the studies related to student impacts report that community service and service-learning lead to positive outcomes for stu-dents, e.g., enhancing career goals, social responsibility, personal efficacy, critical thinking, and problem solving skills, as well as helping students link theory and practice" (Vernon and Ward, 1999, p. 31). While the impact of service learning on student outcomes has been well documented, we continue to need broader studies of the impact of all forms of experiential learning, including the model supported here. And those broader studies must include the community's perspective. As Vernon and Ward point out, the current studies "ignore the community's perspective on service-learning."

Also needed are studies of the impact on the community. Even within the new paradigm of service learning that moves away from a charity model to a collaborative model, we need to measure the impact of faculty and student engagement on social change, or even on changes in behavior, thinking, and acting within a given community organization or agency. The defining of impact measures becomes even more complex in a comprehensive model of service learning that integrates research, teaching, and service. Traditional measures of research (refereed journal articles, for example), of teaching (graduation rates), and of service (numbers of participants) are inadequate for the comprehensive model. This is particularly true if we are to expand the model for the global community in the 21st century. We need to develop measures and studies that demonstrate the benefits to the community, the faculty, and the students.

An example of such impact studies – on the student and on the commu-nity – is demonstrated in the work of a psychology faculty member at MSU who has been involving undergraduates with the families of delinquent youth, abused women and children, and other groups since the mid 70's. The students are involved with a youth and their family referred from the local juvenile court. The students receive intense training prior to their assignment. Once assigned, they work with the youth and their situation 8-10 hours per week while enrolled in two four-credit courses in psychology. They work on family issues, school issues, employment, and free time activities. Although the pro-gram is an elective, it enrolls a majority of psychology majors as well as oth-ers.

Impact on Students in Community Work. The faculty member has conducted many studies on the effect of the work on students. Briefly, students' attitudes towards young people become more positive; their attitudes towards the justice system become more negative; they are more likely to go to graduate school (compared to randomly assigned control students not permitted to enroll in the course); and they are more likely to gain employment in a human service career.

Impact on Delinquent Youth. In terms of benefits to the community, youth handled through the program rather than processed through the court or sent home with a warning are half as likely to be rearrested within the two years following program involvement; youth handled through the program cost the local community approximately 1/4 as much as those handled through the court; youth handled through the program are three times more likely to remain enrolled in school. These observations are based on careful scientifically controlled studies. In addition, there are over 40 articles and two books on the research emanating from this project.

Competing Demands on Student and Faculty Time

A major challenge for a complex institution like the research-intensive, land-grant university is setting priorities for student and faculty time. With the potentials offered by international travel and studies and by technology-enhanced learning and discovery, students and faculty must sort carefully through numerous opportunities. Time is a scarce resource that needs to be carefully apportioned and monitored.

The 21st century student is presented with growing numbers of opportunities for learning: through traditional and mediated course work; through experiential learning activities; through library, laboratory, and community-based research projects; through residential life experiences; and through growing numbers of co-curricular and extra-curricular activities. Many of today's students also hold jobs in order to finance their university studies.

Likewise, expectations on faculty time are increasing, so that the typical workload includes teaching, advising, university committee work, research and dissemination, service to the profession through association activities, as well as public service. As the public demands more direct service from the university and at the same time increases pressure for tenured faculty to teach undergraduates, some synergy of effort is necessary. The challenge is to expand the array of service-learning opportunities while maintaining our commitment to strengthen the university's research and teaching missions.

The advantage of the comprehensive model presented in this chapter is that service learning can be built into the curriculum and into other planned learning experiences. For example, internships – already a requirement in most professional curricula – can be enriched by requiring students to be thoughtful and reflective about those internships, preferably through a written record. Faculty can design community-based or applied research to involve both undergraduate and graduate students, thus augmenting faculty work and giving the student another venue in which to learn. Courses on research methodology can be brought alive by actual practice in a research project. Participating in the presentation of the results of research at conference sessions, or in written artifacts, or at meetings of the local community council, or in interviews with the media, enhances student learning gained through other facets of the curriculum. The challenge is to integrate such experiences into a curriculum that is already full and demanding.

While involving students in their work does provide faculty with additional assistance, doing so comes with its own time demands. Designing research to include students, supervising their work to ensure that there is no harm done in the community and that both the community and the student benefit, and interacting with community organizations and their leaders all take time. Service learning is labor intensive. At the same time, however, community practitioners such as K-12 teachers, social workers, engineers, journalists, and business owners expand the base of "teachers" from whom the students learn, thus augmenting faculty work. In addition, this synergy of teaching-research-service provides a holistic rather than segmented approach to faculty work life. At MSU, we are attempting to assist faculty who wish to engage in this model of experiential learning by hiring academic specialists who are experienced in working with communities, government agencies, and organizations, to help define the concerns of the faculty and the community, attend to details related to logistics, and negotiate finances and contracts.

The momentum is building at MSU as colleagues talk to other colleagues, persuasively explaining the benefits of working with communities and with students as part of their research and teaching. We believe that if we can persuade faculty to carve out time to learn how to undertake this comprehensive model, they will find they are more productive and that both they are their students will find the work to be intrinsically and extrinsically rewarding.

MOVING FORWARD

Although there is work yet to accomplish, particularly in measuring outcomes and impacts, this comprehensive model potentially benefits all participants. Students benefit by applying classroom theory to field research and community service, a process that can carry over to their careers and their community activity. The faculty benefit by expanding their scholarship to include a "scholarship of engagement" and by enriching their teaching as they design active and co-learning experiences for their students. By balancing its tripartite mission, the university recreates the excitement of integrated, multidisciplinary work. And, of course, as a community member, the university benefits from the improvements faculty and student engagement bring about as well as from the enhanced visibility in the community. Finally, the community benefits by collaborating with the university in developing innovative and relevant models of practical, active student learning and in participating in long-term partnerships that serve to strengthen the community and its members. This model, that ties student service learning to the teaching, research, and service functions of the research-intensive, land-grant institution, provides a compelling means by which the public university serves the public and renews its commitment to civic engagement.

As MSU defines its next step forward as a university with practical vision and great purpose, we will continue to evolve the land-grant tradition established in 1855 of integrating practical and theoretical learning. We will combine more current real-world strategies with more conventional textbook and classroom learning experiences. A very substantial portion of the students will participate in real-world service learning as well as research projects with faculty. Critical thinking will be emphasized in problem-based and case-based learning. Additional internships, locally, nationally, and globally, will be added to the curriculum. We will emphasize civility and community to prepare students to be better citizens. Students, staff, and faculty will become even more diverse. The climate among different ethnic groups on campus will be respectful and conducive to a strong learning community. Increased cross-cultural understanding will continue to be a high priority goal. We will remain true to our commitment to access and equity as well as excellence by seeking serious students from all economic backgrounds. We will develop innovative programs for those who are curious and show a genuine interest in learning, who demonstrate leadership in both thinking and doing, and who have a history of active engagement in their communities. In the words of the Kellogg Commission,

> *Close partnerships with the surrounding community help demonstrate that higher education is about important values such as informed citizenship and a sense of responsibility. The newer forms of public scholarship and community-based learning help produce civic-minded graduates who are as well prepared to take up the complex problems of our society as they are to succeed in their careers (February 1999, p. 36).*

REFERENCES

Bringle, R. G., & Hatcher, J. A. (1996, March/April). Implementing service-learning in higher education. *Journal of Higher Education 67*(2), 221-239.

Bringle, R. G., & Hatcher, J. A. (1999, Summer). Reflection in service learning: Making meaning of experience. *Educational HORIZONS,* 179-185.

Bringle, R. G., Games, R., & Malloy, E. A. Eds. (1999). *Colleges and universities as citizens.* Boston: Allyn and Bacon.

Holland, B. (1997, Fall). Analyzing institutional commitment to service: A model of key organizational factors. *Michigan Journal of Community Service Learning,* 30-41.

Kellogg Commission on the Future of State and Land-Grant Universities. (1999, February). *Returning to our roots: The engaged institution.* New York: National Association of State Universities and Land-Grant Colleges.

Michigan State University. (1994). *Framework and guiding principles.* East Lansing: Michigan State University.

Michigan State University. (1995, March 2). *Final report developed by the implementation task group: Involving students in outreach.* East Lansing: Michigan State University.

Michigan State University.(1995, Fall). *Faculty outreach survey.* Unpublished document. East Lansing: Institute for Public Policy and Social Research.

Michigan State University. (1999). *The MSU promise: Focusing the guiding principles.* East Lansing: Michigan State University.

Schneider, M. K. (1998, June). Models of good practice for service-learning programs. *AAHE Bulletin, 50*(10), 9-12.

Vernon, A., & Ward, K. (1999, Fall). Campus and community partnerships: Assessing impacts & strengthening connections. *Michigan Journal of Community Service Learning,* 30-37.

CHAPTER 16

LEARNING TO GIVE: *INCORPORATING THE PRACTICES OF LEADERSHIP AND PHILANTHROPY IN CIVIC EDUCATION AT A METROPOLITAN UNIVERSITY*

Barbara A. Holland[1]
James C. Votruba[2]
Northern Kentucky University

INTRODUCTION

The growing national discussion about renewing the civic mission of higher education has two broad themes: enhancing the role of the university as citizen and creating a college learning experience that prepares students for citizenship. For many universities, especially those that identify with a metropolitan mission, these two themes can become intertwined because of the deep and multi-dimensional relationship between the work of the campus and the characteristics of the region. Consider, for example, that one of the most central and defining characteristics of any metropolitan university is that almost all its students come from the immediate region served by the campus and, most remain in the area after graduation. Thus, by thinking intentionally about the role of civic education in the learning experiences of their students, metropolitan universities have an extraordinary opportunity to have an impact on the social fabric and civic capacity of the region.

As in other academic planning decisions, the choice of a design for civic education must be a reflection of institutional mission and culture as well as community characteristics and traditions. Northern Kentucky University (NKU) is a 12,000 student campus serving a metropolitan population of nearly two million. We are the fastest growing university in Kentucky serving the fastest growing metropolitan area. When the Uni-

---

[1] From 1998-2000, Barbara A. Holland was Associate Provost for Strategic Planning and Outreach at NKU. She is now Senior Scholar at Indiana University-Purdue University Indianapolis and Visiting Director of the Office of University Partnerships for the US Department of Housing and Urban Development.

[2] James C. Votruba is the president of Northern Kentucky University.

versity began anew to explore civic issues of the Greater Cincinnati Metropolitan Area in 1997-98, we came to understand a particular trait of our region that strongly shapes our civic education strategy. In order to respond to public concern about ensuring there will be a new, future generation of committed community leaders for this region, we designed a strategy that will help students understand, through direct practice and involvement, the roles of civic leaders and philanthropists in building successful communities. Not ordinarily a central component of civic education or service learning strategies, the idea of helping students learn about the non-profit sector and the role of philanthropy in community problem-solving caught the imagination of a regional foundation: the Manuel D. and Rhoda Mayerson Foundation. Seeing the possibility of positive impacts on both student learning and civic capacity, the Mayerson Foundation invested in the design and piloting of a curricular model that engages students in a new approach to civic education.

This chapter will describe how NKU, through the "Mayerson Student Philanthropy Project," is creating a model of civic education that is different from many service learning courses. The Project will help prepare our graduates not only to build their careers and to build good lives for themselves and their families, but also to build communities. Unique aspects of the model include giving students real, not imaginary, experiences with philanthropic decision-making, and using project resources so that they have two major impacts: investing in students who then make investments in the community.

THE CIVIC MISSION OF A METROPOLITAN UNIVERSITY

> *Higher education and the larger purposes of American society are inextricably intertwined...A commitment to service as well as teaching and research was never more needed than now...Higher education has more intellectual talent than any other institution in our culture. Today's colleges and universities surely must respond to the challenges that confront society (Boyer, 1994).*

As America has become an intensely urbanized nation and higher education seeks to be more responsive to public needs, universities and colleges located in large urban areas find themselves as early working prototypes of what it means to be an "engaged" institution. All of higher education is exploring strategies for making the knowledge assets of universities more relevant and accessible to society through partnerships that "engage" the university in reciprocal exploration of public issues and purposes (NASULGC, 1999).

For many institutions, this is not new work, though it has never before carried such academic legitimacy and urgency. Universities that think of themselves as urban or metropolitan have long said they are not just located "in" a city, they are "of" the city. Far more than a label of location, "metropolitan" suggests a set of beliefs concerning the social role of the university in the Knowledge Age. Those beliefs emphasize the responsibility of higher education to use its capacity to improve the quality of life, locally and globally, through knowledge relationships. While developing all the academic elements typical of any university, these institutions also demonstrate a commitment to reflect issues and traits of their immediate region through the academic programs they emphasize, the partnerships they cultivate, and the modes and venues through which they make their knowledge assets available in response to community needs and opportunities.

In addition, metropolitan universities strive to model the reciprocal nature of university-community partnerships by recognizing that knowledge is a shared resource, and that knowledge exchanges between campus and the external community must carry mutually beneficial purposes. The community is not a laboratory for academic research, observation or experimentation; the community has its own knowledge assets and expertise that are invaluable in enriching the academic agenda of faculty and students. At NKU, we especially seek to create learning experiences for students that both address community issues and draw student attention to the responsibilities of citizenship in a democratic society.

To capture these more complex tasks that link community goals to higher education responsibilities, academic culture is moving away from the terms *teaching, research and service* and is using the concepts of *learning, discovery, and engagement.* These terms reflect a changing understanding of the shared role academic organizations will play in a high-tech, rapidly changing global economy where knowledge must be shared to ensure individual and collective success and well-being.

Founded in 1968, Northern Kentucky University's history is typical of many metropolitan universities. In our developmental years, we were seen primarily as a valued, but rather generic, institution serving primarily the local high school graduates. The relationship we had with the region was generally positive, but lacked the focus and financial base necessary to illustrate in broad and substantive dimensions the central role of education in regional development and quality of life issues.

With the arrival of a new president in 1997, NKU embarked on an intensive exploration of the meaning of these new knowledge concepts — learning, discovery and engagement — as they might relate to the mission of NKU. Led by the president, a campus team comprised of faculty, staff, students, and community members conducted numerous public meetings as part of a strategic planning process called "Visions, Values, and Voices." Hundreds of citizens of the region, from urban core to rural ex-urban fringe were asked to share their sense of the urgent needs and opportunities of the region, and to explore what the role of NKU might be in addressing those key issues. Through this activity, not only did the campus and community learn more about each other's concerns and condition, but there also developed a stronger, more focused public understanding that NKU was an invaluable asset in planning a bright future for the region.

In addition, we gained a clearer focus of the future of the university that directly pointed to specific directions and strategies for action. The Vision, Values and Voices process inspired NKU to craft a simple, straightforward vision statement that reflects this interactive relationship between the university and the region:

> *Northern Kentucky University will become a preeminent, learner-centered, metropolitan university recognized for its contributions to the intellectual, social, economic, cultural and civic vitality of its region and of the Commonwealth (NKU, 1998).*

Immediately, we embarked on an exploration of what it means to be "learner-centered." On one level, this meant we must ensure that we organize our academic offerings to ensure broad access coupled with the opportunity to succeed. Nearly all of our students are commuters with thirty percent studying part-time in order to balance school with other adult responsibilities. Competition for these students has continued to increase which makes it incumbent upon us to align where, when, and how we offer our curriculum with the needs and preferences of our students. To that end, we have begun to organize ourselves as what we call a "distributed university" with programs available in many locations and through diverse modes of delivery. We believe that, as an industry, higher education is going through a transformation similar to what banking went through thirty years ago when customers were required to bank in one location, during banker's hours, and according to the bank's procedures no matter how inconvenient. Today, customers can conduct a broad range of banking transactions nearly anyplace and anytime. Banks have placed the customer at the center of the enterprise. Universities that hope to thrive in a more intensive competitive environment will do the same.

On another level we realized that being learner-centered meant being more specific about the learning expectations we hold for our students. One of the most central methods for contributing to the vitality of the region is to understand our potential impact on the region through the preparation of thousands of graduates who will live out their lives as residents of our metropolitan area. More than ninety percent of our students come from this region and a similar percentage remain in the region after graduation. Our impact on civic capacity could be enormous. We asked ourselves: What should be the attributes and skills of an NKU graduate so they will have both the capacity and the desire to contribute to building the region's future? How will we be known by the public's experience of the impact of NKU alumni in their communities? As a next step, the campus worked to translate the vision statement into a set of core values, one of which is

> *Public Engagement: We are committed to treating the metropolitan region as an extension of our campus. We will build partnerships throughout the region that both serve the learning needs of the public and enhance the learning opportunities available to our faculty, staff, and students (NKU, 1998).*

Because we wanted the learning objectives for students to reflect the learning needs of the metropolitan region, we drew on the data gathered through the Vision, Values and Voices process. Clearly, the region had evolved quickly since the late 1970s from an economically disadvantaged community into one that entered the 1990s as an economic dynamo with low unemployment and expanding new jobs. What had influenced such a dramatic transition? One of the explanations revealed through community-campus discussions was the central role of a set of self-identified civic leaders — citizens from all sectors of the region who stepped out beyond the work of building their own businesses, careers, and/or families in order to lend leadership to community endeavors and civic decision-making. Overwhelmingly, a message to NKU from the community was this question: "who will be our next generation of civic-minded leaders to guide us into the future?"

We found that citizens of northern Kentucky were experiencing locally the trends we now know to be true across the nation — the growing disengagement of youth with the political process and with civic life. A 1999 survey of college freshmen across the U.S. reported that the percentage of students who believe it is very important or essential for them to influence social issues or to participate in community action programs fell to its lowest level in more than a decade. This was accompanied by declines in factors related to helping others, caring for the environment, or interest in becoming a community leader. Social awareness of attitudes about race also declined. Even among respondents who reported they had engaged in community service, a third said they were not sure they could make a difference (Sax et. al., 2000). These attitudes are reflected in our students as well.

We saw that part of our educational mission must be to try to inspire students to not only explore and understand the responsibilities and skills of citizenship, but to experience their own potential for efficacy through direction action and civic involvement. To inspire the next generation of civic leaders, we believe we must engage students in practicing the work of civic leaders — serving on a board, measuring needs, planning actions, finding funds and other resources. In addition, while we believed this effort might inspire some students to develop a commitment to demonstrating civic leadership, we also hoped it would prepare graduates to at least understand the central role of civic leaders and those who give their time and resources toward community action. In other words, even if some individuals do not take on active leadership roles, they may become supportive advocates and more optimistic participants in political and civic processes.

In 1998, the presidents of the Mayerson Foundation and Northern Kentucky University began discussing the potential of a project designed to give university undergraduates "hands on" experience in inventing in the community. Could such an experience, supervised by a team of instructors from both the campus and the community, help stimulate in the students a greater understanding of and commitment to civic participation? The Mayerson Foundation shares our interest in helping build a future generation of leaders and effective citizens. Through a year of exploratory conversations among campus, community and the foundation, our ideas evolved and we are now embarked on implementation phase of the Mayerson Student Philanthropy Project, described below.

BEYOND SERVICE LEARNING

Our goal was to design a learning experience that would address this need for enhancing student understanding of civic leadership, the role of non-profits and philanthropic organizations, and the relationship of these factors to community capacity and success. Most strategies for promoting civic learning among students focus on community-based learning activities, such as service learning courses, that help students understand links between course work, their chosen profession, and civic life. Edward Zlotkowski says that the goal of service learning is to prepare students to be public problem-solvers (1998). This vision of service learning has two dimensions:

> 1) **Learning** — giving students the experience of translating generalized knowledge and abstract theories into application and direct action (thus promoting fundamental learning of course content); and,
>
> 2) **Community** — helping students "discover the possibility and the importance of simultaneously attending to their needs as individuals and as members of a community. By bringing public work into the very heart of the educational system — i.e., the curriculum — service learning helps students avoid the schizophrenia of private advancement disassociated from public standards and public need" (Zlotkowski, 1998, p. 4).

Thus, service learning has been seen as a tool for building skills of citizenship. The elements of good citizenship can be described as follows.

- Attitudes - "I ought to do."
- Knowledge - "I know what I ought to do and why."
- Skills - "I know how to do."
- Efficacy and self-confidence - "I can do it and it makes a difference."
- Commitment, responsibility, urgency - "I must and will do." (From Giles and Eyler, 1999)

These elements have been translated into a variety of community-based learning experiences for students: extracurricular (volunteer); co-curricular (alternative spring breaks); and course-based (service learning). Service learning, as a distinct pedagogy, is defined as a "course-based, credit-bearing educational experience in which students (a) participate in an organized service activity that meets identified community needs and (b) reflect on the service activity in such a way as to gain further understanding of course content, a broader appreciation of the discipline, and an enhanced sense of civic responsibility" (Bringle & Hatcher, 1995, p. 112).

Service learning courses are a growing element of the learning experience of students at NKU. However, we believed that to meet the local need for building a new generation of leaders and supporters of civic action, we needed an approach that would build on the service-learning model but would go beyond it to engage students more deeply in planning and taking action in the community. Beyond asking students to apply course knowledge toward a community need through a service learning activity, we wanted students to have direct experience of understanding and exploring community needs, analyzing issues, working as a team to plan actions, understanding the resource issues of community-based organizations, and the role of public and private funders. Most of all, we wanted students to have the experience of making tough decisions about investing scarce resources in civic action. This was taking us beyond the most typical interpretations of service-learning. We found ourselves breaking new ground.

To support our exploration of this curricular innovation that might help students practice and master skills relevant to civic responsibility and leadership, the Mayerson Foundation provided a two-year grant of $50,000 each year in 2000-02. As shown below, the curricular design ensures that in each year, $40,000 of the money will be directly invested in community-based organizations, as decided by NKU students.

The Mayerson Student Philanthropy Project — Real Decisions, Real Funds

Our goal was to design a distinctive learning experience that would complement other efforts to prepare students for citizenship through real projects of impact and relevance. We believe that as we expand opportunities for students to develop a sense of civic responsibility, through service learning or other service activities, they will be exploring their individual and collective values regarding the role of volunteerism, leadership, and philanthropy in a democratic society. Community-based organizations, civic leaders, citizen participation, and public-private collaboration have never been more central in addressing the urgent needs of our nation. We sought to create an experience that would prepare students to understand these roles through direct action that imparts an understanding of the responsibilities of community-based organizations and their leaders and members.

After the Mayerson funds were received in January 2000, an open call was made for faculty interested in working as a team to build this course. Faculty response was enthusiastic and a core group of 16 worked through spring and summer 2000 to design the core elements of the course with variations to match up with different departmental learning goals. The faculty who actually teach the class will receive a cash incentive from the Mayerson fund. The proposed model calls for 10 different classes to adopt and pilot the course concepts during the 2000-01 academic year. Faculty will work as a team to design modules, track progress through the year, and recommend improvements as they gain experience. Community members have been invited to participate in the design process and to team teach the courses.

We are creating a curricular model that gives students experience in taking leadership roles in evaluating community needs, soliciting and evaluating competitive funding requests from the community, making decisions about grant awards, making those awards in real dollars, and then evaluating and monitoring the impacts of their decisions. The class focuses on the core concepts of "community investment." Similar to courses in financial investment where students manage a portfolio of investments using real cash, the Mayerson course provides students a real pool of dollars to invest in a community project and/or organization.

In this first phase of design and implementation the course concept is organized both as an independent class and as an integrated module within existing courses that are oriented toward assessing community needs. Faculty believed it essential that the learning goals be integrated wherever possible into required elements of majors or general education so that students would be attracted to enroll. Many faculty also expressed the value they saw in enriching existing courses that contain relevant learning goals similar to the Mayerson Philanthropy Project, and saw this as an enhancement for their students. Our intent is that at least one of the courses offered each year will be an honors course, and the honors course will be an example of creating a new class fully dedicated to the learning goals of the project. The courses vary across the curricular levels; in other words, there will be sections designed for students at the junior and senior levels, but also for students at an earlier stage of study.

The following are the classes being planned for the 2000-01 academic year. All will develop curricular modules in keeping with the Mayerson Project objectives. There are more than 10 classes listed because of high interest among the participating faculty, and we wanted to have backups ready in case some classes don't make enrollment targets or are not able to follow through for some reason:

- Political Science 403 — Public Policy
- Social Work 105 — Community Experience in the Social Services
- Social Work 203 — Social Welfare in Contemporary Society
- Honors 302 — Student Philanthropy: Make a Difference and Invest in Your Community
- Business 306 — Philanthropic Issues and Practical Applications
- Human Services 412 — Leadership Skills
- Human Services 430 — Human Service Administration
- Music/Art/Theater 499 — Philanthropy and the Arts (cross-listed course)
- Nursing 435 — Community Health
- Nursing 441 — Leadership
- Education 646 — Leadership for School-Community Relations

A sample course description for one of these courses is:

Honors 302 — Make a Difference and Invest in Your Community

For more than 6,000 years the power of philanthropy — the desire to help humanity through charitable gifts — has built universities, hospitals and museums; preserved the arts; fed the hungry; housed the homeless and most importantly, made the world a better place. Philanthropy isn't just reserved for the rich, but for anyone interested in serving humanity and making a difference.

This course offers the unique opportunity to be part of an innovative project design to provide students with hands-on experiences in philanthropy and community leadership. Students will explore the non-profit sector, learning not only how it meets the needs of our community, but also how it is governed, operated and funded.

Student participation includes serving on a "community board" which will assess community needs and non-profit organizations, then request and evaluate funding proposals. Students will have the responsibility of actually awarding grant money to a worthy community organization. This chance to make a difference in your community is made possible by a gift to NKU from the Manuel D. and Rhoda Mayerson Foundation.

While these classes illustrate the breadth of courses and faculty linked to the Mayerson learning project in its first year, many other faculty and courses have expressed interest and are seeking to come into the project in the future. For example, so many faculty across departments in the College of Professional Studies are interested that they are initiating discussions to create an interdisciplinary, college-wide course that would encompass the Mayerson Project objectives. Other classes see the Mayerson Philanthropy Project as a different kind of learning resource. The instructor of Sociology 320, Social Research Methods, sees the project as fertile ground for assessment, research, and evaluation projects for her students.

The faculty envision the class as having both common and distinctive elements. Students in each class are convened as a "community board." Each class will cover the following content elements:

- history of non-profit community-based organizations
- techniques for assessing community needs and assets
- non-profit career paths
- the role of civic leaders
- the role of community boards, members, and volunteers
- funding sources for non-profits; the role of government and philanthropy in supporting community action
- grant program design, management, and evaluation
- decision-making in a community setting

These course objectives will be explored through a series of learning experiences that will be guided by NKU faculty in partnership with philanthropic professionals, civic leaders, and non-profit administrators who serve as guest lecturers and co-instructors of each class "board."

Course learning experiences will vary somewhat by the disciplinary home of the course, other relevant goals of the course, and student interests. In general, course activities will include the following experiences for students, their faculty and their community partner/co-teacher:

- Convene students as a "community board" in groups of 15 or fewer
- Identify an area of community need/opportunity about which there is interest from various non-profits, businesses and/or government organizations
- Study the issue in depth; learn about current organizations, projects, activities
- Conduct field visits to assess current conditions, issues, practices, gaps
- Prepare and distribute a request for proposals
- Receive and evaluate proposals
- Make decisions, as a student "community board" about the in-

vestment of $4,000 for each class
- Participate in or design and ensure evaluation of impact of investment decisions
- Maintain individual reflective journals regarding their experience as a member of a "community board" striving to invest in a community issue

Faculty continue to work on strategies to ensure that student "community boards" observe and study the outcomes of their investments (this is discussed further in the Challenges section below). In this pilot effort, faculty propose several approaches for involving students in evaluation activities:

- Some courses will be sequential or are the first of a two-stage course sequence, meaning that in some cases the students who take the Mayerson course in the fall will logically be enrolled in the next sequential course in their major; evaluation can be incorporated into the follow-up course.
- Students in Social Research Methods, Sociology 320, can be assigned as observers/analysts to some or all of the Mayerson courses to coach students on the "community board" regarding assessment and evaluation design; the research students in future semesters would engage in evaluation activities; other research methods classes in other disciplines will join in the future.
- A co-curricular student organization will be created for "alumni" of the Mayerson Philanthropy Project. Students will be encouraged to use the organization as a platform for following the outcomes of their class' investments in the community. The organization may also engage in fund-raising for additional investment projects. It definitely will provide a forum for students to volunteer further to work with community-based organizations.

Challenges and Hopes of the Project

The unveiling of the Mayerson Philanthropy Project has generated an enthusiastic response from students and faculty across the campus, and from the community. Each year, approximately 150 students will engage in deep and direct experience of learning about our region's community challenges and opportunities. Even more important, students will be challenged to make the tough and reasoned choices that real civic leaders and philanthropists face — should they give all their money to one group or divide it among several? Which initiative seems likely to make the most difference? Is it better to invest in an organization with a proven record or in a new organization that is addressing an unmet need? The questions are challenging in every dimension, and will provide the framework students need in order to understand their own commitments, values and goals.

Perhaps the most unique and exciting dimension of the design of this project is that the funds from the Mayerson Foundation will have two direct, measurable, and distinctive impacts. First, the funds help students learn more about themselves and their communities. Second, the funds flow directly through the classes and into community-based organizations in our region to support new and ongoing initiatives. The same dollars will be used two ways to increase the community capacity of our metropolitan area.

As a new, cutting-edge effort a number of challenges are suggested by this project.

Evaluation

The challenge of semester timeframes is daunting. Our learning goals for the course and the reality of the time community work takes to bring fruit tells us it will be difficult to design opportunities for students to be directly engaged in evaluating their own investments. This is a serious challenge that will be a major focus of our pilot courses. Likely, several different strategies will be used, such as the several methods suggested above.

In addition, the design team is thinking about evaluation of the project itself. Does the project have the impact on students for which we hope? Do students achieve the learning objectives as defined? What unexpected outcomes can be identified? The evaluation of course outcomes is more straight-forward since so much work has gone into identifying learning objectives for students and for community and faculty as well. Suggested outcomes include student participation in campus or community volunteer organizations; enrollment in other service learning courses; student intentions regarding career choices or life-long habits of public service; employment of students in community-based organizations; publicity for the course and success in fund raising for additional courses; sustained partnerships between NKU and community-based organizations; the number of sites for service learning, internships, etc. Instruments to assess impact on students regarding social responsibility, awareness of community, commitment to service, and other learning outcomes that already exist in the service learning literature (Driscoll, et. al., 1998) and can be adapted to fit this new project. These methods for assessment also incorporate the perspective of community partners regarding the effect of the course experience on students. In addition, the Northern Kentucky University Mayerson team will engage in continuous assessment of community perception of the effect of the project as a whole on the community.

Rising Expectations and Resources

Faculty and student interest is so high in this early stage, we are already dealing with more courses than the current fund can support. Clearly, NKU leaders and community partners must quickly develop a strategy for identifying sustaining resources to support and expand the program to meet demand and continue the program as it evolves beyond this pilot phase. We believe that the project has great potential for private donor support in the form of endowment.

This need for continuing support includes not only the grant portion of the student learning experience but also the need to support ongoing faculty development. Creating new courses or revising existing courses is labor intensive work for faculty and deserves compensation, especially when the effort is so strongly aligned with institutional mission and strategic priorities. Some faculty are more experienced than others in teaching component elements of this course that focuses on the non-profit sector, leadership and grant-making. Faculty also need access to resource materials, examples of syllabi, and relevant literature to support course design. Mentoring among the faculty participating in this initial group is occurring naturally, and may flourish with a little encouragement. In 2000-01, NKU is also creating and opening a Center for Faculty Development which will include in its charge development activities related to faculty involvement in community engagement.

Turnover

Start up of the project stumbled a bit when several key faculty leading the effort left the institution. As has been shown in other forms of service learning, developing a sufficient core of faculty participants is key to surviving last-minute changes in the availability of particular faculty and their courses. Happily, initial interest at NKU is substantial and we seem to be well-positioned for the first two years of the project. NKU has integrated elements of its vision statement, especially the roles of public engagement and the centrality of being learner-centered, into recruitment announcements. We hope to continually attract faculty, staff, and administrators who resonate to our goals for learning and civic engagement.

Hopes

In addition to these challenges, we have high aspirations for the potential of this project to become a model that will be adopted by other institutions. We hope to find, through our evaluation activities, that we can create a set of course modules and implementation strategies that can be disseminated to other universities and colleges interested in this new variation of the service learning model. Our first endeavors will be to engage other institutions in the Greater Cincinnati Metropolitan region in order to enhance the capacity of our own area communities. Through the national networks of metropolitan universities and other engaged institutions, the lessons we learn through the Mayerson Philanthropy project will also be shared. The Mayerson Foundation also has suggested that a future fund-raising goal might be to build a rotating fund that would assist new institutions in implementing philanthropy courses for their students. Each new institution would raise funds to sustain its own efforts and then extend seed support to institutions that follow in their path.

For any of these fundraising and dissemination ideas to come to fruition, gathering the evidence that the project strategy meets the defined learning objectives for students is critical. We must focus, first and foremost, on monitoring and evaluating our courses as we implement them and using our findings to support continuous improvement and expansion.

The Mayerson Student Philanthropy Project at NKU presents an exciting new variation on the principles and purposes of service learning. Perhaps this is good news, that the service learning movement is maturing sufficiently that new approaches and models are evolving and expanding the potential impacts of service learning on students and communities. It is that dual dimension of impact that is most distinctive of the Mayerson Project — that this curricular endeavor should, in a more direct way than ever — through direct allocation of resources, affect changes in students and in community capacity. Now, there is a return on investment in civic engagement!

REFERENCES

Boyer, E. (1994). Creating the New American College. *The Chronicle of Higher Education*, March 8, p. A48.

Bringle, R. G., & Hatcher, J. A. (1995). A service-learning curriculum for faculty. *Michigan Journal of Community Service Learning, 2*, 112-122.

Driscoll, A. , Gelmon, S. B., Holland, B., & Kerrigan, S. (1998). *Assessing the impacts of service learning: A handbook of strategies and methods.* Portland, OR: Portland State University.

Giles, D.E., Jr., & Eyler, J. (1999). Where's the learning in service-learning? San Francisco: Jossey-Bass.

NASULGC. (1999). Returning to our Roots: The Engaged Institution. Report of the Kellogg Commission on the Future of State and Land-Grant Universities. Washington, DC: National Association of State Universities and Land Grant Colleges.

NKU. (1998). *Strategic Agenda for 2000-2005.* Highland Heights, KY: Northern Kentucky University.

Sax, L.J., Astin, A. W, Korn,W. S., & Mahoney, K. M. (2000). The American Freshman: National Norms for Fall 1999. Los Angeles: UCLA Graduate School of Education & Information Studies.

Zlotkowski, E. (Ed.) (1998). *Successful service-learning programs.* Bolton, MA: Anker Publishing .

CHAPTER 17

PUBLIC SCHOLARSHIP: SERVING TO LEARN

Jeremy Cohen
Penn State University

INTRODUCTION

A set of fundamental axioms occupy center stage at the medley of local and national service learning institutes, workshops and summits that continue, after nearly two decades of germination, to grow in attendance and frequency. Those attending recognize that the cultivation of civic engagement within an environment that nurtures basic research, land grant outreach, disciplinary teaching and learning, and general education is fundamental to the higher education mission. Service learning is an effective incubator for civic engagement. Service learning based scholarship contributes significantly to each of the academy's teaching, research, and service missions, and can facilitate their integration (Astin, Sax, & Avalos, 1999; Cohen, 1994).

Yet back on campus, many of these complimentary objectives compete, not only for resources, but for legitimacy as well. Attempts to integrate research, teaching and service under the rubric of civil society and service learning, although embraced by some, generate perceptions of academic illegitimacy among others. More benignly, Penn State's administrative complexity, mission heterogeneity, and expansive presence — which encompass 80-thousand students and 4,100 faculty at 24 locations spread across diverse rural and urban geographic regions — compound these already complex elements. Even casual observation locates service learning, as a pedagogy for democratic engagement, on the periphery. Why hasn't service learning been embraced with greater enthusiasm at a land grant institution with a mission "To make life better for the people of Pennsylvania, the nation, and the world through integrated programs in teaching, research and public service?"

BARRIERS TO A CURRICULUM FOR CIVIC ENGAGEMENT

Professional considerations play a major role in faculty reluctance to extend further into service learning scholarship. To begin with, little in the way of graduate school preparation for careers in higher education, or in the culture of classroom disciplinary expectations, prepares scholars to explicitly integrate issues of civil education into course syllabi (Cohen, 1997; Kennedy, 1997; Orrill, 1997). Nor can the negative consequences of failure to meet professional scholarly expectations within the research/teaching/service tenure balance be ignored (Fairweather 1995). Untenured faculty who choose teaching and service scholarship over research face significant career consequences. A recent national faculty survey underscores the implications of this academic fact of life. Tenured, full professors, are the least likely among faculty to engage in service learning pedagogies. Those who are not on the tenure track — lecturers, part-time adjuncts and others on contract — are the most likely. "As long as most service activities are being practiced by marginalized faculty, those activities will remain marginalized in academe," the authors conclude (Antonio, Astin, & Crress, 2000, p. 388).

Under current circumstances, mainstream faculty are unlikely to bring service learning into the center. Those who have earned tenure have adapted to the professional expectations of their disciplines — expectations that rarely include teaching for democratic engagement. Among the tenured cohort, the status quo has offered success and limited incentive to stray.

Even so, Penn State faculty recently challenged the teaching status quo in their rewrite of the university's undergraduate general education requirements. Rather than bogging down in a quagmire of *core v. elective* distribution, the faculty breathed life into a student-based learning approach as a fundamental tenet of the university. Now, all general education courses must include several elements of active learning. And, in a research university with an annual freshman class of over five-thousand students at the University Park campus alone, all entering freshmen are expected to take first year seminars limited to 20 or fewer students taught by full-time faculty members. In their inaugural year, the seminars enrolled nine out of ten entering students, a staggering accomplishment at a very large university.

Penn State's general education experience carries implications that bear upon the difficulties of engaging a vast research university faculty in an affirmative program of civic engagement education.

- The shibboleth that tenured faculty are unwilling to undertake major teaching reform is specious.
- Faculty are comfortable when curriculum innovation focuses on scholarship, and ill at ease when academic and student affairs boundaries are crossed. The two year faculty senate committee process from which the first year seminars emerged generated a thoughtful response to the question: What should a first year seminar experience accomplish? Wish-list goals ranged from research technology acquisition, to disciplinary introductions, to life skills courses. Numerous faculty and students believed the seminars should discourage alcohol abuse and tackle other relevant behavioral issues. Many faculty balked, objecting to the notion that scholarship should be replaced by

normative behavioral content. Content decisions finally were left to each academic program and *scholarship* emerged as the common value held among otherwise divergent disciplines.

- The development of keystone educational approaches such as the first year seminar and the active and engaged learning requirements demand a grass roots effort in which faculty are fully vested in the outcome. Once such an initiative is fully underway, it may be naïve to expect close on its heels the commitment of additional resources — either faculty time and energy, or fiscal — focused on yet another fundamental enterprise, such as a curriculum integrating civic engagement through service learning pedagogies.

Other elements effecting the service learning environment at Penn State also are present. Volunteerism, often voiced erroneously as synonymous with service learning, is viewed by many as an issue for student affairs and resident life, not for the academic classroom. Too, volunteerism already plays a significant role at Penn State. Students raise several million dollars toward cancer research annually through a highly publicized dance marathon and more than half of Penn State students recently polled reported participating in community service. Faculty and staff as well join the community yearly for the United Way Day of Caring. There is little demand on campus for still more volunteer opportunities.

Finally, Antonio, Astin & Cress (2000) identified the physical presence of an on-campus service learning center as vital to faculty service learning participation. There is no centralized program of academic service learning support at Penn State. It is worth noting that the university's Schreyer Honors College does have a quarter time service learning director, and the university supports the on-campus AT&T Center for Service Leadership under the auspices of Student Affairs. The AT&T Center focuses primarily on volunteer activities, but is also modestly involved in academic service learning and has been actively involved with the Office of Undergraduate Education and others in the development of Penn State's public scholarship efforts discussed below.

Lacking salience, urgency, and perhaps clarity, service learning remains on the academic margins at Penn State, occasionally punctuated by diminutive offers of faculty support that view it as ancillary to the university's primary mission, scholarship.

Yet, as the observations and examples above suggest, failure to achieve wider integration of civil society, service learning, and research and teaching missions lies neither in a lack of caring, nor in an unwillingness to engage in issues of civic community consequence. The hurdle is instead constructed of a perception of service learning as synonymous with volunteerism, and a disconnect between volunteer work and university scholarship. The need, if our goal is to develop a curriculum of consequence that integrates the theory and practice of higher education with engaged participation in civil society, is a recasting of service enhanced learning within a context of scholarship.

Public Scholarship

A powerful conceptualization and practice called *public scholarship* is emerging and holding fast at Penn State. Rooted in the land grant mission and service learning traditions, *public scholarship* is a highbred that splices several mature higher education goals and practices with the assumptions and implications of recent explications of faculty and student work (Boyer, 1990; Cohen, 1997, 2000; Glassick, Huber, & Maeroff, 1977; Hutchings, 1996; Menges, Weimer, & Associates, 1996; Shulman, 1996, 1997). *Public scholarship* is the scholarly practice of university pursuits, including teaching, research and service, in a manner that contributes to informed engagement in the democratic process. Rather than replacing service learning, the concept of *public scholarship* provides a filter through which to view student and faculty work. *Public scholarship* is a means of conceptually organizing the way we think about the integration of civic participation, research, and general and domain based discovery through teaching and learning. The conduct of *public scholarship* provides a means through which students and faculty can view their work, not as the isolated, self-indulged actions of a campus segregated from society, but as the contributions of scholar-citizens with membership in a larger community.

A review of the rationale for, and the processes and practices of Penn State's program of *public scholarship*, encompasses four elements:

- The conceptual transition from methodology to scholarship;
- The Constitutional lineage of the *public scholarship* mission and the teaching scholarship implications it carries;
- The development of a scholarly *public scholarship* community within the university; and,
- The application of *public scholarship* through a community based collaboration.

From Methodology to Scholarship

Just as statisticians count on precise methodological operations to provide desired outcomes, teachers rely on appropriate methods to develop particular types of learning. Service learning is a pedagogical methodology. Analogous to a chi square in statistics or a particular lab procedure in chemistry, it is employed to accomplish specific tasks. Shulman (1997) describes service learning as a uniquely powerful clinical procedure that enhances liberal arts instruction. Kolb's (1984) experiential learning model underscores the capacity of service learning to generate theory building from concrete experience. Barber (1992) and Ehrlich (1999) focus on the capacity of service learning to engage students in civic and moral learning. Each describes appropriate university objectives. But these worthy goals have been overshadowed in our service learning discussions by an undisciplined use on campus of service learning terminology. Stanton (1987) found conflicting sets of purposes among and within service learning programs and, in the end, little agreement as to whether service learning is at its core a philosophy of education, or a form of experiential learning.

I suggest that too often we have allowed service learning to carry status as an end in itself. Where scholarship requires specificity, we have rested with generalizations. In service learning workshops and symposia and on campus we describe our efforts as *service learning* — too often failing to distinguish between learning *to* serve, and learning *from* service? Do we mean to imply both? The *public scholarship* construct suggests that the answers is, yes. And more. University goals expressed through *public scholarship* encompass the creation of domains of deep learning in a context that treats discovery as a valuable community resource, as well as the purposeful induction of new scholars and their work into the processes of civic community. We have used service learning as shorthand for a variety of scholarly endeavors — the scholarship of civic engagement, the scholarship of general education, the scholarship of discipline based discovery — rather than articulating our explicit educational goals.

Why is this important? One reason is that our in-articulation and our reference to a service learning methodology, rather than to a clearly identifiable scholarship, have contributed to the marginalized placement of the very outcomes service learning methodology is intended to elicit. To clarify this line of thought, I offer two normative observations.

First, as scholars we generally do not seek problems to fit particular methodologies. Instead, we identify a problem and then pursue methods appropriate to solving it. The Penn State adoption of first year seminars — which require significant faculty and administrative resources — did not occur because the application of a curricular methodology (first year seminars) was enticing. Faculty identified problems and goals. Some students were leaving the university in their first year. Some students had only large class experiences. Many students failed to grasp in their freshman year the academic, cultural, and scholarly expectations of the university's academic community. First year seminars took hold as a specific solution to a recognized set of problems. The implication is clear. Faculty have little reason to adapt their courses to service learning methodologies unless they believe that there are pedagogical or curricular problems — problems of scholarship — *and* that service learning is a useful means of addressing those problems.

The likelihood of a Penn State (or any other large research university) service learning problem/solution adoption scenario is even more remote. The problem looks like this. General education theory recognizes the value of interdisciplinary synthesis and problem solving. Teaching scholarship and learning theory provide strong support for the adoption of collaborative and interdisciplinary teaching, cluster courses, and learning communities to address these learning needs. Yet these approaches remain the exception. Why?

Because we often focus on content mastery, rather than on the application of that content. Quite simply, we do not see application as our problem.

One implication of this kind of narrow problem identification is that it is uncommon for faculty to assess individual courses as building blocks within a larger curricular structure (this is less so in disciplinary curriculum, but the norm in general education curriculum). Instead, we make a tautological assumption. I will use my own course as an example. Well educated individuals need familiarity with First Amendment theory and practice. The content of my course is First Amendment theory and practice. Students therefore receive what they need in my course. But absent from this train is a consideration of outcomes. Normative practice tells me that I am responsible for providing an understanding of the First Amendment and not for staying around long enough to know whether my students apply the syllabus readings once they leave my classroom. Simple observation, as well as complex newspaper readership studies (and some would argue as an unobtrusive measure, the quality of candidates for public office), confirm that even after taking courses such as mine, most students have only the shallowest conception of the relation between unfettered speech and democratic practice. They cannot apply what they have *learned*. So long as few faculty identify the dearth of civic engagement among students as a problem relevant to the courses we teach, *or* service learning as a useful means of treating that problem, the adoption of service learning pedagogies will remain infrequent.

Second, faculty accurately perceive that in most instances, professional issues such as tenure and reward are not addressed, at least directly, by pedagogical methodologies. Tenure, promotion, peer status, salary and other rewards are directly linked to traditional measures of scholarly productivity such as refereed publication and conference presentation. As long as service learning is viewed as a methodology, rather than as an element of scholarship, service learning will remain on the margins.

Am I suggesting that service learning is not a scholarly practice or that it does not address important scholarly issues? Far from it. Let me be clear. Service learning is a complex teaching scholarship methodology with the power to contribute forcefully to several university missions.

The message here is that an emerging cohort of Penn State faculty, student affairs professionals and students now view service learning as a valuable methodology within a larger scholarly construct called, *public scholarship*. In doing so, they are explicitly recognizing the primary role of scholarship in the Penn State mission to enable students, faculty and staff to engage in the civic process by contributing to others through *integrated* programs in teaching, research and public service. They are recognizing the necessity of maintaining clear scholarly foundations for their work and in so doing viewing service learning as one of several useful responses to the problem: How can the university best contribute through its teaching, research and public service?

The Public Scholarship Mission

Many scholars, including some of those writing in this volume, point to the mission or duty of universities to educate students for democracy. Where does such a duty originate (Cohen, 2001; Schudson, 1998). Is it an element of scholarship? Does the obligation find meaningful expression beyond the relatively small choir of voices engaged in academic public service? Public scholarship emerges as a rationale response to the intersection of democratic theory and learning theory. The following paragraphs highlight their union.

The American Revolution enabled a sweeping social and political transformation. Radical notions of the relation of individuals to the state that emerged in the Eighteenth Century writing of the European *philosophes* formed the basis of an American Constitution and Bill of Rights in which the nation would be *citizen centered*, rather than *government centered.* Drawing from the declaration, "We the People . . .," the American Constitution created a compact balancing state authority, popular rule, and the rights of individuals — giving greatest weight to the values of individual dignity and liberty. Authoritarian rule was replaced by *citizen centered government.*

The familiar First Amendment command, "Congress shall make no law . . . abridging the freedom of speech, or of the press, or the right of the people peaceably to assemble, and to petition the government for a redress of grievances" is a cornerstone of citizen centered governance, and it is fashioned upon a building block construct. "The critical dimension" of individual liberty, a prominent historian of American rights has written, "is the right to participate in public affairs"(Foner, 1998, p. xvii). And to participate in public affairs? "Freedom to think as you will and to speak as you think are means indispensable to the discovery and spread of political truth," wrote Supreme Court Justice Louis Brandeis (1927). The Brandeis conception views unfettered communication as more than a right. Public discussion is a political duty, Brandeis argued, concluding that "this should be a fundamental principle of American government." (p.375)

The principles of *citizen centered* governance imbedded in this view have four elements:

- The purpose of the State is to enable individual freedom, rather than State sovereignty for its own sake.
- To achieve individual freedom, citizens must enjoy a right to participate in civic affairs.
- Constructive participation in civic affairs is grounded upon free trade in communication that serves as the intellectual roadmap of political, social, and personal discovery.
- The preservation of individual liberty carries the coupled political duties of civic participation *and* acquisition of the knowledge necessary to participate constructively and rationally.

The roots of this inspiration lie deep in America's historical soil. Thomas Jefferson described the value of intellectual and civic education when he wrote, "Were it left to me to decide whether we should have a government without newspapers, or newspapers without government, I should not hesitate a moment to prefer the latter. But I should mean that every man should receive those papers, and be capable of reading them." (1787) Jefferson recognized that individual liberty requires an unfettered press *and* a community capable of reading it.

The growth of a community capable of reading Jefferson's papers – virtual as well as ink — has been nourished by the contemporary recognition of the First Amendment's structural contributions. A longer essay should pause here to document the twentieth century lineage of modern First Amendment theory in which education – civic and intellectual — is no less an element of *citizen centered* governance than is the newspaper. Like the press, education coveys social, political, and cultural expectations. And apart from the press, it is the function of the schools to prepare citizens to read Jefferson's papers critically and to use the knowledge gained in civic participation.

From a constitutional view, the construct *citizen centered* governance provides a rationale for the recognition of an affirmative university duty that goes beyond the preparation of students for employment and commerce. "The primary task of American education is to arouse and to cultivate, in all the members of the body politic, a desire to understand what our plan of national government is," philosopher Alexander Meiklejohn wrote over fifty years ago (1948, p. 3). Do we as educators succeed in that task? Thomas Ehrlich, a founder of Campus Compact, former dean of Stanford University Law School, and now a distinguished scholar at San Francisco State University, is blunt. "The development of moral and civic character in students," Ehrlich wrote, "is not a goal on the radar screens of most colleges and universities — except as a matter of public relations rhetoric." (1999, p.5)

At first blush, Ehrlich 's analysis is forceful. Universities often talk about civic duty. Few universities appear to accept an affirmative obligation to engage students in a learning process in which curriculum matches mission. Portraits of students as politically passive and consumer driven (Levine & Cureton, 1998) and freshman surveys suggesting continuing declines in student interest in courses, race relations, the environment, and voting (Sax, Astin, Korn, & Mohoney, 1999) add a sense of urgency to Ehrlich's condemnation of the shallow *viewbook* spin of campus moral and civic development. A different explanation, however, is plausible — an explanation with scholarship implications, not for *whether* we teach civic engagement, but for *how* we teach it. My thesis begins with two propositions:

- The great majority of American colleges and universities in fact do strive to teach civic engagement, most notably in their establishment of liberal arts and general education requirements. Unfortunately, these efforts often fail. The learning does not produce engagement.

- The failure is the result of a wrong headed, but common, belief about the way students learn.

A great deal of teaching carries an implicit faith in an unbroken **knowledge → belief → behavior** causal chain . Students are expected to acquire the content of the liberal arts through readings, lectures, and writing assignments. Acquisition will cause them to form new belief systems. Students will apply their discoveries to the democratic process. Knowledge in fact may be necessary, but it is not sufficient. The recognition of a direct linkage, however, between the liberal arts and liberty is nowhere better displayed than in the 1792 Samuel Jennings painting, *Liberty Displaying the Arts and Sciences*. With symbols of knowledge and creative talent about her that include a world globe, a lyre and an artist's pallet, Lady Liberty's iron chains of slavery are broken as she hands out books to African slaves newly freed by the abolition movement. The symbolism is strong. The connections are clear. Knowledge enables liberty. Yes. But does knowledge cause liberty? The issue of course is not whether the liberal arts are necessary, but whether such a simple process is sufficient to sustain or even trigger attitudinal and behavioral change and adoption. Does mere exposure to the liberal arts bring about civic engagement?

The curricula in our program descriptions, and the course syllabi we write, often rely on analogous causal chains. We *talk* about the links between liberal arts and democracy. We assume that as students are exposed to the arts of liberty they will understand and adopt behaviors such as voting, volunteerism, and public participation that support the liberty of *citizen centered* governance. In simply *saying* that students must learn and value the liberal arts, however, we don't go far enough. Students need to master the liberal arts, *and* to practice the arts of liberty.

The need to establish clear learning goals that include knowledge and practice is complicated by a related phenomenon familiar to communication scholars, cognitive psychologists, and political propagandists, *schemas*. Students do not arrive empty headed. They carry pictures of the world about them, and beliefs about how things happen. Because of these existing mental pictures, simple exposure to new knowledge — whether through reading, lecture or visual observation — is unlikely to have a significant impact on the way students react to new situations. Put another way, students rarely apply newly acquired classroom knowledge to anything outside the classroom that challenges their long held notions of the world around them.

Lacking a disciplined approach to assist students to transfer their knowledge — from liberal arts to the practice of liberty, from classroom to the world beyond the university — courses become hoops to jump through, but not building blocks for engaging in issues of civic consequence and certainly not practice in applying scholarship to the difficult questions of civil society.

The question before us then is not simply, what are the educational goals suggested by our acceptance of a constitutionally based teaching obligation. What we know about the complexity of learning suggests that teaching the constitutional goal of civic engagement as a public duty requires scholarly practices that go beyond shallow **knowledge→ belief→ behavior** models.

Are there ways to promote a curriculum of consequence and active learning in which faculty and students imagine their courses and research not as disengaged segments of an unrelated set of skills connected by such vague terms as major, minor, discipline and sequence, but as opportunities for students to engage their developing academic talents meaningfully? Can we place experiences such as this into a context in which students can picture their academic capacity as a means to contribute as citizen participants in a community structure in which their intellectual decisions do make a difference?

Crediting John Dewey, Shulman offers a principle that reflects effective teaching and learning as well as the *citizen centered* values of the First Amendment. "We do not learn by doing," Shulman writes. "We learn by thinking about what we are doing." (1997, p.165) The corollary is that students do not master the civic engagement of their university scholarship by volunteering to register voters or tutor children. They learn the integration of scholarship and civic engagement when faculty, student affairs professionals, members of the community, and student peers help them to reflect in ways that identify relationships between the scholarly work they carry on, and the world outside.

The Public Scholarship Associates

The Summer Academy of the American Association for Higher Education selects university teams annually through a process of competitive proposal submissions to participate in five days of plenary sessions and workshops focused on teaching and learning and to develop projects for their home campuses. The 1999 Penn State team, sponsored by the Office of Undergraduate Education, submitted a proposal to AAHE to consider the ways through which students can become further involved in public scholarship.

At the Colorado high mountain retreat, the six member Penn State cohort, which included students, student affairs professionals, faculty, and administrators, began with a self-assessment that elicited a sobering conclusion: Penn State lags behind several other Big 10 schools in its support of the service learning aspects of public scholarship. Our service learning achievements existed only in corners of departmental, college and university efforts, but were nowhere a highly visible, mainstream enterprise. Missing was the administrative and intellectual home necessary to move from the philanthropic volunteerism practiced widely and appropriately by sororities, fraternities, and campus service groups, to a civic participation rooted in scholarship — that is, service grown from the publicly shared discovery and application of knowledge, ideas and skills that underlie the university's educational mission.

Working principles emerged to explicate what remained an incompletely defined construct, *public scholarship*. Public scholarship should not describe a service learning methodology, but an educational philosophy in which the work of the university contributes to the larger society, as well as to the esoteric goals of a modern research institution. Public scholarship should include teaching, research and service focusing on the goal of discovering and the sharing of that discovery, rather than on a given means of inquiry. Public scholarship should enable faculty to make their work available to others and to subject their work to the kinds of disciplined peer review that is the foundation of scholarly work. Public scholarship should place service and teaching squarely within the scholarship paradigm long applied to research, including those elements of recognition and reward that have contributed effectively to the university's productive research environment.

While many forms of pedagogy are appropriate in higher education, service learning within the public scholarship ideal holds out the prospect of especially high return, the team reasoned. It is an effective pedagogy for deep disciplinary learning as well as a form of engaged learning relevant to Penn State's new General Education approach. It encourages time on task, collaboration, problem based learning, external motivation, participation in identifiable communities, and the application of expertise. Too, public scholarship is a useful means of creating the environments highlighted by the National Research Council as key to effective learning. Bransford, Brown and Cocking (1999) focus on the need for environments that are: learner-centered, knowledge-centered, assessment (deep reflection) supported, and community-centered.

The team distinguished public scholarship and service learning as the difference between an educational philosophy, and a teaching methodology subsumed within the larger philosophy. Five recommendations emerged to generate a transformative university environment — one in which initiatives are not isolated, but have the potential to change and then support systemic practices. Acting alone individuals can alter their courses. Together, they can assist in the transformation of the teaching and learning paradigm.

- Recruitment of an active group of faculty, student affairs staff, and students to nurture public scholarship initiatives though shared reflection and scholarship and the development of interdisciplinary initiatives;
- Creation of regular formative opportunities for individuals interested in public scholarship participation;
- A timely follow-up on financial development opportunities;
- Commitment to a Penn State center or institute to foster the practice of scholarship though public service and service learning in teaching, research and service; and

- The sharing of public scholarship teaching, research and service within our own academic community in ways that recognize its scholarly basis for purposes of professional development as well as for tenure and promotion and salary recognition of performance.

The Office of Undergraduate Education acted quickly to execute the first two recommendations with the appointment of five Public Scholarship Associates. Each of the faculty members were tenured. If it is too soon to assess their effectiveness in developing a transformative public scholarship environment, it is nonetheless possible to identify deliberative first steps.

Monthly luncheons created a seminar atmosphere in which to test ideas and identify issues. There were few surprises. Untenured faculty place their careers at risk unless their work is viewed as scholarship within the tenure paradigm. Colleagues outside the Public Scholarship Associates remain skeptical that service learning is, in and of itself , a means to conduct scholarship central to university mission. The standards of scholarship employed in service efforts must be very clear as, lacking a strong constituency, public service may not be afforded the benefit of the doubt.

The naming of Public Scholarship Associates was a step toward creating identifiable academic community. Each involved herself or himself in a successful community-wide summit, *Seeding Partnerships-Growing Community*, detailed below and intended to reach beyond the academy grounds. The faculty and student affairs professionals have been invited to work in a new community-university public service alliance. Each has indicated a desire to continue meeting together, and to work with six additional Public Scholarship Associates during the next academic year. The creation of the named cohort did not, in and of itself, foster new scholarship . But it bestowed a portfolio of institutional legitimacy the cohort is using to broaden a grass roots constituency, both within the university and beyond.

DEMOCRATIC ENGAGEMENT: FROM THE COMMUNITY TO THE UNIVERSITY

CLASS, the Community Leadership Alliance for Service and Scholarship, is a coalition of community, K-12, and university. It is an experiment in democracy . . . and in trust. It is a radical departure from many university to community service alliances in that it does not follow a traditional pattern in which a university service program initiates and then assumes primary responsibility for community outreach.

The non-university based Volunteer Center of Centre County cobbled t ogether the initial outreach that brought together informally members of Penn State's AT&T Center for Service Leadership the Red Cross, and the United Way. Their focused purpose was to facilitate volunteer opportunities among local human service agencies and university students, and to develop shared resources incorporating an *e* database of volunteer opportunities.

The focus, and the membership, expanded. Penn State's Office of Under-graduate Education was invited to join the core group and brought with it the public scholarship recommendations developed at the AAHE Summer Acad-emy. The explicit commitment to teaching and learning complimented the original volunteer opportunity goals of the ad hoc group. More than a dozen human service agencies and university constituencies, including the Public Scholarship Associates, now meet together monthly and the expanded cohort developed the current symbolic moniker, CLASS, to incorporate both scholar-ship and service. The Alliance has adopted four primary goals.

Volunteer Opportunities The first is to continue the work begun, the fa-cilitation of volunteerism throughout the community. The addition of repre-sentation from the Retired Service Volunteer Program, for example, helps to make it clear that students are neither the single source, nor the lone priority, for volunteer recruitment. This is an especially important consideration in an area in which the university is by far the largest employer and the annual autumn arrival of students expands the local population base by nearly fifty percent.

Public Scholarship The Alliance membership, which includes among others, the Retired Service Volunteer Program, , the public schools, the Bor-ough of State College, Pennsylvania Campus Compact, and the Youth Service Bureau, is working with the Public Scholarship Associates to develop public scholarship opportunities. Three observations are especially relevant.

First, neither local agencies nor educators have amassed sufficient experi-ence in establishing a public scholarship philosophy to develop clear imple-mentation maps. While Alliance members support public scholarship principles, each of us encounters new territory in our attempts to bring theory to practice. Traditional perceptions of the role of volunteers remain en-trenched in the community.

Second, the neutral territory on which faculty and community agency leaders meet requires breakthrough diplomacy worthy of any Middle East ne-gotiation. Some faculty have viewed the community as a research laboratory, an attitude that does not encourage residents, students and faculty to regard each other as members of a united public. Some non-university community members have viewed students through polarizing lenses as captive consum-ers for inflated apartment rental leases, and as a drains on civic resources. Al-cohol fueled student riots at the close of the 1998 and 2000 summer arts festivals involved several thousand students and resulted in significant dam-age to property and to trust.

And third, CLASS brings a unique perspective to the university-community service relationship. Traditionally, higher education has thought of service as something it provides *to* the non-university community. Among the many implications of this schema is a tendency to view things as polar in which there are providers and receivers; in which there is knowledge and ignorance; in which there are researchers and clients. The CLASS model is based instead on a foundation of mutual participation, mutual responsibility, and mutual cost and gain. Not only does this view require new attention to listening to the voices of others. It also requires for all concerned a rethinking of roles and goals.

Some important steps have contributed to progress along these lines. CLASS members, from both campus and non-campus, have given joint presentations at Pennsylvania Campus Compact meetings. The experience of working together outside of the immediate community adds to our understanding of each other's needs and goals.

At the end of the first year, consensus was reached by the full cohort on the need for a steering team to set agendas and to shepherd initiatives. To stress the recognition of a variety of interests and views, we agreed to select a balanced team with two members from the university and representing both academic and student affairs, and two from off campus. Beyond symbolism, this structure requires the continuous development of consensus and teamwork.

A non-university member of the CLASS steering team accompanied the university-based Public Scholarship Associates on a cross country site visit to Stanford University's Haas Center for Public Service. The implications of Haplern's work on schema and learning theory are relevant for service leadership groups, just as they are for service learning teaching methodologies. Neither shared understanding nor mutual goals are likely without shared experience at the core. The shared opportunity to engage through observation and discussion the participants in a university-community service relationship outside our own was powerful.

Technical Support There is no desire to establish CLASS as an agency involved in direct service – that is, in directly meeting needs such as hunger, literacy, or health care. The intent is to provide technical support to enable individuals and agencies to get the most out of volunteer opportunities and public scholarship contributions from university and K-12 students, faculty and staff, and from traditional non-student volunteer populations. Toward this end, CLASS contributes to a localized Web based volunteer database and is facilitating the development of volunteer guidelines for local adoption. CLASS also is leading efforts through consultation and workshops to educate both non-university and university members to public scholarship approaches to civic engagement.

Civic Engagement The fourth spoke of the CLASS wheel is civic engagement. Through the creation of forums and summits, the Alliance expects to contribute to the establishment of a community-wide volunteer agenda that increases the sense of shared responsibility and contribution among participants. Through public scholarship partnerships among students, faculty, agencies, and others, the Alliance expects educators to build transformative practices of civic based scholarship.

Seeding Partnerships, Growing Community, the first of what will become an annual gathering, brought together forty community leaders from throughout the region for an eight hour summit. A local corporation, Raytheon, provided neutral grounds on which to meet. The issues were not new. Communication, transportation, continuity, resources, and expectations. Whether the mix — public scholarship associates, K-12 educators, human services agency leaders — will lead to something transformative remains an open question. Yet the summit itself provided a working example of civic engagement in which, at least for the moment, the alliances were inclusive.

The summit also provided the basis for the first cooperative project between the Public Scholarship Associates and CLASS. A working group composed of members of each, as well as a school principle and others from the community, accepted a charge based on their conversations at the summit to develop volunteer principles and guidelines and to draft principles and guidelines that will:

- Encourage beneficial volunteer practices;
- Recognize the diversity of talents and interests, ages and needs, backgrounds and beliefs that volunteers evoke;
- Distinguish among and explain the needs of short and long term volunteer activities, traditional volunteerism, and public scholarship in which student and faculty work becomes a community resource for addressing needs;
- Encourage a view of volunteerism and public scholarship as vital elements of civic participation;
- Promote practices in which volunteers, agencies, students, and others thrive in an atmosphere of respect and learning;
- Recognize and address the complexities of student schedules and academic expectations when establishing relationships with student volunteers.

CLASS served as the facilitator to bring the guidelines group together. The work of the group will form the primary basis of the second *Seeding Partnerships, Building Community Summit.*

CONCLUSIONS

Public scholarship is a philosophy, a way of thinking about the processes and practices of engaged citizenship that the university has an obligation to teach. Recognizing *public scholarship* as an element of professional academic work that is subject to peer review, to disciplinary integrity, and to intellectual rigor, enables faculty to embrace it, to evaluate it, to reward it, and to ask: What kinds of teaching, research, and service help to fulfill the public scholarship obligation we hold?

Service learning, like long held practices of land grant outreach and newer conceptions of action research, provides the means for students, faculty and staff to make their scholarship available to the community at large. *Public scholarship*, as a theory of civic and educational duty, provides a professional home for the expanded mosaic of faculty, staff and student work only now beginning to be appreciated as among the core values of university life.

Several challenges remain. The values of civic engagement hold out the prospect of linking participants from among many communities — academic, lay, professional, and other. Each community will maintain individual and esoteric needs. Promotion and tenure should never be the first concern of a food bank or half way house, but neither should the academic community ignore the importance of its own values or the need to protect and value its own community members.

The most immediate challenge is significant, complex, and embedded within dozens of familiar operational issues such as consistency, funding, structure, adequate student preparation for outreach, authority, and assessment. It is the challenge to maintain communication that will, as a recent Public Scholarship Associates meeting noted, recognize multiple goals, develop relationships, respect differences, foster individual scholarship and creativity, advance disciplinary scholarship, nurture student learning, serve multiple communities and develop civic engagement.

REFERENCES

Antonio, A., Astin, H., & Cress, C. (2000). Community service and higher education: a look at the nation's faculty. *Review of Higher Education, 22*(4), 373-398.

Astin, A., Sax, L. J., & Avalos, J. (1999). Long term effects of volunteerism during the undergraduate years. *The Review of Higher Education, 22*(2), 187-202.

Barber, B. (1992. *An Aristocracy of Everyone: The Politics of Education and the Future of America.* New York: Ballantine Books.

Boyer, E. L. (1990). *Scholarship Revisited: Priorities of the Professorate.* Carnegie Foundation for the Advancement of Teaching.

Bransford, J., Brown, A., and Cocking R. (eds.) (1999*). How People Learn: Brain, Mind, Experience, and School.* Washington D.C.: National Academy Press.

Brandeis, L. (1927) *Whitney v. California 247 U.S. 357, 375-77.*

Cohen, J. (1994). Matching university mission with service motivations: do the accomplishments of community service match the claims? *Michigan Journal of Service Learning, 1*(1), 98-104.

Cohen, J. (1997). Learning the scholarship of teaching in doctorate-granting institutions. *Journalism & Mass Communication Educator, 51*(4), 27-38.

Cohen, J. (2001) "Shouting fire in a crowded classroom: from Holmes to homeroom" in *Communication, A Different Kind of Horse Race: Essays Honoring Richard F. Carter.* Dervin, B. & Chaffee. S. (eds.) Peekskill, NJ: Hampton Press *(forthcoming)*

Cohen, J., Barton, R. & Fast, A. (2000). "The growth of the scholarship of teaching in doctoral granting institutions." Journalism & Mass Communication Educator, 53(4), 4-13.

Ehrlich, T. (1999). Civic and moral learning. *About Campus,* 5-9.

Fairweather, J. (1995) *Faculty Work and Public Trust: Restoring the Value of Teaching and Public Service in American Academic Life.* New York: Allyn & Bascom.

Foner, E. (1998). *The Story of American Freedom.* New York: W.W. Norton & Company.

Glassick, C. E., Huber, M. T., & Maeroff, G. I. (1977). *Scholarship Assessed: Evolution of the Professoriate.* San Francisco: Jossey-Bass.

Hutchings, P. (Ed.). (1996). *Making teaching community property: a menu for peer collaboration and peer review.* Washington D.C.: American Association for Higher Education.

Jefferson, T. "Letter to Edward Carrington, January 16, 1787," in Ford, P.L.. ed., *The Writings of Thomas Jefferson* (pp. 357-361). New York: Putnam.

Kennedy, D. (1997). *Academic Duty.* Cambridge: Harvard University Press.

Kolb, D. A. (1984). *Experiential Learning: Experience as a Source of Learning and Development.* Englewood Cliffs: Prentice-Hall.

Levine, A., & Cureton, J. S. (1998). *When Hope and Fear Collide: A Portrait of Today's College Student.* San Francisco: Jossey-Bass.

Meiklejohn, A. (1948). *Political Freedom: The Constitutional Powers of the People.* New York: Oxford University Press.

Menges, R. J., Weimer, M., & Associates, a. (1996). *Teaching on Solid Ground: Using Scholarship to Improve Practice.* San Francisco: Jossey-Bass.

Orrill, R. (Ed.). (1997). *Education and Democracy: Re-imagining Liberal Learning in America.* New York: The College Board.

Sax, L. J., Astin, A., Korn, W., & Mohoney, K. (1999). *The American freshman: national norms for fall 1999.* Los Angeles: UCLA Higher Education Research Institute.

Shulman, L. (1996). Teaching as community property: putting an end to pedagogical solitude. *Change,* 6-7.

Shulman, L. (1997). Professing the liberal arts. In R. Orrill (Ed.), *Education and Democracy: Re-imagining Liberal Arts in America* (pp. 151-173). New York: The College Board.

Stanton, T.K. (1987). "Service learning: groping toward a definition." InKendall, J.(ed) 1990 *Combining Service and Learning: A Resource Book for Community and Public Service.* Raleigh, N.C.: National Society for Experiential Education.

CHAPTER 18

BUILDING CAPACITY FOR CIVIC ENGAGEMENT AT PORTLAND STATE UNIVERSITY: A COMPREHENSIVE APPROACH

Dilafruz R. Williams[1]
Daniel O. Bernstine[2]
Portland State University

INTRODUCTION

Almost a decade ago, Portland State University (PSU) launched a significant initiative of comprehensive institutional transformation.[3] PSU aligned its curricula, its undergraduate and graduate academic programs, its scholarship and research, and its collaborative community outreach to reflect its commitment to a newly-defined "urban" mission that placed student learning and student experience at the core of the educational enterprise. Located in the heart of downtown Portland, PSU has taken seriously its charge to be *in* and *of* the city and the metropolitan region. Its motto, *Let Knowledge Serve the City,* is visibly embossed on a sky bridge symbolically capturing its commitment to the communities of which it is a part. In Fall 2000, a new year-long series entitled "Great City: Great University" was sponsored by the Office of Academic Affairs to engage faculty and community alike in civic discourse by taking stock of our common purpose and what we aspire to become.

With a student population of over 17,000, most of whom are commuters, PSU has emerged today as a model for the urban research university of the 21st century. The university is frequently cited for its curricular changes related to general education (also called University Studies) and its integration of student learning with service to the community through close ties with the metropolitan region (Ehrlich, 2000; Thomas, 1997). Community-university collaboration facilitates civic involvement that includes not only teaching and learning but also the scholarship of outreach. PSU has participated in several national projects and dialogues on civic learning funded by the Pew Charitable Trusts, W. W. Kellogg Foundation,

---

[1] Dilafruz R. Williams is Professor of Education, and most recently, was the Director of Community-University Partnerships, Office of Academic Affairs, at Portland State University.
[2] Daniel O. Bernstine is President at Portland State University.
[3] For an account of the history of this change process see: Davidson (1997); Driscoll (1998); Reardon & Lohr (1997); White & Ramaley (1997).

Carnegie Foundation for the Advancement of Teaching, Campus Compact and others; these have enabled us to reflect on our work even as we continue to improvise and build capacity for engagement to ensure long-term sustainability of our efforts.

In this chapter we first discuss curriculum design at PSU that includes service-learning. The University Studies general education program[4] explicitly views as top priority "students and their development as moral and educated citizens" (White, Templeton, 1999). We draw upon examples from the University Studies program (Freshman Inquiry courses to senior capstones) and from other programs that address community needs through service-learning courses. This is followed by a section on an initiative that was started two years ago entitled "Practices of Civic Responsibility in Higher Education."[5] The two aspects of this initiative have been the Study Circles and the Breakfast Series that have brought together hundreds of faculty, community partners, administrators, and staff to explore through dialogue the democratic implications of service-learning and partnership pedagogy and our own institutional commitment to this work. We are asking important questions across disciplines and communities such as: How does our mission get implemented? What is our understanding of the knowledge, skills, and attitudes that are being promoted among our students? How do our community partners view our collaborative service work? How is civic learning manifested in practice? Do we embody democratic values on campus? The various participants have found it useful to pause, self-reflect, engage in critical thinking, and share common interests and concerns. In the final section, we present synopses of three new multi-year projects on civic engagement that are providing opportunities for PSU to sustain its capacity further: (1) *Civic capacity initiative* funded by the Fund for the Improvement of Post Secondary Education (FIPSE); (2) *Civic learning cluster* funded by the W.W. Kellogg Foundation; and (3) *Students addressing inequality and diversity through civic responsibility* funded by the Corporation for National Service's Learn and Serve grant. The goals of these projects are in keeping with the argument made by Ehrlich (2000) that institutions such as PSU that have made their intention for civic responsibility clear through structural and curricular trans-

---

[4] The innovative University Studies Program is a four-year general education course of study: Freshman Inquiry is a year-long interdisciplinary thematic course by topic taught by a team of 4-6 faculty. In their sophomore and junior years, students pursue clusters of courses related to a theme. For the senior capstones, interdisciplinary teams of students address significant contemporary issues. For a description see www.pdx.edu.

[5] The Breakfast Series and Study Circles were started and managed by a team that represented faculty, administrators and Student Affairs; Susan Hopp, Associate Vice-Provost and Dean for Enrollment and Student Services, and Michael Flower, Associate Professor in the Honors Program and the University Studies Program assisted co-author Dilafruz Williams in planning and implementing the events.

formation must form a network with other similar institutions to further develop this work through dialogue, assessment, and scholarly exchange.

CURRICULUM AND STUDENT ENGAGEMENT IN THE COMMUNITY

Under the broad umbrella of community-university partnerships, hundreds of students and dozens of faculty from a wide variety of disciplines participate in Portland metropolitan communities every academic quarter. While real-life and community experiences are offered through traditional practica or professional internships, there are a large number of courses that have been redesigned by faculty to intentionally include service as a required component that is connected to academic content. The office of Community-University Partnerships (CUP) at the Center for Academic Excellence, housed in the Office of Academic Affairs, provides curricular, pedagogical, and assessment support to faculty in this endeavor.[6]

It is typical for PSU students at the undergraduate and graduate levels to be engaged in communities beyond the four walls of academia and to address communal and societal issues through direct involvement. Commitment to civic learning via service-learning — which is by no means endorsed or adapted by all faculty — is most clearly found in the general education University Studies program.[7] This general education program has four explicit goals: communication, inquiry and critical thinking, appreciation for diverse experiences, and ethical and social responsibility. The purpose of the University Studies program is:

> [To] facilitate the acquisition of the knowledge, abilities, and attitude which will form a foundation for lifelong learning among its students. This foundation includes the capacity and the propensity to engage in inquiry and critical thinking, to use various forms of communication for learning and expression, to gain awareness of the broader human experience and its environment, and appreciate the responsibilities of persons to themselves, to each other and to community. (www.pdx.edu, 1999)

From Freshman Inquiry courses through the senior-level capstones many of the general education courses provide service-learning experiences that encourage students to extend their understanding of democratic and com-

---

[6] The Office of Community-University Partnerships provides faculty development and support campus-wide for a variety of needs: curriculum design, locating relevant partners, setting up partnerships for service learning, pedagogical support, teaching reflections, assessment of courses, etc.

[7] For the debates related to the University Studies program see *The Chronicle of Higher Education,* July 24, 2000.

munal issues beyond their "personal" experiences enabling them to make informed political choices. As reflected by students in their portfolios, service-learning over the years has made a profound impact on them.

Through service-learning, students are educated in an academic discipline while preparing to be contributing citizens. By becoming involved in community activities students provide benefits to others while learning about teamwork, civic responsibility, and the application of intellectual skills to community issues. Service-learning courses include in-depth theoretical and practical applications that allow for maximum integration of service and classroom work. Through skill building, reflection, generalizing principles, and assessment methods students serve and learn more effectively (CUP, 1999).

Senior capstones are the culminating experience of the University Studies general education curriculum and offer an interdisciplinary approach to addressing community issues. Capstones bring together students from an array of disciplines to apply what they have learned in their major fields of study to solve a "real life" problem in the community. In this context, students develop communication skills and teamwork while actively engaging with their community and critically confronting the social, cultural, economic, and environmental issues facing our society. Almost two thousand students are enrolled in over 150 senior capstones each year.

In the past decade, we have had partnerships with a broad constituency of organizations in the community that actively involve students in service-learning and have made them "participants" in addressing community issues. These partners include, but are not limited to, the following:

- City, county, and regional governmental agencies, e.g. the Bureau of Environmental Services, Parks and Recreation
- Educational institutions, e.g. public schools, museums, after-school programs
- Nonprofit organizations and community agencies, e.g. IRCO (International Refugee Center of Oregon), the Oregon Food Bank
- Watershed stewardship programs, e.g. neighborhood groups, watershed councils
- Businesses, e.g. Nike, Precision Castparts
- Social work and counseling organizations, e.g. Teen Parents Program, Self-Enhancement (for gang-affected youth)

The scope of service through these partnerships varies widely: tutoring migrant children in public schools; community asset-mapping; collaborative research on Welfare-to-Work to support families in need; watershed stewardship activities; conflict resolution for community resource allocation; writing the oral history of the local YWCA; mentoring youth at-risk of dropping out of school; designing and fabricating a wheelchair with potential for curb climbing; designing brochures for nonprofit organizations; addressing affordable housing issues for low-income families; etc.

Next, we present two examples of multi-year partnership projects that have drawn upon several service-learning courses and senior capstones to address community issues.

Service-Learning: Watershed Stewardship

One example of partnership between PSU and the surrounding community that involves both interdisciplinary capstones and other disciplinary service-learning course work is a five-year community watershed stewardship program in which students investigate the effects of urban growth on streams and their surroundings. Since 1995, PSU has partnered with the city's Bureau of Environmental Services, four watershed councils and related neighborhood associations, K-12 public schools, businesses, and local environmental nonprofit organizations to address community watershed stewardship issues. Academic programs in Community Development, Urban Studies and Planning, Teacher Education, Environmental Sciences and Resources, Geography, History, Anthropology, Public Administration, and Conflict Resolution have typically offered service-learning courses that address these issues. Further, in University Studies, Freshman Inquiry courses with themes such as "The Many Places of Portland" or "The Columbia Basin: Watershed of the Great Northwest" have involved students in service related to watershed issues. A Sophomore Inquiry/Junior cluster entitled "Leadership for Change" and several senior capstones have also addressed stewardship matters.

Service-learning with partners in these courses has included long-term goals: to conduct door-to-door surveys of residents to gather data on knowledge of watersheds and stewardship-related habits; to educate school children about their watersheds; to restore and monitor streams, wetlands, and parks; to facilitate discussion sessions on action plans for stewardship at local conferences (organized by Oregon's Congressman Blumenauer); to develop brochures on watershed health; and to design a program for area high school students called "Teens on the Trail," in order to enhance historical knowledge about their school's watershed.

Zenger Farm, a unique parcel of land which lies within the Johnson Creek Watershed in outer southeast Portland, has become a special focus of community stewardship and environmental renewal that brings together diverse partners. Located adjacent to a nature trail and in close proximity to Johnson Creek, Zenger Farm has become the spotlight of neighborhood and city efforts to protect both the watershed and urban agriculture. Students from a capstone entitled "Neighborhoods and Watersheds" work with the Friends of Zenger Farm, the Portland Bureau of Environmental Services, the Environmental Middle School, and the Oregon Food Bank on a broad range of projects. Students' service provides educational opportunities that include the following: management of urban open spaces and wetlands; teaching stewardship to young students in local schools; working on public policy issues with the Johnson Creek Watershed Council to coordinate management of the riparian and wetlands areas and to mitigate winter flooding and runoff; conducting cost and feasibility studies for restoration of existing farm buildings on site; and planting, growing, and harvesting food to serve the needy in the community. The work products resulting from this service-learning opportunity are extensive: oral history recordings in various watersheds; resident survey data on stewardship habits; stream monitoring data fed to the city's Bureau of Environmental Services; videos on watershed restoration activities to be used to educate school children; nature trail signs for native plants; business perspectives on watershed health; and teacher training programs for recycling and composting on school grounds.

Stewardship service activities have developed in our students an understanding of the *complexity* of civic issues related to urban growth, resource allocation, nature/human connections, sustainability, organic food production and marketability, conservation and preservation of open spaces. Feedback from faculty and a survey of students' writing indicate that the degree of understanding varies with the course, the class level, the number of hours spent in service, and the follow-up links and discussions in class. However, students do learn about the difficulties associated with environmental stewardship in urban areas, including the importance of political participation to ensure adequate resource allocations. They begin to see how each individual is implicated in the choices she or he makes. Most important, their simplistic notions of "us" versus "them" are problematized through their active involvement in these complex social, cultural, and environmental issues.

Service-Learning: Addressing Needs of K-12 Children and Families

One of PSU's longest continuous partnerships is with the Portland Public School District and its Migrant Education Tutorial Program. This collaboration between Title 1, PSU, and Portland public schools began in the eighties. The school district benefits from this tutoring arrangement with PSU that provides educational assistance for diverse, migrant populations that are not stable in a given year and not large enough to sustain permanent staffing. Reciprocally, PSU finds a consistent source for students to learn through service. By spending time teaching and mentoring young migrant and Title 1 students, PSU students gain insight into teaching diverse students and an understanding of educational issues related to the intersection of race and class. They also develop an increased sensitivity for and understanding of migrant students and others who need assistance with meeting district or state educational standards. Research shows that tutoring and one-to-one contact has a positive impact on the academic achievement of young students. Individual attention also increases students' self-esteem and confidence in dealing with representatives of the mainstream culture.

PSU also has partnerships with organizations that serve the refugee community. SOAR (Sponsors Organized to Assist Refugees) and IRCO (International Refugee Center of Oregon) find that the involvement of PSU students greatly enhances the services they can provide to recent arrivals who are struggling to adapt to a new culture. By tutoring this multi-age population in subjects ranging from basic English instruction to how to use a post office or a bank, PSU students encounter a multicultural experience far different from that of their daily experience. Their goal is to assist refugees and immigrants in becoming self-sufficient by helping with aspects of American Society that might confuse or frustrate them such as legal and societal views, race relations, health services, and ethnic diversity, etc. Along the way, PSU students improve communication skills while responding to the needs of both the community agency and refugees. Several capstones that deal specifically with the issues of migrant and refugee populations have developed handbooks to meet the specific needs of these communities.

LINKS (Learning Involves Nurturing Kids in the Summer) is an example of a different kind of service-learning that resulted in a multi-year collaboration between PSU, Friends of Children (AmeriCorps/State of Oregon), EnviroCorps, and a Foster Grandparent Program to increase and expand the effectiveness of each program in meeting community needs. It was a collaboration for child care, community pride, and appreciation of the environment and was structured to maximize resources and generate new benefits to the individual partners as well as to the overall partnership. The result was that PSU students joined with members of the Foster Grandparent Program, Friends of Children, and EnviroCorps to provide a month-long camp for 40 five-to-ten year-old low-income students at Lent Elementary School. Through their service, community needs (e.g. after-school child care and support) and children's needs (e.g. secure relationships with responsible adults) were both addressed. Many of the activities involved community development efforts and environmental projects that dealt with real community needs while providing service experiences for the families and children. This partnership instilled appreciation for the environment and pride in the local neighborhood. Through service-learning a number of groups were brought together to create synergy in serving a high-poverty population.

To address the needs of K-12 children and families, several PSU courses have been designed as service-learning courses. Three to four sections of the Freshman Inquiry course on "Pluralism" placed freshmen in public schools that had predominantly low-income and minority students for an entire year so that they could learn through service about issues of pluralism in a democracy. Sophomore and junior students in the "Leadership for Change" cluster learned about transformational leadership issues as they worked with community partners to address assimilation, voice, equity, and social justice. Other academic programs drawn to this domain of service-learning include Teacher Education, Applied Linguistics, Foreign Languages, English, Anthropology, Community Development, Black Studies, and Sociology.

Assessment of service-learning is conducted by the office of Community-University Partnerships. Often, individual faculty members develop their scholarship based on the analysis of student reflections of projects, or on student survey feedback, etc. (Collier, 2000; Gilbert, 2000; Sherman & Williams, 2000; Williams & Driscoll, 1998). Though students consistently complain that service-learning is too time-consuming, the following *categories* of responses have emerged from student surveys conducted in thirty service-learning courses: (1) Development of a sense of personal efficacy. Students speak about becoming aware of developing strengths in terms of interacting with certain groups of people and addressing a variety of concrete issues. They also report becoming aware of their weaknesses and wanting to develop skills to address these weaknesses; (2) Acquisition of skills of communication and problem-solving; (3) Feelings of responsibility toward the communities being served. Hence, students may continue their service in the same community even after completing the course; (4) Understanding the subject matter/academic content better; (5) Development of relationships with diverse groups of people, including better relations with faculty; (6) Having a better sense of career options; (7) Recognizing that the service-learning experience challenges their world-view as they get exposed (many for the first time) to populations in poverty or to environmental issues or to youth affected by gangs.

Service-learning requires that students reflect on their experiences in the community. However, we have found that in their reflection students often simply recycle their prior knowledge and understanding of community issues and, unless challenged, students' stereotypes may get reinforced. For a deeper, more transformative learning, faculty must make the "strange familiar and the familiar strange" by challenging students' taken-for-granted assumptions (Sherman & Williams, 2000). Service-learning is about getting down-to-earth understanding of the "messiness" of our democratic lives. Dewey's democracy is always "in-the-making" (1914). It is among other things, about listening and deliberating; recognizing the complexity of pluralism; becoming open-minded; developing leadership potential to address social issues; and participating actively in the politics of place. Given the large student body at PSU there are some students whose service-learning experience enables them to develop a voice and a vision that goes beyond the particularities of their experience and that also transforms them. While no aggregate data can capture these voices, stories of such student engagement have been shared by faculty, many of whom are themselves connected to their communities.

FACULTY INVOLVEMENT IN DIALOGUE AND CRITICAL REFLECTION ON CIVIC RESPONSIBILITY IN HIGHER EDUCATION

There are several dimensions to the practice of civic learning, ranging from curricular and pedagogical activities to co-curricular activities and research. As seen in the above section, at PSU we have embedded and institutionalized service-learning and the teaching of social and ethical responsibility in our general education program. There are also professional programs that provide service-learning experiences and public service opportunities. Many faculty are involved with and connected to the community as they provide service and also pursue their own research. Furthermore, large numbers of our community partners are involved in co-teaching and in hosting students at their community sites. The community and the university seem to be well-connected in serving one another.

Yet, two years ago, we felt that this was not enough. What was missing was a "culture" on campus that critically examined through discourse the civic and community experiences that were provided to students. Though individual course assessments[8] on service-learning were going on, there was not a collective sense of what we were doing and what the impact of our work was on faculty and community alike. We had not engaged in discussions campus-wide on the intellectual and theoretical underpinnings of our work primarily as they relate to democracy, education, and civic engagement, nor had we shared our practices of civic learning and engagement in "public" ways with one another on and off campus.

Around this time, two national projects coalesced to give momentum to these concerns. First, in July 1999, several college and university presidents gathered at the Aspen Institute on the eve of the birthday of American democracy. There was a sense of urgency in the air. Low voter turnout, public cynicism and distrust in the political process, student apathy, and student alienation from communal and societal interests raised warning flags for the presidents. To address these issues, they committed their institutions to self-examination and self-reflection. In particular, they asked whether the civic mission of their higher education institution was expressed explicitly, and if so how it was manifested in practice. The presidents re-committed their institutions to undertake civic responsibility seriously and to revitalize the role of higher education as agents of democracy. A *Fourth of July Declaration of the Civic Responsibility of Higher*

---

[8] PSU has developed an *Assessment Handbook* that is used nationally; a model for assessment was developed after extensive data collection in a number of courses (see Driscoll et al, 1996).

Education was written and signed (Campus Compact, 1999). To date, almost 300 higher education institutions, including PSU, have endorsed this document. The *Declaration* listed a number of measures as key to determining successful civic undertakings. These measures can be used to reflect on and assess the degree to which institutions are practicing civic responsibility and the kinds of structures that support involvement. We began to use the *Declaration* not as a formal evaluation tool but rather as a springboard for discussions on the status of our civic work at PSU.

Second, Anne Colby and Thomas Ehrlich, senior scholars at the Carnegie Foundation for the Advancement of Teaching undertook a multi-year study of higher education institutions that attempts to promote civic responsibility in students. PSU is part of their study because of our strong commitment to a comprehensive approach to addressing civic engagement. Their overall preliminary findings are presented in *Civic Responsibility and Higher Education* (Ehrlich, 2000). Their site visits for research "triggered" the need for civic discourse amongst ourselves about PSU's civic mission and undertakings.

Thus, armed with a number of questions related to our work, we embarked on a rather unique approach to self-reflection, critical thinking, and the sharing of common interests. Through Community-University Partnerships, we initiated two significant forums under the aegis of "Practices of Civic Responsibility in Higher Education" in the hope of developing a collective sense of our service-related work by linking it to democracy: a *Breakfast Series* and *Study Circles.* Interestingly, as these activities were being undertaken, we wrote and were awarded several grants dealing with the promotion of and building capacity for civic learning and engagement. We used these events as opportunities to share with one another our needs and interests, our curricular and pedagogical insights, and our scholarship on service-learning.

Monthly Breakfast Series: Practices of Civic Responsibility in Higher Education

Over 200 faculty, administrators, community partners, and staff in Student Services have come together in two years to have conversations across disciplines, programs, and communities about our service-learning work and to celebrate the practices of civic responsibility at PSU. For each event, invitations via flyers and e-mails were sent campus-wide to faculty, administrators, and staff and to community partners listed in our database. We also encouraged faculty teaching service-learning courses to invite their community partners. We fore-grounded each event with readings to help focus our discussions. When people signed up each breakfast, they were given the readings in advance so that they could come to the events having given some thought to the topic of the day. 35 to 75 individuals participated on any given day representing most of the schools/colleges and disciplines. This interest did not wane with time. Participants included community partners, Deans, Department Chairs, Faculty of all ranks, and central administrators from Academic Affairs and Student Affairs.

We began the series by addressing such questions as "How can higher education foster democracy?" and "In what ways do our teaching and learning practices on this campus cultivate a sense of civic responsibility among students?" The following represent some of the provocative articles we used as springboards to challenge us and to stimulate conversation about the democratic implications of our university's urban mission:

- Cushman, Ellen. (January, 1999). The public intellectual, service-learning, and activist research. *College English, 61,* 328-336.
- Battistoni, Richard. (1997). Service-learning as civic learning: Lessons we can learn from our students. In G. Reeher & J. Cammarano (Eds.), *Education for Citizenship: Ideas and innovations in political learning* (pp. 31-45). New York: Rowman & Littlefield .
- Video (1997, in conjunction with article): *The public purpose of education and schooling.* A symposium, with participants Benjamin Barber, John Goodlad, Linda Darling Hammond, Donna Kerr, and others.
- Ehrlich, Thomas et al. (2000). Higher Education and the development of civic responsibility. In T. Ehrlich (Ed.). *Civic responsibility in Higher Education.* Phoenix, Arizona: Oryx Press.
- Campus Compact. (1999). *Presidents' Fourth of July Declaration on the civic responsibility of Higher Education.*
- Thomas, Nancy. (1998). *The institution as citizen: How colleges and universities can enhance their civic role.* Paper presented at The Florida State University and commissioned by the ACE Forum on Civic Responsibility.
- Schneider, Carol. (1998). *Core mission and civic responsibility.* Paper commissioned by the Association of American Colleges and Universities.
- Grace, William. (1996). *Ethical leadership.* Seattle: Center for Ethical Leadership.

The readings provided the framework for the topic presented by a guest speaker. In some instances, we had scholars or practitioners--national and local--engage us deeply through the texts and the readings. In other instances, we had panels of community partners that brought new perspectives to our service-learning work and provoked us to think about our taken-for-granted assumptions and understandings, given that in their perception we were still "insulated" and "protected" within the academic walls. Among some of the topics that we addressed were the following:

Values Formation in Higher Education

In his presentation, the Dean of the College of Liberal Arts and Sciences outlined the notion of institutional values, the historical foundations upon which educational values are premised, and the organization of curricula around these values. He led participants through a review of the literature that ties values development and character formation to higher education and discussed the importance of repairing the broken relationship between rights and responsibilities in our citizenry. The Dean challenged the audience to think critically and honestly about PSU's work with community partners in service-learning by asking how exactly PSU puts its motto *"Let Knowledge Serve the City"* into practice. Do we encourage students to develop "habits" of citizenship? What are the ways in which PSU is articulating its institutional values? Is PSU itself a democratic institution? Is service-learning simply about technique of pedagogy or is it being linked with democratic understandings? Among the debates that followed, the audience was left with the realization that for a public institution as large as PSU, while we may not agree about values and character formation as a goal, "openly" having debates about the kinds of values we stand for and teach is indeed healthy.

Martin Luther King, Jr.'s Teachings of Nonviolence and Service: Implications for Civic Engagement

Led by the President of the Urban League, who is also a seasoned community activist with a seven-term membership in the Oregon House of Representatives, this discussion was most provocative. Reflections upon Dr. King's legacy framed the context for a lively session about civic involvement in a democracy. PSU was challenged by this African-American community leader/partner to remain true to its urban mission, urging political action — not merely community service — for bringing about equity and social change. Complementing this session, PSU students, staff, and faculty participated in a variety of service initiatives in African-American communities designed to foster experiential understanding of Dr. King's principles of social justice, nonviolence and service.

The Pleasures and Challenges of Community-Based Learning and Related Activities in the College of Urban and Public Affairs

A faculty member/administrator in Urban Studies and Planning and the coordinator of internship programs, who is also a former state legislator and community leader, reflected upon ways to integrate classroom experience with community-based learning to address the critical social issues facing our urban communities today. As a seasoned activist and politician from Portland, the coordinator reminded participants that a lasting legacy of the 60's was the message to "get involved" to see social change. She is heartened by the political and social involvement of young people at PSU and firmly believes that service-learning promotes the broader habits of civic engagement. The speakers encouraged the academic community to dissolve boundaries created by academe and to make disciplinary knowledge available to local communities through both the activities of students and the scholarship of faculty.

Ethics, Leadership, and Service: Creation of a Just Society

Dr. Grace, the founder and executive director of the Center for Ethical Leadership located in Seattle, Washington, facilitated a discussion on the relationship between values, service-learning and leadership development. Using his theory of "transformational" leadership in contrast to "transactional" leadership, he developed an ethical framework within which individuals can work for the common good. His "4V" model of ethical leadership combined voice, values, vision, and virtue—all of which are possible when we make values concrete and visible. Participants were encouraged to clarify values that come from the heart and to practice congruence in thought and action. Grace believes that ethical leadership on the part of individuals can influence institutional ethics, promoting both civic capacity and social change. The possibility of ethical leadership for the creation of a just society was so encouraging that 99% of the participants have requested a longer, one-day in-depth workshop with him.

Scholarship of Community Outreach

In this session, faculty with experience in the scholarship of community outreach and professional service covering disciplines such as History, Public Health, Art, and Engineering, shared their work and ideas of promotion and tenure portfolios. When the process of institutional transformation began at PSU, new guidelines for Promotion and Tenure were also developed to reflect our commitment to the urban mission and to the scholarship of outreach (Boyer, 1990). Faculty are provided examples in the Promotion and Tenure Guidelines (1996) and are assured that "PSU highly values quality community outreach as part of faculty roles and responsibilites" (p. 10).

The faculty who participated are committed to enhancing "the intellectual, social, cultural, and economic qualities of urban life" reflected in PSU's mission statement. They presented examples of service-learning and community engagement that they have translated into scholarship: the Oral History of the YWCA; Watershed Stewardship Activities and Environmental Education; Technical Support for Graphic Design and Training of Teachers; and Development of Assessment Models for Community-

Based Education. Ways to integrate teaching, scholarship, and professional service were also discussed.

Reflections on the Series: Practices of Civic Responsibility in Higher Education

This session was facilitated by a faculty member and an administrator. Through an introspective look at the themes that had emerged over the term of the series, participants developed the following ideas that they felt needed to be central to future discussions: (1) The role and the responsibility of the University as a community partner in the Portland metropolitan area; (2) The relationship between service-learning and the development of civic capacity and democratic principles; (3) The encouragement of civil behavior (on and off campus) and of leadership as it relates to social justice; and (4) The scholarship of outreach and promotion and tenure issues such as asking whether the institution was "authentic" in valuing non-traditional work among faculty. The session concluded with a sense that the series was helping build community among colleagues beyond disciplinary boundaries; that this was a place where people were intellectually stimulated and could share their work; and that cross-departmental conversations about service-learning had given faculty ideas and also hope to continue to pursue the path they had set for themselves.

Study Circles

Even as the breakfast series was going on, we formed study circles in order to examine the broader theoretical frameworks that help situate higher education's civic engagement. The study circles have drawn 8 to 16 people each—once again, representing community partners, administrators, and faculty from several disciplines. Faculty members and administrators from the University Studies Program, the Honors Program, Urban Studies and Planning, Student Services, and Community Development have volunteered and facilitated discussions. In consultation with faculty who are experienced in service-learning, we selected and read the following books:

- Barber, Benjamin. (1998). *A place for us: How to make society civil and democracy strong.* New York: Hill & Wang.
- Barber, Benjamin. (1998). *A passion for democracy.* Princeton, N.J.: Princeton University Press.
- Briand, Michael. (1999). *Practical politics: Five principles for a community that works.* Urbana: University. of Illinois Press.
- Nussbaum, Martha. (1997). *Cultivating humanity: A classical defense of reform in Liberal Education.* Cambridge, MA: Harvard University Press.

- Putnam, Robert. (2000). *Bowling alone: The collapse and revival of American community.* New York: Simon & Schuster.
- Ehrlich, Thomas. (Ed.). (2000). *Civic responsibility and Higher Education.* Phoenix, Arizona: Oryx Press.

The Study Circles have drawn participants from History, Philosophy, English, Education, Women's Studies, Communication, Urban Studies and Planning, Conflict Resolution, University Studies, Public Administration, Business, Education, Student Services, Center for Science Education, Academic Affairs, Community Development, Extended Studies, and the Campus Ministry.

Faculty, administrators, and community partners have joined in these Breakfast Sessions and Study Circles in order to lend their voices and critically reflect on their experiences. An overwhelming response related to future directions has been — keep it as it is. People simply want to come together across their disciplinary and community boundaries to share their work, to read, to discuss ideas, and to ground their work in broader theoretical and conceptual contexts. These events give them a "bigger" picture of what their own work in higher education is about. And, in the process, they gain communal and collective understanding of PSU's urban mission and the related civic engagement. A sense of reciprocity and inclusivity has begun to emerge.

With sponsorship from various grants, this series continues to address tough questions. For example, using Barber's framework, we ask: Do we practice a dialectic model of education? If, as he says, the university is "civility itself, defined as the rules and conventions that permit a community to facilitate conversation and the kinds of discourse upon which all knowledge depends" (1998, p. 182), where does PSU stand? Do we explicitly foster democracy? If we care about democracy, how do we address diversity of voices and the issues of marginalization? In what ways do our teaching and learning practices on this campus foster a sense of civic responsibility among students? Asking these questions is a first healthy step toward finding the answers.

We are also taking stock of challenges we face at PSU. For instance, the work of civic engagement requires time commitments beyond the normal workload. The logistics of initiating and building partnerships and ensuring the integration of service-learning with academic content can be overwhelming, especially for new faculty. Furthermore, there is no guarantee about the stability of partnerships, since some of the community organizations tend to have high staff turnover; this can discourage faculty from pursuing civic engagement in a sustained way. By the same token, unless a large number of senior and tenured faculty embrace service-learning, it will end up largely within the realm of work done by adjuncts and fixed term faculty. Finally, an on-going challenge is that related to the perception among faculty that only traditional research counts as scholarship. The conversations and study circles have provided impetus to collectively address the challenges that have surfaced.

NEW MULTI-YEAR PROJECTS TO ENHANCE CAPACITY AND SUSTAIN CIVIC ENGAGEMENT

Three new grants provide further opportunities to PSU to enhance its capacity for civic engagement and sustain this work over a long period of time. A synopsis of each project is provided below:

Learn and Serve: Students Addressing Inequality and Diversity through Civic Responsibility

Funded by the Corporation for National Service, this 3-year project starts with the needs of the community and clusters these needs in a focused way around the twin themes of *inequality* and *diversity*. The curriculum of service-learning is also clustered around these needs. Because PSU was funded earlier for two three-year cycles with the Learn and Serve grant, in the new cycle, there is a systemic approach to service-learning that explicitly counts on civic responsibility. Furthermore, the project builds leadership capacity within the institution. Among the anticipated outcomes are the following: enhanced student engagement; increased intellectual understanding of the broader democratic framework for undertaking service-learning and civic responsibility; strengthening of scholarship of outreach; increased faculty expertise in teaching reflection and critical thinking skills; and continued assessment of student, faculty, and community participation in service-learning.

Civic Engagement Cluster: A Model for Multi-Institutional Change

PSU is one of ten higher education institutions to be awarded a Kellogg grant to participate in a Civic Engagement Cluster. This cluster is an inter-institutional learning organization that is committed to undertaking comprehensive institutional transformation to strengthen civic learning. The project will help extend faculty engagement with civic learning; enhance PSU's intentional focus on civic learning throughout the curriculum and co-curriculum; extend the civic learning to graduate and professional education; and clarify and assess expectations related to civic learning *vis a vis* student, community, and institutional feedback.

Civic Capacity Initiative: Integrating Liberal Arts and Professional/Career Education

This 3-year project funded by USDE strengthens the civic capacity of students, faculty, and the university, by expanding the curricular linkages between undergraduate liberal arts programs and the graduate professional schools, and by strategically building bridges to the community. The project seeks to address two growing problems in higher education--decline in civic engagement and erosion of commitment to the liberal arts--through a combination of strategies. Participants will include faculty, community partners, and doctoral students from liberal arts disciplines and professional programs in Education and Urban and Public Affairs. The goals of the Project are: (1) To better integrate liberal arts with professional and career education through curriculum design and collaborations; (2) To inculcate a heightened sense of civic responsibility among undergraduate and graduate students through promotion and strengthening of an institutional ethos of civic engagement; and (3) To deepen and broaden the university's relationship to the larger external community. A Civic Capacity Index (see Table 1) is being designed to measure the civic capacity in students who have completed courses designed as part of this project.

Many of the faculty and community partners involved in the earlier Breakfast Series and Study Circles on "Practices of Civic Responsibility in Higher Education" are participating in these projects. The FIPSE project includes doctoral students with the goal that we can create a new genre of faculty that will be equally interested in the work of building civic capacity at other institutions where they may teach on completing their doctorate. Thus, civic and moral interests in higher education will likely spread beyond PSU.

CONCLUSION

Colby, Ehrlich, and others have provided the following recommendations for "successful" practices of civic responsibility in higher education, based on their research: (1) Institutional intentionality that is clear to all within higher education and out in the community; (2) Conscious connections and links among a wide range of programs—both curricular and co-curricular—to enhance their holistic impact; (3) Clarity and discussion of the conceptual framework that supports these programs; (4) Active pedagogies of engagement and grappling with tough moral and civic issues; (5) Formation of a network of scholars to undertake and share assessment and research; (6) Sharing experiences through site visits, conference presentations, web-based communications; and (7) Inter-institutional sharing of this work (Ehrlich, 2000, pp. xl-xli). While PSU meets several of these criteria, we are aware that our work needs to be enhanced using criteria 5 through 7. A "vibrant" culture cannot be content with being a spectator of events. We are continuing to build capacity by involving faculty and community alike in order to sustain this work of civic engagement for the 21st century. The work of institutional transformation at PSU is ongoing with the new multi-year projects on civic engagement providing impetus to stay on the urban path with our communities.

Table 1: CIVIC CAPACITY INDEX[9]

Types of Capacity

	Beliefs/Values	Knowledge	Skills
Levels of Activity			
1.Individual	• Beliefs/values regarding self-interest, self-confidence • Sense of personal efficacy • Sense of personal responsibility • Attitudes regarding service to society	• Theories of moral development • Ethical Theories of care and justice • Theories of adult learning • Theories of adult development	• Interpersonal communication • Capacity for self-reflection
2.Group/ Team	• Beliefs/values regarding efficacy of group activity • Belief/values regarding diversity • Self-confidence and sense of efficacy when working in groups/teams	• Role theory • Small group behavior • Theories of diversity • Motivation theories	• Collaboration • Conflict resolution • Team leadership • Group decision-making • Group presentation

---

[9] The Civic Capacity Index is our work-in-progress; over fifty faculty, doctoral students, community partners, and administrators are involved in implementing various aspects of the index.

3.Organ-izational	• Beliefs/values regarding role of organizations in society • Efficacy of organizational activity	• Organizational theory & behavior • Theories of organizational leadership • Comparative value of different types of organizations (community groups, political parties, voluntary assoc., etc)	• Planning • Coordination • Project management • Coaching • Mentoring • Facilitating
4.Com-munity/Society	• Beliefs/values regarding society, public/private domains • Beliefs/values regarding social change, i.e. sense of fatalism, confidence about the future, attitude toward politics, etc.	• Public governance processes/structures • Theories of community/society • Origins of modern liberalism • Understanding of comparative role of economics, sociology, political science, anthropology	• Public participation • Meeting facilitation • Use of quantitative/ qualitative techniques for decision-making • Organizing and sustaining community- centered activities

Copyright: Shinn, Morgan, & Williams (2000).

REFERENCES

Barber, B. (1998). *A passion for democracy*. Princeton, N. J.: Princeton University Press.

Boyer, E. (1990). *Scholarship reconsidered*. Princeton, NJ: Carnegie Foundation for the Advancement of Teaching.

Campus Compact. (1999). *Presidents' Fourth of July Declaration on the civic responsibility of Higher Education*.

Collier, P. (October 2000). The effects of completing a capstone course on student identity. *Sociology of Education, 73* (4) 285-300.

CUP. (1999). Community-University Partnerships informational materials, Portland State University.

Davidson, S. (1997). Supporting faculty in educational reform. *Journal of Higher Education (Hokkaido University)*.

Driscoll, A. (1998). Comprehensive design of community service: New undertakings, options, and vitality in student learning at Portland State University. In E. Zlotkowski, (Ed.), *Successful service-learning programs: New methods of excellence in Higher Education* (pp. 50-168). Bolton, MA: Anker Publishing.

Dewey, J. (1914). *Democracy and Education*. New York: Free Press.

Driscoll, A., Gelmon, S., Holland, B., Kerrigan, S. (1996). As assessment model for service learning: Comprehensive case studies of the impact of students, faculty, community and institution. *Michigan Journal of Community Service Learning, 3*, 66-71.

Ehrlich, T. (Ed.). (2000). *Civic responsibility and Higher Education*. Phoenix, Arizona: Oryx Press.

Gilbert, M. (2000). Educated in agency: Student reflections on the feminist service-learning classroom. In B. Balliet & K. Heffernan, (Eds*), The practice of change: Concepts and models for service-learning in Women's Studies* (pp. 117-138). Washington, D.C.: American Association of Higher Education.

Portland State University. *Policies and procedures for the evaluation of faculty for Tenure, Promotion, and Merit increases.* May 17, 1996.

Reardon, M. & Lohr, J. (1997). The urban research university in American Higher Education: Portland State university as a model. *Journal of Higher Education (Hokkaido University).*

Sherman, D. & Williams, D. (2000, April*). When "reflection" isn't enough: Critical pedagogy and transformative service-learning.* Paper presented at the Western Campus Compact Continuums of Service conference, Seattle, Washington.

Thomas, N. (1998). *The institution as citizen: How colleges and universities can enhance their civic role.* Paper presented at The Florida State University and commissioned by the ACE Forum on Civic Responsibility.

White, C. (1999). First-Year Programs: Portland State University. In *Colleges that encourage character development* (p.19). Philadephia, PA: Templeton Foundation Press.

White, C. & Ramaley, J. (1997). Institutional transformation as scholarly activity; The experience of Portland State University. *Journal of Higher Education (Hokkaido University).*

Williams, D. & Driscoll, A. (1996). Connecting curriculum with community service: Guidelines for facilitating student reflection. *Journal of Public Outreach*, 2 (1), 33-42.

CHAPTER 19

EPICS: SERVING THE COMMUNITY THROUGH ENGINEERING DESIGN PROJECTS

Leah H. Jamieson[1]
William C. Oakes [2]
Edward J. Coyle[1]
Purdue University

INTRODUCTION

Undergraduate students in engineering face a future in which they will need more than just a solid technical background. In setting the goals for any system they are asked to design, they will be expected to interact effectively with people of widely varying social and educational backgrounds. They will then be expected to work with people of many different technical backgrounds to achieve these goals. They thus need educational experiences that can help them develop these skills.

Community service and education agencies face a future in which they must rely to a great extent upon technology for the delivery, coordination, accounting, and improvement of the services they provide. They often possess neither the expertise to use nor the budget to design and acquire a technological solution that is suited to their mission. They thus need the help of people with strong technical backgrounds.

The Engineering Projects in Community Service (EPICS) program provides a curricular service-learning structure that enables these two groups to work together and thereby satisfy each other's needs. EPICS enables long-term projects in which teams of engineering undergraduates are matched with community service agencies that request technical assistance. Under the guidance of faculty and industry advisors, these EPICS project teams work closely over many years with their partner community organizations to define, design, build, test, deploy, and support the systems the agencies need. The results are systems that have a significant, lasting impact on the community organizations and the people they serve.

Through this service, the EPICS students learn many valuable lessons in

---

[1] School of Electrical and Computer Engineering
[2] Freshmen Engineering Department

engineering, including the role of the partner, or "customer," in defining an engineering project; the necessity of teamwork; the difficulty of managing and leading large projects; the need for skills and knowledge from many different disciplines; and the art of solving technical problems. They also learn many valuable lessons in citizenship, including the role of community service in our society; the significant impact that their engineering skills can have on their community; and that assisting others leads to their own substantial growth as individuals, engineers, and citizens.

EPICS CONTEXT AND STATUS

In recent years, engineering education has seen a significant increase in emphasis on experiential education and on the "soft skills" that engineering students will need when they enter the workplace (ASEE 1994, Dahir 1993). Among the most dramatic statements about these skills has been the set of program outcomes at the heart of the engineering accreditation guidelines that went into effect in 2000, dubbed "Engineering Criteria 2000" (ABET, 1999). Under EC 2000, in addition to "traditional" engineering knowledge of mathematics, science, and engineering and experience in engineering problem solving and system design, students are mandated to be able to function on multidisciplinary teams, to communicate effectively, and to understand a wide range of issues, including professional and ethical responsibility, the impact of engineering solutions in a global and societal context, and a knowledge of contemporary issues. This sets the stage for engineering courses and curricula that engage students in "real-world" projects.

Many engineering programs have turned to industry as a source of such projects. This approach has been successful; however, community organizations also have a growing need for engineering solutions, and partnerships with the community have the benefit of incorporating service learning into the design experience. Although service learning has been shown to be an effective means of addressing the needs of engineering curricula (Duffy, Tsang, & Lord, 2000), engineering has lagged behind many other disciplines in the integration of service learning into the curriculum (Tsang, 2000). Recent examples of engineering service learning include projects integrated into freshman-level introductory courses (Hobson, 2000; Tsang, 2000), capstone senior design courses (Catalano, Wray & Cornelio, 2000) and multidisciplinary approaches (Nagchaudhuri, Eydgahi, & Shakur, 2000). Other initiatives have sought to integrate the co-curricular activities of student organizations with engineering service learning (Stott, Schultz, Brei, Winton Hoffman, & Marcus, 2000). EPICS has integrated service learning into an ambitious multidisciplinary, vertically integrated course structure that is centered on long-term engineering projects.

EPICS was initiated in the School of Electrical and Computer Engineering at Purdue University in Fall 1995, with 40 students participating on five project teams. The program has grown steadily at Purdue both in size and breadth. In the 2000-01 academic year, 400 students participated on 20 teams, addressing problems ranging from data management for social services to mitigation of agricultural pollution and from designing learning centers for local museums to developing custom play environments for children with disabilities. EPICS spans engineering disciplines at Purdue and includes students from over 20 university departments. By 1997, EPICS programs were under way at the University of Notre Dame and Iowa State University; in 2000-01, programs were initiated at the University of Wisconsin-Madison, the Georgia Institute of Technology, and Case Western Reserve University[2]

CURRICULAR STRUCTURE

Each EPICS project involves a team of eight to twenty undergraduates, a not-for-profit community partner – for example, a community service agency, museum or school, or government agency -and a faculty or industry advisor. A pool of graduate teaching assistants provides technical guidance and administrative assistance.

Each team is vertically integrated, consisting of a mix of freshmen, sophomores, juniors, and seniors. Each team is constituted for several years, from initial project definition through final deployment. Each student may earn academic credit for several semesters, registering for the course for 1 or 2 credits each semester. The credit structure is designed to encourage long-term participation, and allows multi-year projects of significant scope and impact to be tackled by the teams.

Each student in the EPICS Program attends a weekly two-hour meeting of his/her team in the EPICS laboratory. During this laboratory time the team members will take care of administrative matters, do project planning and tracking, and work on their project. All students also attend a common one-hour lecture each week. A majority of the lectures are by guest experts, and have covered a wide range of topics related to engineering design, communication, and community service. The long-term nature of the program has required some innovation in the lecture series since students may be involved in the program for several semesters. This has been addressed by rotating the lecture topics on a cycle of two to three years and by creating specialized lecture supplements called skill sessions that students can substitute for lectures they have already seen. Example skill session topics include learning to operate a mill or lathe, developing effective surveys, and tutorials on multimedia software. We have found that students use the skills sessions as a way

---

[2] The Purdue EPICS web site at http://epics.ecn.purdue.edu includes links to individual project teams, courseware documents, and other universities' sites.

of gaining specific expertise needed for their projects, and also as an opportunity to broaden their experience – for example, a computer engineering student learning to use a lathe or a mechanical engineering student learning web programming.

PHASES OF EPICS PROJECTS

The curricular structure of EPICS enables long-term projects. Over time, each project has five phases: establishing project partners, assembling a project team, developing a project proposal, system design and development, and system deployment and support.

Phase 1 - Establishing Project Partnerships: The university-community partnership is at the heart of any service-learning program. In the context of EPICS, this entails exploring the technology needs and aspirations of local not-for-profit organizations.

When planning for the EPICS Program started in 1994, we were able to contact many different service agencies by making a presentation about the envisioned program and its goals to the directors of all local United Way agencies. This single presentation led to many discussions with individual agencies and a long list of potential collaborations. The community partners, designated *Project Partners*, have been selected based four key criteria:

- *Significance* - not all projects can be undertaken, so partners whose projects should provide the greatest benefit to the community are selected;
- *Level of Technology* -projects must be challenging to, but within the capabilities of, undergraduates in engineering;
- *Expected Duration* - projects that will span several semesters offer the greatest opportunity to provide extensive design experience on the academic side and to address problems of potentially high impact on the community side. It has also proven valuable to achieve a mix of short- (one semester to one year) and long-term (multi-year) projects, in that the short-term projects build confidence and help establish the relationship between the student team and the community partner;
- *Project Partner Commitment* – a crucial element of the program has been the commitment of individuals in the partner organizations to work with the students to identify projects, specify the requirements, and provide ongoing critical feedback.

Each year, EPICS has added new teams using the significance, level of technology, expected duration, and Project Partner commitment criteria. Since the first round of projects that grew out of the United Way presentation, the source of new projects has been varied. Faculty have initiated some projects; students have suggested others. As the program has become known in the community, several projects have been proposed by local community organizations. From five initial teams in Fall 1995, the program has grown to 20 teams for the 2000-01 academic year.

Phase 2 - Assembling a Project Team: Once a project and Project Partner have been identified, a student team is organized. This is done through discussions with academic counselors, advertising the projects in an evening callout and in undergraduate classes, and on the World Wide Web. Eight to twenty students are chosen for each *Project Team*, with assignment of students to teams managed by the EPICS Student Advisory Council, on which each team has a representative.

Depending on the needs of the project, a team may include students from multiple engineering disciplines as well as non-engineering disciplines. During the 2000-01 academic year, over 20 academic majors were involved in the program, including Electrical, Computer, Mechanical, Civil, Aeronautical, Biomedical, and Industrial Engineering, Computer Science, Sociology, Psychology, Education, Audiology, English, Nursing, Visual Design, Forestry and Natural Resources, Chemistry, and Management.

Vertical composition – the mix of freshmen, sophomores, juniors, and seniors – is also a factor in team assignments. Teams need both technically advanced members (typically juniors and seniors) to spearhead technical progress and (academically) younger members to carry the projects into future semesters. The combination of a vertically integrated team and long-term student participation ensures continuity in projects from semester to semester and year to year. Projects can thus last many years if new students, especially freshmen and sophomores, are recruited for the project to replace graduating seniors.

Phase 3 - The Project Proposal: During the first semester of a project, the Project Team meets several times with its Project Partner and the team's EPICS advisor to define the project and determine its goals. During this phase the Project Team learns about the mission, needs, and priorities of the Project Partner. A key aspect of this phase is identifying projects that satisfy three criteria: they are needed by the Project Partner, they require engineering design, and they are a reasonable match to the team's capabilities. This process of project definition culminates in a written proposal and presentation. The proposal must be approved by the EPICS advisor and accepted by the Project Partner.

Phase 4 - System Design and Development: Following acceptance of the proposal, the Project Team's goal is to produce a prototype of the proposed system or service. Regular interaction with the Project Partner continues in order to ensure that the products being designed and developed are as desired. The formal portion of this interaction includes written progress reports, periodic design reviews, and presentations. This phase of a project lasts as many semesters as necessary for the team to complete the project to the satisfaction of the Project Partner.

Phase 5 - System Deployment and Support: The ultimate goal of each Project Team is to deliver a product or service to the Project Partner. The team must train representatives of the partner, collect feedback, and make any reasonable changes requested by the partner. One of the hallmarks of the EPICS Program is that the systems designed and built by the students are deployed in the field, where they provide real, needed service to the community. It has been our experience that after a team fields a project, the team and Project Partner work together to develop new project ideas, in order to continue the relationship. The students on the team in future semesters assume responsibility for supporting and maintaining the fielded projects.

EPICS PROJECTS / COMMUNITY COMMENTARY

In the 2000-01 academic year, 20 Purdue EPICS teams are working with local community partners. The EPICS web site at http://epics.ecn.purdue.edu includes a description of each team. To illustrate the types of projects and work that is done by the teams, four projects with different areas of emphasis and types of partners are summarized here. Since one of the most meaningful assessments of the effectiveness of a service-learning program is the reaction of the community partners, quotes from the Project Partners accompany the summaries.

The Homelessness Prevention Network Project

The Homelessness Prevention Network (HPN) is an alliance of not-for-profit community service agencies in the Greater Lafayette area surrounding Purdue. Current members are the Lafayette Transitional Housing Corporation, Lincoln Center, the Community and Family Resource Center, the YWCA's Domestic Violence Intervention and Prevention Program, the Salvation Army, the Mental Health Association, Home with Hope, and the Area IV Council on Aging. The Network's primary goals are to generate an accurate count of homeless individuals and families and to coordinate services provided by the agencies to each homeless client or family.

To achieve the desired level of coordination of services and sharing of client information, the HPN agencies proposed, as early as 1991, a distributed database linking them together. The purpose of the system would be to help the organizations serving the homeless develop the "Continuum of Care" as defined by the U.S. Department of Housing and Urban Development. The obstacles to establishing such a system included raising the funds for the computers and custom software that would be required, determining how and by whom the system would be maintained, and developing the protocols governing the collection and use of the data.

When the EPICS Program was founded in 1995, the agencies requested that an HPN EPICS team be established to take on the task of designing, developing, deploying, and supporting a custom distributed database system that would allow the agencies to count and characterize their clients, track all services provided to each client, enable case-management that spans all agencies and services, and assemble accurate reports without violating clients' confidentiality. The team that was created has been in operation for over five years. Over this period, the students on the team have come from a wide variety of disciplines, including computer engineering, computer science, electrical engineering, psychology, and sociology. Advisors and teaching assistants for the team have come from Electrical and Computer Engineering and Sociology.

The HPN EPICS team deployed computers and Version 1.0 of its software with the HPN agencies in 1997 and has added capabilities and upgrades with in subsequent semesters. Version 4.3, released in 2000, includes a common client intake form, merging of data across agencies, elimination of duplicate entries, a private email system for the HPN agencies, and custom report generation. The entire system was customized to meet the needs of the agencies. Connections between the agencies' machines and a central server are made at night over standard telephone lines to minimize costs for the agencies. When the database is closed or is transmitted over phone lines, it is encrypted according to the government-approved DES standard to ensure the security of the data. Agencies with very strict confidentiality guidelines can select when and to which other agencies the data they enter will be released. A very user-friendly intake form was developed in close cooperation with the agencies. There are currently more than 4500 homeless clients in the database. The database has also been deployed with five agencies in Anderson, IN, 80 miles southeast of Lafayette.

In 2000, the Purdue HPN team and its project partners in Lafayette, Indiana were awarded a $19,000 grant from the U.S. Department of Housing and Urban Development to participate in a national study of the data on homelessness collected by every city that has successfully implemented a Homeless Management Information System (HMIS). Lafayette is one of only 19 cities in the U.S. with a successful HMIS system. This would not have been possible without the EPICS program.

Joyce Field, former Director of the Homelessness Prevention Network, on the relationship with the EPICS program:

*Agencies receiving Federal grants have witnessed an increasing de-
mand for more accurate information on client management. The
agencies involved in the consortium do not have the resources to either buy expensive software programs on the market or to hire a
company to custom design software. The HPN project team has allowed the agencies to achieve a level of sophistication in data sharing
and client management that would not be possible otherwise.*

*The HPN project team has had a significant impact on the accom-
plishment of the mission of the agencies in the network by providing a
necessary client management system that will help each agency assess the quality of services provided by each agency and the network
as a whole.*

*I am a tremendous supporter of the EPICS program and the way this
program allows students to work in real life settings on real life
problems that affect the community. I have watched students who
have continued in the EPICS program over multiple semesters increase their skill and sophistication in working with community service agencies. The HPN project team has increased the sophistication
and ability of the agencies in the consortium to count the number of
clients being served and to track the quality and quantity of services
being provided.*

Children's Clinic at Wabash Center Teams

The Children's Clinic at Wabash Center is a not-for-profit organization
that provides early intervention programs for disabled or developmentally
delayed children and youths. Many of the young children have cerebral palsy.
The Clinic works with the children and their families to provide therapies and
treatments that enhance opportunities for learning and acquisition of skills.
The EPICS CCWC team began in 1995 with a goal of bringing technology to
bear on both therapy and play activities. The team started with students from
electrical and computer engineering, but quickly expanded to include mechanical engineering students. In 1996, a second team was initiated with the
Wabash Center because of the large number of potential projects. Electrical
and mechanical engineering have remained the core disciplines on the teams;
students from nursing, psychology, and child development have played major
roles in assessing the teams' projects.

The clinicians at the CCWC asked the EPICS teams to develop play environments that would achieve several objectives: provide a rich set of multisensory experiences that could be controlled by the disabled child; allow the
disabled child to interact with the play environment using modalities consis-

tent with the child's abilities; provide experience with "cause and effect" relations; allow disabled and normally abled children to play together in a cooperative way, with the disabled child in control of some aspects of the play; and be easily stored in the clinic's limited space. Although some commercial products are aimed at children with disabilities, they are typically very expensive. Also, the clinicians have found many of them too simple to engage children for long, and few that encouraged interactive play.

The EPICS teams have tackled and delivered several projects to the clinic:

- Custom software that uses a commercial large format input keyboard to allow children to activate animations of faces.
- Animated storybooks using multimedia software.
- Animations of songs and nursery rhymes that incorporate images and voices of the children in the clinic.
- A computer-based sign language tutorial for young children.
- Tutorials on computer use for Clinic staff.
- A "pop box" that speech therapists operate by remote control to encourage correct speech.
- A custom interface and set of interchangeable handles for a commercial toy record player to allow children to activate the record player using motions that don't depend on fine motor skills.
- A toy phone with over-sized buttons and cushioned handset.
- "Dump truck city" -an electrically controlled dump truck that travels forward and backward on a circular track, controlled by a panel of large-format buttons.
- A prototype of a "posture sensor" that interfaces a hat-mounted posture monitoring device with electronic toys. The toy is activated as long as the child maintains an upright posture. The purpose of the system is to build muscle strength in children with cerebral palsy by encouraging good posture.
- Three rooms of a custom multisensory electromechanical dollhouse.

The dollhouse provides an example of an extended, ambitious project that has integrated electrical engineering design, computer interfacing and programming, and mechanical design. The project was initiated at the request of the Clinic's therapists. Several preliminary designs were explored before the idea of a modular, room-by-room construction was adopted. The first system was a kitchen with electronically controlled refrigerator door, lights, and kitchen sounds that a child activates selectively with a large, easy-to-use wired or wireless touch pad. The second-generation system, a bathroom, included an electronically controlled toilet lid, a swimming/singing rubber duck, lights, and sounds, and added a simple speech recognition interface. The third system, a bedroom, includes a ceiling-mounted rotating mobile, a cupboard with two electromechanical doors that open, phone and radio sounds, lights, and (at the request of the clinicians) a vibrating bed, so that the children can feel the motion. In addition to the touch-pad and speech interfaces, it includes a custom "finger sensor" interface that activates the bedroom devices when a child successfully inserts a finger into a hole that detects the insertion with infrared emitters and sensors. This new interface is to encourage children to develop their fine motor skills and practice pointing motions.

Each room is a custom plastic box approximately 24" x 10" x 16", with the electronics and motors and housed in a "subfloor" under the room itself. The rooms are serving several functions. They are used as a part of therapy sessions in which the clinician uses the placement of the touch-pad to encourage specific motions; in cooperative play involving disabled and normally abled children; and as a reward for good progress, because the children like playing with the rooms. In each new room, one of the key design decisions has been considering what aspects of the implementation to adopt from the previous design, which aspects of the system could be improved by modifying the design, and which aspects must be completely new because of new functionality or requirements. The project is expected to continue for several semesters into the future, with the focus of the next generation systems turning to size: the Clinic has requested smaller designs, about the size of a lunch box, so that therapists can easily take dollhouse rooms on home visits.

Comments from **Christina Scheer,** occupational therapist at the Children's Clinic at Wabash Center during the first three years of the EPICS-CCWC partnership:

> *We have greatly benefited from both the groups from EPICS. It has been a joy to work with all the students. I think they are learning a lot about disability. I think all of their projects have been really helpful, and the children just love it.*

From **Sandy Daugherty**, coordinator for the Children's Clinic at the Wabash Center:

> *EPICS has had a positive impact on our programs. Both teams that have worked with the Wabash Center help educate the community about students with disabilities.*

> *EPICS improved our interactions with the kids, which is one of our main missions. In addition, EPICS helped with our recertification from CARF [Commission on Accreditation of Rehabilitation Facilities]. The contact from CARF was impressed with Wabash Center's interactions with the engineering department from Purdue University*

and the projects from both teams that worked with us. In fact, the contact sent information to her husband who works for Los Alamos, which is closely related to New Mexico University, to try do similar programs there.

Both teams have improved the quality for our kids and have improved the overall joy for our students.

The Imagination Station Project

The Imagination Station is a hands-on, interactive children's science and space museum located in Lafayette, Indiana. Its mission is to provide a place for children and their families to explore the worlds of science, engineering, and technology through interactive displays, activities, and workshops. The museum opened in 1996 through the efforts of a volunteer community organization.

The Imagination Station EPICS team began in 1997. The goal of the team is to create interactive displays that enhance the ability of the Imagination Station to accomplish its mission. The team has consisted of students from disciplines including electrical, computer, mechanical, materials, aerospace, chemical, and civil engineering, computer science, sociology, and visual design. Purdue faculty members as well as engineers from Eli Lilly have advised the team. Two local companies have sponsored the team to design and implement displays illustrating technology related to magnet wire and pharmaceutical manufacturing.

The team has worked with the director of the Imagination Station to develop several exhibits, including:

- History of computers — a hands-on collection of hardware and software games showing the evolution of the personal computer.
- Computer operation — An interactive matching game that quizzes children on the components of a computer. The display is run by a computer housed in a clear plastic case so that the child can see the actual computer components as s/he plays the game.
- Electromagnetism — a series of three exhibits that demonstrate the principles of electromagnetism:
- Applications display — a static display of common uses of electromagnets, including a microwave oven and an electric motor.
- Mag Tower — an interactive display that encourages children to explore the properties of magnets by stacking permanent magnets on an electromagnet that they can turn on and off and on which they can reverse the polarity.

- Mag Racer — a 7-foot-long interactive display that challenges children to move a car equipped with a permanent magnet down a track by activating a series of electromagnetic coils distributed along the track.

Barb Pipher-Doran, director of the Imagination Station has summarized the partnership with EPICS:

> *Imagination Station has benefited from their association with EPICS teams in a number of ways. Through the partnership with a local business (Rea Magnet Wire) we have been able to present displays that demonstrate the use of products manufactured in our community. This adds a special dimension to the science concepts presented in the display. Working with the EPICS team has helped Imagination Station focus more clearly on what kind of exhibits are needed in the museum. Discussions with students have provided good feedback and added creative ideas to projects.*

> *The Imagination Station-EPICS partnership has contributed to the museum's mission by allowing the creation of new, and otherwise too costly, displays. The mission, providing opportunities for hands-on science learning, has been enhanced by the contributions of EPICS involvement.*

> *EPICS has provided Imagination Station an avenue to explore exhibit ideas with creative and talented young people who have an understanding of the technical skills needed to make the ideas into reality. The teams have also provided research capabilities and technical assistance that we would not otherwise have been able to afford. Helping the team members understand what "hands-on" entails has made the staff analyze more closely what constitutes good museum practice. We have all gained skills and insight through the process.*

Constructed Wetlands

Purdue University operates a large agricultural facility about ten miles north of West Lafayette, Indiana. In addition to intensive farming activities, there are confined feeding operations for dairy cattle, hogs, and chickens and an aquaculture center for raising fish. Storage lagoons are used to collect the wastes from these operations; the lagoon contents are applied to the farmland by spray irrigation. This common practice can have the negative effect of increasing the levels of nitrogen, phosphorus, and other chemicals in both the surface runoff and the groundwater.

The Constructed Wetlands EPICS team was formed in 1998 to provide engineering support for the planning, design, construction, and operation of a wetland that would treat the agricultural runoff that pollutes Pine Creek. The team has included students majoring in environmental, civil, mechanical, electrical, and interdisciplinary engineering as well as in natural resources and environmental chemistry. The team's advisors have included faculty from civil and electrical engineering, as well as a chemical engineer and an environmental lawyer from local industry; the Project Partner has been a faculty member in Purdue's Department of Forestry and Natural Resources.

At present, little design information exists for constructing wetlands to treat this type of wastewater. The long-range objectives for the project include developing predictive models for pollutant removal performance, engineering design criteria, and good construction and operating cost information. The team has surveyed the site; designed the wetland cells; designed the piping layout and pump installations to carry water from the creek, through the cells, and back to the creek; and designed and constructed a dam to control the water flow. A contractor was hired to excavate the site and to install the large piping and weir boxes. The students worked with a wetlands nursery to determine the type and quantity of plants required, and carried out the planting of 9000 plants.

To allow the wetland to serve as an experimental facility, the four cells of the wetland are arranged into two parallel trains so that the effect of different loading levels can be evaluated. The team has designed and installed flow measurement and sampling equipment to collect data on the effectiveness of the wetland. With construction of the wetland itself completed, the EPICS team has looked to expand the impact of its work. The team is currently constructing an observation deck and educational displays on the ecology of the wetland. This work has spawned interest from local schools and community groups that would like to come and see the wetland. In this way, the project will serve multiple functions for the community's benefit.

George Parker, Professor in Purdue's Department of Forestry and Natural Resources, has been the primary Project Partner for the Constructed Wetlands team. His comments on the project include:

> *The EPICS team has provided valuable assistance in establishment and operation of this project. The work of the EPICS team has been important in developing constructed wetlands to serve as a model of alternative technology to improve water quality within the community. Their work has also provided for increased educational and research activities of the Department of Forestry and Natural Resources.*

Project Partner Retention

One of the key measures of community satisfaction has been the retention of project partners. In the six years since the start of EPICS, teams have worked with a total of 24 different project partners (with some partners, such as the HPN, including several organizations). Twenty-one of the partnerships are still in place. Over half of the teams have completed their original projects; in all but one instance, the community partner has presented the team with new project ideas, in order to continue the relationship. Three partnerships have been terminated. One agency to which three software projects had been delivered reported that its needs had been met. One agency was able to identify funds to purchase a commercial product similar to the one being developed by the team, and deemed this a quicker path to having a system in place. The third partnership terminated when the agency filed for bankruptcy protection.

EPICS has received three awards from the community: a certificate of Outstanding Achievement from the Wabash Center in 1998 and recognition in the 2000 and 2001 West Lafayette Community Honor Roll.

STUDENT EVALUATIONS

On the academic side, indicators of success include measures of student participation and evaluations. In the 2000-01 academic year, 400 students were enrolled in the program, participating on 20 teams. Since the start of EPICS, we have tracked the retention of students in the program: the rate at which students who are able to return to EPICS (i.e., have not graduated or are not off campus on a cooperative industry assignment) do so. The overall retention rate from one semester to the next has been over 78%.

Evaluations of the program have included quantitative evaluation along the specific educational objectives, as well as descriptive formative and summative evaluations. A majority of the students polled have cited the opportunity to obtain "practical, real-world experience in engineering design" as their primary reason for participating in the EPICS Program. A significant number have also identified the opportunity to do community service as a major factor in their participation. Many of the students report that they have done community service in the past, in activities such as tutoring, church work, scouting, soup kitchens, crisis hotlines, and volunteer work for Habitat for Humanity. They have not, however, reported prior experiences that combine community service with engineering.

Quantitative evaluation has focused on specific course/program objectives. Table 1 shows the percentage of students rating the course with an A or B grade for each objective, accumulated over nine semesters starting in Spring 1996. *Ability to Work on a Team* consistently receives the highest grades, followed by *Communication Skills* and *Awareness of the Customer in an Engineering Project*. Table 2 summarizes the students' narrative responses about what they have learned in the program.

Table 1. Percent of students responding with a grade of A or B to the question: "Evaluate the impact that EPICS has had for you on _____." 1078 responses accumulated over 9 consecutive semesters, Spring 1996 through Spring 2000.

	Cumulative %
Your technical skills	67%
Your understanding of the design process *	79%
Your communication skills	84%
Your ability to work on a team	88%
Your resourcefulness	80%
Your organizational skills	78%
Your awareness of the community	74%
Your awareness of the customer in an engineering project	82%
Your awareness of ethical issues	66%
OVERALL EVALUATION	84%

* Question not asked in Spring 96.

As with any program, not all comments have been positive. Most negative comments have addressed the lecture requirement or growth issues. Most comments, however, are extremely positive. Comments from the students include:

> *By far the best engineering class I have had.*
> *Great, I am now thinking about going into engineering outreach as a career, which is what my team does.*
> *It has given me hope because how I see that engineering is not just math.*
> *It has encouraged me to stay in engineering, DEFINITELY.*
> *It is interesting that EPICS takes us as close as any class program would to real life engineering problems.*
> *experience is very precious and the learning of the team communication is even more important.*
> *For first time, again, I was facing such variety of team members from different backgrounds, which helped me realize the importance of trying to understand why other people differ in their ideas, sources, interests and way of thinking in general.*

Table 2. Responses to the question "What are the three most valuable things you have learned from being a part of the EPICS program?"

Course Objectives	Total # Reponses	Type of comments (# of responses)
Technical Skills	83	Design process (35), Applying classroom knowledge to real problems (26), Technical skills (21), Problem solving (2)
Teamwork	191	Teamwork (151), Leadership (30), Accountability (5), Responsibility (3), Cooperation (2)
Communication Skills	99	Communication skills (69), Presentation skills (13), Technical documentation (12), Writing reports (5)
Organizational Skills	68	Organizational skills (39), Time management (14), Long-term project development (8), Dealing with deadlines (7)
Resourcefulness	21	Resourcefulness/ingenuity (11), Research (9), Adaptability (1)
Sponsor Awareness	23	Customer Awareness (23)
Expanded Awareness	17	Community awareness (12), Community impact (2), Helping others (3)
Professional Ethics	4	Character assessment/ethics (4)

This type of interdisciplinary teamwork has been valuable in helping me prepare for a full time job, in fact I think it is more valuable than any other engineering experience I've had at Purdue

I think the learning experience will last a life time. The teamwork

In retrospect, this semester of EPICS has made the team members more aware of the different aspects of product design and development. We are also more equipped to proceed with our projects in the following semesters. Probably the most important beneficiaries of our EPICS project are the people whose lives we enhance with our technical contributions. Our primary goal is to use our technical skills to benefit the community, and the successful completion of these projects will surely enhance the lives of many people who are employed at WCGI [Wabash Center Greenbush Industries]. In addition, by thinking about the many requirements of the workers, we have become more aware of the needs and abilities of people who live in our community.

It has ... made me a little more focused on the moral implications of my professional actions.

It has encouraged my resolve to always be involved in the community.

Makes me want to carry this community service over to my professional experience – organizing community service for my company to participate in.

Open my eyes to the potential to help others.

While most of the students in the program are engineering students, comments from the non-engineering students include:

Well, I think I now care more about what other people want instead of my own interests.

Being team leader has taught me invaluable lessons on positive reinforcement, communication and motivating people to work together. These haven't been easy lessons, but priceless ones.

I have learned to participate in a group and work with team members in doing the projects.

Actually, working on this project has helped me guide the rest of my course work and ideas for a future profession by working on this project in the community.

THE NATIONAL EPICS PROGRAM

The EPICS Program was created at Purdue University in the Fall of 1995. By 1997, EPICS Programs were also underway at the University of Notre Dame and Iowa State University. This demonstrated that the EPICS program satisfied important educational and community needs and was therefore compelling enough to be adopted by other universities.

The existence of EPICS programs at several sites has opened the possibility of addressing community and educational needs that extend beyond those of a university and its local community. Several of the agencies that EPICS teams are working with are national in scope. These include Habitat for Humanity, the Salvation Army, the Red Cross, and the YWCA. EPICS project teams working with these agencies in different cities could address such national-scale problems as homelessness, low-income housing, and disaster relief.

The first multi-site EPICS project, the Homelessness Prevention Network project, was initiated in 1997, when the newly formed HPN team at Notre Dame began working not only with agencies in its home city of South Bend, Indiana, but with the Purdue HPN EPICS team as well. The local goal for each team is to enable its partner agencies to share demographic and services-provided information about their clients. The agencies could then produce duplicate-free counts of homeless individuals and families, meaningful data on the use and effectiveness of services, and a record for each client that can be used for case-management across all agencies and all available services. The common goal of these two HPN teams is the sharing of data on homelessness between Lafayette and South Bend. Success in this task will enable city-to-city comparisons, help track migration patterns, and determine which services are the most effective. The HPN effort is thus on its way towards enabling data collection on homelessness throughout the state. The extension of this project to statewide and national scope could provide the first accurate characterization of homelessness throughout the U.S. and lead to better-informed public policy in the area of homelessness.

The potential benefits of many different national-scale EPICS projects, pursued by a national-scale coalition of EPICS sites, led to the creation in 1999 of the National EPICS Program. The universities currently participating in this program are Purdue, Notre Dame, Iowa State, the University of Wisconsin-Madison, and Georgia Tech. Support for this effort has come from the National Science Foundation, the Corporation for National Service, and Microsoft Corporation. The first two national-scale projects will be the National Homelessness Prevention Network (NHPN) Project that is already underway and the National Habitat for Humanity (NHFH) Project that will begin in 2001.

CONCLUSIONS

The Engineering Projects in Community Service Program has added a new dimension to the educational experience for engineering undergraduates at Purdue University. It represents the first program at Purdue that formally integrates service-learning into the engineering curriculum, and is one of relatively few large-scale engineering-centered service-learning programs nationally. Key features of the program include vertically integrated, multidisciplinary teams and multi-year participation. On the community side, the EPICS structure fosters a long-term relationship between project teams and the community service agency partners, and enables ambitious projects that can have a significant impact. On the academic side, this structure provides students with the opportunity to be involved in all phases of the design process, from project definition through deployment, on projects that are large in scale. Most importantly, the structure encourages an extended service-learning experience, with emphasis on providing a model of how engineers can use their technical skills to benefit the community.

Acknowledgments

The EPICS Program has been supported by grants from the U.S. Department of Education's Fund for the Improvement of Postsecondary Education (grant P116F50129), the National Science Foundation's Instrumentation and Laboratory Improvement Program (grants DUE96-50771 and DUE 98-51200), the Corporation for National Service Learn and Serve America Higher Education Program (grants 97LHEIN025 and 00LHEIN025 00), the National Science Foundation Action Agenda for Engineering Curriculum Innovation Program (grant EEC-0002638), and by grants and donations from numerous companies, including Microsoft Research, Hewlett-Packard, the 3M Foundation, AMD, Eli Lilly, General Motors, the ADC Foundation, United Technologies, Rea Magnet Wire Co., MDBS, Great Lakes Chemical, and Alcoa.

REFERENCES

ABET EC (2000). *Criteria for Accrediting Engineering Programs.* The Engineering Accreditation Commission of The Accreditation Board for Engineering and Technology, 1999, http://www.abet.org/eac/eac.htm.

American Society for Engineering Education (1994). *Engineering Education for a Changing World.* Joint project report of the Engineering Deans Council and the Corporate Roundtable of the ASEE. http:www.asee.org.

Catalano, G. D., Wray, P., and Cornelio, S. (2000). Compassion Practicum: A Capstone Design Experience at the United States Military Academy, *Journal of Engineering Education, 90* (4), 471-477.

Dahir, M. (1993, August/September). Educating Engineers for the Real World. *Technology Review,* 14-16.

Duffy, J., Tsang, E. and Lord, S. (2000, June). Service-Learning in Engineering: What, Why, and How? *Proceedings of the ASEE 2000 Annual Conference,* St. Louis, Missouri.

Hobson, R. S. (2000, June). Service-Learning as an Educational Tool in an Introduction to Engineering Course, *Proceedings of the ASEE 2000 Annual Conference,* St. Louis, Missouri.

Nagchaudhuri, A., Eydgahi, A., and Shakur, A. (2000, June). SLOPE: An Effort Towards Infusing Service-Learning into Physics and Engineering Education, *Proceedings of the ASEE 2000 Annual Conference,* St. Louis, Missouri.

Stott, N. W., Schultz, W. W., Brei, D., Winton Hoffman, D. M., and Markus, G. (2000, June). ProCEED: A Program for Civic Engagement in Engineering Design, Proceedings of the ASEE 2000 Annual Conference, St. Louis, Missouri.

Tsang, E.(Ed.) (2000). *Projects That Matter: Concepts and Models for Service-Learning in Engineering.* Washington, DC: AAHE.

CHAPTER 20

INTERNATIONAL SERVICE LEARNING

Richard J. Kraft
University of Colorado-Boulder

INTRODUCTION

The week following our border immersion service-learning experience on the El Paso/Juarez border between the U.S. and Mexico in April, 2000, a strong wind whipped up the flames from torches used to light the paths in the barrio on the old Juarez dump and seven women and children were killed when their tar paper and cardboard homes were destroyed. My students and I were devastated to learn of the deaths of one of the courageous women and her son with whom we had just interacted at their pre-school and women's center. Our study of critical theory, liberation theology and education, third-world development, immigration, environmental degradation and poverty took on a tragic human face, and punctuated our learning in a manner impossible to forget. This is just the latest of countless examples one could give of the power of international service-learning to affect, and at times even transform, the lives of U.S. college students. A poem by one of my students based on that experience is included later in this chapter.

As a trainer of teachers for almost a third of a century here in the United States and in countries around the world, I have been on a lifelong search for pedagogies that impact teacher behavior and improve their learning and that of the students in their classroom. I have seldom been satisfied with the results of learning in the "closed classrooms" of academe, and found support for those frustrations in the Presidential Address by Lauren Resnick (1987) to the American Educational Research Association in which she explicated some of the differences between "practical and formal intelligence." Using research by anthropologists and psychologists in such disparate settings as navigation practice on U.S. Navy ships, black market lottery bookmaking in Brazil, mathematics knowledge among dairy workers, and arithmetic performance by people in a Weight Watcher's program, she concludes that school learning differs from other learning in four basic ways:

1. *individual cognition* in school versus *shared cognition* outside;
2. *pure experimentation* in school versus *tool manipulation* outside;
3. *symbol manipulation* in school versus *contextualized reasoning* outside school; and
4. *generalized learning* in school versus *situation-specific competencies* outside.

Resnick suggests that school learning often becomes a matter of manipulating symbols rather than connecting with the real world. It becomes the learning of rules disconnected from real life. She concludes that:

> *...there is growing evidence, then that not only may schooling not contribute in a direct and obvious way to performance outside school, but also that knowledge acquired outside school is not always used to support in-school learning. Schooling is coming to look increasingly isolated from the rest of what we do.*

Resnick concludes that we need to help students gain skills even when optimum conditions do not exist. We need learners who can transfer skills from one setting to another and who are adaptive learners. The discontinuity between the worlds of school and work suggest that we should not focus so much on "symbols" correctly manipulated but divorced from experience. Successful schooling must involve socially shared mental work and more direct engagement with the referents of symbols. Schooling should begin to look for like out-of-school functioning and include greater use of reflection and reasoning. With Marshal McLuhan (1964) I have come to believe that children and young people intuitively know that going to school or college is often interrupting their education. Our young people today are "schooling rich," and "experience poor." Service-learning, particularly in an international or cross-cultural context can provide a powerful pedagogy to break the barriers between the in-school and out-of-school experiences, and between practical and formal intelligence.

With the globalization of the world economy and the manner in which events in one part of the world impact on all of us, I have felt for many years the necessity of preparing American college students for this interconnected world of the 21st century. Both K-12 schooling and higher education have felt increasingly disconnected and even irrelevant to preparing young people for a truly global society. Language courses have too often prepared students to master grammar, while being unable to carry on even a minimal conversation with a native speaker. The study of anthropology and sociology leave students unprepared for even the most basic contacts with members of other cultures.

Students in philosophy, religion and ethics courses are unprepared to confront the complexity of cross-cultural ethics and comparative religious practices.

If there is any truth to the belief that formal schooling does not prepare young people for the realities of contemporary American life, it is even more likely that it does little to prepare them for the high tech global world of the next millennium. Finding the traditional classroom insufficient early in my career as a college professor, I sought more impactful teaching methodologies, and came across the concepts of experiential learning as explicated by John Dewey, and the "adventure" education ideas of groups such as Outward Bound. These problem-solving modes of learning in real-life internships and the high mountain or wilderness environment, appeared to be a powerful alternative to the lecture-recitation, teacher-talk modes of learning which still dominate so much of our educational system.

Experiential learning, even outside the classroom, generally failed to meet the important criteria of transferability of knowledge and skills to the solution of problems faced in the real world. In addition, while significantly more motivational than traditional pedagogies, it too often lacked a moral imperative. It was thus that I turned to volunteer community service and eventually service-learning as a powerful pedagogy for students of all ages. Initially, this took the form of local school and community involvement on the part of my students, but having spent 30 years as an international volunteer and educational consultant, I increasingly saw and felt the power of the global setting to radically transform my own ways of thinking and learning. It was in cross-cultural and international settings that I personally experienced and observed in my students the most profound changes, and thus was born my involvement in international service-learning.

MODELS OF INTERNATIONAL SERVICE LEARNING

There are a variety of models and ways to differentiate types of international service learning. One typology differentiates three possible ways of looking at the topic.

1. **Service-Learning Abroad** is one in which students from one or more countries go to another country to be involved in service-learning experiences, closely related to their academic course work. This is similar to the traditional Study Abroad programs run by universities around the world, but with an added component of service, rather than being limited to the more traditional foreign language and culture programs. The most common forms of this type of service-learning are short-term "alternative spring break" activities related to courses in education, environmental studies, sociology, or a range of other

disciplines. Of a longer term nature are small programs run by American universities, and the extensive programs of the International Partnership for Service Learning with its semester and summer-long programs throughout the world.

2. **Service Learning in an International Perspective** looks at the range of community service programs which exist throughout the world, many of them pre-dating the service-learning movement in the United States. Institutions of higher education on every continent to-day have their students out in local communities. Given the "traditional" reputation of higher education in most other countries, there is a surprising array of service-learning programs underway in universities around the world.

3. **National Service** refers to organized programs wherein young people engage in civilian service to the community or nation (Eberly & Sherraden, 1990). While a strong case could be made that national service is not service-learning in the strictest definitions of the term, it does serve as a profoundly educational experience for thousands of American young adults, and tens of thousands or even millions of young people throughout the world. These programs may or may not be connected to higher education institutions, and deal with a wide range of societal needs in health, education, the environment, agriculture, housing, and in almost every sector of society. The purposes of national service tend to be broader than those of most service learning programs, and have their roots in William James 1910 essay on the "Moral Equivalent of War."

A second typology is based on Sigmon's (1996) work which differentiates the types of service-learning based on the emphasis given the words service or learning in a given program. While I and many other practitioners of service-learning have seldom been able to make such clear distinctions in either my national or international service-learning programs, the typology does help to place many of the activities currently going on under the rubric of international service learning.

Emphases of Service Learning Programs

service-LEARNING	Learning goals primary; service outcomes secondary
SERVICE-learning	Service outcomes primary; learning goals Secondary
service learning	Service and learning goals separate
SERVICE-LEARNING	Service and learning goals of equal weight; each enhances the other for all participants

International service-LEARNING: Some Study Abroad programs may include a small component of service in the local communities, but it is generally not a significant part of either the language or culture study or other course work which is the fundamental purpose of most study abroad programs. The learning goals are primary, and service is of only secondary consideration or importance.

International SERVICE-learning: Environmental, social justice, and religious short-term international programs often have a strong service component, but is often only incidental to a program of academic study on the home campus or an overseas institution. While there are several Peace Corps programs closely tied to academic institutions in the U.S. and abroad and while there is undoubtedly a great deal of learning which takes place, Peace Corps volunteers might best be placed in this model. Global volunteers from a wide array of secular and religious organizations also fall under this model of international SERVICE-learning.

International service learning: Each year, hundreds of thousands of students from around the world set off with their backpacks to "see the world." Occasionally, they connect with some volunteer project or stop and take a language or some other course at a local institution of higher education, but while both service and learning may occur, there is no real connection between the service and learning goals. An example of this was my experience on Semester-at-Sea, in which students raised money for various programs visited while on the Semester-long voyage, but there was no real connection to the learning occurring in the shipboard classes.

International SERVICE-LEARNING: The final model gives equal weight to both the service and the learning, and makes a concerted effort to assure that each enhances the other for all participants. It is this model of international service-learning, on which we will concentrate our attention in this chapter.

Berry and Chisholm (1999) in their seminal work, differentiate the models of International SERVICE-LEARNING into the following categories.

1. **Career Related Service Learning**: Unlike the United States with its broad liberal arts tradition, interdisciplinary programs, and open-option majors, in most institutions of higher education around the world, students spend the vast majority of their time within one particular faculty, preparing for a specific career in medicine, law, social work, teaching, engineering, architecture of other professions. Many of these professional schools have a long tradition of practicum experiences or internships. While it is often difficult to differentiate practica and internships from service-learning, some would suggest that the latter is conducted in "non-traditional" settings and that service learning must benefit not only the in-

dividual learning of the student, but in addition the community and agency involved.

2. **Discipline Related**: Berry and Chisholm describe this model as being used by many higher education faculties which have field study components to their programs. Whether it is linguists working with "dying" languages, medical students immunizing poor children, or sociologists working in the urban ghettoes or rural barrios, there are numerous academic departments throughout the world using service-learning to assist their students in mastering their particular discipline.

3. **Course or Module Related**: Perhaps the most widely used form of service-learning is that directly related to a single course (U.S.) or module (Great Britain). The University of Colorado has up to thirty different professors each term using service-learning as a pedagogy in engineering, education, sociology, political science, dentistry, nursing, English, and a wide range of other departments. Examples of course-based service-learning are students in the Foundations of Education who spend time tutoring children in an after school program or engineering students designing a mechanism to assist a physically disabled child perform a particular task. In addition to service-learning directly related to a specific course, many institution have also developed interdisciplinary "stand-alone" service-learning courses.

4. **The Cohesive Curriculum Model**: The International Partnership for Service-Learning is a good example of an organization that uses this model in which two or more disciplines or professional tracks are brought together around a service opportunity, and teams of instructors from different departments coordinate the instruction and service. Students study major concepts in more than one discipline and use the traditional academic course work along with the service experiences to understand the material.

5. **Non-Credited but Part of the Learning Expectations**: While service-learning as it has come to be defined in recent years generally is part of the class expectations and is required and credited, there is a long tradition, particularly in religiously-based institutions of higher education of "mandatory volunteerism." Whether it is built into the values of the institution or into the graduation requirements, professors have for generations sought to have their students "out in the community," with or without a direct connection to the ongoing curriculum or classes.

DEFINITION OF INTERNATIONAL SERVICE-LEARNING

Perhaps the most common definition of service-learning used in the United States is that set out by the Commission on National and Community Service (CNCS; 1993). The CNCS definition states the need for active participation, thoughtful organization, the meeting of actual community needs, collaboration between school and community, integration with the students' academic curriculum, structured time for reflection, opportunities to use newly acquired skills in real-life situations, extension of learning beyond the classroom, and the fostering a sense of caring for others. From and international perspective, the International Partnership for Service Learning (1999) defines service learning as community service that is serious, substantive, and truly useful; that demands responsibility and commitment; and that draws on existing skills and builds new ones. And, as academic study that focuses on the culture in which the student serves; which utilizes the content and methodology of traditional disciplines, especially the liberal arts; that is taught and evaluated by qualified academicians; and credited by a degree-granting university.

Service-learning in higher education which occurs within national boundaries would appear to hold to similar definitions, regardless of where it occurs. There are, of course, numerous cultural and religious differences in motivation and program design, but involving students outside the ivory tower is now becoming a widespread phenomenon on almost every continent. Crossing national boundaries to do "service-learning abroad," however, is more problematic, and in many ways an even more powerful pedagogical tool. Respect for other cultures becomes a critical component of all programs crossing national boundaries, something not always true of service-learning experiences carried out in one's own community. Cultural and linguistic competency become necessary if the service-learning is to be truly effective. Reciprocity between "server" and "served" becomes much more difficult in the international setting, particularly in programs in which students from rich countries serve individuals and organizations in the poorer nations of the world.

EFFECTS OF INTERNATIONAL SERVICE-LEARNING

Research on the effects of international service learning is limited and often anecdotal in nature. However, in the past decade a growing body of research on the effects of service-learning within country, primarily in the United States, has been accumulating and it is possible extrapolate from them some of the effects of international service-learning experiences.

The effects of service-learning on students can be divided into personal, social, learning outcomes, and career development (Eyler, Giles & Gray, 1999). On a personal level it appears to have a positive effect on students' personal efficacy, personal identity, spiritual growth, moral development, interpersonal development, the ability to work well with others, leadership and communication skills. Despite cultural differences, there is likely to be similar effects found among young people in other countries involved in service-learning out in their communities. It is also likely that gains found within country are likely to be even stronger in the international or cross-cultural settings. Kauffman (1982) found that students in the Goshen College Study-Service Program experienced a changed world view, an increased interest in reflective thought in the arts, literature and language, an increased interest in the welfare of others, and increased self confidence, self-esteem, and independence. Social outcomes of service-learning indicate a reduction in stereotypes, a facilitation of cultural and racial understanding, the development of social responsibility and citizenship skills, a commitment to service, and involvement with community service after graduation (Eyler, Giles & Gray, 1999). In one of the few studies to look at effects of international service-learning on social outcomes, Myers-Lipton (1996) found that international service-learning students at my own institution, the University of Colorado, evidenced larger increases in global concern, and cultural respect, but that changes were negligible for cultural interest. He also found significant increases in civic responsibility and significant decreases in racial prejudice among students involved in an intensive international service learning program when compared to control groups who had not had the experiences. The INVST program at the University of Colorado is described later in this chapter as an exemplary program in international service-learning. Follow-up studies with students in that program have found a greater commitment to service and involvement in service occupations following graduation. While international experience can often lead to reinforcing stereotypes, when carefully planned, it can be even more powerful than within country experiences in facilitating greater cultural and racial understanding.

Learning outcomes research indicates that service-learning has a positive impact on students' academic learning, improves their ability to apply what they have learned in the "real world," may positively affect academic learning as measured by grades or GPA, and impacts such academic outcomes as demonstrated complexity of understanding, problem analysis, critical thinking and cognitive development (Eyler, Giles & Gray, 1999). While there is little or no evidence that international service-learning improves mastery of traditional academic subject matter, there is likely a higher motivation for understanding the applications of knowledge in the "real" world. International contexts are also likely to foster a greater problem-solving and critical thinking on the part of students, due to the ways in which culture, language, religion, and beliefs are under constant challenge in "foreign" settings. Finally, research on traditional study abroad programs has found a positive impact on career development for students, and it is thus likely that international service-learning experiences would also affect student career choices.

Qualitative research on service-learning has begun to document the process of student development in service-learning. The following poem by a Master's student of mine at the University of Colorado-Boulder was written during her one-week intensive service-learning experience on the El Paso/Juarez border between Mexico and the United States. It beautifully captures the personal, social and learning outcomes that can result from even a short international service-learning experience. While one cannot claim such power of expression for all students involved in international service-learning experiences, my students have been overwhelmingly positive about the work, and in most cases state that it was the most powerful learning experience of the course or often their whole university experience.

The El Paso/Juarez Border Immersion Experience
By Carrie Symons

The border:
A line drawn in the sand.
Toy soldiers guard the castle walls.
But I can come and go as I wish.
They cannot keep my heart from crossing.

The disparity between the have and "have-nots."
I cling to my "haves."
For fear.
She who has nothing has freedom.
We boast a developed country full of declining spirits
And we spill our toxic vomit into our neighbor's backyard
Only to refuse their children the right to education,
Only to turn our backs on the dependence we have created.

Scraggy trees pose like crotchety old men along the sandy dirt roads.
They are relics of life in this desolate land.
They withstand the dry wind, like skeletons passing the test of time,
Reaching for promise of renewal.
Plastic bags cling to their branches:
Ornaments of emptiness,
First world trash in the arms of Mexico's mother,
Inflating with air like a child's balloon.

But I am the one who's lost, whose identity has been mutated by the border.

Homes made of cardboard boxes, wooden pallets, scraps of wire fences, tarpaper roofs, floors of sand.
Schools made of cardboard boxes, wooden pallets, scraps of wire fences, tarpaper roofs, floors of sand.

Water is scarce, delivered by trucks, pumped into big, black drums.
Electrical wires thrown over power lines,
Like hands of children gripping their father's arm.
Dry, hot, fire hazard, covered in dust...this is home.
Roads rutted like washboards.
No school bus travels down here.

People speak in Mexican tongue,
But poverty translates without words
In those big, brown eyes,
And effortless smiles.
My soul drops to its knees in honor of you,
But the sun can't warm the desert wind.
At the end of the day, I can wash it away.
I can wash away the sand.
At the end of the day, I can wash it away,
But it is I who have nothing.

EXAMPLES OF NATIONAL SERVICE

As indicated in the typologies earlier in this chapter, one form of international service-learning is that of National Service or National Youth Service, found in countries around the world. Over 25,000 young people participate in the Australian Service Cadet Scheme, administered by the Department of Defence, 3500 participate in a Green Corps program, and additional skilled young adults participate in the international **Australian** Youth Ambassadors for Development Programme. The programs are an effort by the government to promote citizenship, develop leadership, develop citizens committed to voluntary work and community service, and provide needed services within Australia and abroad (Gal, 2000).

Katimavik offers young **Canadians** aged 17 to 21 an alternative educational experience to acquire interpersonal and new work skills. This seven-an-a-half month long program has young people live in three different regions of Canada (two English-speaking and one French-speaking) where they work as volunteers on projects submitted by non-profit organizations. Participants are divided into groups of 11 participants, which are made up of men and women and reflect Canada's cultural, economic and social diversity (Gal,2000).

The **China** Youth Volunteers Association began in 1993 and now encompasses thousands of Chinese youth in the Poverty Reduction Program, the Community Development Program, the Green Action Camping Program, and various campaigns to fight calamities and provide relief. Over 70 million young participants had been mobilized in the six years prior to 1990 to provide effective voluntary services to the society (Sherraden & Eberly, 1990).

Germany has a civilian service, which may serve as a substitute to service in the armed forces, and currently enrolls 126,000 German men. In addition, some 13-14,000 serve in the Voluntary Social Year, the Ecological Year, or the volunteer service in foreign countries. There is a wide range of service opportunities including health, education, child-care, work with church agencies, the elderly, ecology, peace movements and international aid and development organizations (Gal, 2000).

Since 1973, the **Nigerian** National Youth Service Corps has played a significant role in post Civil War reconstruction, rehabilitation and reconciliation programs. The scheme mobilizes all University Graduate and Higher National Certificate holder (Nigerians only) from home and foreign institutions for one year of compulsory national service. Participants work in states other their own and within different ethnic and linguistic settings. One purpose of the program is to promote intercultural transformation, inter-tribal marriages, ethnic blending and the mobility of labor to forge national unity and integration. These recent graduates work in rural communities to alleviate poverty, improve health and education, control disease, restore ecological balance, and improve agriculture, among other tasks (Gal, 2000).

Many other nations have national service or national youth service schemes including **Trinidad-Tobago, the United States, Israel, Mexico, Israel, and Russia**. Some of these are open to all youth, others a compulsory for graduates of higher education, and some include service-learning within higher education, a form of international service-learning to which we shall now turn our attention.

AN INTERNATIONAL PERSPECTIVE ON SERVICE-LEARNING IN HIGHER EDUCATION

Colin Bundy of the University of Witwatersrand, perhaps **South Africa's** and the continent's most prestigious university, captures well the changing role of higher education in many of the developing nations of the world.

No university is an ivory tower-even if it wishes to be. Universities are deeply implicated in the modern state and are key agents of modern society. This means that they could be conscious of, and make choice about, the terms of that involvement. Universities can be the brains and the skilled hands of their immediate community; but they can also be the conscience, the source of reflection, and a shaping imagination for change. Higher education must be critically engaged in the needs of communities, nations, and the world: not least because it may just be the last, best hope that communities, nations and the world have for considering what, why and how they do things (Berry and Chisholm, 1999).

The various forms, types and models of service-learning discussed in this chapter and elsewhere in this book can be found on every continent, numerous countries, and countless institutions of higher education. An excellent over-view of many of these programs *is Service-Learning in Higher Education around the World* by Berry and Chisholm (1999), and it is from their work that many of the following examples are taken. The authors point out that service-learning goes under a variety of names in other countries, including extension education (India), study-service (United Kingdom), practical education (Uganda), social service course (Korea), work-study (Jamaica), and programs of education in the community (Mexico). In all countries surveyed, however, service-learning was seen as a means of dealing with educational and communities issues and problems facing their societies. Among the reasons for implementing service-learning given by global participants in a 1998 workshop and in a follow-up survey were reform of the educational system, the development of humane values, leadership, citizenship, cross-cultural communication, tying together theory and practice, expansion of the educational mission of their universities, and student interest and demand.

Three major modes or varieties of service-learning around the world include teaching, health care and community development. An example of a country with a long-history in each of these modes is **Costa Rica.** The country abolished its military in 1948 and began the process or developing voluntary and compulsory programs during and after higher education. Like many developing nations in Africa and Latin America, one of the first programs developed was the "Servicio Social in Medicine," whereby medical graduates repay their training costs by providing one year of health care in rural, under served areas of the country. Trabajo Comunal Universitario (TCU), started in 1972, is required of all undergraduate university student with goals of promoting national social and economic development, social justice, and interaction between the university and the society. In addition to traditional school teaching and literacy programs, TCU includes drama productions, teaching music, conducting research, environmental education and action, consultation with small businesses and municipalities, developing customs procedures, psychological work in penitentiaries and a wide range of other service-learning activities (Sherraden & Castillo, 1990).

A more recent, high profile service-learning program is underway in Argentina, although to date it is primarily in the middle and secondary schools of the country. Many of the higher education service-learning programs around the world are found in private, church-related institutions. This is not unexpected, as service has been a crucial element of most religions and the institutions founded by them. In **India**, many of the Catholic and Protestant colleges have developed extensive service-learning programs. At Kodaikanal College, students work with nearby tribal people to preserve language and culture. Students at Sara Tucker College provides legal assistance for village women to bring their grievances before village officials. Engineering students at American College in Madurai lay roads and de-silt tanks, while biology students from Bishop Heber college conduct study and teaching tours of forests and coastal regions, while protecting and preserving the environment. Students from these and other colleges have set up loan programs for the poor, write letters for the blind, conduct immunization camps for tribal people, and are involved in numerous literacy and numeracy campaigns. Women's leadership and development programs are found in colleges throughout the country (Berry & Chisholm, 1999).

One of the most comprehensive attempts at a university-wide service-learning program is now underway in **Liberia** at Cuttington University College. During nearly 10 years of Civil War much of the staff was in exile in the United States, and it wasn't until 1998 that the staff and administration were able to reopen the institution. Facing the need for a massive rebuilding of the nation, community outreach, of necessity, became a major focus of the newly reopened university, with service-learning at its center. Health care, literacy and economic development have become the three foci of the new curriculum with students and faculty working with nearby towns and villages in the reconstruction and development process. In addition to general and health education, students also are trained to work in animal husbandry, vegetable farming, and water sanitation (Berry & Chisholm, 1999).

Other examples of international institutions of higher education doing interesting things in service-learning are a computer use and maintenance program at St. John's and St. Mary's Institute of Technology in **Taiwan**; a Peer Tutoring Scheme at Imperial College in **Great Britain**; dance classes and medical programs at the Universidad Espiritu Santo and Universidad San Francisco de Quito in **Ecuador**; international service prorrams in Bangladesh, China, Nepal and Russia for **Korean** students at Ewha University; skill building programs in Braille and sign language at Rikkyo University in Tokyo, **Japan;** work at a Care Center in **Jamaica**; and biology and business students at Trinity College in the **Philippines** growing mushrooms for freeze-drying and export (Berry and Chisholm, 1999).

SERVICE-LEARNING ABROAD

The final section of this chapter presents several models of service-learning across national boundaries. As indicated earlier in the chapter, these vary greatly in length of time and intensity. Among the models are a brief one-week "alternative spring break;" 3-9 week projects in other countries; semester-long service-learning experiences with the International Partnership for Service Learning; and one to two year programs involving a combination of campus and international experiences.

The Goshen College Study-Service Program is one of the oldest and largest international service-learning abroad programs. Started in 1968, the program structures overseas experiences for up to twenty-five percent of the student body, primarily sophomores, each year. The 13-15 week program seeks to place students in settings which are significantly different from the U.S. in culture, economic or political terms. Groups of 15-22 students are supervised by a Goshen College professor in residence at each location, but live with local families, typically lower middle class, who speak little or no English. During the initial six to seven weeks, students participate in language and cultural studies, after which students are relocated outside the capital city to a second host family and given a service assignment. Most assignments are in one of five categories: *The Student as Presence*: living in a refugee camp, joining the staff at a reform school, or playing with children in a hospital ward. The *Student as Observer*: being a "gofer" for a research team studying turtles, traveling with a rural health unit, observing classrooms or watching surgical procedures. The *Student as Work Camper*: Building a park, replacing a roof at a school, rebuilding a washed-out road, or digging a foundation. The *Student as Helper*: planting trees in a reforestation project, helping a nurse in a clinic, caring for babies in a shelter, preparing food in a village nutrition center, helping in a community radio station, or tending cattle on an ag-tech farm. The *Student as Skilled Practitioner*: teaching art, literacy, music or some other subject, starting a school computer program, supervising a preschool, translating documents or directing a choir (Hess in DiVitis et. al., 1998).

The International and National Voluntary Service Training Program (INVST) at the University of Colorado-Boulder is a ten-year old interdisciplinary program offered for primarily juniors and seniors. The program's general mission is "to develop well-informed citizens who are trained as leaders to analyze and solve community problems as a lifetime commitment." Four basic courses are offered on campus in Facilitating Peaceful Community Change, Implementing Social Change, Critical Thinking in Development, and

Democracy and Nonviolent Social Movements. Four practicum experiences utilizing a service-learning methodology are offered in conjunction with the campus classes, and students spend the summer prior to entering the program in a wilderness experience designed to develop community and to teach basic survival skills. Students cross social class lines by living and working in a homeless shelter in Denver, followed by a cross-cultural service-learning experience on the Dineh Nation. The second summer program provides students with a global perspective through living and serving in Mexico and in the bilingual and bicultural border area, where community service leadership roles are tested out in a new cultural context. In addition to the course work and national and international service-learning experiences, students are involved in a capstone SOL project, which provides them with an opportunity to design, implement, and evaluate their own community service initiatives. While not as large as the Goshen College program (only 10-15 students per year), INVST has received national recognition for its innovative curricular design and close interaction of service and learning in both campus and off-campus classes and service-learning experiences. Scott Myers-Lipton, whose research is reviewed earlier in this chapter, served as the founder of the INVST program, while completing his Ph.D. at the University of Colorado-Boulder (Scarritt & Lowe, 1999).

St. Olaf College in Minnesota has a wide array of traditional study abroad programs, but has developed a unique Study/Service Program in Indonesia. It is unique in the sense that it is the only St. Olaf program in Indonesia, requires an intensive language and culture course, encourages student independence by having no direct faculty supervision, and is the only study abroad program offering academic credit for service. The "service" offered is primarily the teaching of English at the Satya Wacana Christian University, where St. Olaf students function like teaching assistants in American Universities. Students live in a boarding house surrounded by students not proficient in English, and thus are immersed in the local culture. Students also participate in tutorials on a wide range of Indonesian culture and language topics (Fairbanks & Foss, 1998).

The **International Partnership for Service-Learning** is perhaps the largest and most clearly focused program for service-learning abroad. It has been in existence since 1982, and since that time has placed more than 3,000 students from over 300 U.S., Canadian and other nations' institutions of higher education in service-learning settings for academic credit around the world. Current semester, year, summer and January Intersession programs can be found in the Czech Republic, Ecuador, England, France, India, Israel, Jamaica, Mexico, the Philippines, Scotland and South Dakota (with native Americans). The partnership holds that study and service "is a powerful means of learning; addresses human needs that would otherwise remain unmet; promotes intercultural/international literacy; advances the personal growth of students as members of the community; gives expression to the obligation of public and community service by educated people; and sets academic institutions in right relationship to the larger society." Each of the partnership programs combines academic study, generally at a local university, along with 12-15 hours per week of community service experiences. Many of the service opportunities appear to involve working with children in schools and recreational program, health promotion, language instruction, poverty and homeless programs such as Mother Teresa's Missionaries of Charity in Calcutta, and other community projects for the poor (IPSL, 2000).

In conclusion, it is likely that international service-learning in its three variations will continue to grow in years to come. Every nation in the world is concerned with issues of better preparing its young people in citizenship, passing on the values of the society, and relating its educational system to the needs of global economy and its own society. Issues of poverty and justice will remain at the forefront of most nation's agenda for the foreseeable future, and international service-learning is increasingly being seen as an important component for dealing with these issues. Finally, as more and more faculty in higher education experience the power international service-learning as a pedagogical tool, it is likely continue to grow in numbers and influence.

REFERENCES

Berry, H., & Chisholm, L. (1999). *Service-learning in higher education around the world: An initial look.* New York: The International Partnership for Service-Learning.

Commission on National and Community Service (1993). *What can you do for your country.* Washington D.C: Government Printing Office.

Eberly, D. , & Sherraden,M. . *The moral equivalent of war?: A study of non-military ervice in nine nations.* New York: Greenwood Press.

Eyler,J, & Giles, D. (1999). *Where's the learning in service-learning?* San Francisco: Jossey-Bass.

Eyler, J., Giles, D., & Gray, C. (1999). *At a glance: What we know about the effects of service-learning on students, faculty, institutions and community, 1993-1999.* Vanderbilt University.

Fairbanks, R., & Foss, T. (1998). The global perspective at St. Olaf: Study/service in Indonesia in in DeVitis, J, Johns, R. & Simpson, D. *To serve and to learn: The spirit of community in liberal education.* New York: Peter Lang.

Gal, R. (2000). *Country updates: 5th global INNYS conference on youth service.* Zikhron Ya'akov, Israel: Carmel Institute for Social Studies.

Hess, J.D. (1998). The Goshen college study-service program in DeVitis, J, Johns, R. and Simpson, D. *To serve and to learn: The spirit of community in liberal education.* New York: Peter Lang.

Kaufmann, N. (1982). *The impact of study abroad on personality change.* Dissertation, Indiana University.

Kraft, R. (1992). An inquiry into caring for people and the environment: Closed classrooms, high mountains and strange lands. *The Journal of Experiential Education, 15* (3).

Kraft, R. (1996). Service learning: An introduction to its theory, practice, and effects. *Education and Urban Society*. February, Vol. 28. No. 2.

McLuhan, M. (1964*). Understanding media: The extensions of man*. New York: McGraw-Hill.

Myers-Lipton, S. (1996). Effect of service-learning on college students' attitudes toward international understanding. *Journal of College Student Development,* 37 (6), 659-668.

Resnick, L (1987). Learning in school and out. *Educational Researcher*, 16(9).

Scarritt, J., & Lowe, S. (1999). The international and national voluntary service training program (INVST) at the University of Colorado at Boulder in Weigert, K., & Crews, R. *Teaching for justice: Concepts and models for service –learning in peace studies*. Washington, D.C: AAHE.

Sherraden, M., & Castillo, C. (1990) Costa Rica: Non-military service in a nation with no army in Eberly, D., & Sherraden, M. *The moral equivalent of war?: A study of non-military service in nine nations*. New York: Greenwood Press.

Sigmon, R.(1996). The problem of definition in service-learning in Sigmon, R. et.al. The journey to service-learning. Washington D.C: Council of Independent Colleges.

Symons, C. (2000). *The El Paso/Juarez border immersion experience*. Unpublished poem. Boulder: The University of Colorado.

The International Partnership for Service-Learning (2000*). Service-learning: Combining academic study and volunteer service*. New York: IPSL.

CHAPTER 21

LEARNING TO SERVE: PROMOTING CIVIL SOCIETY THROUGH SERVICE LEARNING, UNIVERSITY OF COLORADO AT DENVER

Andy A. Jhanji[1]
Georgia E. Lesh-Laurie[2]
University of Colorado-Denver

INTRODUCTION

Throughout the twentieth century a debate that has defined the ever-changing world of higher education has surrounded the notion of the importance of service learning. By highlighting issues such as relevance, accessibility, and most importantly, responsibility, the general public has made it clear that accountability will continue to be a theme in the upcoming future. As a result of the external interest in higher education, many institutions are reassessing their core principles in an effort to expand the meaning of excellence. A concerted effort is being made by the higher education community to incorporate service as a component of the learning foundation instead of just an ancillary activity as in the past. This provides evidence that civic responsibility will play a major role in the progression of this new century, whether the institution is a financial services firm, information technology company, or a university.

As educators, it is our obligation to encourage the citizens that we serve to express, revise and refine their ideals. Universities should continue to be the catalyst behind developing solutions for the communities we serve by providing a venue for thoughtful dialogue. It is our hope that as you read this chapter it will become clear that the University of Colorado at Denver is committed to improving the lives of everyone associated with the University. We will try to show that our short history, in terms of educational institutions, is a blessing in that the walls of tradition are only somewhat formed, yet are not unchangeable. It is our goal to also show that as an urban university we feel it is our civic responsibility to provide our students not only a theoretical education but a practical education that is enhanced through problem based

---

[1] Special Assistant to the Chancellor
[2] Chancellor

learning and service. By providing the readers initially with a short synopsis of our institution we expect that a greater understanding and regard will be developed for our undergraduate service programs.

INSTITUTIONAL COMPLEXITY

The University of Colorado at Denver is in the midst of its 25th or silver anniversary. As mentioned above, its youth continues to have both advantages and disadvantages. Having steep traditional values, as a part of the University of Colorado, provides an institution with a very strong structure yet confines it when trying to think "out of the box." CU-Denver has tried to maintain its past while building on its future. Understanding its growth process in the last two and a half decades means reviewing the uniqueness of the campus both in its physical location and student population.

The complexity of CU-Denver is unlike most institutions in the nation. Physically, the University is housed in the Auraria Higher Education Center (AHEC), a unique educational campus that is home to three higher educational institutions serving over 33,000 students making this the largest campus, student population wise, in the state of Colorado. The three Auraria "schools" include a community college, an open admission baccalaureate institution, and the University of Colorado at Denver, a Doctoral/Research Intensive University in the new Carnegie classification system. We feel the greatest benefit of an entity such as AHEC is that any person wishing to continue his or her education can find a niche that meets their needs. On the other hand sharing facilities is never easy. Shared facilities on the campus include a library and media center, student center, recreational complex, bookstore, and child care center, as well as classroom space.

The University of Colorado at Denver is a state-supported institution of higher education enrolling approximately 6,100 undergraduate students and 4,700 graduate students in any given semester. The University concentrates on recruiting undergraduate students from the Denver metropolitan area with the student population consisting of high school graduates, transfer students from two and four-year programs, working students, and returning students. Eighty percent of the student body is employed and the average age of our undergraduate students is 27. In Fiscal Year (FY) 1999, the institution graduated 2,645 students with degrees, including 38 doctorates, 6 education specialist degrees, 1,437 masters degrees, and 1,164 baccalaureate degrees. As is evident from the graduation data, the largest number of degrees conferred at CU-Denver occurs at the masters level.

Institutional Programs and Culture

The undergraduate programs are grounded in a strong tradition of liberal education, the core curriculum is designed to develop students' intellectual skills as critical and analytical thinkers, maximize their effectiveness in written and oral communication, develop their capacity for humanistic and scientific inquiry, foster citizenship through an appreciation of diverse cultures and ideas, and nurture an appreciation of literature and other forms of artistic expression.

Since there is no on-campus housing available for students, CU-Denver has tried to use alternative avenues to provide a holistic educational experience for its student body. This includes maintaining a presence outside of the Denver metropolitan area illustrated by the undergraduate, international programs housed in Moscow, Russia; Beijing, China; Ulaan Baatar, Mongolia; and Kathmandu, Nepal. These international programs provide students an opportunity to grow culturally while giving them a chance for experiential learning through independent exploration.

The University of Colorado at Denver enjoys a significant advantage by virtue of its location in downtown Denver and its proximity to state government, the business community, and non-profit organizations. It has a strong presence in the community, a large array of supportive local constituents, and an alumni base that is developing a high concentration locally.

The work of faculty is recognized for enhancing the human capital of the region and contributing to solutions of urban social problems. Faculty work in key policy issue areas such as smart growth, health care administration, governmental reform and accountability, environmental concerns, and K-12 school issues. Through programs such as music, art, film, theater, history, and modern languages, the University of Colorado at Denver enhances the cultural life of the Denver metropolitan region. Workshops, certificate programs, short courses, retraining programs, and other programs of continuing education are offered to industry, government, and professional associations as well as the general public.

Because of the University of Colorado at Denver's location, opportunities abound for internships and other collaborative arrangements for students and faculty with business, industry, government, and service agencies. The University participates in a number of outreach and enrichment programs, including several to increase minority participation in underrepresented fields. In turn, considerable off-campus talent is available to enrich campus programs through guest lectureships and adjunct faculty appointments, thus giving the students the advantage of learning directly from active practitioners. Furthermore, CU-Denver's regular tenure-track faculty is replete with exemplary teacher-scholars, many of whom integrate the experience of blending theory with practice. Similarly, students are afforded a learning experience that capitalizes on their maturity and their life experiences.

MISSION

As is the case with many public state institutions, the University of Colorado at Denver has been given a statutory mission by the State of Colorado

Legislature. CU-Denver's mission as stated in the Colorado Revised Statutes # 23-20-101b is as follows:

> *The Denver campus of the University of Colorado shall be a compre-hensive baccalaureate liberal arts and sciences institution with high admission standards. The Denver campus shall provide selected pro-fessional programs and such graduate programs at the masters and doctoral level as will serve the needs of the Denver metropolitan area, emphasizing those professional programs not offered by other institutions of higher education.*

The University of Colorado at Denver has taken great pride in expanding the mission of the institution to further clarify the core values and ideals of the campus. By using a strategic planning initiative entitled the "New Urban University," CU-Denver has now become more focused with the service learning component of the institution. The following portions of expanded mission are very relevant to the learning to serve ideal for students: The University of Colorado at Denver is not an institution located in an urban environment – it is an urban university. It is expected by statute and by convention to serve the complex higher education needs of its city, the region which depends on the city and, by extension, cities world-wide. Cities, and their urban areas, are complex centers of commerce, education, government, and the arts. They are also places where urban and non-urban enterprises are centralized and coordi-nated. Significant problems originate there, and other problems are referred there for solution.

The University of Colorado at Denver, as an urban university, represents a significant source of skills, talents, and knowledge that serves Denver, and urban areas everywhere. It is essential that these assets be focused to serve the high priority needs of today's communities. The urban university is uniquely equipped to revitalize the economy of the city and its region, and to help in the solution of difficult problems both because of its resident talent and be-cause it can produce educated citizens that will shape its destiny toward a new and better existence.

Consistent with our mission to educate leaders for future generations and solve difficult problems of urban contemporary life, the University of Colo-rado at Denver commits to:

- giving students the best, and broadest, professional and preprofes-sional education possible. Both undergraduates and graduate students will be well grounded in the professionally-oriented and academic disciplines so that they will be actively recruited by organizations and advanced degree programs throughout the nation;
- developing in graduates the leadership, reflection, ethics, and future-orientation that enable them to become preeminent in their fields and to provide active leadership for the revitalization of cities everywhere.

To add these values to its students, the University of Colorado at Denver excels in building instructional experiences around problems of urban contemporary life as well as traditional disciplines. Students as well as faculty are actively engaged in seeking solutions, through research and service, to the pressing problems of modern urban, contemporary existence. The University of Colorado at Denver explores and incorporates both novel and traditional methods of instruction. Telecommunications and other electronic media are an integral part of the way that CU-Denver transcends geographic space, making instruction more stimulating and available, and connecting faculty, students, and alumni and state, regional, national and international leaders.

By adopting a culture that promotes and rewards civic responsibility, the University of Colorado at Denver has created a community atmosphere for fostering the ideal of moral engagement. Both our Retention, Tenure and Promotion Committee and our annual compensation process have been modified to accommodate faculty's movement into applied research and service areas. As you will see from the examples below this structural reconfiguration has permeated throughout the campus into the work of faculty, staff, and students.

Chancellor's Scholars and Leaders Program

The Chancellor's Scholars and Leaders program (CSL) is an educational program designed to identify students with leadership potential, educate future leaders, create leadership teams that solve problems in the community, and work with current leaders in our community to provide a seamless integration of leadership development both within the University and community. The University of Colorado at Denver is aware that the leaders of tomorrow will require skills and experiences that can prepare them for new challenges in professional and public life.

This undergraduate program uses cooperative learning strategies, practical team projects, seminars, personal contact with leaders, and individual mentoring as vehicles for student growth. For the purpose of this section of the chapter it is our objective to highlight some of the many exceptional projects that have been conducted by the students enrolled in the CSL program.

The **Phoenix** project is an after school program for at-risk teenagers from the west Denver area. The area of concentration for this program is the development of a curriculum that focuses on self-awareness and self-esteem through creative expression in the arts. The aim of the project is to enrich the lives of program participants by providing them with resources and guidance, as well as the freedom and encouragement to explore their individuality. This entails garnering the value of respecting others property, responsibility for oneself, and a desire to learn new fundamentals involving creative discovery. Students from the University of Colorado at Denver work hand in hand with west Denver youths, serving as mentors, providing one-on-one guidance, and developing positive and fun activities in hopes to better the lives of their younger colleagues.

The **Improving Middle Schools One Kid at a Time** or IMSOKAT is a youth mentoring program based at Lake Middle School, a Denver Public School, that focuses on team-building and personal mentoring. IMSOKAT consists of eight middle school students chosen based on their leadership potential. These middle school students in collaboration with students from the Chancellor's Scholars and Leaders program conduct community service projects, utilizing the resources of their school and the University. By providing a personal relationship for these middle school students the program would like to instill the importance of leadership values and a personal reward system for all the participants involved.

The CSL **Auraria Child Care Task Force**, in partnership with the Auraria Child Care Center, has developed an innovative drop-in program for the University of Colorado at Denver students who have young children needing child-care. The program is unique in that it requires no additional funding associated with space or staff by using empty slots at the Center. The Auraria Child Care Center, being one of the largest in the state of Colorado, has an average of 30 children absent from the Center on any given day throughout the year. The drop-in program coordinates these empty slots, filling them with drop-in users and ensuring that the Center is fully utilized. By providing this drop-in service, CU-Denver hopes to alleviate some of the day to day pressures of our non-traditional students while giving them the opportunity to complete their education.

As can be inferred from the title, this program is housed under the auspices of the Chancellor's office. Faculty from many disciplines in the College of Liberal Arts and Sciences, along with community leaders, are asked to spearhead the curriculum and learning activities associated with the program.

The Urban Links Project

The Urban Links Project associates research in the community through interdisciplinary study at CU-Denver. Urban Links is a community-based research and community-service facility using faculty, staff, and students dedicated to research and education in an effort to better understand the patterns of substance abuse and HIV transmission in the local community. It is housed in CU-Denver's Anthropology Department, and works with its Health and Behavioral Sciences degree program. Positive outcomes of this project have included the development of community-focused intervention models aimed at reducing intravenous drug use and its associated health consequences. The students gain practical aspects of learning in a real world situation. They further learn the basic aspects of effecting change within an environment where the population may be disadvantaged. The community is grateful for having a center that deals with issues and concerns of their residents.

West Denver Community Outreach Partnership Center (COPC)

With support from a Housing and Urban Development COPC grant the University of Colorado at Denver has established a neighborhood outreach center that targets three Denver communities: LaAlma/Lincoln Park, Valverde, and Sun Valley. These, collectively, constitute the predominantly Hispanic "Westside" area where significant proportions of the residents are in rental housing. The neighborhoods are some of the most impoverished and troubled in Denver, but they are also some of the most asset-rich in terms of tradition of community.

Our student workers do research for the tenants in the neighborhood and teach them how to express themselves in public meetings. By doing this, the neighborhood gains confidence in their activities and our students learn to, effectively, do research and to write papers. By interacting with residents within a neighborhood outreach center, NEWSED, the students learn culturally about the neighborhood and celebrate cultural events with neighborhood residents. An important activity planned by the students from CU-Denver is the annual Christmas party for the neighborhood at which the children are given an item they desire and the students and children interact using the item. These aspects of the program are within CU-Denver's Political Sciences Department.

The University of Colorado at Denver's College of Arts and Media has also opened studio space on the top floor of NEWSED and gives children an opportunity to make art after school before parents may be at home. Because of this program the University and the neighborhood are able to keep talking whenever a "town and gown" problem arises, and usually this leads to a win-win situation. Students in this program learn the importance of volunteerism, and begin to appreciate the ideal of giving back to the community.

Kids in the City

The Kids in the City project envisions a unique approach to community development and urban planning. By engaging the information and feedback of children and young people living in the neighborhoods affected by planning efforts a more accessible and safer linkage between five Denver neighborhoods and 200 University of Colorado at Denver students has been formed. CU-Denver sees this problem based learning model as a key component of experiential learning in the College of Architecture and Planning.

The students use this opportunity to test their theoretical knowledge toward making improvements to the city while gaining a better understanding of the urban environment where many of these students reside. Students also gain the critical knowledge of working in teams rather than as individuals giving them an advantage when moving into their chosen careers.

Public History Project

Many historians spend their whole academic careers trying to bring history alive. A program at CU-Denver has designed an interesting project whereby history is brought to life by the students. As a capstone to this project each student for his or her final exam is required to pick a character from the semester readings of local Denver history, whether it is a famous personality or a not so famous character, and portray the significance of their existence. Additionally, as the final exam portion of this course each student is asked to research these personalities, dress in costumes relating to the chosen character and then present their findings at the character's final resting spot at the local cemetery. This final exam/recital is open to the public, and usually draws a few dozen spectators and the local media. This project enables students to take part in history and uncover findings that many times might not be available for public consumption in the local community.

Mathematics Clinic

The Mathematics Clinic at CU-Denver provides forums for students in the Mathematics Department to apply classroom knowledge to solving practical problems facing corporations and government agencies. An example of a specific project completed by our students was the development of a grid system, for the city of Denver, that highlights the most effective route for snow removal, enabling traffic flow to be least affected during winter snow storms. One of the underlying goals of this program is to get students more actively involved in their own learning by placing an emphasis on problem solving. The community benefits by not only getting a problem solved but also gaining a better understanding of the benefits provided by the use of mathematical modeling. The students benefit from networking with possible employers, and seeing the correlation between a math degree and future employability.

The Children's Literacy Project

The Children's Literacy Project represents a collaborative partnership between the Tattered Cover, the city of Denver's largest bookstore, and the University of Colorado at Denver's Computer Sciences Department. This project involved these two organizations working together inside and outside the classroom, in the design and creation of computer-based community oriented products that promote children's literacy skills.

This project is also an example of CU-Denver's commitment to provide students with real-world experience in developing a working relationship with a business while designing and creating computer-based tools for promoting literacy skills among children. The initial outcome of the project is KidsTown, an interactive web site that serves as a resource for children, their families, and their teachers as they explore the use of computers to promote literacy through activities that are simultaneously informative, educational and entertaining.

Arts Street

The mission of the Arts Street project is to provide job training and mentoring through the arts for Denver youth in order to develop a disciplined, creative, and culturally competent workforce. Businesses continue to voice the need for workers trained in creative thinking and problem solving. In partnership with the Denver Mayor's Office of Art, Culture and Film, the Arts Street program is an art-based youth employment program which addresses the creative talents of young people.

Through the use of arts curricula, the program engages adolescents ages 14-21 in the acquisition of life skills and workplace skills; and introduces youth in the workforce to become economically self-sufficient. Students work with mentors to deliver quality visual art, performing arts, and media arts products, on time and on budget, through sculpting, carving, painting, theater, dance/music performance, creative writing, computer graphics, publishing, web design and video production. Youth apprentices are involved in project planning, concept developing, and time management while learning industry standards in the business of the arts. The curricula home for Arts Street is in CU-Denver's College of Arts and Media and in our Media Center.

Internship and Cooperative Education Program

In addition to the types of activities described previously, the University of Colorado at Denver also has a very active Internship and Cooperative Education Program. Although we do not require a practical experience, we offer one to any student who requests it. Students throughout our undergraduate (and graduate) programs who wish to have a practical experience may visit our Internship/Cooperative Education office. A very significant number of our students who do participate in the placement program receive employment offers from the companies with whom they have worked. Because of the attractiveness of our Internship/Cooperative Education program employers call us when student assistance is required, and we rarely fill all of our opportunities.

One of the critical components of CU-Denver's strategy for emphasizing service engagement, as is evident from many of the undergraduate service learning projects highlighted in this chapter, is the belief that mentoring plays a critical role in the development of our country's youth. To further foster this tenet, the University of Colorado at Denver is committed to the development of students' character by imploring to our community the importance of civic responsibility through virtues and values. In essence, we believe, it is our moral obligation to foster a democratic philosophy, whereby each and every one of our students have the opportunity to choose in which way they themselves would like to make a difference.

As the higher education community reassesses its mission for future success, each and every institution will require a strong leadership plan that makes strategic decisions based on self-understanding and pragmatic vision. In an effort to follow this underlying principle, the University of Colorado at Denver understands that it must prepare students who are critical thinkers, creative problem solvers, and responsible citizens who make ethical choices. Students must be able to present their thoughts well orally and in writing, develop leadership skills, and work in teams. They should be scientifically, technologically, and culturally literate. CU-Denver must also ensure that students are able to analyze and evaluate important trends in disciplines, comprehend how the world is changing, understand the interconnectedness of knowledge, recognize that there is a blurring of boundaries among disciplines and among nations, and cope with dynamic change. A vision for students includes exposure to multiple viewpoints and the free exchange of ideas, an appreciation for diversity among people of the nation and around the globe, preparation to utilize information technology, and experience with collaborative learning on campus and in the community.

CHAPTER 22

FILLING IN THE MOAT AROUND THE IVORY TOWER

Vachel Miller
David K. Scott
University of Massachusetts-Amherst

INTRODUCTION

Over the past one hundred and fifty years, higher education in America has undergone fundamental changes. After a long emphasis on teaching, the idea of service to society re-oriented higher education in the mid 19th century, highlighted by the creation of the land-grant universities. Then, over the last century and particularly after the Second World War, the focus shifted toward research, and academic subspecialties proliferated. Now the university finds itself with a tri-partite mission and a sprawling accumulation of autonomous units — a multiversity — with no deeper forces of integration guiding its evolution. The splintered forms of inquiry we have inherited from the past do not always serve well a world in which complex problems are not neatly packaged according to academic disciplines.

In response to the fragmentation of our era, the third transformation of higher education, we submit, will involve the formation of the Integrative University, with deep dialogue among disciplines and rich connection with diverse constituencies in government, business, and communities. In this pending transformation, the university will become a more dynamically networked community of learning.

One of the most fundamental questions we face as we enter the twenty-first century is this: how can we preserve what is best of our pluralistic society while overcoming the fragmented human isolation of modernity? At the University of Massachusetts, we believe that we can answer that question, not through a return to the past or through a descent into relativism or nihilism, but through the bold step of embracing the complexity of our world — by creating new methods of inquiry for dealing with our seemingly intractable social problems and finding new forms of learning that can foster both community and diversity.

The Kellogg Commission on the Future of State and Land Grant Universities recently introduced the idea of the Engaged University (Kellogg Commission, 1999), a concept closely related to that of the Integrative University. For a university to become deeply engaged with society, which is central to the idea of service learning, we believe society must also be engaged with the university. There must be outreach and inreach. But that engagement is more likely if the university is also engaged internally — across disciplines, across cultures, across organizational units. As the barriers are overcome in one dimension, it becomes easier to cross the boundaries in other dimensions. Often we tend to tackle each barrier in isolation, whereas we actually need to unfreeze the organization and let it flow to a new level. This movement of energy and ideas across old barriers is what we mean by filling in the moat around the ivory tower and creating an Integrative University.

The most promising pedagogical practice for the formation of the Integrative University may prove to be service learning. This chapter will briefly outline the contours of the Integrative University, then discuss the role of service learning in preparing students for engaged citizenship in an integrative age. We will describe the structure of service learning at the University of Massachusetts Amherst, focusing on several innovative service learning programs.

CREATING CONVERSATIONS AND SOCIAL CAPITAL

At a recent conference on spirituality in higher education and worklife held here, poet David Whyte and organizational visionaries Margaret Wheately and Peter Senge spoke about the power of conversations as a force of change: conversations bring us together to share worldviews, concerns, and visions for the future. Change leaders are those who know how to convene communities around conversations of shared significance.

One hallmark of the Integrative University will be conversations that flow in all directions, across all institutional boundaries — both within the university and between the campus and the community. Service learning is one catalyst for such conversations, since students move between classroom-based and practice-based learning about issues of common concern. "What does your world look like?" is a fundamental question service learning teaches students to ask, a fundamental question of transformative conversation.

The value of connections forged by service learning is underscored by the concept of social capital. Social capital refers to the level of reciprocity and voluntary associations between individuals in a community. A good stock of social capital makes it more likely that people in a community will assist each other in times of need and trust each other in business dealings. Thus, social capital is seen as foundational to economic prosperity (Fukuyama, 1995). In the United States, many analysts feel social capital is lacking due to the decline of voluntary association in communities (Putnam, 1995). In his recent book, *The Fourth Awakening*, Robert Fogel (2000) writes that the most intractable maldistribution of resources in rich countries like the U.S. is in the realm of spiritual and immaterial assets, which are the central assets in the struggle for self-realization, self-confidence, self-esteem and a vision of opportunity.

Social capital accrues as a result of social engagement, and service learning increases the potential of relationships to form between students and the larger world. As pointed out by Eyler and Giles (1999), service learning connects people in multiple ways: student to student, student to campus, student to faculty, student to community, and community to university. Service learning, then, can be seen as a key means by which universities can enrich themselves and their surrounding communities by expanding the stock of available social capital.

One of the most direct benefits of service learning is students' encounters with difference. In service learning studies, students consistently note that service learning brings them into contact with people whom they would not otherwise meet. Service experiences encourage students to confront their generalizations about people different from themselves (Rhoads, 1997). Thus, service has the potential to transform stereotypes and biases. Research on altruistic behavior offers a further insight into the impact of service: we value those we help and are more likely to help them in the future (Staub, 1989). Learning to value others, students who serve often develop life-long service orientations. They enjoy the positive feelings of self-worth that result from service (Eyler & Giles, 1999). Caring about the welfare of others becomes part of what they value in themselves: service can "compel students to rethink their lives in terms of connection and relationships with others" (Rhoads, 1997, p. 94).

In a society marked by persistent racial and ethnic divides, this is an important outcome of service. According to a comprehensive study of over 3,000 students by the Higher Education Research Institute, an increase in civic responsibility was one of the strongest changes associated with service learning (Sax & Astin, 1997). Students with service experiences had a strengthened commitment to promoting racial understanding and participating in community action programs. In a longitudinal study, the same researchers found that, regardless of pre-college service experiences, service in college was positively associated with life-long commitment to volunteerism and community action.

In the Integrative University, preparing students for positive social engagement must become a more intentional goal. It would be naïve to imagine that students, after years of schooling that disconnects them from community life, would leap into community service after graduation. In order for a service-orientation to become an enduring dimension of learning outcomes in college, we must model community engagement, value community engagement, and provide structured opportunities for community engagement. In short, without service learning, it is unlikely that students will learn to serve.

LEARNING FOR AN INTEGRATIVE AGE

Service learning develops in students the learning arts of an integrative age. Traditional pedagogies in western universities have assumed that the motivation to learn arises from the desire for individual achievement, mastery, or economic gain. In contrast, service learning emphasizes that learning occurs in community. This position is gaining support from studies of learning in organizations. Cognitive researchers now believe that the social context of learning is critical because we learn what enables us to contribute to a community, a community which values our activity and informs our identity (Wenger, 1998). Against the institutionalized bias toward individualized learning, runs a strong desire for learning in community, for reciprocal relationships, for partnership.

Historically, the national mood and with it, organizational culture, swing between periods of community caring and periods of great individual selfishness. In *The Cycles of American History*, Schlessinger (1986) describes this phenomenon as shifts between centralization and diffusion of energy. He was building on an idea of his father in an essay entitled "Tides of America Politics" (Schlessinger, 1939). From 1765 onwards, there have been periods of community ascendancy, lasting for about 16 years, followed by comparable periods of individual ascendancy. These swings transcend political parties and reflect reactions of society to either extreme.

During this century, for example, Roosevelt's accession in 1901 heralded the sweep of reform measures comprising the Progressive Era and the Square Deal. Another two cycles of community ascendancy were the New Deal in the '30s and the New Frontier/Great Society in the '60s. Schlessinger (1986) predicted that, at some time in the '90s, another burst of innovation and reform would take place. The rhetoric of reform is certainly present. President Bush called for a "kinder, gentler nation," and Clinton spoke of a "new covenant with society." Today we hear about "compassionate conservatism." Slogans, by themselves, are merely "words marching across the landscape in search of an idea." The idea may be discernible on college campuses, which are often the bellwethers of imminent transformation.

In the book, *When Dreams and Heroes Died: A Portrait of Today's College Student*, Levine (1980) also describes periods in universities and colleges of community ascendancy which are future-oriented and ascetic, and periods of individual ascendancy which are more present-oriented and hedonistic, more concerned with duty to self than to others. In a more recent work, Levine and Cureton (1998) analyze student activism during the century by using data gathered from measures of organizational strength, viability of student publications, and participation in demonstrations. The high points of these movements coincide with the swings in national mood described earlier. These historical cycles predict that we should now be in a period of community ascendancy; but this time, a greater transformation may take place. As Tarnas (1991) has suggested, humanity may be gathering for a denouement, a unification of knowledge, of cultures, of faith and reason, of matter and spirituality, of art and science and religion, which have been increasingly fragmented and separated for almost 300 years. Collective frustration with such fragmentation has generated great interest in transformative perspectives on higher education (see, for example, Kazanjian and Laurence, 2000). People everywhere are searching for greater meaning, wholeness and relatedness in their lives and in their interactions with others.

Our organizations are modeled on the industrial, machine age. Indeed, to some extent our universities and educational paradigms are also. The modern university has its genesis in the middle of the last century when rational, scientific approaches to knowledge began to emerge in all fields and a mechanistic worldview prevailed. Our education prepares us to function in an organization that is mechanical and ordered. However, modern science has long moved from a mechanistic model of the universe to one that is more holistic, more organic — a web of connections. How would our educational paradigm change if we prepared students to function successfully in a living, breathing organism in which everything is connected? Management theorists, taking inspiration from the natural sciences, are pointing out that living beings desire greater connection: life seeks partners and membership in larger wholes in order to make more life possible (Wheatley & Kellner-Rogers, 1996). By providing ways for students to learn through active participation and partnership with a community group, service learning taps our deepest motivations for the kind of learning which transforms us and our worlds.

Service learning is attuned to a holistic understanding of the way the world works. Whereas traditional pedagogies are grounded in an understanding of knowledge as a rarified commodity extracted and refined by experts for consumption by amateurs, service learning seeks other grounding in an understanding of the world as interconnected, as a place where knowledge arises out of relationship, engagement, and mutuality. Indeed, service learning brings students into a dialogic relationship with the world. They cannot stand objectively apart from the subjects of inquiry; service entangles students in the social, economic, and political complexities of knowing and, in turn, reveals who they are as knowers to themselves and others.

TOWARD SITUATED LEARNING

As universities have matured over the last one hundred and fifty years, we established a pedagogical approach grounded in the separation of the university from society. At the same time, we espoused the belief that, ultimately, the mission of the university is to improve the world and enable people to live better and more fulfilling lives. The approach to knowledge embedded in higher education has typically involved the assembly of facts and databases, from which theories are derived and applied to society. Following the tenets of modernism and the Enlightenment, this approach insists that knowledge should remain sanitized: the world and its confusing problems must be excluded from the processes of knowledge production. Meanwhile, we see that outside the university, there is another orientation, one concerned with the messy problems of life and policies that can be applied to remedy them. Service learning begins to bridge the two worlds and creates the possibility of building a better and a wiser world more rapidly. This approach to knowledge is based on wisdom in conjunction with rational inquiry (Maxwell, 1984; Scott & Awbrey, 1993).

Service learning suggests a fundamental question: are we teaching students simply to play the "game of school" (Resnick, 1987) — to function well within a closed academic system — or are we preparing them for success in the more open learning systems of adult life? We often forget that, after students graduate, they continue learning. They learn in many ways: by doing what matters to them and their communities, by conversing with friends, and by asking questions they want to answer. They may consult subject experts, of course, but such experts are only one type of resource available for forming new knowledge.

From this perspective, service learning provides students with practice in the kind of learning they will undertake once they leave the university. Embedding knowledge in practical contexts, service learning helps overcome the problem that philosopher Alfred North Whitehead identified as "inert" knowledge, i.e., information stored in memory but unavailable for application to new situations. Following Whitehead, Eyler and Giles point out that "if knowledge is to be accessible to solve a new problem, it is best learned in a context where it is used as a problem-solving tool" (1999, p. 64). With a strong blend of conceptual learning, experience, and reflection, service learning can help students gain knowledge that is more richly indexed, linked with other learning, and available for addressing matters of public consequence.

Service learning invites us to broaden our notions of learning and bring new voices into campus discussions of accountability. How well are we preparing students for community engagement? How well are we addressing the pressing questions of the diverse communities around us? Taking the perspective of communities into account can open new dialogue about the purpose of learning: for whom and for what is higher learning? Service learning makes it possible for students to create knowledge of consequence to communities, moving beyond the traditionally passive role of knowledge consumers.

In this light, rather than seeing service learning as a special form of pedagogy, we might view it as a turn toward a more integrated mode of learning that we are beginning to reclaim as we develop an Integrative University.

SERVICE LEARNING AT THE UNIVERSITY OF MASSACHUSETTS - AMHERST

At the University of Massachusetts Amherst, the value of engagement in local communities is central to our land-grant mission. As we become a more integrative institution, we see engagement not merely as helping those outside the campus, but entering into transformative relationships of mutual learning. We value what Rhoads calls "critical community service", i.e., service grounded in reciprocity and reaching toward constructive social change (1997, p. 216). The goals of the service learning program here are indeed transformative:

- Develop social consciousness, foster civic responsibility and a better understanding of democracy, and develop and nurture the future community leaders of the Commonwealth and the nation;
- Meet community needs and appropriately connect the university to its communities within the context of the university's overall outreach efforts;
- Enrich and enhance classroom-based courses and programs through the process of reflective practice and community-based learning.

At the University of Massachusetts, there is a powerful interrelationship between these three goals. They are complementary, emphasizing the relationship of the university and students to its social ecology. Service learning at the university is understood as a means of transforming lives and organizations.

Program Structure

Like other such programs, service learning at UMass grew out of the vision and passion of committed faculty. After several years of growth, the structure of the service learning program is more networked than centralized, more organic than pre-designed. Emerging from different parts of the campus at different moments over the past several years, service learning efforts have connected with each other to form a dynamic system.

The components of the program are detailed below:

- **The Provost's Committee on Service Learning.** This group provides overall leadership for the Community Service Learning Faculty Development program. It is comprised of faculty, deans, other administrators, and graduate students.

- **Service Learning Faculty Fellows Program.** As of fall of 2000, there are fifty-six Service Learning Faculty Fellows, faculty members from every school and college who have participated in service learning training and seminars. Fellows are selected by the Provost's Committee to receive $2000 awards in support of the integration of service into their courses. Fellows meet monthly to discuss shared curricular and pedagogical questions.

- **Faculty Initiated Service Learning Courses.** A recent survey indicated that there are nearly seventy-five service learning courses offered by faculty each academic year. This number includes courses offered by the Service Learning Fellows.

- **Departmental Fellowship in Community Service Learning.** To enhance the influence of the work of individual Faculty Fellows on departmental curricula, a one-year pilot is being tested during the 2000-2001 academic year. Departments were invited to submit proposals for the incorporation of service learning as a major departmental learning strategy. Nine departments applied, and two (Communication and Marketing) were selected for funding. Each received about $10,000 to fund faculty release time, a teaching assistantship, or other costs.

- **The UMass Office of Community Service Learning at Commonwealth College.** Created as part of the new honors college, Commonwealth College, in the 1999-2000 academic year, and staffed with a full-time director and a group of graduate assistants beginning in the fall of 2000, this office serves to support service learning both within the honors college and across the entire university.

- **University Community Service Learning Resource Center.** Housed in the Center for Teaching, the Resource Center is a collection of books, syllabi, faculty reports, student papers, proposals, and other materials on service learning for use by campus faculty and staff.

- **The Citizen Scholars Program.** This two-year program, supported by Commonwealth College, includes at least five service learning courses, a minimum of 60 hours of community service in each of the four semesters students are in the program, and a summer service project or internship with a community or government agency. Fourteen students began the program in fall, 1999, and 16 more joined it in fall, 2000.

- **IMPACT! The First Year Service Learning Community.** To build upon the growing community service movement within high schools, a new initiative was launched in academic year 1999-2000. IMPACT!, which is available only to first year students, will aid recruiting by positioning the campus as a place to continue the integration of learning and serving and will act as a feeder program for the Citizen Scholars program. Students belonging to this learning community live together in a residence hall, take a service learning course together each of their first two semesters, work together to process the role of service in their lives and plans for the future, and design and implement service projects in addition to the service they perform through their courses.

- **Curricular Alternative Spring Break.** Led by faculty mentors, student teams travel to American communities (in 2001, rural Virginia, Tennessee, North Carolina, Alabama — and Holyoke, Massachusetts, 20 miles away from our campus) during spring break to engage in direct service with local community development groups as an integral component of a comprehensive academic course. Over one hundred students participated in these trips during the 1998-1999 academic year. The success of the alternative breaks has fostered creative new programs and partnerships. Recent innovations include "reverse alternative spring break" in which high school students from partner communities come to our campus as guests to learn about college life, as well as "alternative summer break," a week-long summer camp for youth in a Virginia community.

Program Development

Service learning took root at UMass Amherst in December of 1993 with the formation of the Provost's Committee and extensive collaboration between Student Affairs and Academic Affairs. The first set of service learning courses emerged in 1994-95, and the program has flourished in recent years. During the 1998-1999 academic year, 1,000 students enrolled in service learning courses offered by Service Learning Fellows, and 2,400 students participated in co-curricular community service activities, offering an estimated 165,000 hours of service to local communities.

With initiatives such as the Service Learning Fellows and Department Fellows programs, UMass has attempted to create conditions supportive of the spread of service learning. It has also maintained a vibrant system at a relatively low cost, thriving on the goodwill, enthusiasm, and extra effort of faculty and staff. In recent years, the program has had a budget of approximately $50,000, which has supported publications, memberships, gatherings, faculty grants, and graduate students.

To ensure its sustainability, university resources committed to the program have increased over the past two years. The program made a great stride forward when the Dean of Commonwealth College established service learning as a core value of the college. By centering service learning within the new honors college, the university has affirmed its academic legitimacy and enabled linkages with departments across campus.

Commonwealth College has strongly supported service learning, committing funds to hire a full-time director, as well as providing financial awards for the Citizen Scholars. In 2000-2001, a budget of approximately $50,000 supports the Citizen Scholars Program. Another $100,000 supports the Office of Community Service Learning (with a director and two graduate assistants) and the Departmental Fellows in Service Learning. These resources are currently augmented by Massachusetts Campus Compact, which is providing two VISTA volunteers, and the Corporation for National Service, which has given a "Learn and Serve" grant of $125,000 for support including three additional graduate assistantships and funds to compensate each of four core partners for joint planning and supervision of service learning students.

At the level of executive leadership in the university, the new Vice Chancellor for University Outreach has been appointed, signaling that the idea of service is given the same visibility and administrative focus as research and teaching, although with emphasis on the increasing integration of all three. In order to make service learning an integral part of the university, systemic changes like these are essential.

Another systemic change involves the convergence of learning communities and service learning. Learning communities come in many forms. They may involve a group of students who live together and study issues of common interest; alternatively, learning communities may refer to groups that gather around shared activities such as a student business. In their varied forms, learning communities can be a powerful vehicle for integrative learning, nurturing connections among students and disciplines. Such communities provide practice in working with others, weaving together a social ecology of learning and action. At the University of Massachusetts, one of our goals is to enable every first-year student who would like to join a learning community to do so. At present, about one-third of all first year students belong to some form of learning community. Although service is not yet a standard feature of living/learning communities at UMass, there is interest in this direction and one service learning community has been created.

Ultimately, both learning communities and service learning enable students to live their learning. Rather than centering learning exclusively in an academic discipline, they focus learning on the formation of community. In the future, as we move toward greater integration in our thinking and working, we should always ask ourselves: what are the conditions that support shared inquiry and action? Gathering a community around compelling problems, visions, ideas, and activities, we nurture the roots of life-long and integrative learning.

An Education in Engagement: The Citizen Scholars Program

Among the many outcomes of service learning, one of the most important is a strengthened capacity for meaningful participation in democratic society. If we deeply value social engagement, how might undergraduate education be redesigned to promote both learning and service? What are the elements of a transformed and transformative experience? In sum, how do we train leaders for an integrative age?

The Citizen Scholars program at the University of Massachusetts is designed to equip students with a full toolbox for the practice of engaged citizenship. It prepares students to become community leaders who have the commitment, the competence, and the experience to solve community problems through citizen action.

The program emerged in 1999, as a response to the limited capacity of the traditional academic course structure to provide students with deeper critical understanding of complex social issues. Although semester-long service learning courses introduced students to local problems, they did not provide opportunities for a variety of service experiences or sustained, systemic analysis of the underlying social and political dimensions of those problems. Students were unable to generate a collaborative project or policy proposal aimed at problem solving. To overcome that limitation, the Citizen Scholars is designed to be a comprehensive leadership development program, enabling students to explore multiple perspectives on complex issues over an extended period within a supportive learning community.

The two-year program includes several related features: 60 hours of community service each semester, five service learning courses, a major research paper, a collaborative service project, and an integrating seminar. These elements are described in further detail below:

- **Courses.** Participants take a minimum of five service learning courses. "The Good Society" is the first course and asks students to think creatively and critically about the elements of an ideal society. During the semester, students study and analyze current and past community efforts in the U.S. and abroad to achieve social justice.

  In addition to service learning courses offered by departments across campus, students can develop service learning independent study projects in collaboration with a faculty sponsor and community agency that can substitute for one of the courses. "Public Policy and Citizen Action: Leadership in Community Service" is the capstone course taken during the final semester of the program. During the course, students are challenged to develop strategies and skills to enable them to translate their ideals into a realistic program in collaboration with others. Part of the course will analyze the failures as well as the successes of programs intended to promote social justice. In each service learning course, students will keep journals reflecting on their service and on its relationship to the course content and classroom discussions.

- **Service.** Students are expected to engage in 60 hours of service each semester. The bulk of this commitment can be completed in conjunction with service learning courses. In addition to direct service, the program expects students to participate in intensive "immersion" experiences such as alternative spring break trips. Further, students are encouraged to complete a summer internship, ideally working with the director of a community agency to learn about the challenges of raising funds, recruiting volunteers, and trying to meet community needs with a limited budget and staff. Such an internship, combined with four semesters of direct service, gives students a broader perspective on the financial, legal, administrative, and public policy aspects of solving community problems and serving people in need.

- **Research paper.** Each student is expected to prepare and present a paper examining local, state, and national policy related to their community service and to a major public policy concern.

- **Service project.** Based on their research and service, teams of three to five students will work with a community agency to identify a project that they can implement. The project is to be designed, implemented, and evaluated in close collaboration with a community partner. Alternatively, students may prepare a draft proposal dealing with an issue of social justice in collaboration with a state legislator to be considered by a committee of the Massachusetts House or Senate.

- **Integrating Seminars.** Each semester, citizen scholars will participate in a bi-weekly seminar that will both supplement and complement their courses. The seminars have three foci: first, they introduce students to representatives of local community agencies; second, they introduce students to faculty from diverse disciplines who teach about critical social issues; third, students will meet local and state legislators and government officials who can discuss how individuals and groups can influence legislation and government action. In addition, the seminar will give students the opportunity to share perspectives on their individual service assignments and to collaborate on their research and group service projects.

By combining these five features, the Citizen Scholars program offers a unique, comprehensive approach to educate and support students who plan to become effective leaders in community service. According to Citizen Scholars program co-director David Schimmel, "community service will not be an atomized part of the student's experience but for at least two years will be infused in much of what the student does. The multiple components of the program enable the student to break free of the compartmentalized atmosphere of the university to approach the question of justice and citizenship holistically and consequently much more effectively."

The Citizen Scholars program is distinctive in its integrative approach to educating students for citizen action. By involving students in direct service, indirect service, and policy work, it trains students analytically and practically for effecting change on multiple levels. It makes students aware of the multifaceted nature of service and helps them find ways to incorporate service within different career paths. Whichever career path they ultimately choose, we expect graduates to be sensitive to the needs of their community and to take a leadership role in mobilizing private and public resources to meet those needs.

Because the citizen scholars program is new, it has not been formally evaluated. Nevertheless, studies of other service learning programs suggest that the program's goals are realistic. Based on extensive survey data and intensive interviews of students across the country, Eyler and Giles (1999) found that service learning extends students' abilities to solve complex, unstructured social problems. Experienced service learning students had far more sophisticated analysis and convincing approaches to change than other students. They were sensitive to the value of community voice, of assessing available resources, and respecting the limitations of action. Unlike some students without service learning experience, they did not espouse a strategy of creating change by simply "telling people what to do." In their study of service learning outcomes, Sax and Astin (1997) also noted gains in students' understanding of community problems, acceptance of differences, cooperative work, and sense of leadership.

CHALLENGES AND OPPORTUNITIES FOR CHANGE

One of the most important directions for the program in upcoming years is to strengthen its sense of partnership and reciprocity with the community. The program is thinking carefully, in the words of new director John Reiff, about "how the energy and intellectual resources of the university can be applied to community needs, and how the leadership and wisdom in the community can contribute to the learning and development of students as citizens."

With funding from the Corporation for National Service, the program will have the capacity to nurture core partnerships with local organizations and actively involve them in program development. The question now being asked of agencies is this: "How can the university contribute to your work?" Through this dialogue and active co-planning, the university intends to better support the objectives of local agencies and provide reliable information about volunteer support from students. The program also is interested in assisting community agencies gain access to university resources, especially research related to pressing concerns, and bringing agencies into discussion of research agendas. The program believes that transformative conversations and actions can occur when faculty and community partners have time to talk together.

Overall, it is important for universities to think more carefully about the conditions of reciprocity they offer to community partners. How does the university acknowledge the costs agencies incur in mentoring our students? How do we honor their role as "community teachers"? How might the vast learning resources of the university — the computer laboratories, libraries, classrooms — become a shared resource for community-wide learning, especially in a digital age in which physical barriers to the movement and storage of information are shrinking daily?

On campus, barriers remain to the wider promulgation of service learning. The endorsement of service learning by the Provost and other academic leaders at UMass has signaled its importance to the faculty. Nevertheless, preparing service learning courses is hard work for faculty, and many wonder how such effort will be evaluated in tenure reviews. In a research-oriented academic culture, service learning has not yet won widespread respect as a valuable form of outreach scholarship. It is interesting to note that schools and colleges such as education, nursing, and public health are those most deeply engaged in service learning. The more traditional areas of knowledge and the "core" areas of academic inquiry are those that tend to be most deeply involved in the traditional approach that developed over the last centuries. For service learning to continue making inroads, faculty from the higher prestige disciplines must be engaged in the conversation about the social application of knowledge and more integrative, situated forms of knowing.

Another challenge the program faces — a challenge to the entire service learning movement nationally — is recruiting a more diverse group of student participants. Historically, service learning at UMass has been the domain of white students, especially women. For the Citizen Scholars program, it is especially important that different experiences of race, class, and gender enter into the dialogue about the formation of a "good society." The program has worked intensively to recruit men and students of color. Of the fourteen students in the first cohort, 31% were students of color and 21% were male.

Transformative Service Learning for Newcomer Communities

In response to the challenge of diversity in service learning, a highly innovative form of service learning for engaged citizenship has arisen from the Center for Immigrant and Refugee Community Leadership and Empowerment (CIRCLE). This program, known as Students for Education, Empowerment and Development (SEED) links refugee and immigrant students to newcomer youth. The CIRCLE initiative originated in 1994, as a collaboration between three campuses of the University of Massachusetts system, with funding from the Massachusetts Office for Refugees and Immigrants. The SEED program evolved as an alternative service learning model at UMass Amherst, through the efforts of faculty and graduate students at the Center for International Education. Program staff worked with newcomer undergraduate students and local communities to shape the program and develop courses to institutionalize it within the School of Education.

The SEED program addresses a key problem faced by typical service learning programs: how to attract non-majority students. Rather than assuming identity has no relevance, this program acknowledges that refugee and immigrant students have a different relationship with the institutions and identities of mainstream American higher education than do majority students. The SEED program affirms students' identities and offers opportunities for intensive sociocultural reflection and engagement with local community issues. As noted by the founders of CIRCLE, "Redesigning a service learning program or course to be relevant and appropriate to immigrant students requires an alternative model that educates and empowers them to become active citizens *and builders of their own communities* as well as the larger society" [italics theirs] (Arches, et al., 1997).

Unlike conventional service learning, this program is grounded in the more radical participatory research and critical pedagogy traditions. Rather than prescribed academic material, students' lives and the concrete realities of their communities are the subject matter of the courses. Taking an ethnocultural perspective, this program invites students to reflect on issues of identity and cultural values. For many, it is the first time in college they have been able to explore the complexities of bi-cultural or bi-racial identities and the tensions between the demands of their familial cultural traditions and the expectations of mainstream youth culture. They have space to explore their roles as both cultural insiders and cross-cultural mediators. In many other university courses, newcomer youth might be perceived as lacking the "cultural capital" to succeed academically. In the SEED program, however, students' lived realities become a valued source of knowledge and space of action.

Parallel to the focus on identity is an emphasis on mentorship and leadership. In their service learning courses, students learn the skills of facilitation, conflict resolution, and teambuilding. In the community, they work with youth at local social service agencies to help them explore their own questions of identity and develop community-building projects such as photographic collections, scholarship funds, and ethnic dance performances.

The SEED program is built upon multiple layers of mentorship and collegial connection. A faculty member mentors a team of graduate students who teach the courses; graduate students mentor the undergraduates enrolled in the courses; the undergraduates mentor local youth, who, in turn, form new layers of relationship with their families and friends. Thus the program nurtures dialogue and learning-rich relationships, affirming that all participants are teachers and learners. In a tightly woven web, the program combines community research, skill building, self-knowledge, and action for social change.

CONCLUSIONS

In an integrative age, the educational outcome perhaps most urgently needed is that of wisdom. We believe that service learning is a powerful means of moving the university toward the cultivation of wisdom. As philosopher Nicholas Maxwell (1984) states:

> *We urgently need a new, more rigorous kind of inquiry that gives intellectual priority to the tasks of articulating our problems of living and proposing and critically assessing possible cooperative solutions. This new kind of inquiry would have as its basic aim to improve, not*

just knowledge, but also personal and global wisdom — wisdom being understood to be the capacity to realize what is of value in life. (p. 3)

He goes on to point out that "a basic intellectual task of philosophy-of-wisdom inquiry is to help all of us imbue our personal and social lives with vividly imagined and criticized possible actions, so that we may discover, and perform where possible, those actions that enable us to realize what is of value."

Service learning enables students to discover what is of value — to themselves and to the communities they serve. It prepares them for public deliberation about complex issues and for taking full responsibility for the well-being of the whole community. When focused on engaged citizenship, as at UMass, service learning can also equip students with the tools of wise action — the insight into identity and the understanding of community dynamics and political processes necessary to take real steps toward the formation of a better and wiser world, and the development of more complete and integrative human beings. These outcomes are, after all, the high purposes of a university and always have been.

References

Arches, J., Darlington-Hope, M. Gerson, J., Gibson, J., Habana-Hafner, S., & Kiang, P. (1997, January/February). New voices in university-community transformation. *Change, 29*(1), 36-41.

Eyler, J. & Giles, G. (1999). *Where's the learning in service learning?* San Francisco: Jossey Bass.

Fogel, R. (2000). *The fourth great awakening and the future of egalitarianism.* Chicago: University of Chicago Press.

Fukuyama, F. (1995). *Trust: The social virtues and the creation of prosperity.* New York: Free Press.

Kazanjian, V. H. & Laurence, P. L. (2000). *Education as transformation: Religious pluralism, spirituality, and a new vision for higher education in America.* New York: Peter Lang.

Kellogg Commission on the Future of State and Land Grant Universities. (1999, February). *Returning to our roots: The engaged institution.* New York: National Association of State Universities and Land-Grant Colleges.

Levine, A. (1980). *When dreams and heroes died: A portrait of today's college student.* San Francisco: Jossey Bass.

Levine, A. & Cureton, J. (1998). *When hope and fear collide: A portrait of today's college student.* San Francisco: Jossey Bass.

Maxwell, N. (1984). *From knowledge to wisdom: A revolution in the aims and methods of science.* London: Basil Blackwell.

Putnam, R. (1995). Bowling alone: America's declining social capital. *Journal of Democracy, 6*(1), 65-78.

Resnick, L. (1987, December). The 1987 presidential address: Learning in school and out. *Educational Researcher, 16*(9), 13-20.

Rhoads, R. (1997). *Community service and higher learning: Explorations of the caring self.* Albany: State University of New York Press.

Sax, L. J. & Astin, A. W. (1997, Summer/Fall). The benefits of service: Evidence from undergraduates. *Educational Record*, 25-32.

Schlessinger, A. Jr. (1986). *The cycles of American history*. Boston: Houghton Mifflin.

Schlesinger, A. (1939). Tides of American politics. *The Yale Review, 29*(2).

Scott, D. & Awbrey, S. (1993). Transforming the university. *In Proceedings of the Conference on Women in Science and Engineering.* Bloomington, IN: Committee on Institutional Cooperation.

Staub, E. (1989). *The roots of evil: The origins of genocide and other group violence.* Cambridge: Cambridge University Press.

Tarnas, R. (1991). *The passion of the western mind: Understanding the ideas that have shaped our worldview*. New York: Harmony Books.

Wenger, E. (1998). *Communities of practice: Learning, meaning, and identity.* Cambridge: Cambridge University Press.

Wheatley, M. & Kellner-Rogers, M. (1996). *A simpler way*. San Francisco: Berrett-Koehler.

CHAPTER 23

UNIVERSITY OF NEBRASKA - LINCOLN

Eric Hartman
Diane Podolske
James Moeser
University of Nebraska Lincoln

> *May the warp be the white light of morning,*
> *May the weft be the red light of evening,*
> *May the fringes be the falling rain,*
> *May the border be the standing rainbow.*
> *Thus weave for us a garment of brightness.*
> *Song of the Sky Loom, Native*
> *American Origin (Tewa)*

INTRODUCTION

Several in service learning yearn for a panacea, a brilliant burst of programmatic pontification that yields the ultimate answer for small offices with mighty tasks. At the University of Nebraska – Lincoln (NU), we have yet to unearth the end all in service learning programs, however, we have developed several replicable programs that address challenges familiar to practitioners of service learning. The types of difficulties we face are well-known throughout much of the profession. We work at a Research One, land-grant institution where research is pragmatically prioritized, but service to the community is included in the mission. Our office is young, struggling to gain footing and recognition on a campus of over 18,000 undergraduates and over 4,000 graduate students.

Our programs must create a significant impact on a limited budget. We strive to foster positive relationships with community members despite some recent town gown antagonism. Our efforts are broad and our goals are sometimes disparate. We work in a region where the individual, autonomy, and independence are mythological aspects of popular culture. This wide variety of challenges has influenced us to approach service learning with an early emphasis on experimentation, followed by thorough evaluation, necessary reformulation, and finally program solidification to the extent that our programs become an integral part of the university infrastructure.

While developing service learning at NU, we have drawn from every available resource: disparate disciplines, student organizations, community agencies, and university departments. Our multiple efforts combine to form a common fabric of service learning. In areas where programs have developed, the fabric has become progressively stronger, but the pattern that succeeds in one area is never precisely the same as the pattern that succeeds elsewhere. This loose structure is due to the purposely alterable nature of service learning, which rightly calls for practitioners to solicit and address community needs in a manner that considers the unique characteristics of situations, resources, and participants.

In this chapter we will discuss the goals that guide our efforts and four programs that reflect our distinct approach and unique institutional factors. The first section includes our definition of service learning, a description of our administrative location within the institution, and an explanation of our objectives: student development, civic and community development, and institutional integration. We move on to describe four unique programs that could be replicated elsewhere. These include: an emphasis on developing student-initiated service visions; a service learning scholarship program supported by the private sector; a credit-bearing course that serves as training for service learning teaching assistants; and an effort to create a state-wide infrastructure for service learning. Before concluding we discuss several obstacles that we have dealt with or continue to struggle with in our efforts to weave the tapestry of service into the university and community.

DEFINITION AND GOALS

The absence of a single, universally accepted definition of service learning is often vexing for service learning professionals. Myriad acceptable definitions exist, including focused models intended particularly for school-based, community-based, academic and co-curricular service learning. After considering numerous definitions and approaches, we developed our own model in the spirit of the oft-cited National and Community Service Trust Act definition (Education Commission of the States, 1993). The SERVE model (Hampton, 1999) is brief, concise, understandable, and accurate, yet it is still broad enough to envelop service learning's countless possibilities.

The **SERVE** model represents five steps to successful service learning projects: **S**elect service; **E**ducate and inform; **R**espond to need; **V**alue significance and reflect; **E**valuate and celebrate. Select service refers to the initial step of identifying and focusing on a community need. Educate and inform describes the process of learning about the need. In this step volunteers gain a greater understanding about the extent, causes, and hopeful solutions to the community issue that they are addressing. This may be part of an academic course or it may be part of volunteer training sponsored by a community agency or student organization. Respond to need refers to direct service. This is the action step, when students perform the actual service.

Value significance and reflect describes activities that encourage students to make linkages between their education, their service, and their daily lives. This is accomplished through any number of reflection activities, including group discussions, games, personal journaling, mirroring, and many more. Evaluate and celebrate refers to the final assessment of the volunteer experience as well as some form of recognition or celebration for those that have given their time. Evaluations should be thorough and include recommendations for future improvements. The SERVE acronym provides a simple memory tool that illustrates the steps of a quality service learning program and is useful when training faculty, agency staff and students who wish to contribute to service learning projects.

Program Goals and Previous Research

The SERVE model is a critical tool to further two of our main objectives: student growth and civic and community development. In addition to the body of research that justifies its inclusion, student development is an objective of our service learning program due partly to our administrative location in a student affairs department.

Student Development

Student development, as an articulated goal, refers to a plethora of student characteristics including academic, psychological, social, career, and skill development. Academic development through service learning has been the focus of several studies in which researchers have found a correlation between service learning participation and increases in students' grades (Dean & Murdock, 1992; Markus, Howard & King, 1993; Shumer, 1994; Yates & Youniss, 1996). Additionally, research suggests service learning increases students' likelihood of reporting that they performed to their potential, ability to apply course principles to new situations, and classroom learning (Markus et al., 1993). Related findings suggest a correlation between service and decreased truancy (Yates & Youniss, 1996). Still others have demonstrated a relationship between service learning participation and an increased likelihood of course completion, as well as an increased ability to link course lessons to civic or career situations (Axsom, 1999).

Additionally, students' improved self-concept has been correlated with service learning. Maton (1990) found that meaningful activity is positively related to life satisfaction and self-esteem. Not surprisingly, then, a correlation has also been found between service learning and the development of mature interpersonal relationships (McGill, 1992). Further, Calabrese and Schumer (1986) have demonstrated a relationship between service and reduced levels of alienation, improved school behavior, and acceptance by the adult community. Finally, Schine (1989) suggests that service learning challenges students to work collegially, to compromise, to communicate effectively, to confront problems and to find solutions to those problems. This substantial body of research justifies our view that service learning enhances student development academically, socially, and psychologically.

Only a small number of research studies have focused on the relationship between service learning and career / skill development. Still, it has become trite for employers to complain about graduates' lack of practical skills, teamwork experience, and leadership ability. Further, in one of the few studies completed on the subject, Schine (1989) reported that students who participate in service learning have increased opportunities for career exploration and self-report more positive attitudes toward the work world. Service learning allows students to gain tangible experience in academic areas and professional skills before leaving the academy. Though our program is too young to offer significant quantitative outcome measures, the aforementioned studies and volumes of anecdotal evidence allow us to confidently refer to service learning as a significant factor in many areas of student development.

Civic and Community Development

Encouraging students' civic and community development is another key objective of our service learning program. The NU mission includes the following statement about civic responsibility, "The land-grant tradition creates for the University of Nebraska-Lincoln a special statewide responsibility to serve the needs of Nebraska and its citizens." Service learning answers the call for civic development in two critical ways. First, service learning programs result in immediate, tangible benefits, as students are engaged in direct service to affect areas as disparate as human services, public safety, education, the environment, and many more.

Second, the educational and reflective components of service learning help students link their efforts to larger social issues and increase the likelihood that these students will participate and contribute to the community in the future. The second contribution is less tangible, but it is crucial. Students who participate in service learning during their formative years are much more likely to counter the current societal trends against participation, against community, and against generosity in general. This creation of engaged citizens helps NU fulfill its role as an active institutional citizen, in line with the vision for higher education posed by Ernest Boyer, who called for universities to recommit to their communities (Rothman, 1998).

Numerous studies have substantiated the claim that service learning improves civic attitudes (Batchelder & Root, 1994; Corbett, 1977; Giles & Eyler, 1994; Krug, 1991; Markus, Howard & King, 1993; Myers-Lipton, 1998; Schmiede, 1995). Many studies that emerged in the early 90s were criticized for small sample sizes, were only conducted at one institution, and sometimes did not control for possibly mitigating background factors. These criticisms led to two large-scale studies concerning service learning and civic attitudes.

Eyler, Giles, and Braxton (1997) gathered data from over 1,500 students at 20 colleges and universities. Astin and Sax (1998) gathered data from 3,450 students at 42 different institutions. Both studies controlled for potentially influential background factors such as propensity to engage in service and demographic variables such as gender and race. Astin and Sax also controlled for the student's major as well as structural characteristics of the institution, such as size, type, and selectivity. Both studies concurred with previous, less extensive research and concluded that service learning has a significant positive impact on civic attitudes. These findings, as well as the research on student development, provide us with sufficient data to confidently conclude that the fabric of service learning should be inexorably intertwined with the campus culture at NU.

Institutional Integration

Institutional integration, then, is our third objective for service learning at NU. Focusing on institutionalization is driven by the common sense notion that further integration begets further legitimacy, acceptance, and respect. Currently, we are focused on institutionalizing service learning infrastructure by designing a course that will educate and train participants to become more effective campus and community service leaders. The course, which will be thoroughly discussed in the second section, is a pilot program that will allow us to test a new area for service learning at NU. Because we are consciously creating a solid institutional structure, we carefully and continuously experiment, evaluate, reformulate, and solidify. As long as steady and careful institutionalization remains one of our three main objectives, we will continue to consistently create programs that further holistic student development, civic development, and community improvement. Four of our current programs are exceptional due to their congruence with our objectives and for their uniqueness among service learning programs.

SUCCESSFUL PROGRAMS AT NU
Supporting Student-Initiated Service Learning: History

Student Involvement staff at NU have always encouraged and supported student-initiated ideas and proposals. In the service-learning program, we are consciously committed to the tradition of facilitating, rather than dictating. Our focus is on recruiting students with visions to improve their communities. This emphasis on students initiating, implementing, and leading also allows us to stretch the efforts of our limited staff and resources. Instead of directing programs, we engage and motivate students to direct their own. Two highly successful transitions from student vision to service learning program have encouraged us to design a non-credit course to institutionalize the transition from vision to implementation.

Vision creation is already part of an annual institutionalized program at NU. Prospective student leaders are invited to participate in LeaderShape Nebraska during spring break. The program objective is, "to develop a growing nucleus of campus leaders who understand the necessity and process of defining personal values, developing a vision and creating a plan of action for the realization of that vision" (The LeaderShape Institute, 1998). During the LeaderShape Nebraska experience, students are asked to develop a vision to improve their campus or community. They are encouraged to have a healthy disrespect for the impossible, and their visions are purposefully bold and daring. Visions from the LeaderShape Nebraska 2000 class include everything from volunteer service to elder care to the quality of life in Third World countries. Some examples include:

> "To help others realize the true benefits of community or volunteer service and to help bring effective awareness of service in the community; To help people become better stewards of the environment to make the world a cleaner, safer, more productive place for the future; To educate people about diversity; To create a society where all children regardless of social class, ethnicity, or race, have an equal opportunity to be successful; To increase appreciation and importance of the elderly in our society; And to improve the quality of life in Third World Countries."

This sample represents the diverse and hopeful nature of the dozens of visions produced each spring. During the past two years, two LeaderShape Nebraska visions have completed a successful transition from conceptualization to implementation. In 1998, sophomore Adam Pfeifer had a vision to create a system that would help middle school children perform successfully in school and develop an appreciation for the importance of education. The following year sophomore political science major Jake Wobig sought, "to work to improve the lives of those less fortunate, who are put at an unfair disadvantage by the system."

Pfeifer's vision developed into a successful, completely institutionalized program that creates mentoring relationships between college students and disadvantaged grade school children and provides the children with a positive introduction to higher education. Pfeifer's program, from conception to implementation, followed the SERVE model. Select service: Pfeifer selected a service based on what he perceived to be a critical time in young people's lives. He felt that attitudes toward education were formed and solidified during the vital early adolescent years and he wanted to encourage students to succeed.

Educate and inform: Pfeifer developed a thorough understanding of trends in American education. He examined programs designed to combat high drop out rates and poor attitudes toward education, which led him to College Bound. College Bound is a nationwide program that was created in 1994. Respond to need: Pfeifer orchestrated College Bound's implementation at NU so effectively that in its first year on campus NU College Bound was the largest College Bound program in the nation. Since that time, NU College Bound has touched the lives of over 400 grade school students in the Lincoln area, motivating them to stay in school and encouraging them to strive for a higher education in the field of their choice.

Value significance and reflect: Although the national College Bound program does not include a reflection component for the college student facilitators, we have successfully incorporated journal writing and evaluation. This helps engender greater personal growth, development, and increased awareness of the linkages between the program, academic coursework, and daily decisions. Evaluate and Celebrate: A celebratory event is planned for College Bound facilitators at the end of the program. We include both evaluation activities and recognition. Evaluations are thorough, involving careful analyses of the insights that volunteers have gained about how to improve the program and thoughts the facilitators would like to share with the national College Bound office.

Wobig's vision developed into NU's first campus and community wide Students in the Streets service program. Students in the Streets contributed to the community by soliciting service project requests from Neighborhood Associations and local nonprofits, then fulfilling those requests to: help rejuvenate community parks; restore a historic building; contribute to activities at a local youth center; scrape, prime, and paint rooms at the local YWCA; perform outside home and yard tasks for elderly residents; install park benches and playground equipment; and help local AmeriCorps volunteers and school children paint playground lines, games, and art on the blacktop at Lincoln's most impoverished elementary school. Students in the Streets also followed the SERVE model. Due to the broad student and community support of the Students in the Streets program, it is likely to become an annual program that will be further institutionalized with each passing year.

Supporting Student-Initiated Service Learning: Institutionalization

To institutionalize the transition from vision to implementation we have created a noncredit, bimonthly course entitled Civics and Service. We invite students who demonstrate an unwavering commitment to service to participate in the course. Inviting a select group of students is advantageous for three reasons. First, we are able to target groups that are underrepresented among volunteers. Research has shown that men are more likely to volunteer when leadership positions are available. We have lower rates of volunteerism among males, and we hope to attract men into the program because leadership position creation is inherently part of vision development. Second, we are able to ensure that students who receive the rather substantial investment of human resources are committed to public service. Finally, we benefit from the visions and opinions of students from diverse backgrounds and experiences. We actively seek participants from student organizations, the LeaderShape Nebraska class, residence halls, off-campus housing, and Greek houses. This diversity of participants allows us to maintain a balance of perspectives.

The course objective is, "to impart the resources and training necessary to ensure implementation of service learning visions." Initially, participants are required to research the issue they wish to address. They develop a thorough understanding of the issue, possible causes, attempted solutions, associated organizations, and local efforts already established that are working to ameliorate the problem.

With a growing understanding of their chosen issue area, students receive training from guest speakers and service learning staff on areas such as: leadership, grant writing and fundraising, management, planning, writing mission statements, motivating volunteers, public relations and advertising, working with government agencies, and political participation. Though the course is only offered during the fall semester, the implementation plans continue according to each student's vision. Due to the pragmatic consideration that these bold visions will not offer tangible results until some time after the Civics and Service course ends, we schedule a banquet for the end of the spring semester, at which time students are asked to report on their successes and congratulate their colleagues. The banquet serves as a motivational deadline for students to produce some tangible results.

By harvesting student visions and acting as an incubator for service-oriented ideas, we are able to make substantial strides toward our stated goals of student development, community and civic development, and institutional integration. Student development takes many forms. Certainly, the experience of taking a bold idea from conceptualization through implementation is a valuable personal leadership experience, as well as a crucial resume piece for students entering the professional world. Our Civics and Service course seminars amount to an intensive workshop on Public or Nonprofit Administration, a growing field with numerous valuable employment opportunities. The seminars also cast a practical light on many of the lessons learned in management, communications, administration, political science, and several other courses.

Because the SERVE model ensures that both education and reflection are ongoing components of the Civics and Service experience, students also benefit from increased personal and community efficacy, or an increased belief that the community can solve its problems (Eyler et al., 1997). While many Civics and Service lessons are designed strictly to improve students' ability to realize their visions, the ultimate objective is to create engaged citizens who recognize the myriad connections between their lives, their community, and their political system. The course operates on a continuum from articulated vision, through implemented vision, to vision realization combined with related political activism.

Encouraging activism is an additional unique aspect of Civics and Service. While service learning often emphasizes identifying linkages between service and the larger political picture, few programs provide political training. As students steadily gain greater appreciation for the importance of public policy in addressing, lessening, or creating public problems, they simultaneously receive seminars on: the legislative process, lobbying, influencing policymaking, working with elected officials and government agencies, and other associated areas.

The ultimate end of the course continuum, the completely conscious person who realizes and acts upon the numerous connections between life, values, and political participation, is to some extent an exalted ideal, but the direct service that students provide, and the deeper understanding of the problem gained through reflection and education, are significant moral victories in their own right.

At first glance, the desired course outcomes are predominantly qualitative, and therefore difficult to measure. However, we plan to use two quantitative measures to index program success, in addition to the vast amount of qualitative input that we are sure to receive. Those measures are: First, Civics and Service participants will complete a thorough course evaluation. Our initial goal is that at least eighty percent of participants will report: a significant learning experience, increased ability to develop projects, and a strong belief that the course was exciting and professionally valuable. Second, we will track participants' success regarding vision development. Our goal in this area is that at least fifty percent of participants will make tangible progress toward completing their vision.

We have high expectations for Civics and Service as a model program because we are able to simultaneously pursue each of our three main objectives - student development, civic and community development, and institutionalization - while also addressing many of our more vexing difficulties. We are able to stretch our budget and staff by combining dozens of projects into one course that gives students the ability to follow through on their ideals. This contrasts starkly with the image of student affairs employees working to develop projects for students. We strive instead to develop students for projects, personal growth, and empowerment. We address broad and disparate needs because we assemble a diverse group of students with varying concerns.

We are able to incorporate the cultural emphasis on the individual because we ensure that visions and plans originate with individual students. Town gown tensions are tempered as students strive to solidify relationships with community members. In addition to the relationships formed, part of the course deals with public relations and press releases so the students are able to advertise their efforts effectively. The institutional emphasis on research is sidestepped because we gather eager students for our own course, rather than relying only on faculty to develop courses in their specific areas. Civics and

Service enables us to overcome limitations and hurdles by empowering students to set and achieve exceptional standards of service on their own.

Training the Next Generation of Service Learning Scholars

The service learning scholarship program at NU was created as a result of beverage contract negotiations between the Pepsi Cola Co. and the University. Pepsi agreed to fund forty $1,000 scholarships for incoming Nebraska students who had performed outstanding service and leadership projects during high school. The scholarship was named the Pepsi Scholarship for Outstanding Leadership and Service, and Student Involvement was chosen to host the program and provide additional educational and social opportunities for these exceptional students. This is the third year of the program, and funding for the scholarships will continue until the end of the twelve-year beverage contract.

The mission of the Pepsi Scholars program is to promote social change by encouraging students to become trustees of the NU campus and community. The program has evolved into a one semester, non-credit course focused on educating these new students about each other, service learning pedagogy, community agencies in Lincoln, and large-scale service event program planning. The Pepsi Scholars also plan and implement a large-scale children's literacy event for the National Day of Service and a senior citizens prom. Pepsi Scholars benefit from a wide variety of leadership and personal development activities while fostering within each other a life-long commitment to service.

The Pepsi Scholar alumni also play an important part in the program by mentoring the new students and alerting them to co-curricular and academic opportunities. Alumni serve as teaching assistants in the class, and they often bring application forms, event flyers, and student government information to the Scholars' attention. Program staff also are available to help Scholars write resumes and to provide letters of recommendation as the new students apply for their first involvement positions on campus.

The response to the Pepsi Scholar program has been overwhelmingly enthusiastic. Evaluation data show that the Pepsi Scholar program is a formative experience for these students, as it reintroduces the concept of service during a developmental period when many students decrease their outreach into the community. The Scholars report benefits from meeting other service-minded students, learning about the needs of the Lincoln community, understanding community agency efforts, planning events on a large campus, and awareness of their options for involvement. Community agency staff welcome the influx of trained volunteers, many of whom are among the best and brightest of the new class of students. After the formal program ends, Pepsi Scholars often return to the agencies to volunteer on their own. University administrators value the recruitment aspect of the program and the high retention rate of these exceptional students. Last, but not least, Pepsi enjoys the benefit of the on-going positive publicity surrounding all Pepsi Scholar events, including publicity in every Scholar's hometown newspaper.

This service learning scholarship program model can be replicated at universities or community colleges where new funds are available for scholarships or existing funds can be redirected for service learning. Many institutions of higher education are forming exclusive contracts with corporations for beverage pouring, computer services, food service, etc. or soliciting financial contributions from alumni and other benefactors who potentially could contribute to a service scholarship fund. A scholarship that provides a student with the opportunity to receive education and experiences leading to ongoing service in the community multiplies the effect of the initial scholarship contribution and may prove persuasive to donors and corporations.

Our goals of student development, civic development, and institutional integration are realized through the Pepsi Scholar program. The Pepsi Scholars develop academic, interpersonal, and career skills that advance them to leadership positions on campus and in the community. A senior honorary recently named their NU Freshmen Notables – students recognized for their academic and co-curricular achievements and potential – and all four of the Notables were Pepsi Scholars. Pepsi Scholars have encouraged student organizations, residence halls and Greek houses to perform meaningful service projects that address true community needs.

One Pepsi Scholar influenced Greek houses, multiple student organizations, and residence hall floors to pioneer an unprecedented program to collect unwanted food, personal items, and clothing as students moved out at the end of the academic year. Another Pepsi Scholar challenged his fraternity to complete hundreds of direct service hours in addition to their traditional philanthropic projects. NU has integrated these talented students by asking them to provide campus tours for prospective students and to represent the University at statewide events. Though we have not developed a quantitative instrument to measure the longitudinal impact that the Pepsi Scholars program has on participants, the qualitative evidence is unmistakable and nearly unanimous: The program helps solidify lifelong commitments to service. Pepsi Alumni are not only regulars on the service circuit; they are often the leaders.

Developing a Service Learning Teaching Assistant (TA) Course

Careful preparation for academic service learning includes investigating community needs, building relationships with agency partners, researching reflection activities, rewriting course syllabi and expectations, and attending to the myriad logistical details of a service learning project. We have encountered interested faculty who would like to add service learning to a course, but already feel overtaxed by our Research One university's expectation for research, teaching, advising, and the inevitable committee work. Our task as service learning professionals was to devise some form of assistance that would diminish the logistical tasks for the faculty member, freeing him or her to adjust their curriculum to ensure that a service learning project would meet the academic expectations for the course.

We are currently developing a credit-bearing class that would educate students to serve as TAs for faculty willing to try academic service learning. The semester long course will include sessions on service learning pedagogy, event planning, reflection methods, advocacy techniques, and evaluation methodology. The diverse curriculum will provide the students with a foundation of service learning knowledge that can be applied across specific course content and across academic disciplines. The students will also be introduced to a variety of community service agencies and staff in the Lincoln area who have expressed an interest in hosting service learning projects. Faculty and student teaching assistant partnerships will be established mid-semester, so the students can begin to aid faculty in developing service learning projects. The partnership will continue throughout the semester in which the new service learning course is offered, with the student assisting with the logistics, reflection activities and evaluation of the project.

The service learning TA program will provide valuable help for faculty, and it will also provide academic, civic, and personal development opportunities for the students. The TAs will gain knowledge about service learning pedagogy, community needs, personal leadership skills, and building relationships with both faculty members and agency partners. The assignment of academic credit will provide motivation for student commitment and achievement. The TAs will also attend a regional service learning conference to learn about best practices from other higher education institutions, to create information networks, and to build cooperative partnerships.

Institutional integration will occur through departmental support because each service learning course must have a sponsoring department and faculty in multiple departments will participate in the program. We plan to offer the course every year to build a cadre of teaching assistants to assist faculty and also to assist other co-curricular service learning programs on campus.

CREATING A STATEWIDE INFRASTRUCTURE FOR SERVICE LEARNING

In May of 1996, representatives from several colleges and universities from across Nebraska met to participate in a daylong workshop on service learning. Following this workshop, ten institutional representatives continued discussions about the power of this pedagogy and envisioned the formation of a collaborative unit to develop and coordinate the efforts of service learning in Nebraska higher education. The representatives also discussed a desire to form a complete Stream of Service beginning with the K-12 educational system, through higher education, and moving beyond to rural governments, school boards and other community-based service organizations. Fueled by passion, the spirit of possibility, and the commonality of institutional mission statements that reflect a commitment to develop citizens who are serving members of the community, the Nebraska Consortium for Service Learning in Higher Education was born (Nebraska Consortium, 1999). Invitations to partner with the new Consortium were extended to every higher education institution in the state. All but three of the higher education institutions in Nebraska have joined the Consortium, including private and public, four year and two year, research and teaching focused institutions (Nebraska Consortium, 1999).

To establish goals and objectives for the newly formed Consortium, the founding group conducted a needs assessment exploring and prioritizing the service learning related needs of higher education in Nebraska (Nebraska Consortium, 1999). This study resulted in the development of eight statewide objectives to guide the efforts of the Consortium during its first three years and to serve as the basis of a request to the Corporation for National Service for start-up funding. The objectives are as follows:

1. Statewide faculty training on service learning pedagogy.
2. Subgrant awards for faculty members to integrate service learning into courses.
3. Statewide student leadership institutes on service learning, incorporating the social change and servant leadership models.
4. Demonstration of replicable models for utilization of Federal work study funding for service.
5. Creation of a sustainable infrastructure for higher education service learning in Nebraska.
6. Institutional subgrant awards for the development or continuation of service learning efforts.
7. Collaboration with agencies to assess needs and assets and establish plans for continued collaboration.
8. Creation of a dissemination vehicle for all higher education institutions in Nebraska and surrounding states (Nebraska Consortium, 1999).

The objectives combine and interact to address four areas of need: faculty development, student leadership, institutional development, and community development. Programs were then created to address the eight objectives and four areas of need determined by the needs assessment. All objectives relate to the Corporation for National Service emphasis on education, public safety, the environment, and other human needs.

The Consortium is currently in its third year of Corporation for National Service funding. NU acts as the conduit institution for the grant funds and provides a significant cash and in-kind matching commitment to the work of the Consortium. NU Chancellor James Moeser initiates the yearly drive for recommitment by member institutions, and he fully supports the Consortium's

goals and efforts. The Consortium office is housed within the NU Student Involvement offices, and the Program Director for the Consortium is a member
of the Student Involvement staff.

The strength of the Consortium is built on three key factors: collaboration
of the individual member institutions; support of quality institutional and faculty grant projects; and a strong, unified voice from Nebraska's higher education institutions to advocate service learning. Member institutions have
generously shared curriculum plans, provided physical and personnel resources, and invited other institutional members to attend service learning
training sessions and speakers. All member institutions are involved in the
process of reviewing both faculty and institutional subgrant applications, with
the goal of providing ideas and support to the grantees in addition to the grant
funds. The Consortium has a World Wide Web homepage and it serves as a
central source of grant project information and provides links to the member
institutions' service learning programs. The Consortium is building the capacity to serve as a recognized resource on academic and co-curricular service
learning for our state and beyond.

We are making slow but steady progress on understanding our role as the
Streams of Service link between our K-12 partners and our community partners. Consortium institutions have begun to form support linkages for service
learning with K-12 schools through after school programs, teacher education
practicum that feature service learning, and assisting with the coordination of
service learning conferences for youth. Consortium members provide programmatic support for the AmeriCorps National Service Members serving in
Nebraska, including the recruitment of new Members from our universities.
We are exploring ways the Consortium can assist with Nebraska's rural development efforts to reenergize and rebuild stagnant rural economies. The
progress on the Stream of Service efforts is slow, as we struggle with competing priorities, lack of funding and staff time, and less than enthusiastic
support from our Legislature, however, we continue our efforts toward the
goal of a seamless service environment for our state.

OBSTACLES

We have described four increasingly strong service learning efforts in the
preceding pages. However, we have also experienced a number of disap-
pointments and setbacks that, like our positive experiences and lessons, may
serve as a learning tool for others who engage similar obstacles.

First, it has been difficult to gain access to university committees that
oversee curriculum development and tenure processes. We need to continue to
build faculty alliances to develop a strong voice for service learning in these
committees. Building trusting relationships with faculty takes focused time
and effort, and the recognition of service learning as a valuable learning pedagogy and as a consideration in the tenure process may not come for years.
This may be especially true at land grant universities, where the service men-

tioned in the mission statement often refers to agriculture extension programs. Unfortunately, one of our own weaknesses only perpetuates this problem. Due to pressing community needs, we have a tendency to focus on filling immediate volunteer opportunities, rather than spending time to effectively plan institutionalized and regular partnerships between university faculty and the community. This is a serious difficulty, as neglecting to fulfill a volunteer need can quite literally mean that someone will go without a meal. However, focusing on effective planning and partnerships would likely enable us to have a broader and more effective impact in the future.

Second, the Nebraska University system has experienced a less than friendly relationship with our state legislature during the budget request process. Recent legislative budget cuts have forced the Nebraska University system to develop funding priorities and reduce budgets in non-priority areas. It is certainly a time when faculty and staff are again asked to do more with less. The climate on campus is less receptive to new service learning initiatives that need funding when existing programs are being eliminated. Just as political scientists speak of post-materialist values emerging only with a strong economy, ostensibly idealistic initiatives are less likely to meet with a favorable reception when established departments feel threatened. Our service learning programs currently receive funds through student fees and federal grants, but we lack administrative recognition as an important priority for university support.

Finally, it is taking more effort and energy than expected to develop community agency partnerships for service learning. There is no strong history of partnerships between our office and community agencies, and therefore our agency relationships do not always have the requisite level of trust that would characterize a true partnership. While our relationships are steadily improving, we realize that community agency positions often offer the combination of low pay and demanding work, so many staff members leave their jobs after a year or two. The service learning program staff is constantly in the process of training new agency staff members about service learning, updating mailing and contact lists, revisiting board members, and renegotiating service learning partnership agreements with community agencies. The process can seem never ending and it sometimes is difficult to measure progress despite our best efforts.

CONCLUSIONS

Universally, our programs reflect a constant commitment to do less with more. We are acutely aware of the idealized expectations that encumber service learning offices everywhere. Often, it seems, we are asking ourselves to prevent poverty, house the homeless, end environmental degradation, dispel domestic violence, and ameliorate everything else. During particularly lucid times, our most honest hours, we recognize that we are but few in a formidable field.

This understanding drives us to stretch our resources, to itemize, and to categorize. One, two, three, we must focus on: First, student development because it benefits our students, our university, our community, and our society as a whole over the long term. Second, civic and community development because it is significant in creating close communities and it ensures that students are regularly engaged in direct service to those who benefit from immediate assistance. Third, institutional integration because we are serious about our goals and we are constantly creating a legacy of service, community, generosity, and empathy.

The programs that we discussed are four key threads in the fabric of service learning at NU. Each program has its own unique pattern or structure, yet the resultant effects are often the same. Civics and Service, Pepsi Scholars, the Service Learning TA Program, and the Nebraska Consortium for Service Learning in Higher Education all create structures through which individuals committed to service may collaborate with like-minded individuals while they lead others to become more involved in service activities. The emphasis on: growing programs through volunteers; developing servers into service leaders; striving to create Streams of Service that will solidify lifetime commitments to service; motivating students to implement their own programs and inspire others; and training teaching assistants to implement service learning; enables us to serve a large campus and community with limited resources.

REFERENCES

Astin, A., & Sax, L. (1998). How undergraduates are affected by service participation. *Journal of College Student Development, 39*(3), 251-262.

Axsom, T., & Piland, W.E. (1999, Summer). Effects of service learning on student retention and success. *National Society for Experiential Education Quarterly*, 15-19.

Batchelder, T.H., & Root, S. (1994). Effects of an undergraduate program to integrate academic learning and service: cognitive, prosocial cognitive, and identity outcomes. *Journal of Adolescence, 17*(4), 341-355.

Calabrese, R.L., & Schumer, H. (1986). The effects of service activities on adolescent alienation. *Adolescence, 21*(3), 675-87.

Corbett, F.C. (1977). The community involvement program: Social service as a factor in adolescent moral and psychological development. *UMI Dissertation Reproductions.*

Dean, L., & Murdock, S.W. (1992, Summer). The effect of voluntary service on adolescent attitudes toward learning. *Journal of Volunteer Administration*, 5-10.

Education Commission of the States (1993). *Higher education and national service: A Campus Compact guide to the National and Community Service Trust Act of 1993.* Denver: Author.

Eyler, J., Giles, D. & Braxton, J. (1997). The impact of service learning on college students. *Michigan Journal of Community Service Learning, 4*, 5-15.

Giles, D., & Eyler, J. (1994). The theoretical roots of service learning in John Dewey: Toward a theory of service learning. *Michigan Journal of Community Service Learning, 1*(1), 77-85.

Hampton, L.R. (1999). *The SERVE Model.* Unpublished manuscript, Student Involvement, University of Nebraska-Lincoln.

Krug, J.L. (1991). Select changes in high school students' self-esteem and attitudes toward their school and community by their participation in service learning activities at a Rocky Mountain high school. *UMI Dissertation Reproductions*, No. 9318063.

LeaderShape Institute (1998). *Program Management Manual.* Champaign, IL: LeaderShape, Inc.

Markus, G.B., Howard, J., & King, D. (1993). Integrating community service and classroom instruction enhances learning: Results from an experiment. *Educational Evaluation and Policy Analysis, 15*(4), 410-419.

Maton, K.I. (1990). Meaningful involvement in instrumental activity and well-being: Studies of older adolescents and at risk urban teenagers. *American Journal of Community Psychology, 18*(2), 297-320.

McGill, J.C. (1992). The relationship of community service learning to developing mature interpersonal relationships in a sample of university students. *UMI Dissertation Reproductions*, No. 9312235.

Morgan, W., & Streb, M. (2000, April 27-30). *Effecting efficacy through service learning.* Paper presented at the Midwest Political Science Association Conference, Chicago, Illinois.

Myers-Lipton. (1998). Effects of a comprehensive service learning program on college students' civic responsibility. *Teaching Sociology, 26*, 243-258.

Nebraska Consortium for Service-Learning in Higher Education (1999). *Member Handbook*. Lincoln, NE: Author.

Rothman, M. (ed.). (1998). *Establishing universities as citizens*. Indianapolis, IN: Indiana Campus Compact.

Schine, J. (1989). *Young adolescents and community service*. Washington, DC: Carnegie Council on Adolescent Development.

Schmiede, A. (1995, Fall). Using focus groups in service learning: Implications for practice and research. *Michigan Journal of Community Service Learning, 63-71.

Shumer, R. (1994). Community-based learning: Humanizing education. *Journal of Adolescence, 17*(4), 357-367.

Yates, M., & Youniss, J. (1996). A developmental perspective on community service in adolescence. *Social Development, 5*(1), 85-111.

CHAPTER 24

ACADEMICALLY-BASED COMMUNITY SERVICE AND UNIVERSITY-ASSISTED COMMUNITY SCHOOLS AS COMPLEMENTARY APPROACHES FOR ADVANCING, LEARNING, TEACHING, RESEARCH AND SERVICE: THE UNIVERSITY OF PENNSYLVANIA AS A CASE STUDY IN PROGRESS

Lee Benson
Ira Harkavy
University of Pennsylvania

INTRODUCTION

The service-learning movement has nearly arrived.[1] Witness this volume, the 18 volume series on service-learning and the disciplines, the extraordinary growth of Campus Compact from 12 member institutions in 1985 to nearly 800 colleges and universities in 2000, and the focus on service-learning by influential national higher education associations such as the American Council on Education, Association of American Colleges and Universities, National Association of State Universities and Land-Grant Colleges, and American Association for Higher Education. Although relatively silent on service-learning, the prestigious Association of American Universities, an organization of 61 American and two Canadian research universities, has recently focused on issues of community service and university-community relationships.[2]

---

[1] In a 1996 issue of *Metropolitan Universities* (vol. 7, no. 1) entirely dedicated to service-learning, Deborah Hirsh, the issue editor, begins her excellent introductory essay by stating that "service-learning has arrived." *Nearly* arrived, in our judgement, more accurately reflects the current state of the field and the movement. See Hirsch's (1996) essay as well as a number of other useful articles in that issue.

[2] Campus Compact is, in our judgement, the organization most responsible for the growth and development of community service and service-learning across higher education. A compact of college and university presidents, Campus Compact explicitly defines its goals as a com-

This increased acceptance is all to the good. Service-learning is one of a handful of creative, active pedagogies (among them collaborative, peer-assisted, and problem-based learning) that enhance a student's capacity to think critically, problem solve, and function as a citizen in a democratic society.[3] Although all to the good, it is not as good as it could be. The advance of service-learning would, we believe, have better results if service-learning practitioners asked and answered, in a reiterative fashion, this simple question: What are the goals of the service-learning movements?

This is a difficult question indeed, requiring lots of hard thinking and rethinking. It is certainly not meant to be an academic (in the pejorative sense) question. "Know thy goals" is surely a first principle for any movement. "It is," as Francis Bacon stated in 1620, "not possible to run a course aright when the goal itself is not rightly placed."[4]

In our judgement, the service-learning movement has not "rightly placed" the goal. It has largely been concerned with fostering the civic consciousness, moral character, and academic learning of college students. (Needless to say, highly significant, extremely worthy goals.) Providing

---

mitment to "supporting students in the development of skills and values to promote citizenship through participation in public service" (document, 1997 Campus Compact governing board meeting).

Indications of the increased focus on service-learning by influential national higher education associations include these: the American Council on Education's (ACE) co-sponsorship with Florida State University of a June 1998 national conference on "Higher Education and Civic Responsibility," which set an agenda for a new ACE National Forum on Higher Education and Civic Responsibility; the Association of American Colleges and Universities' Program for Health and Higher Education, which has highlighted the potential role of service-learning in effective AIDS education and prevention; the National Association of State Universities and Land-Grant Colleges's Kellogg Commission report on the "Engaged Campus"; and the American Association for Higher Education's sponsorship of an 18 volume series on *Service-Learning in the Disciplines* and its appointment of Edward Zlotkowski as a senior associate to edit the series as well as to advance service-learning in general. Since 1996, under the leadership of Tulane University, an ad hoc working group representing 26 Association of American Universities (AAU) institutions have convened to address the role of research universities in serving their local and regional communities. Among the working group's goals is to support federally funded community service programs, strengthen the connections between government agencies that support community service, and address problems related to the administration of community service programs. Moreover, the October 1999 meeting of AAU presidents was significantly devoted to university-community relationships.

[3] For an illuminating discussion of "active" pedagogies, see Carol Geary Schneider and Robert Shoenberg, "Contemporary Understandings of Liberal Education," Academy in Transition Discussion Paper, (Washington, DC: Association of American Colleges and Universities, 1998)

[4] For the citation to Bacon and a discussion of his work, see Lee Benson, "Changing Social Science to Change the World: A Discussion Paper," *Social Science History* 2 (1978): 427-441.

service to the community has obviously been an important component of the movement. Community problem solving and making a difference in the actual conditions of communities, however, have tended to play minor roles in service-learning programs.

In its classic form, service-learning may function as a pedagogical equivalent of "exploitative" community-based research. Academics, of course, have often studied and written about poor, particularly minority, communities. The residents of these communities have largely been subjects to be studied, providing information that would produce dissertations and articles that someday, somehow would contribute to making things better. Meanwhile, the poor have gotten poorer and academics have gotten tenure, promoted, and richer.

Similarly, advocates and practitioners of service-learning have tended to agree that the goal of that pedagogy is to educate college students for citizenship. Citizenship is learned by linking classroom experience to a service experience that is at best seen as doing some good for the community. The real beneficiaries are, however, the deliverers, not the recipients, of the service. Someday, somehow when we have effectively educated a critical mass of the "best and the brightest" for citizenship, things would be made better. Meanwhile, the causes of our societal problems have remained untouched, the distance between the haves and have nots has widened, and universities have continued to largely function as institutions engaged in symbolic actions rather than institutions producing knowledge for (to use Bacon's phrase) "the relief of man's estate."[5]

Urban colleges and universities are in a unique position to "rightly place the goal" and "run [the]…course aright" by going beyond traditional service-learning (and its inherent limitations) to strategic, academically-based community service, in which contributing to the well-being of people in the community (both in the here and now and in the future) is a primary goal. It is service rooted in and intrinsically tied to teaching and research, and it aims to bring about structural community improvement (e.g., effective public schools, neighborhood economic development, strong community organizations) rather than simply to alleviate individual misery (e.g., feeding the hungry, sheltering the homeless, tutoring the "slow learner"). Strategic, academically-based community service requires a comprehensive institutional response that engages the broad range of resources of the urban college or university (including the talents, abilities, and energy of undergraduates involved in traditional service and service-learning activities) to solve a strategic problem of

---

[5] Ibid.

our time—the problem of creating democratic, local, cosmopolitan communities.

Why will urban "higher eds" go beyond service-learning to strategic, academically-based community service? Most centrally, they will increasingly have no choice. The need for communities rooted in face-to-face relationships and exemplifying humanistic values is most acute in the American city. The problems of the American city have increasingly become the problems of the urban college and university. Since they cannot move (as more mobile institutions have done), there is no escape from the issues of poverty, crime, and physical deterioration that are at the gates of urban higher educational institutions. The choice is to hold on to a mythic image of the university on the hill and suffer for it, or to become proactively, seriously, fully, effectively engaged. Summarily stated, the future of the urban university and that of the American city are intertwined.

For Penn, as well as all other urban universities, one if not *the* strategic real-world and intellectual problem it faces is what should be done to overcome the deep, pervasive, interrelated problems affecting the people in its local geographic areas. This concrete, immediate, practical, theoretical problem, needless to say, requires creative, interdisciplinary, interactive, democratic scholarship. It is a problem that can help to transcend traditional boundaries between academics and practitioners and among disciplines, leading to a level of mutual understanding, innovation, and cooperation rarely achieved in the past.

The Center for Community Partnerships at the University of Pennsylvania is founded on the idea that the vast range of resources of the American university, appropriately and creatively employed, can help us figure out how best to proceed. Over the past number of years, colleagues at the Center have been working on the problem of how to create modern, cosmopolitan local communities. It is within the American city that the need for communities based on face-to-face relationships and exemplifying humanistic universal values is most acute. The problem of the city is the strategic problem of our time. As such, it is a problem most likely to advance the university's primary mission of preserving, advancing, and transmitting knowledge. This resonates with John Dewey's claim that real advances in knowledge occur through a focus on the central problems of society.

Much of the Center's work has focused on the public school as the educational and neighborhood institution that can, if effectively transformed, serve as the catalytic hub of community change and innovation. The Center has worked to create university-assisted community schools that function as centers of education, services, engagement, and activity within specified geographic areas. With its community and school collaborators, the Center has developed significant academically-based community service programs that engage young people in creative work designed to advance skills and abilities through serving their school, families, and community.

In this article, we discuss Penn's work to create university-assisted community schools as an example of a much broader development, a "democratic devolution revolution." We also discuss academically-based community service learning as a particularly useful approach for advancing scholarship, improving communities, and forging democratic, mutually beneficial, mutually respectful university-school-community partnerships.

PENN'S ENGAGEMENT WITH LOCAL PUBLIC SCHOOLS AS A PRACTICAL EXAMPLE OF "DEMOCRATIC DEVOLUTION REVOLUTION"

Since 1985, Penn has increasingly engaged itself with its local public schools in a comprehensive school-community-university partnership, the West Philadelphia Improvement Corps (WEPIC). In its sixteen years of operation, the project has evolved significantly. Moreover, it has helped spawn a variety of related projects, which also engage Penn with public schools in its local community, West Philadelphia. From its inception, we conceptualized Penn's work with WEPIC as designed to forge *mutually beneficial and mutually respectful* university-school-community partnerships. In recent years, we have begun to conceptualize that work in much broader terms; namely, as part of a (literally) radical attempt to advance a "democratic devolution revolution."[6] It is from that "lofty perch," we believe that an overview of Penn's work (and the work of many other higher educational institutions increasingly engaged with their local public schools and communities) is best comprehended.

For nearly a generation, John Gardner, arguably the leading spokesperson for what we lengthily call the "New American Democratic, Cosmopolitan, Civic University," has been thinking and writing about organizational devolution and the university's potential role in it. For Gardner, the effective functioning of organizations requires the planned and deliberate rather than *ad hoc* and haphazard devolution of functions:

---

[6] Discussion of the concept of a democratic devolution revolution is found in testimony by Ira Harkavy before the Subcommittee on Housing and Community Opportunity of the Committee on Banking and Financial Services of the House of Representatives, 105 Cong. 1 sess. (Washington, DC: U.S. Government Printing Office, 1997).

We have in recent decades discovered some important characteris-tics of the long large-scale organized systems—government, private sector, whatever under which so much of contemporary life is organized. One such characteristic, perhaps the most important, is that the tendency of such systems to centralize must be countered by deliber-ate dispersion of initiative downward and outward through the sys-tem. The corporations have been trying to deal with this reality for almost 15 years and government is now pursuing it . . . .

What this means for government is a substantially greater role for the states and cities. And none of them are entirely ready for that role. . . . [L]ocal government must enter into collaborative relations with non-governmental elements.

So how can colleges and universities be of help?[7]

In effect, Gardner proposes a multisided involvement in "contemporary life" for "higher eds," including building community, convening public dis-cussions, educating public-spirited leaders, offering continuing civic and leadership seminars, and providing a wide range of technical assistance (broadly conceived). An effective, compassionate, democratic devolution revolution, he emphasizes, requires much more than practicing new forms of interaction among federal, state, and local governments and among agencies at each level of government. For Gardner, government integration by itself does not meaningful change make. New forms of interaction among the pub-lic, for-profit, and non-profit sectors are also mandatory. Government must function as a collaborating partner, effectively *facilitating,* rather than im-posing, cooperation among all sectors of society, including higher educational institutions, to support and strengthen individuals, families, and communi-ties.[8]

To extend Gardner's observations about universities (and similar obser-vations by such highly influential thinkers as Ernest Boyer, Derek Bok, Lee Shulman, Alexander Astin), we propose a democratic devolution revolution.[9]

---

[7] John W. Gardner, "Remarks to the Campus Compact Strategic Planning Committee," San Francisco, 10 February 1998.
[8] Ibid.
[9] See Ernest L. Boyer, "Creating the New American College," *Chronicle of Higher Education,* 9 March 1994, p. A48; Bok, *Universities and the Future of America;* Lee Schulman, "Profess-ing the Liberal Arts," *in Education and Democracy: Re-imagining Liberal Learning in Amer-ica,* ed. Robert Orrill (New York: College Entrance Examination Board, 1997), pp.151-173; Alexander W. Astin, "Liberal Education and Democracy: The Case for Pragmatism,"

In our proposed "revolution," government serves as a powerful catalyst and largely provides the funds needed to create stable, ongoing, effective partnerships. But government would function only as a second-tier deliverer of services, with universities, community-based organizations, unions, communities of faith, other voluntary associations, school children and their parents, and community members functioning as the first-tier operational partners. That is, various levels and departments of government would guarantee aid and significantly finance welfare services (broadly conceived as "promoting the general welfare"). Local, personalized, caring services, however, would actually be delivered by the Third (private, non-profit, voluntary associations) and Fourth (personal, i.e., family, kin, neighbors, friends) Sectors of society. Put another way, government would not be primarily responsible for the delivery of services; it primarily would have macro fiscal responsibilities, including fully adequate provision of funds.

The strategy we propose requires adapting the work of local institutions (e.g., universities, hospitals, faith-based organizations) creatively and intelligently to the particular needs and resources of local communities. It assumes that colleges and universities, which simultaneously constitute preeminent international, national, and local institutions, *potentially* constitute very powerful partners, "anchors," and creative catalysts for change and improvement in the quality of life in American cities and communities.

For colleges and universities to fulfill their potential and really contribute to a democratic devolution revolution, however, will require them to do things very differently than they do now. To begin with, changes in "doing" will require higher eds to recognize that, *as they now function*, they constitute a major part of the problem, not a significant part of the solution. To become part of the solution, higher eds must give full-hearted, full-minded devotion to the hard task of transforming themselves and becoming socially responsible civic universities. To do that well, they will have to change their institutional cultures and structures and develop a comprehensive, realistic strategy.

A major component of the strategy being developed by Penn (as well as by an increasing number of other higher educational institutions) focuses on the development of *university-assisted community schools* designed to help educate, engage, activate, and serve *all* members of the community in which the school is located. The strategy assumes that universities can help develop and maintain community schools which function as focal points to help create healthy urban environments and that universities find that worth doing because, among other reasons, they function best in such environments.

---

in *Education and Democracy*, Orrill, ed., pp. 207-223.

Somewhat more specifically, the strategy assumes that, like higher eds, public schools can function as environment-changing institutions and become the strategic centers of broad-based partnerships that genuinely engage a wide variety of community organizations and institutions. Public schools "belong" to all members of the community. They are particularly well suited, therefore, to function as neighborhood "hubs" or "nodes" around which local partnerships can be generated and formed. When they play that role, schools function as community institutions *par excellence*; they then provide a decentralized, democratic, community-based response to significant community problems and help develop the democratic cosmopolitan neighborly communities John Dewey envisioned.

The university-assisted community school reinvents and updates an old American idea, namely that the neighborhood school can effectively serve as the core neighborhood institution—the core institution that provides comprehensive services and galvanizes other community institutions and groups. That idea inspired the early settlement house workers; they recognized the centrality of the neighborhood school in community life and hailed its potential as the strategic site for community stabilization and improvement. At the turn of the 20th century, it is worth noting, deeply-motivated, socially-concerned, brilliantly-creative settlement house workers such as Jane Addams and Lillian Wald pioneered the transfer of social, health, cultural, and recreational services to the public schools of major American cities.[10] In effect, theoretically-guided, caring, socially engaged, feminist settlement leaders recognized that though there were very few settlement houses, there were very many public schools. Not surprisingly, Dewey's ideas about "The School As Social Centre" (1902) had been strongly, directly shaped by his enlightening experiences and inspiring discussions with Jane Addams and others at Hull House. In a highly influential, theoretically-creative, address Dewey explicitly paid homage to them:

> *I suppose, whenever we are framing our ideals of the school as a social Centre, what we think of is particularly the better class of social settlement. What we want is to see the school, every public school, doing something of the same sort of work that is now done by a settlement or two scattered at wide distances through the city.*[11]

---

[10] For a fuller discussion, see Ira Harkavy and John L. Puckett, "Lessons from Hull House for the Contemporary Urban University," *Social Service Review*, 68, no. 3 (1994): 299-321.

[11] From John Dewey's 1902 essay, "The School as Social Centre," as reprinted in *John Dewey: The Middle Works, 1899-1924*, vol. 2, 1902-1903, ed: JoAnn Boydston, (Carbondale: Southern Illinois Press, 1976) pp. 90-91.

Dewey failed to note, however, two critically important functions that community schools could perform: 1) the school as the core community institution actively engaged in the solution of basic community problems; 2) the school as a community institution that educates young children, both intellectually and morally, by engaging them in real-world, community problem-solving. He did recognize that if the neighborhood school were to function as a genuine community center, it needed additional human resources and support. But, to our knowledge, Dewey never identified universities as a key source of broadly based, sustained, comprehensive support for community schools.

To suggest the contributions that university-assisted community schools can make to an effective, compassionate, democratic devolution revolution capable of achieving Dewey's utopian goal of democratic cosmopolitan neighborly communities,[12] we summarily cite some results of the "community school-creating" efforts presently being undertaken by higher eds across the country: Undergraduates, as well as dental, medical, social work, education, and nursing students, are learning as they serve; public school students are also connecting their education to real-world problem solving and providing service to other students and community members; adults are participating in locally-based job training, skill enhancement, and ongoing education; effective integration (as distinct from co-location) of services for school children and their families is now significantly under way in many communities.

It is critical to emphasize, however, that the university-assisted community schools now being developed have a very long way to go before they can effectively help mobilize the potentially powerful, untapped resources of their communities and thereby enable individuals and families to function both as deliverers and as recipients of caring, compassionate local services. To make the point concretely, we briefly recite the "narrative history" of our experience at Penn; it suggests how far we have come *and how far we have to go.*

---

[12] For a fuller discussion of Dewey's utopian goal of cosmopolitan democratic communities and our proposal for university-assisted community schools, see Lee Benson and Ira Harkavy "Progressing Beyond the Welfare State," *Universities and Community Schools*, 2, no. 1-2 (1991): 2-28; and Benson and Harkavy, "School and Community in the Global Society," *Universities and Community Schools*, 5, no. 1-2 (1997): 16-71. We created *Universities and Community Schools* in 1989 as a means to advance mutually beneficial, innovative partnerships between universities and local schools in general, and university-assisted community schools in particular.

Penn and West Philadelphia Public Schools: Learning by Reflective Doing

Following the brilliant lead provided by Gardner, we believe that, as is true of all American universities, Penn's highest—most basic, most enduring—responsibility is to help America implement in practice the democratic promise of the Declaration of Independence; to become an optimally democratic society, a pathbreaking democratic society in an increasingly interdependent world, an exemplary democratic "City on the Hill." Granted that proposition. The hard operational question then becomes: How can Penn best fulfill its democratic responsibility? For reasons sketched below, we believe it can best do that by effectively integrating and radically improving the entire West Philadelphia schooling system, *beginning with Penn but comprehending all schools within its local geographic community, West Philadelphia, i.e., all schools, including itself, within the complex urban ecological system in which it functions as the strategic component.* Stated more generally, and at the risk of sounding sanctimonious; true democratic responsibility, like true patriotism, begins at home.

The history of Penn's work with West Philadelphia public schools has been a process of painful organizational learning; we cannot overemphasize that our understanding and activities have continually changed over time.[13] For example Penn has recently embarked on two new, highly ambitious, ventures: 1) leading a coalition of higher educational institutions, medical and other nonprofit institutions, for-profit firms, and community groups, to improve 25 West Philadelphia public schools; 2) developing a university-assisted public school adjacent to campus, in partnership with the School District of Philadelphia and the Philadelphia Federation of Teachers.

Reaching that level of activity has been neither an easy nor a straight path. Moreover, Penn is only now *beginning* to tap its extraordinary resources in ways which eventually will *mutually benefit Penn and its neighbors* and result in substantial school, community, and university change. Significantly, we have come to see our work as a concrete example of a general theory of democratic, action-oriented, integrated, real-world problem-solving teaching, learning, research, and service. Our real-world strategic problem, we have come to see, has been, and continues to be, radically improving the quality of the entire West Philadelphia schooling system, beginning with Penn. Coming to see our work in terms of what we now conceive as the strategic schooling

---

[13] For an illuminating discussion of the concept of organizational learning, see William F. Whyte, ed., *Participatory Action Research* (Newbury Park, CA: Sage Publications, 1991), pp. 237-241.

component of a remarkably *complex urban ecological system*, we are convinced, constituted a major conceptual and theoretical advance for us.

Ironically, and instructively, when we first began working to change university-community relationships in 1985, we did not envision it in terms of schools, problem-solving teaching and learning, or universities as highly strategic components of urban ecological systems. What immediately concerned us and gave us some reason to think that Penn's traditionally indifferent (hostile?) attitude towards its local community might change for the better was that West Philadelphia was rapidly and visibly deteriorating, with devastating consequences for the University. West Philadelphia's deterioration, therefore, might be used to spur Penn to creative action to overcome it. But what specifically could Penn do and how could it be induced to do it? (Necessity *sometimes* is the mother of invention.)

Committed to undergraduate teaching, convinced by our experiences during the 1960s that undergraduates might function as catalytic agents to help bring about university change, we designed an Honors Seminar which aimed to stimulate undergraduates to think critically about what Penn should do to remedy its "environmental situation" (broadly conceived). For a variety of reasons, the president of the university, Sheldon Hackney, himself a former professor of American history deeply interested in and strongly moved by the 1960s, agreed to join us in giving that seminar in the spring 1985 semester. The seminar's title suggests its general concerns: "Urban University-Community Relationships: Penn-West Philadelphia, Past, Present, and Future, As a Case Study".

When the seminar began, we didn't know anything about Dewey's community school ideas. We literally knew nothing about the history of community school experiments and had not given *any thought* to Penn working with public schools in West Philadelphia. For present purposes, we need not recite the complex, painful processes of trial, error, and failure which led us, President Hackney, and our students to see that Penn's best strategy to remedy its rapidly-deteriorating "environmental situation" was to use its enormous internal and external resources to help radically improve West Philadelphia public schools and the neighborhoods in which they are located. Most unwittingly, during the course of the seminar's work, we reinvented the community school idea!

Public schools, we came to realize (more or less accidentally), could effectively function as core community centers for the organization, education, and transformation of entire neighborhoods. They could do that by functioning as neighborhood sites for a West Philadelphia Improvement Corps (WEPIC) consisting of school personnel and neighborhood residents who would receive strategic assistance from Penn students, faculty, and staff. Put another way, the seminar helped invent WEPIC to help transform the traditional West Philadelphia public school system into a "revolutionary" new system of university-assisted, community-developing, community-centered, community resource-mobilizing, community problem-solving, schools.

Translating the University-Assisted Community School Idea into Practical Action

Given Penn's long, deep-rooted, institutional resistance to serious involvement with West Philadelphia's problems, the limited resources available to us, and the intrinsic difficulty of transforming conventional, inner-city public schools into community schools, we decided that our best strategy was to try to achieve a visible, dramatic success in one school rather than marginal, incremental changes in a number of schools. While continuing the WEPIC program at other schools, therefore, we decided to concentrate initially on the John P. Turner Middle School, largely because of the interest and leadership of its principal.

Previous experiments in community schools and community education throughout the country had depended primarily on a single university unit, namely, the School of Education, one major reason for the failure, or at best limited success, of those experiments. The WEPIC concept of university assistance was far more comprehensive. From the start of the Turner experiment, we understood the concept to mean both assistance from, and mutually-beneficial collaboration with, *the entire range of Penn's schools, departments, and administrative offices*. For a variety of reasons, however, it soon became apparent that the best way to develop and sustain the Turner project would be to initiate a school-based *community health program*.

Given the development of a community health program at Turner in the summer of 1990, Professor Francis Johnston, Chair of the Anthropology Department, and a world leader in nutritional anthropology, decided to participate in the project. To do that effectively, for the Fall 1990 semester, he revised Anthropology 210 to make it what we have come to call a strategic, academically-based community service seminar.[14] Anthropology 210 has a

---

[14] For more complete accounts of Professor Johnston's work, see Lee Benson and Ira Harkavy, "Anthropology 210, Academically Based Community Service and the Advancement of Knowledge, Teaching, and Learning: An Experiment in Progress," *Universities and Community Schools*, 2, no. 1-2 (1994): 66-69; and Ira Harkavy, Francis E. Johnston, and John L. Puckett, "The University of Pennsylvania's Center for Community Partnerships as an Organizational Innovation for Advancing Action Research," *Concepts and Transformations*, 1, no. 1 (1996): 15-29.

long history at Penn and focuses on the relationship between anthropology and biomedical science. An undergraduate course, it was developed to link pre-medical training at Penn with the Department of Anthropology's major program in medical anthropology. Premed students are highly important in Penn undergraduate education and the Department's program in medical anthropology is world-renowned. Professor Johnston's decision to convert Anthro 210 into a strategic, academically-based community service seminar, therefore, constituted a major milestone in the development of the Turner community school project, in Penn's relation to the Turner School, and in our overall work with West Philadelphia public schools.

Since 1990, students in Anthro 210 have carried out a variety of activities at Turner focused on the interactive relationships among diet, nutrition, growth, and health. Designed to contribute to the moral as well as the intellectual development of undergraduates, the seminar is explicitly, and increasingly, organized around strategic, academically-based community service. After Professor Johnston began to focus his own research and publications on his work with Turner students and community residents, he increasingly came to function as a noteworthy example for other anthropology professors and graduate students; they are now integrating their teaching and research with the Turner program, or with other WEPIC programs in West Philadelphia public schools. Even more significantly, Anthro 210 not only affected the anthropology department (which has recently developed an academic track in Public Interest Anthropology);[15] its success has radiated out to other departments and schools. Undoubtedly, it—and Professor Johnston—have played major roles in the increasingly successful campaign to expand strategic, academically-based, community service at Penn.

At present, 125 such courses, working with schools and community organizations, have been developed and are "on the books" at Penn, with 40 offered during the 2000-2001 academic year. Moreover, an increasing number of faculty members, from an increasingly wide range of Penn schools and departments, are now seriously considering how they might revise existing courses, or develop new courses, which would enable their students to benefit from innovative curricular opportunities to become active learners, creative

---

[15] A fuller definition of Public Interest Anthropology can be found in Peggy Reeves Sanday's "Opening Statement: Defining Public Interest Anthropology," presented at Symposium on Defining Public Interest Anthropology, 97th Annual Meeting of the American Anthropological Association, Philadelphia, December 3, 1998. Sanday's statement is located at http://www.sas.upenn.edu/~psanday/pia.99.html.

real-world problem solvers, and producers, not simply consumers, of knowledge.

THE CENTER FOR COMMUNITY PARTNERSHIPS AND PRESIDENTIAL AND FACULTY LEADERSHIP

Encouraged by the success of the university's increasing engagement with West Philadelphia, in July 1992, President Hackney created the Center for Community Partnerships. To highlight the importance he attached to the Center, he located it in the Office of the President and appointed one of us (Ira Harkavy) to be its director (while continuing to serve as director of the Penn Program for Public Service created in 1988).

Symbolically and practically, creation of the Center constituted a major change in Penn's relationship to West Philadelphia/Philadelphia. The university as a corporate entity now formally committed itself to finding ways to use its truly enormous resources (broadly conceived) to help improve the quality of life in its local community—not only in respect to public schools but to economic and community development in general.

Very broadly conceived, the Center is based on the assumption that one efficient way for Penn to carry out its academic missions of advancing universal knowledge and effectively educating students is to function as a "cosmopolitan community school of higher education." Stated somewhat more specifically, Penn's research and teaching would focus on universal problems, e.g., schooling, health care, economic development, as those universal problems *manifest themselves locally in West Philadelphia/Philadelphia*. By efficiently integrating general theory and concrete practice, Penn would symbiotically improve both the quality of life in its local ecological community and the quality of its academic research and teaching. Put another way, the Center assumes that when Penn is creatively conceived as a "cosmopolitan community school," it constitutes in the best sense both *a universal* and a *local* institution of higher education.

The emphasis on *partnerships* in the Center's name was deliberate; it acknowledged, in effect, that Penn could not try to go it alone, as it had long been (significantly) accustomed to do. The creation of the Center was also significantly internally. It meant that, *at least in principle*, the president of the University would now strongly encourage all components of the University to seriously consider the roles they could appropriately play in Penn's efforts to improve the quality of its off-campus environment. Implementation of that strategy accelerated after Judith Rodin became president of Penn in 1994. A native West Philadelphian and Penn graduate, Rodin was appointed in part because of her deeply felt commitment to improving Penn's local environment and to transforming Penn into *the* leading American urban university.

Rodin made radical reform of undergraduate education her first priority. To achieve that far-reaching goal, she established the Provost's Council on Undergraduate Education and charged it with designing a model for Penn's undergraduate experience in the 21st century. Following the lead of Penn's patron saint, Benjamin Franklin, the Provost's Council emphasized the action-oriented union of theory and practice and "engagement with the material, ethical, and moral concerns of society and community defined broadly, globally, and also locally within Philadelphia." The Provost's Council defined the 21st century undergraduate experience as:

> . . .*provid[ing] opportunities for students to understand what it means to be active learners and active citizens. It will be an experience of learning, knowing, and doing that will lead to the active involvement of students in the process of their education.*[16]

To apply this Franklinian-inspired orientation in practice, the Provost's Council designated academically-based community service as a core component of Penn undergraduate education during the next century.

Building upon themes identified by the Provost's Council, Penn's 1994-95 annual report was entitled, *The Unity of Theory and Practice: Penn's Distinctive Character*. Describing the university's efforts to integrate theory and practice, President Rodin observed that:

> *there are ways in which the complex interrelationships between theory and practice transcend any effort at neat conceptualization. One of those is the application of theory in service to our community and the use of community service as an academic research activity for students. Nowhere else is the interactive dimension of theory and practice so clearly captured [emphasis added].*

For more than 250 years, Philadelphia has rooted Penn in a sense of the "practical," reminded us that service to humanity, to our community is, as

---

[16] Provost's Council on Undergraduate Education, "The 21st Century Penn Undergraduate Experience: Phase I," in University of Pennsylvania, *Almanac*, (May 1995): S-I.

[Benjamin] Franklin put it, "the great aim and end of all learning." Today, thousands of Penn faculty and students realize the unity of theory and practice by engaging West Philadelphia elementary and secondary school students as part of their own academic course work in disciplines as diverse as history, anthropology, classical studies, education, and mathematics.

> *For example, anthropology professor Frank Johnston and his under-graduate students educate students at West Philadelphia's Turner Middle School about nutrition. Classical studies professor Ralph Rosen uses modern Philadelphia and fifth century Athens to explore the interrelations between community, neighborhood, and family. And history professor Michael Zuckerman's students engage West Phila-delphia elementary and secondary school students to help them un-derstand together the nature—and discontinuities—of American national identity and national character.[17]*

The 1994-95 annual report illustrated and advanced a fundamental, far-reaching cultural shift that had *begun* to take place across the University. By the end of her first year in office, Penn's president had significantly increased the prominence of undergraduate education, defined the integration of theory and practice (including theory and practice derived from and applied within the local community) as the hallmark of Ben Franklin's University, and iden-tified academically-based community service focused on West Philadelphia and its public schools as a *powerfully-integrative* strategy to advance univer-sity-wide research, teaching, and service.

In an August 2000 letter to Penn parents, faculty, and alumni, President Rodin extended this argument even further, calling for Penn and universities to become "the exemplars of a new kind of civic activism" through "the con-tinuing development of 'academic service-learning courses'."

> *Penn and universities like it can become the exemplars of a new kind of civic engagement that is neither easy no accidental, but rather is strategic, comprehensive, intense, and purposeful. At its best, it weaves itself in and through every aspect of campus life, from medi-cal research and particle physics to classical studies, student volun-teerism, and economic development. It must become not a second thought, or an afterthought, but a matter of forethought and persistent commitment [emphasis added].*

---

[17] University of Pennsylvania, *Annual Report*, 1994-1995 (President's Report), Philadelphia, 1996.

There are many ways to promote this kind of engagement. One is through the continuing development of academic "service-learning" courses that find synergy in the courses that feature a direct and conscious link between the application and social value of knowledge and the academic core of the University....

> ... we have the work of geologist Bob Giegengack, chair our department of Earth and Environmental Science, whose class in Environmental Studies pursues basic research in environmental toxins. Then members of the class help West Philadelphia public school students and their families, many living below the poverty line, to identify sources of lead in and around their homes. The undergraduates work with students from a nearby middle school to test soil samples from their yards and dust and paint samples from their homes and assist in mapping the risk of lead exposure in the neighborhood. In addition, the middle school students work with the undergraduates to design materials that are disseminated to parents and neighbors warning them of the dangers of lead exposure and how to decrease the chances of lead ingestion by the group most at risk of its ill effects, pre-school toddlers.
>
> This kind of education is transformative. At its best, college should offer transformation: the transformation of facts into knowledge, potential into reality, the old into the new, history into the future [emphasis added].[18]

Presidents can provide leadership. But it is faculty members who develop and sustain the courses and research projects which durably link a university to its local schools and community. More specifically, it is through faculty teaching and research that the connection to local schools and communities is ultimately—and durably—made. We gave high priority, therefore, to increasing the number and variety of academically-based community service courses. Thanks in large measure to President Rodin's strong support, the number of academically-based community service courses has grown exponentially; from 11 when the Center was founded in 1992 to 125 in the Spring of 2001.

---

[18] Judith Rodin, "Letter to Parents, Colleagues, and Friends of Penn," Philadelphia, 17 August 2000.

As a result of the highly positive reaction to those courses, the long term process of radically changing Penn's undergraduate curriculum has gained accelerating momentum. In addition to the development of the Public Interest Anthropology track cited above, after years of complex negotiations, two new interdisciplinary programs, a minor in Urban Education and a major in Health and Societies with a concentration in Urban Health, have been created. Academically-based community service courses are core components of both the Urban Education minor and Urban Health concentration. At a "higher level," the College of Arts and Sciences has recently implemented (Fall, 2000) a pilot curriculum for 200 entering freshmen which will serve as a primary center for innovation in undergraduate education. The pilot curriculum highlights community-based research, thematic clusters, and thematic semesters as particularly attractive free elective options for students in the program to consider. At a still "higher level," affecting graduate and undergraduate education, the Deputy Provost convened a university-wide Provost's Seminar in Academically-Based Community Service. Approximately sixty faculty members attended the inaugural meeting in the Spring 2000. During the 2000-2001 academic year, the Provost's Seminar explored how academically-based community service courses and projects might be developed and connected along the themes of Health and Society, Schooling and Society, Environment and Society, and Culture and Society.

CONCLUSIONS

In an article written nearly a decade ago, we described our work as a "long march" through the institutions.[19] Although we are still on that long march and have very far to go, we have made some real advances in the past 16 years. Academically-based community service focused on creating university-assisted community schools has shown significant promise as a strategy for advancing school, community, and university change. Perhaps even more important for long-term school, community, and university change (i.e., for a successful long march), Penn has put an urban agenda at the core of its academic/institutional mission. And even more important, Penn and a number of other higher educational institutions across the country are *beginning* to make progress toward functioning as New American Democratic, Cosmopolitan, Civic Universities dedicated to the practical realization of the democratic promise of America *for all* Americans. We find this development, needless to say, to be truly encouraging.

---

[19] Ira Harkavy and John L. Puckett, "Toward Effective University-Public School Partnerships," *Teachers College Record* 91, No. 4 (1991): 556-581.

CHAPTER 25

PUTTING PASSION IN ACTION: SERVICE LEARNING AT WHEELOCK COLLEGE

Marjorie Bakken*
Wheelock College

INTRODUCTION

Lucy Wheelock, the founder of Wheelock College, saw service as the essence of her individual calling to work with children. She said, upon entering a kindergarten, reminiscent of her early biblical training, "I have found my kingdom." The mission of Wheelock College, to improve the quality of life for children and families, continues to express service in the academic work of Wheelock students. The field work that students undertake in their professional study, and often in their liberal arts preparation as well, will be described elsewhere in this chapter.

Adding a service learning component to the already existing, multiple experiences that students had with children was not an easy decision to make at Wheelock – and may still remain not always a popular one. When I became President of Wheelock College in 1993, I initiated a community service learning project. This project was named Connections by popular choice of the first students in the program, and was an attempt at creating non-curriculum related service experiences that resonated with the Wheelock mission. A young woman who had done many hours of community service herself and was eager to work with students was hired to be the coordinator of the program. At the end of the first year – in intensive evaluation sessions — the students and the coordinator wondered if it would be possible to expand the opportunities for students beyond working with children. The students wanted to work across the life span in a greater variety of settings.

The field work that students undertake is focussed on the professional areas, increasingly, as the student completes the four years, in the student's chosen professional career area. Why did students want additional field work experiences as volunteers?

- Before students come to Wheelock, they have what some people think of as a gift for or a calling to work with people. Wheelock students are not cynical about their ability to change the lives of other people.

They have often had multiple experiences working in recreation centers, homeless shelter, camps, hospitals – a wide range of settings and a vast array of experiences.

- In their field work, students work in settings where they had to respond to a supervisor or did not have the authority to set the parameters of the experience. In the volunteer setting, they were able to determine their level of involvement and take things at their own pace, without external expectations. Students focussed on the relationship with the individual with whom they were working. For example, one of the most popular Connections programs was "Best Buddies," a program in which students developed relationships with handicapped adults. Wheelock students relished this particular experience.

- Although students understood that their work would eventually be in classrooms or in hospital settings, students wanted to experiment with a range of activities in which they might never have a professional career. They wanted to experiment, stretching their skills and their inclinations to work with people.

After the second year of Connections, faculty members came to me explaining that Connections was too intensive and too difficult for students to manage in their already full academic and work lives. Many students are scholarship students and, in addition to their academic and field experiences, spend up to 35 hours each week at work. The students who were devoted to their Connections projects did not reflect the faculty sentiments. If they could not handle the demands of their current Connections projects, they chose other projects that were less intense and without long-term commitments. For example, they would engage in special projects to prepare holiday events for hospital patients or make bookmarks, work on food drives, or participate in other projects that did not involve their personal time so intensively.

The students won us over with their desire to serve and their skill at managing their own lives. Generally, the students in Connections stay in Connections and, a year ago, participated in a five-year celebration of their work.

I speak from a presidential perspective. In this chapter, a current student, two alumni (Class of '99), a faculty member, advisors to the Connections program, and a member of the Student Development department at Wheelock College will give their perspectives on service learning at Wheelock.

ADVISOR PERSPECTIVE: PROGRAM STRUCTURE AND EVALUATION

The advisor's role in a student organization is influenced by the strengths and needs of its members. An effective advisor provides guidance for organizational structure, supports student initiatives, and empowers students to assume new and increased responsibilities. As organizations grow and develop, the advisor's role changes. In the early years of Connections, the advisor, in a systematic method, supported students' creativity. In later years, the advisor's role was modified to provide opportunities for student initiative and leadership.

The foundation of the Connections organization is sustained by the academic programs and mission of the college. One of the advisor's main goals is to assist in continuing this approach in order to build a strong service learning program. The advisor strives to help students understand the presence of community on the local, state, national, and international levels. Ideally students experience these levels as they become involved in community outreach. The advisor attempts to guide students as they learn about the important role they play as a member of this community. Through developing leadership positions for participants, setting organizational goals, providing opportunities for ongoing leadership skills training, and facilitating the generation of ideas for volunteerism, the advisor plays an integral part in the growth and continuity of the service learning component of the Connections organization.

Program Structure and Evaluation: The First Year

The Boys & Girls Club of Boston was identified as the community partner for the inaugural year of Connections. Students were active participants in program development. Nine student leaders collaborated with Wheelock administrators and faculty and clubhouse representatives to identify program goals, assess agency needs, and develop an orientation program for volunteers. Student surveys and an End-of-the-Year Reflection/Recognition Reception illustrated program success and satisfaction. Through volunteering, students not only gained a better understanding of the issues faced by children in an urban setting but also developed valuable professional and leadership skills.

Program Structure and Evaluation: The Later Years

During the next several years, the mission of Connections was expanded and the organizational structure was modified. These transformations occurred for multiple reasons: (1) to more effectively meet the diverse needs of the Boston community, (2) to respond to the numerous interests of volunteers, and (3) to address student leaders' strengths. More specifically, Connections expanded to include service opportunities in the following areas: seniors, health, the environment, hunger and homelessness, and social issues. In addition to the multiple possibilities to serve children and families at the Boys & Girls Club, after-school programs created alternative opportunities for youth-related service.

To successfully manage Connections, a leadership structure was developed and implemented. The early structure was informal; student leaders shared responsibilities for tasks. Due to the challenges presented by this arrangement, distinct roles and responsibilities were created. The present structure consists of nine student leaders: two Fellows who chair the weekly meetings and assist with administrative responsibilities, and seven Area Directors who are responsible for coordinating volunteer opportunities at local agencies.

Effectiveness and Evaluation

Connections began as an organization of nine student leaders and twenty volunteers. During the past six years, student leaders have successfully recruited over 100 volunteers per year. Through Connections, students, faculty, administrators, and alumni have contributed over 10,000 hours of service *to improve the quality of life for children and families.*

Student surveys and written and oral reflections remain the primary tools for program evaluation. Additionally, comments and suggestions are requested of program affiliates — agency staff as well as individuals, families, and communities served by volunteers. This information is used to assess the impact of the service performed and the extent to which needs are met.

Service Learning

Wheelock's unique curriculum includes several opportunities for students' professional development. Off-campus professional training begins during students' first semester at Wheelock as part of a required course entitled, Children and their Environments. This trend of experiential education continues in their following semesters, initially as part of a Human Development course and eventually in their professional concentration. Connections allows students to expand on what they are learning in class and in their placements by adding a different type of fieldwork component.

Traditional volunteer opportunities provide extensions to students' coursework. Students studying Early and Elementary Education can participate in tutoring programs, such as America Reads, or in the annual book drive or even holding a Halloween Party for children from the Boston area. Social Work students often work with Social Issues or Hunger and Homelessness volunteer opportunities. Some of these have included clothing drives, the annual Oxfam Hunger Banquet, Christmas in April, the Walk for Hunger, and volunteering at Rosie's Place, an organization that provides services for women. Students from the Child Life concentration are often involved in opportunities from the Health area. Since Wheelock College is located close to several world-renowned hospitals, students can participate in blood drives, Make-A-Wish fundraisers, and creating decorations for the children's wing during the holidays. Each of these service opportunities allows Wheelock students the ability to develop as responsible members of the community and make a difference in the lives of children and families as they begin to make decisions regarding their own professional futures.

Opportunities for leadership development are further supported by strong student participation in local and national conferences, including those sponsored by COOL (Campus Outreach Opportunity League) and MACC (Massachusetts Campus Compact). Through conferences students not only gain an increased understanding of the service movement, but also learn valuable leadership skills and new strategies for the recruitment and retention of volunteers. Wheelock students have facilitated a variety of workshops for students and advisors from other colleges and universities. Some of these presentations have included the following: *Learning How to Talk Teen*, *Volunteers: How to Get Them and How to Keep Them*, and *Two Thumbs Up*. These learning experiences have further prepared students to be effective volunteers and knowledgeable human service professionals –individuals who have the tools to *improve the quality of life for children and families.*

STUDENT PERSPECTIVE

Students at Wheelock College spend many hours in the Boston community at various settings that include schools, social service agencies, hospitals and many other sites. Each student will spend a maximum of 16 hours per week in fulfilling college and course academic requirements in their field of study. Field placement hours range from 56 hours per semester freshman and sophomore year, 75 hours for juniors, and a total of 400 hours in field experience during senior year. The hours that students devote to completing academic requirements remain separate from the number of volunteer hours that students dedicate to activities and agencies in their personal time.

Student organizations that include groups like Connections and Wheelock's Women's Center offer a variety of volunteer opportunities opening the door for volunteering within the community. What is the catalyst for this type of prosocial, altruistic behavior exhibited by the Wheelock student body? According to Harowitz and Bordens (1995) altruism is a type of behavior that helps a person in need and is motivated purely by the desire to help the other person. An altruistic person is concerned and helpful even when no benefits and/or rewards are offered or expected in return. This still does not answer the question of why we help others. Altruism is often compared with what is simply known as helping behavior. Helping behavior is different from altruism in that it is a type of behavior that is motivated by the desire to attain some personal reward in return for helping. But for many the drive to volunteer is the belief that we offer help to others not for our own personal benefit but rather because something inside tells us that this is something that should be done. Whether it is the belief of student volunteers that people should help those who need help without thinking of retribution or that they volunteer to learn or benefit from additional contact with community agencies the fact remains that there is a win win situation for both student and community.

The importance of community service and service learning is engrained into the social and educational fabric of Wheelock College. As students enter Wheelock College, they are assigned a book to read, and those books have included *The Call of Service* by Robert Coles, *Amazing Grace* by Jonathan Kozol and *The Power of Their Ideas* by Deborah Meier. These books have a profound impact on us and set the tone for how we begin to shape our lives as well as the ways in which we see ourselves beginning new roles as members of a larger community.

To be a volunteer on the Wheelock campus does not require 10 hours a week every week. Connections, the community service organization at Wheelock arranges activity calendars with scheduled volunteer activities in the areas of Health, Youth, Seniors, Environment, Social Issues, and Hunger and Homelessness. These calendars are distributed monthly through a mailing list and are posted around the college campus. The goal of Connections has been to highlight the importance of volunteering in community service projects and to bring students in the three Wheelock disciplines-education, child life, and social work, together to work on projects in interdisciplinary teams. Connections has always been a resource for imaginative volunteers to present their own service projects as well as to show their interest in working with specific populations.

There are endless benefits from volunteering within the Boston community. Learning new skills and applying them to meet the needs of others bring feelings of accomplishment and pride. The act of volunteering allows individuals to feel a sense of accomplishment while expanding our awareness of our social environment. By testing new waters and experiencing others beyond our comfort levels, past experience and our own expectations can give us a new outlook and perspective on the communities and the world in which we live. Through student run organizations, like Connections, students have planned and organized many community projects. Students do their volunteer work on many different levels. Opportunities vary from working with individuals, with groups, and with community organizations. The range in volunteer opportunities allows students to begin to test new knowledge and skills in different arenas.

On my return from a conference on student volunteering, I said, "I feel like putting my passion into action. The energy that volunteers have is awe inspiring and the spirit very contagious." Attending annual conferences allows for students to network with other volunteers and discuss new ideas and ways to transform ideas into reality. By assisting students in putting passion into action, colleges like Wheelock recognize how community service serves an essential role and helps students develop a sense of shared responsibility in the community. Students continue to volunteer and start their own projects because they are connected to and concerned about the world around them. As students continue to grow and take on new roles, share their excitement and show their commitment, they continue to make small deliberate steps in making a difference in the world through service and continued awareness and activism within the community.

STUDENT DEVELOPMENT PERSPECTIVE

The connection between service learning and student leadership has only recently become an area of study. While the links within the student development community have long been evident, only recently have the benefits and outcomes been quantified. It is only within the past decade that research has taken place to look at links between a student's volunteer work at the local elementary school and the benefits to his or her academic performance. One did not consider the benefits of teaching swimming to disabled students and how to quantify that in term of values or moral development. Yet it has become increasingly more apparent through the annual Cooperative Institutional Research Program (CIRP) surveys at multiple colleges and universities nationwide that students involved in service projects perform better academically and are more likely to be involved in leadership activities (Astin et al, 2000).

Within the Wheelock Community, the connections between service and student development are evident in countless ways. Students take the mission of the institution — to improve the quality of life of children and their families — very seriously and their works can be seen in a myriad of arenas. Although Connections, the service learning organization, has made their commitment to service the club's mission, service based organizations are evident in other campus organizations and student-generated programs. Even before the creation of the Connections program, service has played a key role in Wheelock students' lives.

Peace and Social Action active in the early 90's brought the issue of social justice to the forefront of the community. They were the first organization to initiate the Oxfam Hunger Banquet on campus and address issues of hunger in global terms. They instituted recycling on campus by setting up recycling stations in all administrative offices, recommended the use of scrap paper for drafts, and encouraged the reduction of campus-wide memos through posting of announcements in high-traffic areas.

Pi Gamma Mu, a national honor society on campus, has made service a major component of the organization's mission. Members are required to participate in numerous service projects each semester to remain in good standing and to carry on the idea of service to others. Projects have ranged from sponsoring blood drives for Children's Hospital, hosting children from a battered women's shelter for a Halloween party, participating in charity walks, as well as co-sponsoring events with other campus organizations. Pi Gamma Mu and the Women's Center jointly raised money and participated in a 10K walk for the Jane Doe Safety Fund.

The Women's Center at Wheelock has also incorporated social justice into projects that they have held both on and off campus. This small but dedicated and extremely active group has continued to link issues of feminism with broader issues of social justice. They have mobilized the campus to participate in Take Back the Night, a program that takes place on college campuses across the county protesting violence against women. They also organized a bus trip to Washington, D.C. to participate in a national march protesting violence against women. They have participated in grass-roots efforts to make issues of social justice prominent within the community. They have also connected issues to the academic work of the community and with the professional lives of students. Child pornography, women's health and sexuality are all topics relevant to work that human service providers may face that the Women's Center has addressed.

The residence life staff took on the theme of service not only in the context of the service that they provide to the community as student leaders, but also in a larger community context. For the 1999-2000 year, the staff adopted the theme "Helping Hands." At the beginning of the year, they incorporated service projects into their staff training. Staff volunteered at the Recording for the Blind and Dyslexic, sorted food at the Greater Boston Food Bank and worked on a Habitat for Humanity project.

Residence life staff was also expected to incorporate a service project into the programming requirements within the residence halls. Resident Assistants sponsored programs such as pumpkin decorating for a children's home, volunteering for the Big Sister's program Haunted House and organizing a clothing and toiletry drive for a residential facility for adolescents.

Anthony Shriver began Best Buddies as an undergraduate at Georgetown University in 1987. Best Buddies' mission is to enhance the lives of the mentally challenged through opportunities for socialization and employment. Students hosted pizza parties, swimming outings, bowling trips, etc. and made one-on-one connections with mentally impaired adolescents and adults.

Wheelock students' commitment to service especially as it relates to children and families was most evident in the leadership role they assumed for the first Stand For Children rally in Washington, D.C. In 1996, a contingency of over 100 students, alumni, and staff attended the Stand to advocate for children. Wheelock students took leadership roles locally and nationally to produce, organize and promote the march. In Washington, Wheelock students were photographed with Marian Wright Edelman, Stand for Children founder, due to their outstanding commitment and work with the march.

The Student Government Association has made service a part of the work that they do within the community. Each spring the SGA hosts "Kids' Day", an event for children from the surrounding community, placement sites, baby-sitting charges, staff and alumni children and the younger relatives of current students. The day is set up as a carnival filled with clowns, games, music and food. Each campus organization is required to participate by hosting a booth, organizing an activity or providing entertainment.

The highlight of the spring semester has become the "Make A Wish" Benefit Talent Show. In 1995, a student rallied support from the entire community to found the talent show to benefit terminally ill children. This student organized event has consistently raised over $1500 each year to donate to the Make A Wish Foundation to fulfill children's dreams. Campus clubs and organizations donate time and resources to field the numerous committees needed to produce the show. Raffles, ticket sales to the talent show and donations from local businesses have made this event an integral part of the Wheelock community. This event in particular serves as a model for student leadership and community service at its best. Students are able to use leadership skills acquired through club and organization involvement and translate those values in a service-oriented activity.

The commitment to service extends beyond the Wheelock students, faculty, staff and alumni. In 1996, as a part of Make A Difference Day, a national day of service, Wheelock hosted its first service learning project for the Fall Family Weekend. On a beautiful autumn afternoon more than 60 students and their families chose to make decorations for the Massachusetts General Hospital children's ward, assemble toiletry kits for a homeless shelter and make reading packets for an after-school program rather than taking one of the excursions planned into the city. The first year we were totally unprepared for the large number of family members who showed up to participate in the service projects. We anticipated less than two dozen participants and projects were expected to fill a 90-minute time slot. The projects were completed in less than 30 minutes due to the large turnout. The service learning component is now led by the Connections team and has become an integral part of the Fall Family Weekend. Families look forward to participating in the projects and to become re-acquainted with other families that they're sure to see each year during the service learning activity. We now plan to have more projects than we could possibly expect to be completed, but families continue to amaze us by the numbers that come to participate with their daughters and sons each fall.

It comes as no surprise that students who are active leaders on campus contribute their time and energy to a variety of service oriented projects.

These are not always organized by an organization, but can be generated by them seeing a need or a desire to make a change. Students take the initiative to implement service related activities on campus without the guise of an academic or co-curricular requirement. Recently a student requested permission to solicit age-appropriate book donations for her under funded placement site. She took on the task to solicit, collect and sort books without the benefit of a campus-sponsored organization. Because of the institution's mission to improve children's lives, she did what she felt needed to be done—and that philosophy is echoed in the work of many students on campus. Connecting to the community and providing service to others makes them better leaders within the classroom, hospital settings, and as social workers. Wheelock students live the mission of the institution in many aspects of their lives. Wheelock will continue to challenge students academically and personally to improve the quality of life of children and families. We will also continue to provide them with opportunities to connect service with their personal development as students and as leaders.

FACULTY PERSPECTIVE

From my perspective as a faculty member at Wheelock College, I have seen service learning enhance the educational process along several dimensions. These include the creation of a vital learning environment that supports the personal and professional development of both students and faculty, the strengthening of the relationship between students and instructors when engaged in this work together, and the expansion of the systemic field in which the academic institution and the community interact.

One of the biggest educational challenges faced by any teacher is to create a medium through which the two-dimensional learning that emanates from the ideas of books and classroom discourse can fully come alive. The incorporation of service learning can be just this life-giving force. It is a way of connecting ideas in the abstract with concrete experiences in the here and now, it arouses emotional as well as intellectual response, it supports hands-on development of skills, and it provides students with an opportunity to observe and evaluate their own actions. As such, this learning can be a powerful vehicle for the development of three major educational objectives: knowledge, competence, and self-awareness.

For students in the helping professions, such as those at Wheelock, service learning also provides a valuable opportunity to learn about the human condition. Some of the specific lessons there for the taking include direct contact with: 1) the two-way interaction between large, bureaucratic institutions and the daily lives of children and adults, 2) the uniqueness of individuals and the existence of strengths in all human beings, 3) the devastating effects of discrimination and oppression, and 4) the efficacy of even the smallest of "helping" actions.

In the characteristics described so far, service learning and the learning that culminates from formal field placements, internships, or practica possess many qualities in common. As vehicles for the integration of theory and practice, both are extremely important; however, they are not the same. In order to parallel academic content and to monitor individual student progress, field placements are planned, supervised, and evaluated, often by an instructor and an agency staff member working together. This carefully coordinated educational component is essential to the professional development of students in many fields.

Since by its very nature service is a voluntary activity, chosen and engaged in freely by the individual, the learning it generates can be a unique mechanism for the development of self-direction, self-regulation, and empowerment. The contract is between the student and the agency and is not connected to course requirements or to external review by an instructor. This quality of autonomy places the responsibility for both performance and learning squarely in the hands of the student. Given agency guidelines and needs, it is up to the student to determine the frequency, duration, and intensity of participation. Similarly, it is the student's own choice to bring the observations, ideas, and questions that stem from the service experience into the classroom. The sense of initiative and ownership thus generated serves to synthesize and consolidate the learning that takes place and also contributes to the upsurge of excitement, energy and passion which often follows.

Students are not the only ones who gain from active participation in service learning. Since personal and professional development is a dynamic, ongoing, lifelong process, service provides an optimal means through which faculty members can stay grounded in the real world and can continue to learn, grow, and rekindle their own experience of passion. For the past three years, I have been volunteering on a weekly basis at Rosie's Place, an outstanding organization that provides a multitude of services for poor and homeless women in the Boston area. Here, I have seen time and time again that it is one thing to read treatises about poverty and homelessness, yet very much another to prepare meals for real women and children who have far too little to eat. Similarly, it is one thing to study the components of the legislative process, yet very much another to go to the State House to lobby busy senators and representatives about food stamp access. In these situations, the interdependent connection between life learning and classroom teaching has become readily apparent as the meaningfulness and freshness of direct experience has provided me with an unending supply of rich material to share.

Alongside its power to enhance individual functioning, service learning represents a unique opportunity for the development of student-faculty relationships. Students engaged in service activities at Wheelock regularly come with me to Rosie's Place — on a one-time basis, for a semester, or even for a whole year. In this context, students and I see each other through a widened lens. Instead of viewing me as an all-knowing and powerful authority figure, students are able to work alongside me as a peer who has similar hopes, needs, and uncertainties. By the same token, I have been able to experience students more fully as the young adults that they are, with multiple strengths, interests, talents, and intelligences.

Since there are no grades at stake, the students and I are on a level playing field, united by experiences that transcend the classroom and the generations. The relationships that develop in this context of parallel experience and collaborative effort contain a naturalness and openness that also foster learning. Such is the effect of a moment in time when I see a student overcome her hesitation, take the risk to engage in contact with another human being, and then glow in the aftermath of a positive encounter. In this split second of shared experience, I witness and support the development of mastery taking place within this particular student, tune into my own parallel experiences in the past and the present, and observe in bold relief the value of service as a tool for the provision of care. Although I cannot speak for the students, I imagine that a similar process takes place when they view me in comparable critical moments. No written or verbal report can ever do the same.

Finally, because it creates new connecting linkages for people within Wheelock College and between the institution and the outside world, service learning has the ultimate function of expanding the environmental field of the college itself. Participation in service activities brings together students, faculty, administration, staff, and alumni whose paths might not otherwise cross, it connects this internal group with peers they might never meet from other educational settings, and it brings both of these groups into the community where life is actually taking place - where those who are the beneficiaries of service are the ultimate teachers. In this way, the boundaries for the exchange of information, ideas, and actions are opened wider and the impact of service learning can continually reverberate in multiple directions.

CONCLUSIONS

The authors of this article represent voices of different constituencies of Wheelock College and on- and off- campus individuals who have contributed to service learning at Wheelock and created a more civil society.

The primary benefits of service learning at Wheelock College included the following:

- Changing the concept of service to include people and organizations beyond the usual groups served so well by the mission of the College, to improve the quality of life for children and families. Families became a more comprehensive concept and allowed our students to interact across the generations to enact and enhance the mission of the College.

- Involving all constituencies in similar events. Some service learning projects included the students, the students' families, the faculty, alumni, and other members of the community.

Civil society at Wheelock was increased through service learning for the following reasons:

- More people – across the College, from all constituencies – assumed responsibility for community work and participation.
- Establishing greater connections between students and alumni, both of whom become attracted and stay attracted to Wheelock for the compelling reason of the service component of the mission of the College.
- Increasing communication between and among the students and the administration. The President, for example, became more directly involved in the students' co-curricular activities. Because of the inaugural initiative, the President became part of a broader community-wide effort.
- A sense of equality emerged among those who participated in community service projects. Everyone was a learner at the same level.

The challenges of having service learning at Wheelock College included the following:

- Setting priorities for service learning in the midst of already crowded academic and co-curricular lives for faculty and students on campus.
- Compelling the College to set priorities for service learning in the context of the already crowded academic and co-curricular lives of faculty and students on campus. Faculty began to understand that students' service commitment extended beyond work with young children. Particularly, undergraduate students, who were embedded in communities as high school students, came to college having had strong commitments to work in nursing homes and shelters, and their interest in people extended throughout the life cycle.
- By including interprofessional contexts in the ways it conceptualized professional practice, the service learning project compelled the Office of Field Experience and the various coordinators and heads of professional programs to take note of each other's work more thoughtfully.

Service learning at Wheelock College is historical and multlidimensional, and has a strong place in the lives of students, even beyond their field work and career preparation. Service becomes part of the lives of students and continues throughout their lives, no matter what career paths they take.

REFERENCES

Astin, A., Vogelgesang, L., Ikeda, E., and Yee, J. (2000). *Executive Summary: How Service Learning Affects Students*. Los Angeles: Higher Education Research Institute.

Horowitz, I. & Bordens, K. (1999). *Social Psychology*. Mountain View, CA: Mayfield Publishing Company.

AUTHORS

Introduction and Conclusion	Marjorie Bakken, Ed.D. President Wheelock College
Advisor Perspective	Clare M. O'Brien, B.A., MS.Ed, Ph.D. Director of Academic Advising and Academic Assistance Wheelock College
	Effimia Parpos, B.A., M.S.W. Assistant Director of Admissions and Financial Aid Wheelock College
Student Perspective	Allison Marie Carlson, B.S.W. Wheelock College, '00
Alumni Perspective	Jennifer A. Bean, B.S., M.S. Special Education Teacher Manville School, Boston
	Jessica Palmer, B.S., CCLS Child Life Specialist Children's Hospital at Dartmouth
Student Development Perspective	Pamela Pleasant, A.B., Ed.M. Dean of Students Wheelock College

Faculty Perspective   Deborah Lisansky Beck, M.S.W.
Instructor in Social Work and Human Development
Wheelock College

CHAPTER 26

THE MASSACHUSETTS CHILDREN'S TRUST FUND: PARTNERSHIPS WITH UNIVERSITIES IN THE CONTEXTS OF POLICY AND FAMILY SUPPORT

Gretchen Biesecker
Suzin Bartley
Children's Trust Fund

INTRODUCTION

Today's society faces the enormously complex problem of child abuse and neglect—a crisis that touches every community. Between 1986 and 1996, the number of U.S. children who suffered serious injuries through child abuse and neglect quadrupled (Sedlack & Broadhurst, 1996). In 1999, over 30,000 reports of child abuse in Massachusetts were confirmed by the state Department of Social Services. Clearly the issues of child abuse and neglect and their associated costs challenge the resources and sustainability of a civil society (Lerner, Fisher, & Weinberg, 2000).

The Massachusetts Children's Trust Fund (CTF) was created by the Massachusetts legislature in 1988 to implement the Commonwealth's mission to strengthen families and prevent child abuse. CTF is funded by state and private monies, as well as by federal matching funds. Our organization has grown tremendously since its inception, and we currently employ over 20 staff members and operate under a budget of approximately 19 million dollars. The notion of a Children's Trust Fund is credited to pediatrician, Ray Helfer, who noted that just as there are trust funds to maintain our nation's highways, there should be trust funds to care for children. Today there are Children's Trust and Prevention Funds in every state, which vary in size and the scope of their activities.

In Massachusetts, CTF researches national strategies that strengthen families and prevent child abuse, looking for programs with proven track records. To implement these model programs in local communities, CTF offers funding to community-based organizations. Local service providers are selected carefully through a proposal review process for their ability to deliver outstanding services and to reflect the cultural and ethnic diversity of the parents they will serve. Programs address some of the known factors contributing to child abuse and neglect, including social isolation of parents, stress, and lack of knowledge of child development and parenting techniques.

CTF provides technical assistance and training for family support professionals in a variety of ways, including two annual conferences, curriculum-focused workshops, and monthly networking and informational meetings focused on the needs and interests of fathers. We also provide comprehensive and ongoing training for staff of our statewide, universal home visitation program for first-time teen parents (Healthy Families). In fiscal year 2000, for example, we provided over 11,058 hours of training for 297 Healthy Families staff. An overview of our mission and programs appears in Figure 1.

Figure 1

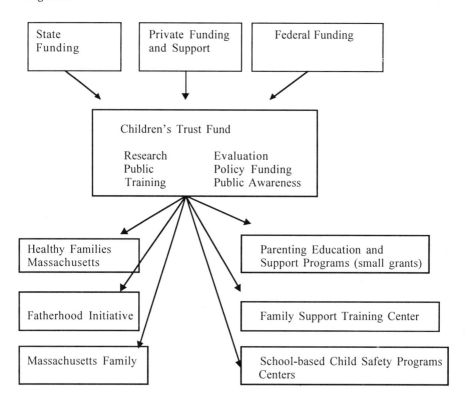

In addition, CTF educates and informs Massachusetts public policy makers and human service providers about effective family support strategies. CTF works with the media, legislature, and local providers to raise public awareness about the availability, and importance, of strengths-based family support programs. In partnership with communications professionals, CTF also seeks to encourage public attitudes that are more responsive to the needs of families.

As part of our mission to prevent child abuse and neglect, CTF addresses the practical problems of families, parenting, and communities.

Through a variety of relationships with local universities and colleges, CTF has engaged students and faculty in approaches to working with families, direct service providers, and communities. Our recent collaborations have included students and/or faculty from a variety of departments from: Boston College, Boston University, Harvard University, Northeastern University, Simmons College, Tufts University, Wellesley College, and Wheelock College. These relationships have provided university faculty and students with opportunities to contribute to the lives of people in communities throughout Massachusetts and inspired them to investigate new areas of research. The Children's Trust Fund, in turn, has enhanced its knowledge of child development and evaluation, and derived benefit from the expertise and resources that students and faculty bring. Four main areas illustrate the mutual utility of our partnership: expertise and training, internships, evaluation, and research.

EXPERTISE AND TRAINING

Faculty and staff from local colleges and universities contribute regularly to CTF's knowledge base, training, and decision-making about programs. One vehicle for this has been our Program Evaluation and Development Committee (PDEC), which provides input and guidance for CTF's family support programs, Training Center, and evaluation activities. The Committee meets regularly and several members are affiliated with colleges and universities. CTF depends on the Committee to solve problems and questions about the directions programs should take, especially during CTF's growth over the past few years, and members also review grant applications from prospective family support programs. In turn, experts who participate in activities such as PDEC, find a connection to real-life programs and what is happening on the front lines of family support, and they grapple with solutions to the practical problems of these programs and the communities served.

In addition, CTF relies on local universities to provide experts for trainings and conferences. Each year, CTF and Wheelock College co-sponsor a statewide conference for parenting education professionals. Furthermore, faculty and graduate students from a number of institutions have conducted trainings on topics such as evaluation and cultural competence and participated in the development of a 3-part video series on parent-infant interactions. University experts who conduct trainings gain experience teaching beyond the college classroom, applying and adapting their knowledge to meet service providers' needs and interests and learning from the experiences these students in the "real world" can share. Their knowledge of topics such as child development can reach a broader audience of professionals and paraprofessionals, outside of the academy, affecting direct service work with families and children. Listening to the stories of direct service providers during the trainings CTF provides, ideas for research emerge and questions arise about the relevance of higher education to the issues of society.

Academic experts have collaborated with us in additional varied roles, e.g., as consultants to special projects, and as experts providing testimony to the state legislature. Consultants from local universities have designed an array of materials for training and other purposes, including a manual to assist school personnel when they see signs of child abuse or neglect and an assessment tool for home visitors to use during their initial visits with families. Using consultants from university settings helps ensure that CTF is drawing on the latest research to create and disseminate credible, theory-driven materials and creates opportunities for academic consultants to work with program staff to solve real-life problems and add value to services. Additionally, bringing together the voices of university experts with others who are influential to the state legislature helps us make the case for support of our programs.

A good example of the success of combining testimony of university experts with that of community leaders occurred in May 1997, when CTF held a highly successful hearing before the state legislature's Committee on Health and Human Services to propose the creation of the Healthy Families program. Academic experts in early literacy, brain development and parent-child attachment provided testimony on behalf of the program in concert with influential leaders from the business, church, and labor communities, pediatricians, and state and local government officials. The academic voices lent additional credence to the perspectives presented by the diverse and powerful leaders noted, and helped CTF demonstrate its unique ability to draw on all segments of the community to mobilize on behalf of children. This hearing was a significant event in securing state funding to launch our Healthy Families program.

Furthermore, the relationships CTF builds through collaborations with universities help to expand our mutual reach and vision. Recently, for example, a faculty member at Tufts University arranged a meeting between the Director-General of the Ministry of Labor and Social Affairs from Israel, CTF staff, a Tufts doctoral student, and a CTF-funded program in a local community. The relationship between Tufts and CTF created this valuable interaction. CTF had the unique chance to exchange ideas and experiences about family support and organizational strategies with delegates from another country and to influence program development and policy decisions there. The Tufts faculty member was able to meet the requests of the delegates to see prevention programs in action because he had a relationship with CTF; his relationship with CTF had broadened his access to community-based programs in neighborhoods he would not have known otherwise.

EVALUATION

In particular, the context of evaluation has been a critical area of collaboration for CTF with university faculty and students. A collaboration with Dr. Francine Jacobs, her colleagues, and students from Tufts University has built CTF's capacity to evaluate its programs in new, rigorous, and meaningful ways. Tufts' participatory, utilization-focused approach to evaluation has become part of the expectation of CTF for its programs and part of our way of thinking and understanding of how to use evaluation in meaningful ways. In our smaller programs, customer satisfaction surveys have become a simple way to gather data about parents' experiences and expectations of our grantees, and a way to help us monitor and improve the quality of our programs. Tufts has helped us to develop basic tools for data collection that work for us and allow us to compare data with others in the field. For example, CTF and Tufts staff collaborated to create a tool to track services in our Family Centers, many of which are also funded through the state Department of Education (DOE). This tool was so successful that DOE adopted it as well, which means that local programs do not have to duplicate their evaluation efforts to meet the needs of both of their funders and that we can more effectively share and compare data.

In turn, the programs that CTF has developed have created new research opportunities and directions for Tufts. For example, the Healthy Families newborn home visiting program in Massachusetts, and its evaluation, is providing numerous possibilities for the intersection and exchange of ideas between child development researchers, policy makers, and providers. This initiative links faculty and students from Tufts, the Children's Trust Fund, community-based program sites, and policy makers in a partnership.

Healthy Families offers home visiting services to all first-time parents under 21 in Massachusetts, through 29 community-based collaborations of health and human service organizations. Families can enroll and begin services during pregnancy and continue until their child is three years old. The goals of the Healthy Families program are to:

- Prevent child abuse and neglect;
- Achieve optimal health, growth, and development in infancy and early childhood;
- Promote maximum parental educational attainment and economic self-sufficiency; and
- Prevent repeat teen pregnancies.

Tufts University, the outside evaluator for the Healthy Families program, applied to do this research because of its relationship with CTF and because the program offered a unique experiment — a statewide parenting program for adolescent parents. This program, aside from being the largest of its kind in the U.S., lends itself to the exploration of numerous theories and topics of interest to Tufts, e.g., risk and resilience, how therapeutic relationships affect parenting, adolescent parenting, the role of fathers in infant development, and cultural differences in the acceptance of family services. Involvement in the evaluation of the program provides a multitude of tangible resources, opens a world of research questions, and connects Tufts to diverse programs and families across the state.

The evaluation uses the Jacobs' Five-Tiered Approach (Brady, Easterbrooks, Jacobs, & Mistry, 1998; Kapuscik & Jacobs, 1998). The FTA dictates that it is important to be responsive to program variations (environmental context, age and developmental stage, and evaluation resources and capacity) and evaluation issues (multiple stakeholders and their concerns, different evaluation questions, need to build evaluation capacity, and preparation to assess outcomes) in making decisions about which evaluation activities are appropriate for a given program. The evaluators are involving stakeholders in all steps of the process to ensure that the evaluation addresses the questions stakeholders want to know about home visiting. Key informant interviews conducted during the design phase of the evaluation included, for example, state legislators, state budget analysts, and home visitors. Massachusetts' state legislators consider evaluation to be an essential element of their decision to fund and sustain programs such as this one, and the Tufts' evaluation has been critical to CTF's legislative advocacy efforts to fund this program.

Furthermore, Healthy Families' evaluation has enabled graduate students to involve themselves in various aspects of the research process including focus groups, selection of instruments, ethnography, and data collection and analysis. Typically, graduate students in policy and child development may take courses in program evaluation or social policy for children and families, but they rarely get the chance to immerse themselves in large-scale, long-term evaluation projects and to see a program in operation with a diverse group of families. Data collection itself is providing an opportunity for Tufts students to receive valuable training in interviewing techniques and coding of parent-infant interactions. Several masters theses and doctoral dissertations will emerge from this evaluation, adding value to the work the evaluators can accomplish and providing students with new data and an opportunity to see the effects of their research on program delivery. Students participating in the evaluation do not only gain research experience, however, because this project also places many of them in the homes of young parents in communities across Massachusetts — a unique view into a world otherwise far removed from the academic community.

Healthy Families has not been the only CTF program that has benefited from collaborative evaluation efforts. We would like to share at least one other example of how CTF has used the work of a university partnership in this context. In 1998, Fran Basche, a masters student in the departments of Urban and Environmental Policy and Child Development at Tufts, conducted a study of parent involvement in the governance of family support programs in our seven Massachusetts Family Centers for her thesis. Her study included an extensive literature review on parent involvement in other fields, a survey and interview of program directors, telephone interviews with parents serving on Family Center boards, and interviews with senior staff at CTF. Based on what she learned, Basche offered a series of recommendations to improve the structure and process of parent involvement in the governance of the Family Centers. This study was an incredibly valuable tool to CTF for all of its programs and to others in the field. The recommendations it yielded were implemented in our programs and shaped our expectations of all of our programs. A regular part of our grant proposal review process for new programs requests information on parent involvement in program governance based on this study. Subsequent to her thesis, Fran Basche began her post-graduate career working with related programs at the state Department of Education. Clearly, this study influenced both CTF's program development as well as one student's career development and involvement in the field.

DISSEMINATION OF RESEARCH

The Children's Trust Fund is also discovering the potential for the utilization of graduate students in the process of informing and educating legislators about family support. Graduate students in child development know how to read the academic literature, but need to learn to summarize it clearly and truthfully for advocacy purposes. They must learn how to deal with the potential conflicts of interest entailed. Rarely can students hone these skills through coursework alone. Rarely do professors in the field even know which skills their students will need in order to provide these experiences in the coursework.

Several years ago an issue of the Society for Research in Child Development's Social Policy Report described training and career options for developmental scientists (Susman-Stillman et al., 1996). The authors noted the need for skill-building to formulate research that is meaningful to policy makers and that anticipates their needs and to communicate findings in non-academic ways. In graduate programs, they lamented the lack of training and practice provided in writing policy briefs and executive summaries and in writing for non-technical audiences.

Some of the skills graduate students learn in transmitting their knowledge at CTF include: learning to adjust language and content to the interest of a range of audiences (media, legislature, service provider), anticipating needs and questions and answers, placing data in a larger context, being able to discuss research in shorter or longer time periods, and thinking how data and theory from multiple disciplines relate and can be put together.

One of the authors of this chapter, Gretchen Biesecker, is a doctoral student in Child Development at Tufts University. Beginning as an intern, and then working as the Research and Policy Coordinator at CTF, I have learned these skills and my efforts to make research useful to policy makers and program staff are an important component of CTF's advocacy efforts. I have used my skills as a child development researcher to gather, evaluate, and distill research on topics including home visitation, parent-child relationships, and father involvement, into fact sheets and other publications, trainings, and presentations. Some of these tools helped CTF influence policy makers to create and grow the Healthy Families program and informed CTF's own decisions about program design. Others, such as a fatherhood resource kit, video series, and workshops, helped me to share my knowledge with family support staff in this state and nationally. Thus, among many others benefits, I have received a rare gift of being able to see my academic knowledge and skills make a very real impact on the lives of young parents and all those who are necessary to sustain these programs to help them. Furthermore, in working to disseminate my research in ways that are useful and meaningful, I have gained a unique and complex understanding of the state legislative process and what is needed to influence the policy process for children and families. My ability and set of strategies to teach adult learners from a variety of educational and cultural backgrounds have also been enhanced through opportunities to provide trainings and presentations for providers representing diverse disciplines. These are skills and experiences that could only be gained by an experience outside the university, made possible because my department at Tufts fosters and values these relationships and the application of research.

INTERNSHIPS

One of the best ways, in fact, to create these sorts of outreach scholarship and leadership opportunities is through internships. Internships that allow students to draw from their deeper understanding of child development, social work, family ecology, and evaluation, and related fields strengthen the abilities of future leaders and develop students more fully as individuals.

CTF's numerous partnerships with graduate and undergraduate interns from local universities provide mutual benefits. Internships vary according to the requirements of the different university programs who partner with us. Students represent an array of disciplines, including social work, child development, policy and management, public health, and journalism. Many interns typically work at CTF for one academic year, receiving supervision at CTF and at their home institutions. Their responsibilities vary according to our mutual needs and strengths. Interns have assisted all aspects of our mission, including public relations and development, legislative advocacy, public awareness, program administration, and training. Working with staff and other CTF colleagues, interns have written pieces of legislation, press releases, and reports to programs. They have gained experience in fundraising, aiding in the planning of a gala event each year and cultivating potential donors to CTF and to our programs. Interns interact with program staff, participating in site visits to monitor our funded programs and assisting with trainings. Many learn a great deal about reviewing grants and the necessary components of a successful family support program.

Opportunities such as these enable students to connect their learning within their university settings to the outside world, in tangible products and policies that programs and communities can use. Interns can literally see their work in print, in action. This enhances their learning, their focus, and helps them to find new meaning in their coursework. More concretely, internships provide students with other benefits: course credit; income, in some cases; fulfillment of degree requirements; contacts in the field for future employment; and access to data and support for theses, qualifying papers, and dissertations.

It is also clear, however, that many interns enjoy the work beyond these benefits, because several core staff members started at CTF as interns and grew into key positions within the organization. Cassie Mitchell, one example, was CTF's first intern when she was a graduate student in social work at Boston University. She stayed at CTF for seven years, playing a critical role as Director of Programs and Evaluation in the development of CTF's program and evaluation efforts. The longevity of intern involvement and growth within CTF suggests that we are truly engaging students in this work and that they are experiencing personal benefits of service to communities.

CTF, as well, needs its interns. Benefits to CTF include: affordable access to expertise and labor, new perspectives, and current knowledge in several fields. In most cases, student interns bring skills that are up-to-date and ready for our use: they typically write well, are comfortable learning or sharing new computer skills, and they bring an access to the latest in research and theory. These skills mean that CTF can often rely on interns not just for the necessary "grunt work" that we all need to do at times, but that we can use interns to accomplish projects that are necessary to our work but that we otherwise truly could not do.

The value of a non-profit organization's ability to tap into university expertise at such a low cost should not be underestimated. We have been surprised, however, at how often we suggest the idea of engaging students to work on program evaluations or legislative advocacy, for example, to other colleagues and find that they have never considered contacting their local universities before. This happens every year when we present a workshop on building relationships with legislators to family support staff at a national conference. Typically, this suggestion is met with delight and many questions about how to set up these relationships, but it is unfortunate that what seem to be obvious places for connection to us are brand-new, untapped resources to others.

CHALLENGES

Collaborations are never easy, and despite the rosy picture we have painted, some challenges should be noted. First, faculty, students, and CTF staff all experience competing demands at times. Consultants and students, for example, are usually working on other projects and courses outside of CTF and at times these make them less accessible than we would like. Similarly, CTF staff members often feel overburdened by the demands of their jobs, and finding time to orient, train, and supervise students and overseeing their projects can be difficult. This is especially true of internships that are relatively short in duration or where hours per week devoted to the internship are minimal.

Second, the language of academia and our agency sometimes are not immediately translatable. Much has been said about the unique language or style that academic journals value and how it is not always accessible to those outside the academy. On the other hand, the abbreviations and acronyms tossed around CTF and other state agencies can be so confusing that one intern created a guide to our lingo as part of an intern orientation manual. Both partners in university-community partnerships, therefore, need to be sensitive the language of others and communication needs of others. It helps when both partners take time to understand each others' styles and can articulate questions or suggestions for adjustments to content or format.

Third, the goals of the parties involved in these collaborations may be quite different and not always complementary. Again, communication of these goals and expectations of each member of the collaboration must be made clear at the beginning and revisited over time. Students, for example, may hold different goals for themselves than an organization such as CTF can provide during the time of an internship. Additionally, not all universities and programs always understand or define clearly exactly the kind of work we do. For example, CTF is not a direct service provider, and students who seek clinical experience and direct contact with families would be disappointed with an internship experience here. This highlights the importance of defining the internship site's mission and activities clearly and outlining expectations and tasks for interns early in the process.

The challenge of differing goals extends beyond internships. Faculty members may find adjusting a training to meet the needs and interests of service providers, for example, a difficult challenge. Clarifying goals is especially important in the area of program evaluation and research, so that programs such as CTF can collect the kinds of data that are most useful to their programs and stakeholders and so that university partners can find places to investigate questions and theories of interest. When a program expects to achieve certain goals, and an evaluation finds evidence contrary to these goals, other related challenges arise. These questions relate to the very meaning and use of evaluation, but can be difficult to negotiate and have an impact on relationships.

Fourth, for us as a field, a challenge to universities and to communities is how to better engage and sustain men in community service and work with families. Our work in the field with programs, in our own agency, and with students and faculty is predominantly with women. Finding ways to meet the personal and professional needs of men in this field, and making their worth clear, requires changes in our culture and forces that may feel beyond our control. Reaching young men, as students, may serve a valuable initial step in engaging them in this work as they experience the satisfaction of using their knowledge to benefit society.

CONCLUSIONS

In fiscal year 2000, CTF provided direct service to over 5,000 families in our Family Centers, reached over 4,800 young families in Healthy Families, and funded 7 parenting education groups serving 970 parents and 1,363 children. We offered two statewide parenting education and family support conferences, each of which provided training to over 750 participants. We doubled our state funding for Healthy Families. These are just a few of our accomplishments last year. Each of them was in some way strengthened by partnerships between CTF and local universities, with direct benefits to the partners and society. We hope that the examples we have provided will suggest ideas to others and promote the growth and development of families, children, and the professionals who work with them.

REFERENCES

Brady, A.E., Easterbrooks, M.A., Jacobs, F.H., & Mistry, J. (1998, February). Evaluating Healthy Families Massachusetts: Building on the past and charting the future. Unpublished manuscript.

Kapuscik, J.L., & Jacobs, F. (1998, Winter). Evaluation that works for you: A practical, useful model from the field. *Family Resource Coalition of America Report: Family Support Evaluation, 16(4)*, 25-28.

Lerner, R.M., Fisher, C.B., & Weinberg, R.A. (2000). Toward a science for and of the people: Promoting civil society through the application of developmental science. *Child Development, 71(1)*, 11-20.

Sedlack, A.J., & Broadhurst, D.D. (1996). Third National Incidence Study of Child Abuse and Neglect. Washington, D.C.: U.S. Department of Health and Human Services.

Susman-Stillman, A.R., Brown, J.L., Adam, E.K., Blair, C., Gaines, R., Gordon, R.A., White, A.M., & Wynn, S.R. (1996). Building research and policy connections: Training and career options for developmental scientists. *Social Policy Report: Society for Research in Child Development, Vol. X(4)*.

CHAPTER 27

ACADEMIC SERVICE LEARNING: DEVELOPMENT FOR SYNTHESIS AND SYNERGY

W. George Scarlett
Erin Cox
Marisa Matsudaira
Jumpstart and Tufts University

INTRODUCTION

At the heart of academic service learning is the notion that community programs and academic programs can and should be synthesized to create synergy (Furco, A.,1996; Howard, J., 1998; Zlotkowski, E.,1999). But how does this occur? Based on our own efforts to promote academic service learning, we have some answers that might prove helpful. Our programs have to do with children, and some of the lessons learned are lessons about child-related programs. However, there are general lessons here as well — lessons about synthesis, synergy, and development. To define these lessons, we need first to describe our two programs — beginning with the community program. In each description, what is important to notice are the ways that academic service learning can address limitations and help everyone.

Jumpstart is an early literacy program for preschoolers from low-income families. Many of Jumpstart's children also attend Head Start. The goal of both Head Start and Jumpstart is school readiness[1], As such, much of the work with Jumpstart children has to do with laying the foundation for reading.

To get children ready for school and to lay the foundation for reading, Jumpstart pairs each child with one undergraduate whose responsibility it is to nurture a positive relationship that will in turn nurture a love of books and a beginning interest in reading. But Jumpstart differs from other early literacy programs in several important ways. First, the undergraduates become "Corps" members because Jumpstart is part of the federally sponsored com-

---

[1] Recently, there have been efforts to de-emphasize this goal of getting children ready for schools and to emphasize instead that schools should be getting ready to serve diverse populations of children. However, getting children ready for schools was central to justifying Head Start's beginnings, and it continues to be central to justifying its funding as a federal program.

munity service program known as AmeriCorp. Second, Corps members are paid — usually from work-study money provided through university partnerships. Third, Jumpstart provides teacher training leading to an early childhood certificate. Fourth, Jumpstart demands a commitment in time far greater than the average internship: nine hours per week during the academic year and 40 hours per week during the summer —— for a total of 900 hours of service in all.

Jumpstart's features make it a potentially ideal partner for academic service learning having to do with children. It is a program where students at every level take on meaningful work and responsibility. Furthermore, it is a program where students can get first hand knowledge of serious issues discussed in coursework, issues having to do with early literacy, immigrant status, poverty, and children who are at risk for school failure. Finally, Jumpstart is a program where students have the time needed to develop connections between their fieldwork and their coursework. Nevertheless, developing even this potentially ideal partnership has not been easy. Just as students often leave their academic minds in the classroom as they engage in community service, so too do students often leave their service experience in the community as they engage in coursework — as can be seen when turning to the academic side of the community-university partnership. The Eliot-Pearson Department of Child Development is our example.

The Eliot-Pearson Department of Child Development at Tufts University is an inter-disciplinary academic community offering an undergraduate program in child development. The overall goal of the Department is to prepare students for life-long study and service related to children. The Department's focus has been on practical questions understood from the vantage point of both research and theory. To promote this focus, the Department requires students concentrating in child development to take research methods and theory courses as well as courses on specialty topics. Furthermore, the Department encourages students to gain first-hand experience with diverse populations of children.

In the past, students' experiential learning has come mostly through single semester internships and field placements which have provided on-site, as well as on-campus supervision and which have required written and spoken reflections in order to harvest the experiential learning. For the most part, these internships and field placements have worked well. Students have gained valuable experience, provided thoughtful reflections, and been quite satisfied with what they have learned. However, despite their success, these internships and fieldwork placements have often run parallel to academic learning. Even good students have left theory, research and their "academic minds" in the classroom as they worked with children and childcare agencies.

Take, for example, one excellent student at the very end of her student career at Tufts. This student showed herself to be quite capable of explaining theory and understanding research within the context of her coursework, and yet, when carrying out her internship in a residential school for troubled children, she still had difficulty distinguishing tactical from theory-driven thinking. For her, changing from the tactic of guiding a child to thinking about alternatives to hitting to the tactic of sending the child to time-out for hitting constituted not simply a change in tactic but also a change in theory. What she understood in her coursework (or so it seemed), she did not understand in her fieldwork. She did not understand that time-out, which normally is associated with a behavioral approach, can sit comfortably within a developmental education or ego analytic or any other approach — though its meaning and character is determined by which approach is adopted. In other words, she did not understand that one need not change theories when changing tactics — an invaluable lesson if one is to develop a consistent and powerful approach to complex problems such as how to manage behavior problems and still help troubled children learn and develop.

Or take another example of the same phenomenon, again of a good student who proved herself capable of explaining theory within the context of her coursework. This student had learned a good deal about family systems theory, in part because her long-term goal was to become a family therapist. And yet, in the context of her internship in a charter school where there were chronic behavior problems by acting out teenagers, she could not recognize her own family systems way of thinking. To her, these problems stemmed not so much from teachers being inconsistent in administering consequences as from teachers trying to befriend students in ways that undermined teachers' authority. This was a valid point of view, however, she did not see how easily it could be made into a family systems theory point of view, one focusing on issues of roles, boundaries, and sub-systems. Had she realized that her own spontaneous way of explaining was consistent with family systems theory, she could have drawn upon that theory to expand her explanation in ways that might have led to more meaningful explanations and to useful interventions.

Academicians have traditionally expressed concern over students working in parallel and putting theory, research, and academics to the side while they engage in community service. Non-academicians have not been so concerned and some have responded with the disdainful question, "So what?" There are, of course, compelling arguments in response to this question of "So what?" We need not go into them in detail. The gist of these arguments is summarized by Kurt Lewin's famous line; "There is nothing so practical as a good theory." That this is so in virtually every applied field is easily demonstrated by the contributions and thinking of both leaders and accomplished practitioners.

What most students do not fully appreciate, then, is the fact that theories guide the inevitable struggles necessary in every responsible and difficult practice. What most students do not realize is that theory and research equip the mind not so much with answers and directives as they do with good questions and useful hunches. And what most students rarely realize is that the process of defining problems is a theory-laden process that deeply influences where and how solutions are found. These arguments about the utility of theory and research are central arguments for academic service learning. The question, then, is not why we should institute academic service learning but "How?" To answer this question, we need to adopt a developmental perspective.

REDEFINING LEARNING AND TEACHING TO UNDERSTAND HOW ACADEMIC SERVICE LEARNING WORKS

So far, we seem to have argued that community service learning and coursework run mostly parallel to one another — making it difficult to find examples of academic service learning. We have used the Jumpstart and Tufts programs as examples. But looking closer at these two examples and with a developmental perspective, this appearance of parallel work takes on a different meaning — a meaning that helps us better define what we should mean by academic service learning and how it works. Let us first revisit the Jumpstart example — then revisit the examples of the two Tufts students doing internships in schools. In revisiting, we can better appreciate the often hidden contributions of academic service learning and the fact that learning and development are dependent upon one another.

The Hidden Meanings In Academic Service Learning

To investigate what students felt they learned and got from their Jumpstart community service experience, Marisa Matsudaira conducted a survey and found that Corps members did not feel their Jumpstart experience had a significant impact on their coursework. In this survey, corps members emphasized the "authentic learning" and value of the one-on-one work with their individual child. They also emphasized the value of working as a team and making connections both with other Corps members and with members of the community. Finally, they emphasized the value of their having a voice in the way work got done and, at times, the value of their having a leadership role —— something not common to most internships and field placements.

What should we make of these survey results? If we take them at face value, it would seem that Jumpstart and programs like it provide valuable opportunities for service learning but *not for academic service learning.* Just as many faculty say their students do not apply coursework to their community service, so too the students in this survey seemed to say they did not apply their service learning to their coursework. But is this really the case? We do not think so, and for two reasons: the first has to do with semantics, and the second has to do with development.

According to the Jumpstart survey, students did not see their community service learning as effecting their academic learning. But what did they mean by "not effecting"? When interviewed later, it became clear that most meant they did not see Jumpstart as leading to their getting higher grades or performing better on the usual "objective" measures of academic success. However, many students related that they did bring their Jumpstart experience into their coursework — whenever courses required observation reports or encouraged students to make use of examples from their community work. Furthermore, students reported that their Jumpstart work gave meaning to their coursework — even if that meaning was not reflected in higher grades. The following account of one Corp member's experience provides a clear example.

> At Jumpstart, I came in contact with Jean, a five year old who was of Haitian Kreyol descent. He stood out for being tall, for having large glasses, and for always wearing the same string around his neck. But he stood out even more because his speech was slow and garbled, because he was relatively isolated, and because he often resorted to physical means to get attention and what he wanted. Jean puzzled me until I was further along in my course on bilingual education that I was taking at Tufts.

> In this course, we studied Patton O Tabors' theory of children who are raised having to speak two languages – children she called "Omega" children (Tabors, P.O., 1997). According to Tabors, Omega children often remain silent during their early schooling — because they are not sure which language to use and because they have not developed far enough in either of their two languages to be able to express themselves well. As a result, Omega children become somewhat isolated as other children ignore them. And, after awhile, to get at least some attention and to feel somewhat connected, Omega children often become physical with others – which wins them the label of being "problem children".

> Tabors' description of Omega children fit Jean exactly. Furthermore, it helped me understand that there were reasons for Jean's behavior, reasons having to do with problems communicating rather than with problems being aggressive or misbehaving. With these reasons in mind, I was able to work more effectively with Jean.

There is, we believe, a significant lesson to be learned from this example, namely, that the contribution of community service to academic learning can be quite valuable without being what professors normally mean by learning.

Professors see class discussions and their course material as being about reality; many college students do not. That is, for many students, academic discussions have an air of unreality about them — not because professors live in ivory towers but because the reality that professors speak of is a reality that students have not *lived*. However, community service offers opportunities for students to live the realities spoken of by professors — as the previous example clearly demonstrates. When this happens, that is, when students sit in class and find themselves referring to their own experience in response to their professors' points, distinctions, and examples, then the coursework takes on a new meaning, namely, the meaning of being "real".

We do not ordinarily put the label of learning on this experience, but, in fact, it is indeed learning and significant learning at that —— the kind of learning leading to students internalizing coursework and making it their own. However, academic service learning can and should do more — by stimulating critical thinking and scholarly work. For this to happen, professors teaching courses related to community service need to do more.

Promoting Academic Service Learning

There is an analogy between promoting academic service learning and promoting good writing. In many colleges and universities, freshman take special courses focusing on how to write — courses that do, in fact, promote good writing through demonstrating the necessity of re-writing (i.e., writing multiple drafts). However, in subsequent courses, indeed throughout their entire college career, most students rarely have instructors who design their writing assignments to encourage re-writing. The result is that instructors blame students' poor writing on the freshman courses that they believe should have "fixed" the writing problems.

However, many problems (e.g., being overweight, keeping a house clean, balancing a budget) are not of the to-be-fixed type. They are of the to-be-constantly-worked-on type. That is, many problems demand on-going attention and support. If courses do not support re-writing, then students' writing will suffer, and the fault will lie not in the freshman course but in subsequent courses and in the poor way that writing assignments are designed.

Something similar can be said about academic service learning. If students are not bringing their service learning into the classroom and if their coursework seems unaffected by their community service, then the fault may lie not so much with students or with community programs as with the way courses are designed. Putting this positively, if professors and courses encourage students to make use of their service learning and community experience, they will.

Learning And Development

Returning to our opening examples of the two Tufts students who failed initially to connect their academic learning to their community service, we find a different lesson. Not every instance of learning is of the same type — as we have already seen. Much of what we call learning is better defined as development — because what we at times refer to as learning is actually a newly developed structure in the mind, a structure born of long-standing, active struggles by students in partnership with mentors who guide. The problems defined in the examples of the Tufts students are problems of development as well as of learning. We need to explain.

The problems defined in the examples of the Tufts students were not problems about facts and information. Rather, they were problems about thinking. The first example was about thinking hierarchically inasmuch as thinking about theory can be metaphorically relegated to a higher, more abstract, and superordinate level while thinking about tactics can be relegated to a lower, more concrete, and subordinate level. This thinking on different levels is more a matter of development than of learning. Many beginning college students are simply not ready to think on multiple levels about theoretical issues pertaining to areas in which they have little or no experience. Given this situation, professors can be crystal clear about the distinction between theoretical and tactical matters and still, many students will not learn because they are not ready to learn.

However, after developing further, students may indeed be ready to learn, as was the case with the first Tufts student. Because she was an experienced student who had developed her thinking, she could easily learn the distinction between theory and tactics when provided a clear explanation that included a single example. If she had not yet been capable of thinking simultaneously on abstract-theoretical and concrete-tactical levels, teaching the distinction between adopting a theoretical approach and choosing a tactic would likely have fallen on deaf ears. The point is that learning depends on development.

But the reverse is true as well: Development depends upon learning — as illustrated by the second student. This student could not have developed a practical theory about behavior problems had she not already learned a good deal about family systems theory with its concepts of boundary, role, subsystem, and the like. What she had learned and not simply her overall cognitive development made her "ready" for development.

CONCLUSIONS

From these discussions of the different contributions of academic and community service learning, we can draw several conclusions. First, students must have community service experience that is applicable to coursework, even if only to make coursework seem more "real". Second, for there to be true academic service learning, professors must re-design their courses so as to help students make use of their community service in their coursework. Third, professors, students, indeed everyone involved, must understand that the task of implementing academic service learning is not simply about having experience or imparting information but about supporting development.

This last point has implications for how we define and understand academic service learning. The beginning student need not apply theory to practice. At this stage, community service and coursework need only support a student's emerging identity — in the Eliot-Pearson program that would mean supporting an identity as someone committed to the life-long study and service of children. With subsequent development, service and coursework can be gradually integrated to form the synthesis and synergy that defines mature academic service learning. This gradual development of academic service learning will depend on varied and sustained support more than on didactic teaching. Furthermore, this varied and sustained support will depend on there being close-knit partnerships between community programs, academic programs, and the students themselves — partnerships that do more than provide information, develop skills, and offer opportunities to gain experience. These partnerships will support the development of academic service learning mainly through the way they encourage and guide.

REFERENCES

Furco, Andrew (1996). *Service Learning: A Balanced Approach to Experiential Education*. Washington, D.C.: The Corporation for National Service.

Howard, Jeffrey (1998). "Academic Service Learning: A Counternormative Pedagogy" in *Academic Service-Learning: A Pedagogy of Action and Reflection*. R. Rhoads & J. Howard (Eds.). San Francisco: Jossey-Bass.

Tabors, Patton O. (1997). *One Child, Two Languages: A Guide for Preschool Educators of children Learning English as a Second Language*. Baltimore, MD.: Paul H. Brookes Pub.

Zlotkowski, Edward (1999). "Pedagogy and Engagement" in *Colleges and Universities as Citizens* Boston: Allyn & Bacon.

CHAPTER 28

4-H: AN ADAPTABLE MODEL FOR YOUTH DEVELOPMENT AND SERVICE LEARNING

Donald T. Floyd
Leigh McKenna
National 4-H

Ever since its scattered beginnings over a century ago, 4-H has been more than an organization devoted to serving youth — it has also provided youth a forum in which to serve. This important distinction has been the principle that has shepherded 4-H from its beginning as a loosely linked assembly of narrowly focused clubs to a national movement involving over 6.8 million American youth today.

Those people who were instrumental in the creation of 4-H believed that youth possess tremendous capacity for serving their communities. This belief has been proven through action, time and again, as 4-H has developed over the years. As an organization, 4-H has consistently been an effective mechanism for channeling the civic-minded interests of America's young people, and our communities have been the better for it.

Although its official mission has occasionally been modified over the last 100 years, 4-H has always been and remains deeply committed to a single objective — youth and community development. Author Scott Peters describes it as, "both the individual development of youth and the tangible improvement or enrichment of a larger public world beyond the self." (Peters, 1999, p. 17). 4-H has been able to remain on task and be successful in achieving its objective because of its continued commitment to a few basic ideas:

1. the belief that youth are a powerful, capable resource;
2. the value and advantage in having youth and adults work together;
3. the use of the club structure at the local, grassroots level; and
4. education based largely on a "learning by doing" method.

These fundamental building blocks are the foundation on which 4-H was built and they remain instrumental to the success and vitality of 4-H work today. To know the 4-H organization of the 21st century, it is helpful to understand its beginnings. First of all, 4-H was not created or started by one individual, but rather, it evolved as a product of the contributions and collaborations of many. As author Franklin M. Reck states, "4-H club work is too great a movement to be claimed by any one man."

The changing culture and needs of rural American communities at the close of the 19th century played a significant role in the formation of 4-H. The early 1900's ushered in a time of relative prosperity for American agriculture. "Farmers were not only making more money, they were emerging from frontier isolation. Mail was now coming to them by rural free delivery. The crank telephone...was becoming more and more common." (Reck, 1951, p. 6). The favorable economic conditions and advancements in communications, together with the dramatic growth of cities and industry began to transform the future that many rural people envisioned for themselves.

Public schools and the educational opportunities they offered children, reinforced the shift to urban culture and industrialization. School curricula did not stress the study of agriculture and domestic science, but instead emphasized subjects like reading, writing, and arithmetic, with few examples of practical application for rural schoolchildren. These communities were beginning to recognize the real threat of losing their children and culture to the lure of the city.

There were efforts to inspire youth to embrace and advance agricultural life in the face of these changes. In particular, a number of documented public contests were held in the mid- to late 1800's that encouraged youth to demonstrate their farming talents. However, these contests were seldom repeated and lacked consistency and coordination across the country. (Reck, 1951, p. 5) Their immediate impact was limited but they laid the groundwork for a form of educational development based largely outside of the classroom.

Then, in 1896, Liberty Hyde Bailey of Cornell University in New York used a state appropriation to create a series of nature study leaflets for distribution to rural schools. Bailey had recognized the lack of value placed upon environmental and agricultural sciences in traditional school settings. He also prescribed to the belief that nature is a classroom in itself where scholarship can be attained. In order to disseminate the information provided in the leaflets, various Nature Study clubs for youth were organized with success. (Reck, Wessel, & Wessel).

It was at the convergence of these events and circumstances that 4-H began to take form. Following in the footsteps of Bailey, men such as Albert B. Graham, superintendent of schools for Springfield Township, Ohio, and O. J. Kern, county superintendent of schools in Winnebago county, Illinois, recognized the void of rural education in school systems dominated by the urban perspective. They began to embrace and actualize the concept of non-formal (out-of-school) education as a method for studying agriculture.

At about the same time in 1902, both Graham and Kern began organizing youth experiment clubs. They wanted to apply to agriculture, the same principles of manual training that they had witnessed being used successfully in industrial education. The work of their clubs employed the "learning by doing" concept. The club activities that young people participated in were directly applicable to their own lives and the lives of their families, thus providing value to their communities. This coupling of community service with academic objective was an early example of the educational philosophy known today as service learning.

During its first year, Graham's club members participated in activities such as performing litmus tests on the soil of their families' farms. This hands-on work established a discernible link between science and the farm-life these youth had always known. In 1903, Graham began partnering with the Agricultural Experiment Station in Wooster, Ohio, and Thomas F. Hunt, dean of agriculture at Ohio State University. College experiment stations had been searching for ways to disseminate their knowledge to individual farms and Graham's club seemed a viable mechanism. With the support of the experiment station and the university, Graham's club conducted various projects including corn growing, soil testing, vegetable garden growing and flower garden growing.

Kern received the support of colleges and the state Farmers' Institute in the formation and activities of his club. Projects included growing corn and beets and surveying oats for smut, a disease-causing fungus that affects plants. In calculating the percentage of oats affected by smut or determining the amount it cost to cultivate, harvest, and rent land for growing beets, the club members were discovering practical applications for arithmetic.

The partnering of Graham, Kern and others like them, together with agriculture experiment stations and universities led to the eventual association of 4-H clubs with the Federal Government's Cooperative Extension System. Today, this relationship is important for many reasons, but at the time it was particularly significant because of the Extension System's use of demonstration programs. New and improved methods of farming were being introduced to communities through public demonstrations, and youth, with their eagerness for learning and capacity for change, were well suited to teach their communities through showing.

Having young people conduct publicly visible demonstration projects was unique because it cast them in a dual role as student and teacher. Not only were they learning, but they were also demonstrating their value to their communities by passing along what they learned to their families. Put simply, communities were being taught things by their young people that could improve the lives of everyone.

The work of early 4-H pioneers employed many of the same beliefs and concepts that are still being used by 4-H today. First, they recognized the promise of youth and the tremendous value they could bring to their communities. Engaging young people proved highly effective in the transfer of knowledge from the university system to the farm. They also realized the advantage of having youth and adults work together as partners, resulting in a much richer exchange than if they worked in isolation of one another. Adopting the club structure enabled young people to address the specific issues of their communities, creating a personal connection or "buy in." This grassroots format also allowed for flexibility and rapid change. Finally, using experiential learning provided the action step necessary to actualize the first belief, that youth are a valuable resource. Young people were empowered to identify problems that affected themselves and their communities, thus establishing a vested interest in finding the solution. These early clubs were certainly successful in advancing the development of youth, but the methods they employed ensured that the community would advance too.

Today, the 4-H name and emblem is federally authorized by Congress and managed by the Families, 4-H and Nutrition unit of the Cooperative State Research, Education and Extension Service of the U.S. Department of Agriculture. At the state level, 4-H is sponsored by the Cooperative Extension Service offices of the 106 land grant Universities located throughout the U.S. and its territories. Private sector organizations work with these public sector organizations to provide a collaborative network to strengthen the 4-H movement. New management systems and structures are emerging to provide the leadership for the movement. The success of the organization is partly attributed to the uniqueness of its non-formal educational network that combines the expertise and resources of the university system, federal, state, and local governments, and private sector partners like the National 4-H Council.

One hundred years after it began, 4-H remains staunchly committed to encouraging and promoting the power of America's youth to actively engage their communities, with over 6.8 million young people involved today. Through its historic association with extension education and its unwavering commitment to civic engagement and collaboration, 4-H has become America's only youth development organization extending across the entire nation, reaching into every county in America. Presently, 4-H receives support from both public and private resources.

One of the most notable 4-H achievements has been its success in helping young people take active leadership roles in civic life. During its formative years 4-H was grounded in the belief that "youth have creativity, talent and energy that can be developed, tapped and organized for serious, constructive public contribution." (Peters, 1999, p. 17). This civic-minded focus was affirmed in a 1935 report commissioned by the Department of Agriculture, titled "Recommended Policies Governing 4-H Club Work." It concluded that a major objective of 4-H was to "train rural boys and girls in cooperative action to the end that they may increase their accomplishments and, through associated efforts, better assist in solving rural problems."

A continued commitment to the central concept of "cooperative action," rather than to a particular issue or way of life, is what has allowed 4-H to remain adaptable in a rapidly changing world and still be relevant. Persistent utilization of the local club structure has rooted 4-H's power in grassroots efforts, encouraging 4-H'ers to customize their work to meet the specific needs of their communities. This type of forum inspires youth to not only consider, but also adopt, the concerns, problems, and challenges that influence their own lives in order to affect change.

The same basic principle on which 4-H was founded — youth and community development — remains unchanged. However, the modern scope of 4-H work has broadened far beyond all things rural. Certainly, agriculture and domestic science continue to be major focus areas for 4-H. But the 4-H of today has broadened its scope enormously to include over 130 curriculum categories, including things like citizenship and civic education, service learning, performing arts, visual arts, safety, waste management, and reading literacy.

A century ago, regular mail delivery helped lessen the isolation of farming communities, contributing to the creation of 4-H. Today, the modern advances of the Internet and e-mail have enabled isolated individuals and communities to participate in dialogues that previously excluded them. In fact, the digital age is witnessing the creation of a new kind of "community" linked by common interest rather than shared borders. The line between rural and urban has become progressively indistinguishable as many of the same concerns and issues are shared by both. As the world has changed, so too has 4-H. Regardless of the topic area, be it improved farming methods or computer literacy, 4-H has successfully been able to adapt its youth development and service learning models to produce results.

Just as those early farming demonstration projects enabled youth to be the teachers as well as the students, 4-H continues to employ the same approach today. For example, in Oregon, 4-H agents are working with the children of migrant farm workers to help them develop computer and Internet skills. The youth are then able to pass those same skills on to their parents, who might otherwise have no way to attain them. In this example, young people benefit from their experience but they also play a crucial role in the community.

This demonstrates that including youth in solving community problems isn't a courtesy afforded by well-intentioned adults, but a smart and just use of human resources. If America is to achieve its democratic ideals, youth need to be granted their rightful place as contributing members in society.

National 4-H Council, a partner in the 4-H movement, has chosen to empower youth, and consequently itself, by involving young people as full partners in the governance of the organization. Today, a quarter of the board of trustees consists of young people (ages 12-21), serving as equal partners with their adult counterparts. The sensibility of this decision is supported by a study commissioned by National 4-H Council and done by the University of Wisconsin-Madison, which found that "the mutual contributions of youth and adults can result in a synergy, a new power and en-

ergy that propels decision-making groups to greater innovation and productivity" (Zeldin et al., 2000, p.5).

4-H will continue to change in order to meet the needs of today's
youth. In fact, the commencement of the 21st Century prompted 4-H to
yet again reevaluate its mission and focus. It has adopted five priority areas that will guide its work in the next many years:

1. The Power of Youth — Do what it takes to allow youth to become
   fully engaged as valued partners.
2. Access, Equity, and Opportunity — Serve all communities by providing equitable access and opportunity for diverse youth, volunteers, and 4-H staff and be aggressive in reaching under-served and
   under-represented children and their families.
3. An Extraordinary Place to Learn — Build upon past success and
   continue to use the model of experiential learning.
4. Exceptional People, Innovative Practices — Enable youth, volunteers, and 4-H staff to flourish with their involvement in the important work of youth development.
5. Effective Organizational Systems — Consider approaches to
   achieve the mission through new ways of thinking and working.
   Marshal our resources, talent, and respect to create a cooperative,
   futuristic, and accountable network.

With 4-H's long history, far-reaching presence in American culture,
extensive pool of resources, and commitment to a few basic principles, it
serves as an excellent model for service learning and civic engagement.
The areas of focus for 4-H may change, but the foundation on which the
organization is built remains sound. The 4-H pledge embodies the organization's most basic objective — youth and community development — and it
continues to be as meaningful and relevant today as it was when first
adopted in 1927[1]:

> "I pledge my Head to clearer thinking,
> my Heart to greater loyalty,
> my Hands to larger service,
> and my Health to better living
> for my club, my community, my country and my world."

The first four lines stress the value, capacity, and promise of the individual. The final line delineates the layered context in which the individual
exists with other individuals. This simple idea — that the self is important
and capable, but becomes more so when applied to a civic purpose — is
what has enabled 4-H to continuously re-invent itself and still be a vital
force supporting the development cf millions of youth today.

---

[1] the pledge was revised in 1973 to include the phrase, "and my world."

REFERENCES

Annual 4-H Youth Enrollment Report, 2000 Fiscal Year (2001). United States Department of Agriculture, Cooperative State Research, Education and Extension Service and Land-Grant University Cooperating Extension Service.

Ehrlich, T. (2000). Civic Engagement. *The National Center for Public Policy and Higher Education*, pp. 177-179.

Flanagan, C. A., & Faison, N. (2001). Youth Civic Development: Implications of Research for Social Policy and Programs. *Social Policy Report*, 3-15.

4-H Information, Fact Sheet (2001). National 4-H Council website, www.fourhcouncil.edu/Market/4hinfo/4hfactsheet.htm.

4-H Information, History of 4-H (2001). National 4-H Council website, www.fourhcouncil.edu/Market/4hinfo/NHISTORY.HTM.

Peters, S. (1999, winter). Organizing Head, Heart, Hands and Health for Larger Service: The Public Value of 4-H Youth Development Work. *The Center, A Publication of the Center for 4-H Youth Development at the University of Minnesota*, 16-25.

Recommended Policies Governing 4-H Club Work. (1935). Report of the National Committee of the Land-Grant Colleges and the United States Department of Agriculture on 4-H Club Work.

Reck, F. M. (1951). *The 4-H Story, A History of 4-H Club Work*. Ames, Iowa: National Committee on Boys and Girls Club Work and the Iowa State College Press.

Wessel, T., & Wessel, M. (1982). *4-H: An American Idea 1900-1980, A History of 4-H*. Chevy Chase, Maryland: National 4-H Council.

Zeldin, S., Kusgen McDaniel, A., Topitzes, D. & Calvert, M. (2000). Youth in decision-making: A study on the impacts of youth on adults and organizations, The Innovation Center for Youth and Community Development, a division of National 4-H Council, Chevy Chase, Md., and the University of Wisconsin-Madison in partnership with the Youth in Governance Taskforce of the National Association of Extension 4-H Agents, and supported by the Surdna Foundation, Inc.

CHAPTER 29

SEARCH INSTITUTE'S EVOLVING APPROACH TO COMMUNITY–BASED HUMAN DEVELOPMENT AND THE ROLE OF SERVICE LEARNING

Marc Mannes
Search Institute

INTRODUCTION

Service learning is increasingly being viewed by the academy as a way of building meaningful partnerships between institutions of higher education and communities. It is seen as a form of pedagogy capable of linking lecture hall and mall, laboratory and basketball court, seminar and family room. Students benefit from experiential learning and community members gain from the services students' render.

Nearly 600 cities, town, suburbs, and neighborhoods throughout America are using Search Institute's developmental assets framework to mobilize communities and implement initiatives on behalf of positive child and adolescent development. Community-based human development is an emerging conceptual formulation framing Search Institute's efforts to encourage, study, and understand, community and social change rooted in civic action that is intended to establish and maintain developmental attentiveness. Developmental attentiveness reflects the consciousness and mindset needed to initiate and maintain a community-wide focus on positive growth for young people. Community-based human development is dependent upon the degree of personal, group, and organizational readiness and capacity to create environments, resources, and opportunities that foster healthy, caring, and competent young people, and the extent to which service agencies, civic organizations, and socializing institutions take action to support positive development.

This chapter identifies the importance of service learning and describes Search Institute's developmental assets framework and initial thinking about the concept of community-based human development. The chapter also makes the case that service learning experiences focusing on positive child and adolescent development create a significant bridge between university and community and enhances students' capacity to create social environments that enrich and reinforce the well-being of all young people long after they graduate. The chapter concludes with an assessment of the prospects and challenges associated with securing developmental attentiveness.

THE SIGNIFICANCE OF SERVICE LEARNING

According to Ehrlich (1996), John Dewey's position that intellectual study needs to be fundamentally connected to practical endeavors and social problems confronting society serves as the historical and theoretical basis for service learning.

Service learning can be understood as the lynchpin integrating community service and academic study so that they strengthen and reinforce each other. For Jacoby (1996), service learning is defined as:

> ...a form of experiential education in which students engage in activities that address human and community needs together with structured opportunities intentionally designed to promote student learning and development. Reflection and reciprocity are key concepts in service-learning (p. 5).

A growing body of resources and services dealing with the topic of service learning is available. The Compact for Learning and Citizenship, which operates out of the offices of the Educational Commission of the States (ECS), has been a leader in assembling materials on the subject. The Campus Compact, which is housed at Brown University and is also an offspring of ECS, has helped design service learning programs for hundreds of thousands of college students. The Campus Compact also distributes a vast collection of resource materials which gives educators and administrators ideas, suggestions, and approaches to developing and implementing service learning programs. The National Youth Leadership Council brokers training and technical assistance on school and community-based service learning.

There have been efforts to study service learning. Keith (1995) demonstrated how a service learning initiative has flourished in one academic setting. Kraft and Swadener (1994) reviewed a state's experience with implementing a service learning orientation in its higher educational institutions. Kraft (1996) noted the potential and possible benefits of service learning, but suggested we are too early in its evolution to understand how it might effect higher education's instructional and curricular reforms and the relationship between colleges and universities and the communities in which they reside.

While we await additional inquiry to help us more fully understand the impact and implications of service learning on "town" and "gown", there is evidence suggesting its promise. Schlossberg (1989) discusses the duality of "marginality" versus "mattering" in relation to building a sense of shared purpose, motivation, and commitment among students within the confines of the academic community. "Mattering" is indicative of meaningful student involvement, and "marginality" represents being disconnected and feeling alienated from the mainstream of campus life. Schlossberg (1989) cites the work of Astin (1977, 1984) to document how students' active involvement in campus life is related to all kinds of positive outcomes such as satisfaction with the higher educational experience, retention, and academic achievement. Perhaps student "mattering" via service learning endeavors will cause community life to flourish in the same way in which campus life appears to have been enhanced and enriched through students' substantive participation.

Studies of specific service learning projects along the K-12 portion of the educational continuum have pointed to positive markers such as improved grade point averages for participating students, decreased drop-out rates, and increased percentages of students moving on to higher education. It is possible that similar beneficial results would materialize among baccalaureate level and graduate degree seeking men and women participating in service learning programs.

THE DEVELOPMENTAL ASSETS FRAMEWORK

Search Institute is an independent, nonprofit, nonsectarian, organization whose mission is to advance the well-being of children and adolescents by generating knowledge and promoting its application. The institute has addressed the topic of service learning in several of its publications. It has developed a resource on the importance of service learning for youth (Benson & Roehlkepartain, 1993), and another on the relationship between asset building and service learning for children and adolescents (Search Institute, 2000). Most relevant to this chapter is Search Institute's effort to identify the elements of a strength-based approach to development. Search Institute created the framework of developmental assets which identifies 40 critical factors for young people's healthy growth. The assets offer a set of benchmarks for positive child and adolescent development. The framework also points to the additive nature and cumulative value of these developmental resources for children and youth. The assets themselves demonstrate the important roles that families, schools, congregations, neighborhoods, youth organizations, and others in communities play in shaping young people's lives. The developmental assets framework is presented in Figure 1. You will note in Figure 1 that there are two categories of assets, external and internal.

Figure 1

**Evolving Approach to Community-Based
Human Development**

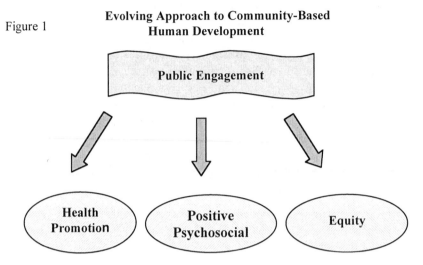

Search Institute Research & Evaluation, Minneapolis, MN September, 2000

External Assets

The first 20 developmental assets focus on positive experiences that young people receive from the people and institutions in their lives. Four categories of external assets are included in the framework:

- Support-Young people need to experience support, care, and love from their families, neighbors, and many others. They need organizations and institutions that provide positive, supportive environments.
- Empowerment-Young people need to be valued by their community and have opportunities to contribute to others. For this to occur, they must be safe and feel secure.
- Boundaries and expectations-Young people need to know what is expected of them and whether activities and behaviors are "in bounds" and out of bounds."
- Constructive use of time-Young people need constructive, enriching opportunities for growth through creative activities, youth programs, congregational involvement, and quality time at home.

Internal Assets

A community's responsibility for its young does not end with the provision of external assets. There needs to be a similar commitment to nurturing the internal qualities that guide choices and create a sense of centeredness, purpose, and focus. Shaping internal dispositions that encourage wise, responsible, and compassionate judgments is particularly important in a society that prizes individualism. Four categories of internal assets are included in the framework:

- Commitment to learning-Young people need to develop a lifelong commitment to education and learning.
- Positive values-Youth need to develop strong values that guide their choices.
- Social competencies-Young people need skills and competencies that equip them to make positive choices, to build relationships, and to succeed in life.
- Positive identity-Young people need a strong sense of their own power, purpose, worth, and promise.

STUDYING DEVELOPMENTAL ASSETS

Since 1989, Search Institute has measured developmental assets in more than 1 million 6th to12th graders in communities across the United States, using the survey *Profiles of Student Life: Attitudes and Behaviors*. In addition, the institute has blended the literature on child development with the framework to suggest developmentally appropriate sets of assets for infants, toddlers, preschoolers, and elementary-age children (Roehlkepartain and Leffert, 2000). The institute is launching new, long-term applied research initiative to study positive human development and the emergence of developmental assets across the first decade of young people's lives. We are particularly interested in investigating when, where, and how assets emerge in relationship with primary and professional caregivers and the larger community setting.

The Significance of Developmental Assets

On one level, the 40 developmental assets represent everyday wisdom about positive experiences and characteristics for young people. Search Institute's research has found that these assets appear to be highly correlated with adolescent behavior— linked to the protection of young people from many different problem behaviors and tied to positive attitudes and behaviors (Benson, Scales, Leffert, & Roehlkepartain, 1999). Moreover, as the number of assets young people say they possess or have experienced increases, many forms of high-risk behavior decrease. Also, as assets increase in number, many aspects of thriving increase. This relationship is evident across cultural and socioeconomic groups of youth (Benson et al., 1999).

Yet, while the assets seem to be strongly related to young people's lives and choices, too few young people experience enough of these assets. The average young person surveyed experiences only 18 of the 40 assets (Benson, Leffert, Scales, and Blyth, 1998). Overall, 62 percent of young people surveyed experience fewer than 20 of the assets (Benson et al.,1999). In short, many young people in the United States do not experience or possess the basic building blocks of healthy development in their lives.

A Positive Community Vision for Young People

At a time when people in many places feel overwhelmed by the problems and challenges facing children and adolescents, communities across the country are discovering new energy and strategies for working together toward a positive vision for young people. Instead of focusing exclusively on reducing risks and resolving problems, these communities are mobilizing around the developmental assets framework to rebuild the foundation of development that all young people need — a foundation that has crumbled in far too many places and for far too many young people in our society.

Since 1993, Search Institute has been working with communities toward that positive vision, expanding upon a 40-year tradition of applied research into youth development.

In 1996, the institute launched a national Healthy Communities - Healthy Youth (HC♦HY) initiative to support communities use of the developmental assets framework. The intent is to motivate and equip individuals, organizations, and their leaders to join together in nurturing the well-being of children and adolescents. The nearly 600 communities implementing asset-building initiatives has prompted Search Institute to think more fully about the community and social context for promoting developmental strengths at the interpersonal, group, and institutional levels.

Thinking About Community-Based Human Development

The idea of community-based human development is rooted in ecological approaches to human development (Bronfenbrenner, 1979), individual-environment dialectics (Riegel, 1975, 1976), developmental contextualism (Lerner, 1992), and neighborhood effects on child and adolescent development (Sampson, Morenoff, & Earls, 1999). It is also grounded in recognition of the increasing importance being attached to overall societal responsibility for successfully rearing youngsters. This sentiment is represented in the overly cited African proverb "it takes a village to raise a child". Excessive usage, however, does not diminish the importance of the idea imbedded in the proverb, and there remains a conviction on the part of many to move beyond rhetoric and engage in community action (Benson et al. 1998).

In presenting the concept of community-based human development we acknowledge the current dominance of an orientation that concentrates on individual risk and to a somewhat lesser degree on individual protective factors for each particular young person. Yet, we also feel compelled to raise the concern that this preoccupation with individuals and their deficits makes for residual social policies triggering responses only when emergencies appear and there are breakdowns in the operation of primary systems such as family (Wilensky & Lebeaux, 1965), a program landscape dominated by prevention and/or risk-reduction ventures (Roth, Brooks-Gunn, Murray, & Foster, 1998), and a service environment in which success or failure is assessed on the basis of reductions in the risk producing behaviors of individuals being served (Goodman, Wandersman, Chinman, Imm, & Morrissey, 1996). Parents, teachers and other child and youth workers spend inordinate time and energy striving to eliminate, or preclude the formation of, risk behaviors instead of devoting attention to fostering health, caring, and competence.

Community-based human development is offered in contrast and as an alternative to this prevailing ethos and its social, developmental, and delivery system implications. There is a growing call to move beyond risk and prevention-oriented strategies and attend to positive development (Pittman, 2000). Search Institute's interest in a community oriented approach is also in part a response to growing dissatisfaction with the effectiveness of traditional responses to child and adolescent outcomes which tend to focus on individuals (Dryfoos, 1990). Community-based human development certainly recognizes the value and importance of individuals, but argues there is a compelling case to be made for a more expansive perspective that takes into account and pays particular attention to the environment in which child and adolescent development transpires. It readily acknowledges the influence of community and societal forces on developmental processes.

Wynn et al. (1987) clarify that communities can encourage and facilitate healthy development by allowing youths to participate in various group activities and organizations, provide them with access to community facilities and events, offer them personal support through positive interactions with peers and adults, and allow them to benefit from the welfare of others through active involvement in prosocial activities. Stevenson's (1998) research on African-American adolescents suggests that the intersection of family and neighborhood networks provide a valuable framework from which to understand emotional adjustment across cultural contexts. Rodriguez (1999) points out that a major developmental task for the Hispanic parent and child is to reconcile the conflict between the young person's sense of self rooted in community as family and the way in which the dominant social norm defining success undervalues a sense of the collective.

Community-based human development takes the position that there is a role for professions and professionals to play in fostering positive development, but there must also be the complimentary engagement of "everyday people" to create a healthy habitat for young people. It affirms that redundant messages must permeate all of the entities responsible for effective socialization of young people (Damon, 1997). Community-based human development ascribes to Coleman's contention, cited by Sampson et al. (1999), that social capital, which is so essential to positive development, is…"lodged not in individuals but in the structure of social organization" (pg. 302).

Civic Action Supporting Community-Based Human Development

Civic action is essential to accomplish community-based human development. The public needs to be effectively engaged around three types of civic action: (1) promoting health, (2) seeking positive psychosocial growth, and (3) striving for equity.

In calling for public engagement, community-based human development recognizes and affirms collective responsibility for supporting the positive growth of young people and active involvement in initiatives to see that it occurs. It is predicated in the recognition that all adults – and not just parents – need to participate in building developmental strengths. Public engagement has received considerable treatment in the arena of public education reform. The Annenberg Institute on Public Engagement for Public Education has concentrated on involving the public in school reforms and made it clear every American needs to get involved (Annenberg, 1999). Similar levels of civic involvement on behalf of positive development are needed in schools and all other socializing institutions in communities.

Support for health promotion means that education about health matters and social conditions supporting health are of central importance to positive human development. While the developmental assets framework tends to emphasize socio-emotional health, we understand that health promotion attends to issues of lifestyle, environments, policies, resources, and social norms (Green, 1992). For Green and Kreuter (1999), community exists as the "center of gravity for health promotion." (p. 14) Encouraging health promotion also makes the point that community-based human development is about more than just the absence of disease and illness, and is instead about intentional steps to actually establish the health of youngsters (Green & Potvin, 1996).

Seeking positive psychosocial growth means confronting a society which is woefully neglectful of its young. The rates at which children are born into poverty, reported as abused and neglected, run away, drop out of school, and bear children are staggering (Edelman, 1999). An emphasis on the positive and having young people meet their full potential instead of, and in spite of, these daunting negatives is being touted more frequently. It is consistent with an emerging consensus that development for youth is best undertaken when they are seen as resources and not as manifesting difficulties needing to be "fixed" (Roth et al.,1998). In calling for positive psychosocial growth efforts need to be undertaken so that young people experience relationships, competencies, values, and self-perceptions that help them succeed (Scales & Leffert, 1999).

Civic action regarding equity is based in the premise that '"All Kids Are Our Kids" (Benson, 1997) and addresses fundamental matters of resource distribution. According to Aaron and Lougy (1986) in an attempt to move to greater equity one needs to take into account the beneficiaries, the actual items being equalized, and the process used for reallocation (in Stone, 1988). Action on behalf of equity seeks to minimize existing inequalities and implores communities and the society to actively work on behalf of all young people so they have a greater degree of equal access to resources, opportunities, and experiences that allows them to attain their full developmental potential.

Contemporary America appears to be lacking in the civic exercise of getting actively involved in positive child and adolescent development and reluctant to make the commitment to greater equality in its attainment. One of the biggest hurdles is helping community members come to understand what is meant by being developmentally attentive. Developmental deficits and the associated emphasis on the prevention and/or the reduction of risks have dominated professional thinking, academic research, and public discourse about how to best serve children and youth for an extended period of time. Reshaping thought, redirecting research, and recreating public imagination about positive development and healthy growth are riddles needing to be solved.

The issue of citizen estrangement has received significant coverage (Elshtain, 1996; Putnam, 2000) and complicates matters even more. While many explanations for this condition have been put forth, one of the more intriguing is presented by Cortes Jr. (1996), who argues that the dominance of marketing and its incursion into all spheres of American life including politics has transformed citizens from being producers of political activity into consumers of political affairs. Attempts to correct this condition and rally the public by employing traditional publicity and marketing methods based in treating people as consumers have fallen short. "Public relations campaigns can persuade people and gather support for causes, but they can't create genuine publics" (Mathews, 1994 pg. 18), because genuine publics are an outgrowth of people "banding together" to engage in collective decisions and behave and live together in a certain way.

Instead of business oriented strategies which operate on the basis of public relations premises, a more meaningful approach to engagement is based in recognizing the importance of actions grounded in forceful deliberation. This attention to forceful deliberation is also in marked contrast to misguided nostrums regarding community espoused by numerous modern day communitarians. For Sennett (1998), communitarians incorrectly see unity as the source of strength in community and inaccurately believe conflict undermines community social bonds. Instead, Sennett (1998) cites Lewis Coser's classic essay entitled "The Functions of Social Conflict" in which Coser makes the case that people wind up being connected more fully through verbal disagreement than by agreement. Conflict makes communicating more difficult and harder, but it is out of the hard work associated with actively listening and trying to get one's message across that a sense of community is forged. Coser argues that community cannot really exist until differences are delineated and dealt with.

Civic action tied to community-based human development needs to allow for the expression of very different opinions regarding collective responsibility for the healthy development of young people, and then tackling those issues head on so community members can work together to rebuild the developmental infrastructure for all young people. According to Gates (1999), tackling differences of opinion in this way brings about a true "citizen democracy", because even with the extra time and messiness involved in working through diverse perspectives and eventually securing agreement, new relationships and networks to help build and enhance a community's civic infrastructure are established. Gates (1999) speaks of "community guardians" who are able to transcend the various factions and bring people together to focus on the larger sense of community good. In terms of community-based human development we speak of "asset champions" who bring a message of community unifying around positive development for children and adolescents.

It is essential that this deliberative strategy be extended to youth as well. Nightingale and Wolverton (1993) remind us it is youth feelings of not having a meaningful role in the wider community that has often been identified as leading to numerous adolescent problems.

In calling for public engagement around community-based human development, however, we must remain sensitive to deep seeded social and cultural forces that reduce America's comfort level with the very idea of shared responsibility. A majority of American voters have never demonstrated a willingness to accept the tax consequences of public policies that happen to be standard child and youth investments in most advanced nation-states (Mannes, 1997).

Despite social and political challenges, public engagement to support healthy development must be implemented with a commitment to equity. Some such as Lawrence (2000) take solace in the fact that inequality has not continued to worsen. Others, continue to raise concern over existing inequities in wealth and education (Edelman, 1999). Equity, though, becomes very tricky because as Stone (1988) reminds us, people tend to be of two different minds about it. One perspective, dating as far back as James Madison, views differences among people around basic resources such as property, income, and education as the norm and interprets any attempt to alter the situation as subversive. The other perspective sees equality as the norm and believes deviations from it require remedial action.

Equity in relation to positive child and adolescent development would require some form of redistribution. Daunting policy and financial reallocations would have to be calculated, agreed to, and then put into place. This wouldn't necessarily result in perceptions of equal treatment (think Affirmative Action) and certainly wouldn't make everyone happy. Given the likelihood of civic engagement primarily by the well-to-do and the well-schooled, and in the absence of their firm resolve in the value of equity, maintenance of the status quo is likely to prevail. With Search Institute's data suggesting that the developmental picture for most young people in contemporary American society is fragile (Benson et al., 1999), attention must be devoted to ensuring that commensurate resources and opportunities are available to support community-based human development in the urban cores, isolated rural settings, and suburban enclaves. In the final analysis, equity and public engagement are closely tied because the possibility of attaining a greater degree of equality can only come about through diverse and spirited citizen involvement.

The institute's perspective on community-based human development is depicted in Figure 2. Community-based human development operates on the assumption that public engagement around health promotion, positive psychosocial growth, and equity fosters the developmental strengths of all young people.

Search Institute's Contribution to Community-Based Human Development

Communities often use Search Institute's *Profiles of Student Life: Attitudes and Behaviors* survey as a prime mechanism to engender civic engagement. Literally hundreds of communities have used public meetings in which survey results depicting the collective profile of developmental assets among adolescents have been communicated in order to build energy and serve as a springboard for citizen creation of a better setting for positive development. The forty elements contained in Search Institute's developmental assets framework provide communities with clear ideas about what actually constitutes the promotion of health and positive psychosocial growth. The external and internal assets provide individuals, agencies and institutions with the items they need to deal with in order to address positive child and adolescent development. The developmental assets serve as growth goals for cities and towns, and the framework is regularly used as the basis for conducting community dialogues on the roles people can play in bringing about support, empowerment, boundaries and expectations, constructive use of time, commitment to learning, positive values, social competence, and positive identity for all young people. Various groups of citizens and professionals working within socializing institutions such as schools and congregations tap resources produced by Search Institute for ideas, suggestions, and techniques on how to promote developmental strengths. With more than 600 communities across the nation currently using the developmental assets framework to guide their community transformation work, Search Institute has a deep and abiding interest in studying strength-based community and social change leading to developmentally attentive community and social growth for young people. The institute has designed and is implementing a field research program to investigate and learn about community-based human development. One of the first lines of inquiry of the field research agenda is to conduct a set of place-based case studies examining the personal and asset-building initiative induced changes that occur as communities, towns, and cities emphasize the positive development of young people. The objective is to establish an initial understanding of how community-based human development is unfolding in various settings. We are interested in studying how communities move through phases of receptivity, awareness, mobilization, action, and continuity along the pathway to becoming developmentally attentive, how they engage citizens, and what they do to promote positive growth.

Using Service Learning to Foster Community-Based Human Development

Kendall (1990), saw service learning at its core being predicated upon "human growth and purpose, a social vision, an approach to community, and a way of knowing" (p. 23). Kendall's approach to and conceptualization of service learning provides the bridge for its relevance and application to the evolving field of endeavor and applied research agenda that we at Search Institute are defining as community-based human development.

The relationship between service learning and community-based human development plays out differently for various groups of students. We concur with Nakkula and Ravitch (1998) that helping professionals such as social workers, educators, and allied health personnel serve as "applied developmentalists." These helping professionals play a vital role in maintaining the fabric of communities and have a responsibility to create caring, healthy, and responsible young people. In lieu of service learning, students seeking careers in the helping professions have practicums and internships to prepare them for their careers. The more these students deal with development issues as part of their experiential learning activities, the more a value base is reinforced, a mindset imparted, and a repertoire of professional skills cultivated all in the name of developmentally attentive practice.

The bigger challenge lies in raising the consciousness and enhancing the abilities of other higher education students to support community-based human development. It rests in creating service learning experiences to help these students also become applied developmentalists and understand how for the remainder of their lives they have an obligation to make meaningful contributions to the developmental strengths of young people. Student exposure to situations where they can think about, acquire, and employ developmental skills set the stage for them to be able to infuse a developmental perspective into their daily activities. Service learning experiences tied to positive child and adolescent development helps produce college graduates more sensitive to and equipped with a better understanding of how they can maximizing human potential.

Search Institutes' survey instrument, its developmental assets framework, and resource materials offers students participating in service learning experiences the tools they can use to engage in applied human development work with young people and adults in schools, homes, agencies and on playgrounds. Students who participate in these service learning efforts, and take the time to engage in the reflection that is a core part of service learning (Jacoby, 1996), are becoming a part of a developmentally attentive community that they can then help perpetuate throughout their lives. The exposure to developmental assets through an applied development service learning experience can transform these students into "asset champions". In the course of actually engaging in positive development activities students will likely become more aware of and more thoughtful about how they are being changed as a result of their involvement. Ideally they will come to appreciate the nature of reciprocal exchange and transformation that transpires in the course of conducting applied developmental work (Nakkula & Ravitch, 1998).

CONCLUSIONS

Search Institute maintains strategic priorities to utilize the developmental assets framework and its evolving thinking around the concept of community-based human development to foster and study civic action in support of the positive growth of young people. Search Institute's advocacy of and support for community-based human development contributes to an enhanced civil society. For O'Connell (1999), "Civil society represents the balance between the rights granted to individuals in free societies and the responsibilities required of citizens to maintain those rights" (page 10-11). Search Institute emphasis on creating developmental attentive community enlists community members to balance their individual rights with an assumption of responsibility for and taking steps to insure the developmental well-being of children and adolescents.

We contend that institutions of higher education have a stewardship role regarding the integration of service learning, community-based human development and civil society. Establishing positive development oriented service learning experiences for students contributes to producing citizens with sensibility to the values, issues and concerns embedded in the idea of community-based human development.

Marshall (1949) identified the three core elements of citizenship in western civilization as civil, political, and social. The civil aspect is comprised of individual liberties regarding property and contracts and includes freedom of speech and religion. The political element consists of the right to exercise political power as a voter or elected official. The social aspect incorporates economic welfare, security and the right to fully share in the social heritage and live in accordance with the prevailing standards of one's society. Marshall (1949) proposed that civil rights emerged in the eighteenth century, political rights in the nineteenth, and social rights in the twentieth. In our opinion, the twenty-first century needs to be about the extension of social rights to encompass positive human development.

The path in America will not be an easy one. Galbraith (1992) has derided the presence of a politics and a constituency of contentment in our culture that is consumed by personal financial gain at the expense of holding a larger social vista. Brooks (2000), in his biting critique of the new upperclass and their fusion of that which is bohemian and bourgeois, laments the emergence of an era of complacency. For Brooks (2000) this period of complacency shrinks our national life, renders our public spirit threadbare, and poses as great a threat to our collective well-being as does the specter of imperial overreach or a crushing military defeat.

Brooks (2000) call on all of us — and especially those in the educated class — to engage in reform at home and activism abroad. We would argue that both activism and reform are needed on the domestic front to bring about community-based human development, and that service learning experiences serve as fertile grounds to stimulate both meaningful involvement and progress. Reforms would be dedicated to strengthening our primary socializing institutions — making them more developmentally attuned. Activism would motivate individual and collective attitudinal and behavioral change — making people more developmentally attentive to children and youth.

Search Institute, along with colleges and universities, must pay attention to the study of applied development service learning experiences and the awakening and unleashing of community members in support of developmental strengths. Research and scholarship determining the contributions of service learning and civic action to community-based human development must be carried out in ways that ties the science to the real world in a real way. Zigler (1998) lauds the growing acceptance of applied research and policy studies by traditional basic research professional associations such as the Society for Research in Child Development. For Lerner and his associates (2000), the learning derived from an applied development research orientation grounded in community promotes civil society.

The increased attention being paid to applied development research and policy is significant for a number of reasons. It increases the importance of viewing communities as developmental laboratories. It also enhances the value of exploring and understanding the developmental possibilities that emerge from the power of community members to identify and make use of their inherent and natural wisdom. Finally, it creates the possibility of linking knowledge derived from community-based study with the formation of a public science of development.

REFERENCES

Aaron, H.J., & Lougy, C.M. (1986). *The comparable worth controversy*. Washington, DC: Brookings Institution.

Annenberg Institute for School Reform. (1999). *Reasons for hope; voices for change*. Providence, Rhode Island: Annenberg Institute for School Reform.

Astin, A.W. (1977). *Four critical years: effects of college on beliefs, attitude, and knowledge.* San Francisco: Jossey-Bass.

Astin, A.W. (1984). Student involvement: A developmental theory for higher education. *Journal of College Student Personnel, 24,* 297-308.

Benson, P. (1997). *All kids are our kids.* San Francisco, CA: Jossey-Bass, Inc.

Benson, P., Leffert, N., Scales, P., & Blyth, D. (1998). Beyond the "village" rhetoric: Creating healthy communities for children and adolescents. *Applied Developmental Science, 2*(3), 138-159.

Benson, P., & Roehlkepartain, E. (1993). *Beyond leaf raking.* Nashville, TN: Abingdon Press .

Benson, P.L., Scales, P.C., Leffert, N., & Roehlkepartain, E.C. (1999). *A fragile foundation: The state of developmental assets among american youth.* Minneapolis, MN: Search Institute.

Bronfenbrenner, U. (1979). *The ecology of human development.* Cambridge, MA: Harvard University Press.

Brooks, D. (2000). *BOBOS in paradise.* New York, NY: Simon and Schuster.

Cortes, J. (1996). Community organization and social capital. *National Civic Review, 85*(3), 49-59.

Damon, W. (1997). *The youth charter, how communities can work together to raise standards for all our children.* New York, NY: Free Press.

Dryfoos, J.G. (1990). *Adolescents at risk: Prevalence and prevention.* New York, NY: Oxford University Press.

Edelman, M.W. (1999). *Lanterns: A memoir of mentors.* Boston, MA: Beacon Press.

Ehrlich, T. (1996). Foreward. In B. Jacoby (Ed.), *Service learning in higher education: Concepts and practices.* (pp. xi-xvi) San Francisco, CA: Jossey-Bass, Inc.

Elshtain, J.B. (1996). Democracy at century's end. *Social Services Review 70,* (4), 507-515.

Finkelstein, B. (2000). A crucible of contradictions: Historical roots of violence against children in the united states. In V. Polakow (Ed.), *The Public Assault on America's Children; Poverty, Violence, and Juvenile Justice.* NY: Teachers College Press.

Galbraith, J.K. (1992). *The culture of contentment.* Boston, MA: Houghton, Mifflin, Co.

Gates, C.T. (1999). Creating a healthy democracy. *National Civic Review, 88* (4), 259-264.

Goodman, R.M., Wandersman, A., Chinman, M., Imm, P., & Morrissey, E. (1996). An ecological assessment of community-based interventions for prevention and health promotion: Approaches to measuring community coalitions. *American Journal of Community Psychology, 24*(1), 33-61.

Green, L.W. (1992). The health promotion research agenda revisited. *American Journal of Health Promotion, 6,* 411-413.

Green, L.W., & Kreuter, M.W. (1999). *Health promotion planning: An educational and ecological approach.* Mountain View, CA: Mayfield Publishing Company.

Green, L.W., & Potvin, R.L. (1996). Ecological foundations of health promotion. *American Journal of Health Promotion, 10,* 270-281.

Jacoby, B. (1996). *Service learning in today's higher education.* San Francisco, CA: Jossey-Bass, Inc.

Keith, J. (1995). Introducing a campus to service learning. *Journal of Career Development, 22*(2), 135-139.

Kendall, J.C. (1990). Combining service and learning: An introduction. In J. C. Kendall (Ed.), *Combining Service and Learning: A Resource Book for Community and Public Service.* Raleigh, NC: National Society for Experimental Education.

Kraft, R.J. (1996). Service learning: An introduction to its theory, practice, and effects. *Education and Urban Society, 28*(2), 131-159.

Anonymous. (1994). *Building community; Service learning in the academic disciplines.* Denver, CO: Colorado Campus Compact.

Lawrence, R.Z. (2000). Inequality in america: The recent evidence. *The Responsive Community: Rights and Responsibilities, 10*(4-10)

Lerner, R.M. (1992). Dialectics, developmental contextualism, and the further enhancement of theory about puberty and psychosocial development. *Journal of Early Adolescence, 12*, 366-388.

Lerner, R.M., Fisher, C.B., & Weinberg, R.A. (2000). Toward a acience for and of the people: Promoting civil society through the application of developmental science. *Child Development, 71*(1), 11-20.

Mannes, M. *The evolution and implications of reforms for public child welfare and community-based family support.* (1997). Summary of proceedings 1.N.R.S.o.F.G.D.M. Denver, CO: American humane association children's division.

Marshall, T.H. (1964). Citizenship and social class. In T. H. Marshall (Ed.), *Class, Citizenship, and Social Development.* Garden City, NY: Doubleday.

Mathews, D. (1994). Community change through true public action. *National Civic Review, Fall/Winter*, 400-404.

Nakkula, M.J., & Ravitch, S.M. (1998). *Matters of interpretation:reciprocal transformation in therapeutic and developmental relationships with youth.* San Francisco, CA: Jossey-Bass, Inc.

Nightingale, E.O., & Wolverton, L. (1993). Adolescent rolelessness in modern society. In R. Takanishi (Ed.), *Adolescence in the 1990's: Risk and opportunity* . (pp. 14-28). New York, NY: Teachers College Press.

O'Connell, B. (1999). *Civil society: the underpinnings of american democracy.* Hanover, NH: University Press of New England.

Pittman, K. (2000). Balancing the equation. *CYD Journal-Community Youth Development, 1*(1), 32-36.

Putnam, R.D. (2000). *Bowling Alone: The collapse and revival of american community.* New York, NY: Simon & Schuster.

Riegel, K.F. (1976). The dialectictics of human development. *American Psychologist., 31*, 689-700.

Riegel, K.F. (1975). Toward a dialectical theory of development. *Human Development, 18*, 50-64.

Rodriguez, G. (1999). *Raising nuestros niños:Bringing up latino children in a bicultural world.* New York, NY: Fireside.

Roehlkepartain, J.L., & Leffert, N. (2000). *What young children need to succeed.* Minneapolis, MN: Free Spirit Publishing.

Roth, J., Brooks-Gunn, J., Murray, L., & Foster, W. (1998). Promoting healthy adolescents: Synthesis of youth development program evaluations. *Journal of Research on Adolescents, 8*(4), 423-459.

Sampson, R.J., Morenoff, J.D., & Earls, F. (1999). Beyond social capital: Spatial dynamics of collective efficacy for children. *American Sociological Review, 64*(October), 633-660.

Scales, P., & Leffert, N. (1999). *Developmental assets: A synthesis of the scientific research on adolescent development.* Mpls, MN: Search Institute.

Scales, P.C., Benson, P.L., & Roehlkepartain, E. (2001). *Grading grown-ups: American adults report on their real relationships with kids.* Minneapolis: Lutheran Brotherhood and SearchInstitute.

Schlossberg, N.K. (1989). Marginality and mattering: Key issues in building community. In D. C. Roberts (Ed.), *Designing campus activities to foster a sense of community: New directions for student services.* (pp. 5-15). San Francisco, CA: Jossey-Bass, Inc.

Search Institute (2000). An assets builder's guide to service learning. Minneapolis, MN. Aufhor.

Sennett, R. (1998). *The corrosion of character: The personal consequences of work in the new capitalism.* New York, NY: W. W. Norton and Company.

Stevenson, H.C. (1998). Raising safe villages: Cultural-ecological factors that influence the emotional adjustment of adolescents. *Journal of Black Psychology, 24*(1), 44-59.

Stone, D. (1988). *Policy paradox and political reason.* (ed.). Waltham, MA: Harper Collins Publishers.

Wilensky, H., & Lebeaux, C. (1965). *Industrial society and social welfare.* New York, NY: Free Press.

Wynn, J., Richman, H., Rubinstein, R.A., & Littel, J. (1987). Communities and adolescents: An exploration of reciprocal supports. *William T. Grant Foundation Commission on Youth and America's Future,*

Zigler, E. (1998). A place of value for applied and policy studies. *Child Development, 69*(2), 532-542.

SEARCH INSTITUTE'S 40 DEVELOPMENTAL ASSETS

Search Institute has identified the following building blocks of healthy development that help young people grow up healthy, caring, and responsible.

EXTERNAL ASSETS

Support

1. **Family support-**Family life provides high levels of love and support.
2. **Positive family communication-**Young person and her or his parent(s) communicate positively, and young person is willing to seek advice and counsel from parents.
3. **Other adult relationships-**Young person receives support from three or more nonparent adults.
4. **Caring neighborhood-**Young person experiences caring neighbors.
5. **Caring school climate-**School provides a caring, encouraging environment.
6. **Parent involvement in schooling-**Parent(s) are actively involved in helping young person succeed in school.

Empowerment

7. **Community values youth-**Young person perceives that adults in the community value youth.
8. **Youth as resources-**Young people are given useful roles in the community.
9. **Service to others-**Young person serves in the community one hour or more per week.
10. **Safety-**Young person feels safe at home, school, and in the neighborhood.

Boundaries and Expectations

11. **Family boundaries-**Family has clear rules and consequences and monitors the young person's whereabouts.
12. **School boundaries-**School provides clear rules and consequences.

13. Neighborhood boundaries-Neighbors take responsibility for monitoring young people's behavior.

14. Adult role models-Parent(s) and other adults model positive, responsible behavior.

15. Positive peer influence-Young person's best friends model responsible behavior.

16. High expectations-Both parent(s) and teachers encourage the young person to do well.

Constructive Use of Time

17. Creative activities-Young person spends three or more hours per week in lessons or practice in music, theater, or other arts.

18. Youth programs-Young person spends three or more hours per week in sports, clubs, or organizations at school and/or in the community.

19. Religious community-Young person spends one or more hours per week in activities in a religious institution.

20. Time at home-Young person is out with friends "with nothing special to do" two or fewer nights per week.

INTERNAL ASSETS

Commitment to Learning

21. Achievement motivation-Young person is motivated to do well in school.

22. School engagement—Young person is actively engaged in learning.

23. Homework-Young person reports doing at least one hour of homework every school day.

24. Bonding to school-Young person cares about her or his school.

25. Reading for pleasure-Young person reads for pleasure three or more hours per week.

Positive Values

26. Caring-Young person places high value on helping other people.

27. Equality and social justice-Young person places high value on promoting equality and reducing hunger and poverty.

28. Integrity-Young person acts on convictions and stands up for her or his beliefs.

29. Honesty-Young person "tells the truth even when it is not easy."

30. Responsibility-Young person accepts and takes personal responsibility.

31. Restraint-Young person believes it is important not to be sexually active or to use alcohol or other drugs.

Social Competencies

32. Planning and decision making-Young person knows how to plan ahead and make choices.

33. Interpersonal competence-Young person has empathy, sensitivity, and friendship skills.

34. Cultural competence-Young person has knowledge of and comfort with people of different cultural/racial/ethnic backgrounds.

35. Resistance skills-Young person can resist negative peer pressure and dangerous situations.

36. Peaceful conflict resolution-Young person seeks to resolve conflict non-violently.

Positive Identity

37. Personal power- Young person feels he or she has control over "things that happen to me."

38. Self-esteem-Young person reports having a high self-esteem.

39. Sense of purpose-Young person reports that "my life has a purpose."

40. Positive view of personal future-Young person is optimistic about her or his personal future.

Name Index

Subject Index